C0-APB-917

ALSO BY LELAND STOWE

NAZI MEANS WAR

"An excellent account of Nazi militarism by a careful and reflective journalist."

FREDERICK L. SCHUMAN
in the *New Republic*.

NO OTHER ROAD TO FREEDOM

". . . he possesses all the qualities of the glamorous war correspondent. Among these are the gifts of vivid description and dramatization, warm emotional sympathy for the peoples whose struggles he is reporting, and a remarkable knack of being in the most exciting place at the right time."

W. H. CHAMBERLIN
in the *Atlantic Monthly*.

They Shall Not Sleep

. . . We are the Dead. Short days ago
We lived, felt dawn, saw sunset glow,
Loved and were loved, and now we lie
In Flanders fields.

Take up our quarrel with the foe:
To you from failing hands we throw
The torch; be yours to hold it high.
If ye break faith with us who die
We shall not sleep, though poppies grow
In Flanders fields.

Captain John D. McCrae

THEY SHALL NOT SLEEP

Leland Stowe

ALFRED A. KNOPF
NEW YORK
1945

PUBLISHED JANUARY 17, 1944
REPRINTED NINE TIMES
ELEVENTH PRINTING, JANUARY 1945

THIS BOOK HAS BEEN PRODUCED
IN FULL COMPLIANCE
WITH ALL GOVERNMENT REGULATIONS
FOR THE CONSERVATION OF PAPER, METAL,
AND OTHER ESSENTIAL MATERIALS

TO

MY FATHER AND MOTHER

Frank Philip Stowe

AND

Eva Noe Stowe

Acknowledgments

The major portion of the material in this book is based upon the unpublished notes in my war diary from July 1941 to December 1942. In a few chapters, however, I have rewritten incidents and data which were contained in my dispatches to the *Chicago Daily News.* I am also indebted to Paul Scott Mowrer and Carroll Binder, respectively editor and foreign editor of the *Chicago Daily News,* for their constant co-operation while I was abroad and for the leave of absence which has enabled me to complete these pages. Most of the chapter on the evolution of the Red Army was published in *Foreign Affairs* and is included here with the kind permission of Hamilton Fish Armstrong.

At various stages in my travels I have been fortunate to receive the aid or advice of American officers and officials in posts or places widely separated. Among these were Colonel Joseph Twitty, Lieutenant Colonel John K. Gowen, Jr., Colonel Louis Johnson, Colonel Arthur W. Herrington, Colonel Frank Hayne, Major Gordon Enders, Clayton Lane, U. S. consul in Calcutta, Byron D. McDonald, and the members of the United States Army (General Magruder's) mission in China and Burma. I am also much indebted to the friendly counsel of Colonel Philip Faymonville, formerly Brigadier General and chief of the American supply mission in Soviet Russia; and for the numerous courtesies of Admiral William H. Standley, former American Ambassador in Moscow; of Llewellyn Thompson, Jr., first secretary in our Moscow Embassy; and of the American Minister to Iran, Mr. Louis Dreyfus, and Mrs. Dreyfus.

In the preparation of this manuscript Blanche Knopf and Bernard Smith have given numerous suggestions and assistance which cannot be overstated. Throughout the writing of this book I have been helped immeasurably by my firmest friend and best critic, my wife. After such unfailing interest and support the limitations which remain must be regarded as those which the author, as yet at any rate, has been unable to grow out of. He lives in hope.

L. S.

CONTENTS

PART V — ALL OF US

Foreword

Since September 3, 1939 I have completed two assignments — each of more than seventeen months' duration — reporting the war for the *Chicago Daily News* and some fifty American and Canadian newspapers which subscribe to its foreign news service.

A by-product of my first close-up of the war, entitled *No Other Road to Freedom,* was written in the late spring of 1941 in the conviction that the United States could not escape armed conflict with the Axis coalition. I had scarcely remailed the last galley proofs to Alfred Knopf when Carroll Binder, my foreign editor, assigned me unexpectedly to cover the Orient. Thus my second wartime odyssey eventually took me around the world. It provided the material for these pages, which seem, in both content and theme, a natural sequel to the preceding volume.

This book is primarily a piece of reporting. It is not a repetition or rehash of dispatches which have already appeared in newspaper columns. For the most part it contains the kind of frank, factual, and detailed reporting which censorship would not permit at the time the events occurred. In this respect I believe many of the facts recorded here are more important than anything I was able to write from China, Burma, or some other war zones. Some of these facts may still be comparatively new to Americans, or even completely new. Yet they apply sharply to the problems of postwar international co-operation. For that reason perhaps it is better that they can now be presented with the perspective of elapsed time, with a greater degree of objectivity, and with an honest effort to record them without bitterness or recrimination.

Not long ago Hanson Baldwin, military authority of the *New York Times,* wrote: "It is obvious that not only in the Pacific, but all over the world, the censorship is keeping from the American people many facts that they are entitled to know and is covering up mistakes and inefficiency." Although Mr. Baldwin referred to a widely recognized shortcoming of censorship in our American armed services, what he said has been equally true of the censorship exercised by most of our allies. Yet any serious observer must admit that official refusal to publicize numerous instances of Allied "mistakes and inefficiency" again and again has greatly delayed corrective measures and has merely served to encourage a dangerous false optimism among our home publics. The same sort of excessive censorship, with its clouding of political and social realities, can only serve to endanger equally the negotiation and construction of a stable, workable postwar settlement. This is why a more accurate knowledge of what happened one or two years ago in China, Burma, India, Russia, or the Near East has an extremely vital bearing upon the United Nations' definitely uncertain chances of winning the peace. To this end one war correspondent's report cannot be more than a very small contribution, but it can be as honest and dispassionate as a man is capable of making it. This I have tried to do.

This book is likewise an effort at reporting-plus. I do not use this phrase with either presumption or false modesty. In wartime the straight reporting of facts, policies, and situations is an absolute necessity. But from anyone who possesses a reasonable experience and background as a foreign correspondent the mere reporting of day-by-day developments is not enough. Any alert police reporter can do that kind of job. In a global conflict and a world-wide revolution, such as exist at present, it seems clear that the American and Allied publics have a right to expect reporting-plus from their war correspondents — and especially from those newspapermen who have worked abroad for a number of years previous to the war. It is not enough to find out what happens. It is essential to endeavor to understand how what is now happening may or will affect developments next month, next year, or perhaps even several years from now. In other words, it is necessary to have learned the lessons of the past and to learn, in some measure and as fully as possible, the lessons of the present. In times as confused and complicated as these it is not likely that many correspondents (nor many diplomats, generals, or congressmen) will emerge with marks of 98 or 99. Our limitations are all too obvious. Nevertheless that will not excuse the failure of any of us to strive to apply yesterday's and today's lessons to the severe demands of tomorrow.

Accordingly, and without any nuance of disparagement, this

is not intended as another war correspondent's report of the battle fronts and nothing more than that. Its goal is more difficult and for that reason I am the first to appreciate, all too ruefully, that it may fall pitifully short of its mark. For all that, these pages constitute an effort to shed a little more light on some phases of the war and of our postwar problems; and to provide, if possible, a somewhat sounder basis for judging the difficulties as well as the opportunities which confront Americans in tomorrow's world. I have not written as a mere spectator who happened to draw a front observation post at Armageddon, but with a point of view. The viewpoint is grounded in the extended liberties, welfare and self-expression of common men and women throughout the world, regardless of race, creed, or nationality. To my mind this is the essence of a progressive democracy and the prerequisite of any democracy worth fighting for or worth attempting to preserve — of any democracy which *can be* preserved.

For there is no choice for democracy in this unprecedented world revolution in which we live. Either democracy, in the United States and also outside America, will set its course along progressive lines and will progress commensurately with our machine-dominated civilization. Or democracy will perish through its failure to improve its functioning and through its refusal to speed its gait. If our own democracy perishes, it will not be in the next century — but in our time.

LELAND STOWE

Bronxville, New York

October 1943

They Shall Not Sleep

Part I — China

Chapter I

THROUGH CHINA'S BACK DOOR

One generation opens the road upon which another generation travels.

Chinese proverb

During fifteen years of newspaper wanderings, across five continents and scores of national frontiers, it had never happened before. And now it happened with a country at war — the country which has been much longer at war than any of the others.

Charan Singh, our Sikh driver, turned his green-turbaned head just long enough to flash a smile above his majestic black beard. "Now come Wanting," he said, pronouncing it as the Chinese do: Wan-ding.

With that our Lend-Lease caravan of twenty-eight handsome new station wagons lurched down into the cramped little valley. Bamboo sheds and rough wooden buildings littered the valley's uneven sides. It was more a gulch than a valley, really: a hodgepodge of shelters dumped into the depression beside a half-dried-up stream. The trees, the huts, the road — everything was powdered pasty-gray with dust — and the dust spurted wildly upward from our tires and from the naked feet of Chinese or Kachins or other Shan tribal folk as they hopped out of our path.

The road, already too narrow, was transformed here into a grooved gantlet by dozens upon dozens of battered dust-laden trucks which stood parked tightly, head to tail. Beyond the bridge, where the road twisted sharply into the midst of the crowded mass of drab structures, the trucks were simply jammed in at all angles regardless of traffic. Somehow our lead car shoehorned along, and we followed, toward the only official-looking building in the place. A red flag with a blue field, embossed with a symbol which looked like a white sunflower, hung above the steps and served notice that we were now in China. Lashio, back in Burma, lay six hours behind us. This was the beginning of

Yunnan; Wanting, where the tough part of the Burma Road begins.

For the next twenty minutes we seemed bogged down in the middle of an unbreakable traffic jam. Burmese and Hindu chauffeurs rushed here and there or formed queues under signs lettered in bewildering Chinese ideographs. Evidently these were inspection offices. There must be a passport control office here somewhere. Peter Rowland, the English Quaker and Red Cross man, joined me in trying to locate it. Of course we couldn't read the Chinese signs and in the general hubbub and confusion we got nowhere so fast that we finally gave it up. Undoubtedly the leader of our caravan would get around to us once he got the cars checked in and cleared. Our leader was rushing about like mad. He was pint-sized but he moved faster than any Chinese I had ever seen in my life. In no time at all he was waving us back into our station wagons, yelling at the last laggard drivers, and then, suddenly, all our cars were bouncing over the ruts, twisting and pushing and climbing out of the town. "Petrol station next," said Charan Singh. "This leader very quick man."

Then it dawned on me that we had finished with Wanting. Most caravans were stuck in Wanting for ten or twelve hours at least, yet our midget dynamo up front had got us through in twenty minutes. He must have an amazing amount of pull or something. But what about our passports? Not a single official had talked to us or examined our kits and baggage or seen our passports. So here we were, jouncing and rolling through clouds of Yunnanese dust — inside China — inside wartime China — and we hadn't so much as shown our passports at the border. Nothing like that had ever happened to me before. But it merely seemed to fit with the general scheme of things. Nothing, apparently, was orthodox on the Burma Road. And the more we saw of the road, the truer we found that to be.

From Wanting the road traverses the first plateau, threading toward Mangshi, sixty miles away. I thought about that congested border control station behind us, clogged with scores of trucks all day and all night. What a bombing target for the Japs! Of course it was still out of reach of the Japs, but they had already bombed more than half-way along the road from Kunming. Anyhow, Wanting was a terrible bottleneck by its very conformation, and so a costly waste of time in getting war supplies into China. No wonder the American traffic experts had urged that the control station be moved inland. And supposing the Japs did bomb Wanting? Naturally, it never occurred to me that Japanese troops could ever *occupy* Wanting. After all, Wanting lies deep in the upper Shan Mountains, with the great gorges of the Salween and Mekong rivers protecting it from the Japs in Indo-China, hundreds of miles away. On that early October day in 1941 how were we to guess that in six months' time Hirohito's warriors would hold Rangoon itself? That the Burma Road would be cut at its outset and that shortly thereafter the Japs would be pressing up from Lashio, through the seemingly impregnable mountains, over the very route we had traversed, up and ever upward, that very morning?

We forgot Wanting in the excitement of seeing this first remote hinterland of Free China. Now the road scaled well above the tree level. Our caravan snaked to right and left until, precipitately, the earth fell away beside us — a sheer drop of some eight hundred feet into a green river valley. And as we squirmed downward for miles, the empty trucks, Burma-bound from Kunming, roared up at us through the blinding dust. Farther on we met a fleet of nondescript old commercials. These were the first with their tops covered with branches as camouflage, the first intimation of a country at war. Then the road cut through and beneath a gigantic red earth embankment with huge trees towering at a risky slanting angle above us. Then again we meandered across another plateau. Beside the highway an old Chinese woman, little more than skin and bones, walked painfully toward us. She was carrying a big load of wood on her back and she wore only a ragged skirt. She had no other garment and her naked breasts hung shriveled against her upper ribs. She did not look at us. It required all her waning strength to stumble forward. Now, near a tiny village, a litter of young pigs scrambled squealing out of our path. Tiny Chinese children chased them, shouting shrilly. Somehow that fleeting stark picture of the gray-haired bent old woman and her tortured body remained long after we had passed. In a single flash how much of the real China had we seen!

Peter Rowland and Dr. Hu, just graduated as a veterinary

from Edinburgh University, and I had had great luck in hooking up with the station-wagon caravan in Lashio. These de luxe American station wagons, destined for the Chinese air force and for those young American fliers who were now secretly training in Burma, could travel two or three times as fast as the ordinary Burma Road caravan. So we reached Mangshi at dusk that evening, wondering what a typical town of China's interior might be like, but amply forewarned to expect things plain, rough, and skimpy. Mangshi, it also happens, has one of the highest malaria rates in all China. Well, we had the absolutely indispensable mosquito netting and folding camp cots, quantities of canned goods, canteens filled with boiled water, cups and knives and forks — all those things which constitute a minimum kit for the Burma Road. That is, the essential minimum for soft Occidentals like ourselves. And Mangshi quickly demonstrated that we had been well advised.

Any Chinese town seems much more crowded than a New York or Chicago slum area, but in this respect we found every inhabited point along China's supercharged lifeline simply overflowing with human beings and paralyzed with motor vehicles. They said there was a hostel in Mangshi, and there was — of sorts. It was a two-storied decrepit affair, a combined office and living-room filled with tables and wooden benches and several dormitory-like rooms, each holding eight or ten beds. Rowland and I took one look at the dirty floors and soiled bed covers and were thankful we had lugged in our bedding rolls. By the light of a kerosene lantern we set up our cots and netting while Dr. Hu ruefully selected one of the few hostel beds that remained unoccupied — unoccupied, that is, so far as one could observe. It was a bad night for poor Dr. Hu. Perhaps the tiniest guests of our Burma Road "guest house" scented the fact that Dr. Hu was spending his first night in his native land for several years; or that his blood, during his stay in England, had become richer than ever. At any rate, we had scarcely blown out the lantern and settled down under our nets — stifled with the humidity, and with mosquitoes buzzing greedily by the hundreds, beating in incessant assaults against the netting — when Dr. Hu and his flashlight snapped into action. The netting formed a canopy directly above Dr. Hu's head and there, inside the canopy, he found two exceedingly fat nocturnal ramblers. At intervals all night Dr. Hu was up and after the bedbugs with his flashlight. So we slept very little and dressed gingerly, to discover that not a cup of tea (let alone coffee) could be purchased in the grimy little holes in the wall which passed for restaurants in Mangshi. Finally we located some cocoa for breakfast; then hurried out of town to where Chinese drivers would take over our station wagons from the Hindoo chauffeurs. Charan Singh told us the Indian and Burmese drivers refused to go beyond Mangshi. Too many of them had been beaten up or robbed by the Chinese gangsters, many of them drivers, who infested the Burma Road.

2

That morning at Mangshi we began to learn about the time problems of transportation over China's saw-toothed lifeline. It was "Double Ten" (the Chinese way of expressing the tenth day of the tenth month) and, being the nation's independence day, none of the war-supply caravans planned to move on that day. Fortunately a co-operative Chinese colonel agreed to permit three of our station wagons, our own three, to proceed without the others. But each must carry a huge fifty-gallon drum of gasoline, and that meant unloading our cargo of extra tires, taking out the rear seats, and some rejuggling of our loads. It also provoked as much general debate as a similar task would have touched off in a crowd of talk-loving Greeks. So it took three solid hours to get our three wagons reloaded and I then understood why the rest of our caravan would probably lose two days at Mangshi. Neither Rowland nor I, and least of all bite-scarred Dr. Hu, had any desire to spend another night in bug-ridden, malaria-infested Mangshi. In addition to that, the mountains, the truly formidable Yunnan Mountains, now lay directly ahead.

As we set out on the 3,800-foot ascent to Lungling, their first gigantic shoulders rose sprawling across the horizon, shimmering mirage-like through a haze of heat. Winding upward toward Lungling, however, the red-brown earth still clung to the hilly slopes on either side. Carefully piled stone walls, crisscrossing the slopes, held the soil in place; and the terraces thus formed, yellow with ripe wheat or green with young corn, marched up and up to the very crest of lofty ridges. In the Andes I had seen similar terraces, now in ruins, built by the Incas. These terraces spoke of Chinese frugality and patience. Not even a dozen square feet of tillable soil, however inaccessible it might seem to wasteful Westerners, was ignored. Along the roadway, too, we saw the patience and the inner strength of China. Little men and women, clad in faded blue overalls and jackets, labored steadily with heavy sledges crushing rocks. As the rocks were crushed into pieces suitable for repairing the truck-torn highway, small boys and girls piled the pieces into baskets. They labored stolidly and steadily. These, in tens of thousands, are the anonymous and unsung people who had kept the Burma Road open and passable ever since its completion in September 1938.

I had chosen to come in through China's back door because most of the problems and difficulties of continued Chinese resistance to Japan hinged upon the amount of weapons and war materials which were being transported — or could be transported — over the Burma Road. In Rangoon I had been told that only two American newspaper correspondents had traveled over the road in the past fifteen months. Of course one of these had been A. T. Steele of my own newspaper, the *Chicago Daily News*. Inevitably Arch Steele had investigated China's lifeline at first hand, this during the previous April, because he had worked that way for years in every corner of the Orient. By that kind of reporting (as I was assured by foreign ministers, cabinet members, ambassadors, and his fellow craftsmen with extraordinary unanimity wherever I went) Steele had long since established himself as the most authoritative American journalist in the entire Far East. As his temporary successor, and a newcomer to the Orient, I was bound to rattle around like a dry bean in Arch's seven-league boots. Nevertheless the importance of the Burma Road had changed in one tremendous way since Steele went over it last. The United States government had appropriated half a billion dollars or more as its first installment of Lend-Lease aid to China. Now the first trickle of vital supplies which might some day turn the tide of war against the Japs was coming up over the fabulous mountain-bucking, gorge-diving highway that stretches 1,445 miles from Rangoon's docks to Kunming in the heart of distant Yunnan. At least I could be the first correspondent to make this trip with a Lend-Lease caravan.

So here we were now, taking the first great downward dip from Lungling to the Salween River. The road coils tightly around the barren, granite-lined pyramid of the mountain. It rolls forward to one promontory, then swerves sharply back along the mountain's upper chest; back and forth and back again. Dust from the car in front of us clogs our throats and our vision, but there are no protecting walls on these cramped curves and as I look down over one edge after another the only alternative to remaining in line is all too plain. Our station wagon, if it should be pushed over, would drop and somersault at least four hundred or five hundred feet before it could meet anything as solid as a single dwarfed pine tree. We are thinking in terms of being pushed over, Rowland and myself, because dozens of trucks are now grinding fiercely and indiscriminately around these curves.

"Those drivers are mad — they're lunatics," growls my Quaker companion.

At that moment it seemed only too true, but in reality they were merely typical Chinese drivers of the Burma Road. For the one supreme slogan of the Burma Road has always been: "To hell with everybody except yourself." Here everything is as ruthless as an early American gold rush — a gold rush on wheels. And for most of the road's drivers, as we gradually discover, that is exactly what it is.

As we creep down into the rocky well of the Salween gorge, zigzagging interminably back and forth and ever downward, there comes a realization of what deep down really is. It takes us more than two hours to descend these 3,500 feet, catching a glimpse again and again of the turbulent yellow torrent of the Salween and looking with sudden live delight at the mighty lifts of sheer granite and the tumbled crags across from us. But the roadbed underneath us is remarkably good here. It is hard and strong and there are no washouts whatever. What a tremendous job of engineering and road-building! This highway has been hewn out of the sides of these vast mountains without the use of a single steam shovel or rock-crusher or tractor. It has been built completely by hand, by the same incredibly small and incredibly strong and deft hands that once built the Great Wall of China. Even now, three years after its completion, we have traveled the Burma Road for almost two days, yet we have seen only one machine shovel in all this time. Precisely one steam shovel. But the road itself, for all that and for all this undisciplined, insanely plunging traffic, remains in remarkably good condition so far.

At last, from the bottom of the gorge, our station wagon slides out on the tracklike groove of Kweitung Bridge and as its full weight hits the groove we feel the bridge's floor sinking beneath us, sinking down toward the roaring yellow torrent. This Salween bridge has an up-and-down play of at least two feet and behaves like a boa constrictor writhing across rough ground. We are relieved to be back on solid earth again, with the road serpentining upward as sharply as it descended. This time it's a long climb of 3,300 feet, but on every side the vistas hold an untamed and awesome beauty. At some moments the gorge below rivals the Grand Canyon, and then the tumbling profusion of mountain peaks, lifting successive elbows and shoulders and profiles across a vast horizon and far into the distance, claims all our attention. Burrowing through the passes and slicing around countless ridges, the highway ultimately cuts out into a lofty and opulent upland valley.

Once there we race the gathering dusk into the walled and ancient city of Paoshan. At this altitude of nearly 6,500 feet the evening air pierces lungs, too long half-smothered in the tropical straitjackets of Siam, Indo-China and Lower Burma, with a wonderful coolness. A great brick entrance house straddles the gateway of the city, and its archway is so narrow that our car passes through with but a few inches to spare. By this time night has fallen, but the cramped streets are nothing less than a human beehive and the buzz of humanity livens the night air. Small wonder, too; for Paoshan, surprising as it may be, somehow houses a population of more than 370,000.

We ferret our way into cobbled rough streets which are much quieter; and here is a house of pure ancient style which merits the name of hostelry. Its rooms open on a central courtyard where large plants and flowerpots and several young fig trees create an atmosphere curiously like that in a Spanish patio in Córdoba or Seville. The ridgepoles of the roofs on all four sides hang swaybacked, rising skyward at each end with an impeccable delicacy and grace. This is an old and lovely house where some wealthy Mandarin family must have lived for several centuries. Now it has become the one real sanctuary on the Burma Road. Here we slept well, while the rain commenced and poured down steadily, easing our nerves by night but placing a new and greater strain upon them for tomorrow and after tomorrow.

3

Beyond Paoshan the valley spreads out into thriving rice-fields dotted with roomy houses, all speaking of well-to-do farmers and a prosperity we had not dreamed could exist in the mountain fastnesses of Yunnan's interior. But the roadway is now filled with deep puddles and greased with mud from the rain which still falls from a slate sky. Even so, men and women, using their wide sombrero-type hats partially as umbrellas, labor uninterruptedly at cracking rocks. From the shoulders down they are soaked to the skin, yet we come upon groups of such workers, including many children, every few miles along the way. Then the fog and the mists close in around us as we start downward once more toward the deeper gorge of the mightier and more grandiose Mekong River. Much to my relief, Peter Rowland, sturdy and soft-spoken and calmly efficient, has taken the wheel again.

"Why on earth do these Chinese drivers always coast out of gear down these mountains?" Peter demands. "They don't save any petrol to speak of, and they ruin their engines."

"Well, the Arnstein committee says the Chinese learned to drive that way, and there's nobody here to force them to change. After all, there's no traffic control on the road. Plenty of tax-collection stations, but no policemen."

"I don't think we'll have much fun today," Peter replies. "Soon we'll be meeting the Burma-bound trucks again. Why don't they have one-way traffic on this road? There's no reason why the loaded ingoing trucks couldn't travel by day and the empty outgoing trucks by night. that would prevent a lot of smash-ups and save a great deal of time."

All of which seemed very sensible, except that this was the Orient, the Burma Road was a wartime improvisation, and even after three years there still existed no over-all supervision to correct costly habits which were now ingrained. So our car sloshed between tight hills at the valley's end and we started sliding downward, past red hills and hills of rock and then alongside twisting ravines which were soon smothered in mist. Above us now the white clouds blanketed out the mountains. A little farther on we came upon an abandoned truck. It lay teetering on its belly, its front wheels projecting out into emptiness—hanging over nothing at all but gaping space. We wondered how its driver felt as he crawled back from the eyelash edge of that 300-foot drop.

Half-way down the gorge we overtook a large Chinese convoy and paused to chat with an American missionary and his wife. They had been riding one of these trucks all the way from Lashio, and thus far it had taken them eight days to cover what we had traversed in only two and a half days. So this caravan would probably require two weeks to reach Kunming. That was the measure of the heart-breaking task of getting war supplies over the road.

We had a steady ten-mile, 3,700-foot climb with the rain now at a downpour tempo and the road's surface thick with menacing juice. There was another bridge at Shingpi. We reached it at six o'clock and already it was dark. Yet there was nothing to do but to grind our way upward for as many hundred feet as we had just descended; and after that a three-hour nightmare, over unseen ridges and ghostly valleys, through a fog so dense that our headlights rarely pierced more than thirty feet in front of us. That was the last treacherous lap into Hsiakwan (pronounced Shah-gwan), and when we reached that darkened walled city we had behind us eleven tense hours of ceaseless battle over one of the most dangerous roads in the world.

But unwashed and grimy as we were, the morning was something to remember; and so was Hsiakwan. At six in the morning the sky already wore a gown of robin's-egg blue. The mists were rolling up the valley and a single scarf of white cloud encircled a shining green hill beyond the city's rooftops as I stepped out of the garage door. Directly opposite stood a gilt-and-garnet old pagoda, with a hawk perched lazily on a corner of its low roof. Our drivers had slept in the cars; but they had vanished, so I strolled into the center of the town. The tile roofs of the tightly packed houses were Oriental picturesqueness itself, one ornamental kind of extra roof being set upon and several feet above a larger and more projecting main roof underneath. The roofs were so old that grass and even daisies grew in little bunches between the cracked tiles, and the sun shone on weathered walls of mauve and brown.

Several women passed me, hobbling in tiny steps on feet that looked like sticks. I gazed, half-incredulous, at the distorted little lumps of flesh which made it impossible for them ever to run or walk swiftly. These were the women with bound feet; elderly women, the last and fortunately vanishing victims of a horrible medieval custom. I saw a good many of them that morning in Hsiakwan, but once I understood what caused their crippled, teetering gait I could not endure looking at them. On all sides unfamiliar things and curious scenes quickly commanded my attention. Here is an old woman deftly rolling balls of dough and tossing them into a kettle of hot fat. When they are done she fishes them out and sprinkles them with a brown substance. Some kind of Chinese dumpling, I suppose they are. In these Yunnan towns almost anything is prepared, cooked, and sold on the narrow sidewalks. Regardless of dirt, dust, and incessant traffic, hunks of dried meat dangle on strings and are brushed by pedestrians' elbows.

Here comes an old fellow right out of a Chinese print, from his black skullcap and drooping black mustache down to his slippers. And here I meet another patriarch whose chin sprouts such a thin driblet of white hairs as to be startlingly effective. His cap is of faded black velvet and he wears a long blue shirt-tailed gown with patched trousers underneath it. The streets are festooned with decorations and ideographs for yesterday's Double Ten festivities. Several times I nearly stumble over live chickens where they lie tied together on the sidewalk waiting for marketers to come and bargain for them. As I start back toward the cars, a baby's anguished wailing suddenly strikes my ears. A few steps forward and my eyes trace the sound through the window of a tiny shop. A baby, perhaps twenty months of age, is sitting on a crude bed. It is naked and its entire body and face are covered with great festering sores. The baby sits bolt upright, sobbing its heart out, tears coursing down its diseased cheeks. A woman, thin and drooping, stands at a table close by. She is stirring rice—stirring slowly and mechanically. The baby's cries pound at my eardrums. Its body is terrible to see. The woman does not look at the child. She stirs slowly, slowly, her head bowed. This, all this, is the real China which quick-trippers and distinguished visitors seldom see.

4

We were inexcusably late in starting that fourth morning on the road. Our drivers had been up before six, yet they had neither fueled the cars nor eaten when eventually they reappeared about eight thirty. Rowland, Hu, and I were fuming to get under way in order to avoid another nightmare on the highway after dark. But the Chinese chauffeurs were full of bland excuses. "Monkey business of some kind," said Dr. Hu. In the course of a long day's ride the monkey business became perfectly clear in the shape of dozens of cartons of English cigarettes, which jounced out from under seats, bedding rolls, and other places of concealment in the station wagons. English cigarettes brought handsome prices in Kunming and beyond. This was where part of the Burma Road drivers' "squeeze" came in.

We drove over the highest point on the road that day, with magnificent panoramas of humpbacked mountain ranges visible at times for more than fifty miles without a break. Finally, in mid-afternoon, we struck a long level valley. Dr. Hu had his station wagon rolling cozily along at some thirty-five miles an hour and was just in front of us, rounding a curve and hugging it, when the Burma Road law of averages caught up with him. Of course, the big truck was far over on Dr. Hu's side of the road. Rowland and I saw a Chinese coolie sail off the top of the truck and land on his head and shoulder twenty feet away. Several other coolies cluttered up the landscape in those few seconds, yet picked themselves up immediately. Peter Rowland, a Red Cross man who knew his job, reached the injured Chinese in a flash. A long deep gash in the coolie's head was bleeding profusely. I suppose none of these Chinese had ever seen a first-aid job done in the long and callous history of the Burma Road. A score of natives watched wonderingly while Peter shaved the man's scalp and dressed his wound expertly. Meanwhile the truck-driver vociferously blamed Dr. Hu for a crash which was palpably his own fault; and meantime the front end of one of our fine new $1,200 station wagons was reduced to a pulp. Meanwhile, too, the cars piled up behind us on both sides. Characteristically, no one paid any attention to the traffic jam. If I couldn't mend heads or carburetors, at least I could shout. Eventually, with resort to the most emphatic sounds and sign-language in my repertoire, I got the trucks moving again. But the wrecked station wagon had to be towed by our number-two car and the process would be so slow that we might reach Chu 'Hsiung too late to find any place to sleep. So I went on ahead to hunt for a hostel with our own driver, Yang, and one of the others.

Yang was an amiable, shrewd-eyed young roughneck, reckless and devil-may-care, and his friend was of precisely the same stripe. The valleys were longer and wider now, so Yang drove at a fast pace, all the while chattering, joking, and gesticulating with his pal. Hitting it up in this fashion, we burst suddenly over a slight rise in the highway and a sickening sight struck my eyes. Exactly in the middle of the road lay the body of a man. The side of his head was bashed wide open. His face and shoulders were covered with blood. He was trying to crawl — to lift the upper part of his body on his hands. I saw all this in a split second as Yang jerked the wheel to the right and we sped past. I grabbed the knee of the driver, who sat between Yang and me. "Stop! He's dying. We've got to help him! Stop!" I cried again. Though they couldn't speak a word of English, of course they knew what I meant. But Yang pushed his foot down on the accelerator. We were making fifty miles an hour now. I looked back. I thought I had seen pieces of brain bulging from the wound in that man's head. Yang and his partner were jabbering to me in great seriousness now. The gist of their gestures was plain enough. Their gestures said: "If we stop we will be blamed. People will say that we ran him down. If you try to help people, you only get into trouble. The only thing to do is to get away fast." Yang drove on faster than ever. In a few minutes the two Chinese were chattering and laughing together as lightheartedly as ever. In the Orient you seldom worry about a dying man or a dying animal. Here, and most of all on this Burma Road, it is every dog for himself. Yang and his partner had simply followed a rule of the over-populated, misery-ridden East, a rule which is thousands of years old.

An ancient walled-in Chinese city can look like a small town and still contain more than 140,000 Chinese. Chu 'Hsiung was like this, and you understood how it could be so once you got inside its very thick and hoary walls. In the main street Yang led me to a narrow doorway and into a cramped corridor. Upstairs I found a dirty front room with three beds made of boards and covered with soiled matting and sheets. I piled all that in one corner so we could put up our own cots. Then the proprietress showed me a kettle of boiling water where we could heat our beans. We ate at the rough table in the front corridor, a dozen Chinese youngsters crowding around us. They cackled with delight when they sampled our beans. One was a very bright-eyed little chap who looked no more than five years old. I taught him to say "eeny, meeny, miney, mo," and he roared with pleasure when he repeated the strange sounds after me. Eeny-meeny and I became friends at once, so he asked immediately for our first empty can. We had eaten so little for so long that tomato soup and beans tasted like a dinner at LaRue's in Paris. Toward the end of our meal I noticed Eeny-meeny making a swift motion near a paper picture that hung on the wall. Behind the picture I discovered he had hidden two more of our empty cans. For all his wide eyes and childish capers, and despite his diminutive size, little Eeny-meeny was an expert at looking after himself. He was remarkably intelligent; he had great charm and his laughter was contagious; and at the age of four or five he was well versed in taking care of number one. This, we had noticed, was equally true of Dr. Hu and of Yang — it seemed to be true of all the Chinese we had yet met. I liked Eeny-meeny and, within the limits of his opportunities, I'm sure he will become a successful man. I still think of him as typical, in many respects, of his country and his countrymen. Among other things Eeny-meeny was much more grown up than his outward appearance.

5

On our fifth and last day on the Burma Road there was only one more 1,500-foot climb, going up to Ipinglang. Then we started winding down a rock-bitten gorge where the highway hugged the cliffs above a swift-flowing river. Now all our thoughts were concentrated upon getting through to Kunming without an accident. The strain of the endless hairpin curves and the constant narrow misses from wildly driven trucks had put my nerves on edge. It didn't help very much to look down and see a big truck astride a bunch of rocks in the middle of the river, a good four hundred feet below the roadbed. And the dozens of trucks which now roared up at us around a series of dastardly curves strongly reinforced that too vivid reminder of what could happen at almost any moment. Peter Rowland laughed uneasily.

"I don't know which song to sing—'Scatterbrain' or 'I'm heading for the last round-up,'" he said.

So we rode on in a prayerful mood, thinking of only one thing—if only we could get to Kunming without another smash-up. But the worst of the road's terrors were all behind us now. By early afternoon we reached the village of Lufung, a madhouse of parked trucks and shouting Chinese drivers. But Lufung actually had a neat and relatively clean coffee house, where we obtained excellent cocoa for twelve Chinese dollars. I figured it out that this amounted to forty American cents per cup, or thereabouts, but to us it was more than worth it. Strange that Yang and our other drivers had still shown no interest in getting some food. When we returned to the station wagon the explanation was evident. There was Yang just concluding a transaction for his last five cartons of cigarettes. When we started on, with Peter driving, Yang pulled two huge rolls of Chinese dollars out of his pockets and began to count them, his face glowing with pleasure. They had unloaded the cigarettes at Lufung to escape the customs inspection at the outskirts of Kunming. Someone else would do the smuggling from Lufung, getting a bigger profit the nearer he got to Chungking. But Yang was happy. After all, on this one trip his profit in "squeeze" amounted to as much as a Chinese professor earns in salary for three months or more.

The road was still devilishly slippery from recurring showers; and once, just as I was thinking that you needed a new prayer on every curve, a speeding truck missed us by less than two inches. I cursed and Peter, being a good Quaker, merely tightened his lips in a grim line. We had both lost all interest in the scenery or in anything except getting to Kunming all in one piece. Nevertheless, after another fifty miles of riding on tenterhooks, the highway at last struck a wide plateau and cut straight across a friendly plain, broken by occasional hillocks of red and mauve earth. For the first time, on a trek which had now brought us seven hundred miles from Lashio, the road ran straight for two or three miles at a stretch. Here, too, it was hard-surfaced; and beyond the mud-walled town of Anning the highway was lined with towering and lovely eucalyptus trees, the same trees which had stood so majestically along many of the roads in Greece.

At every rise or turn we looked eagerly ahead for a first glimpse of Kunming. And at last, pushing through a great red gap, we had it. There lay the broad peaceful lake and on its lower shores the great huddle of buildings which was Kunming — and for us the end of the Burma Road odyssey. Nearing the town, the highway became cluttered with coolies carrying long planks on their backs and all sorts of heavy objects. Then suddenly a great hole marred the high wall along the roadside and through it we saw the skeleton of a house and several shell-holes in the adjoining field. In another ten minutes we were waiting for the customs inspection at the entrance to Kunming. We had made it in five days, remarkably fast traveling, and it had been a lucky trip in every way. But just how lucky I did not fully appreciate at that time.

A few weeks later William Dunn of the Columbia Broadcasting Company journeyed over the road from Kunming to Lashio. En route Dunn's chauffeur was assaulted by eight government drivers because he had told them there was no room for them in his car. The gang of eight men beat the driver with clubs and with a spade. Then one thug seized a rock and smashed the defenseless chauffeur on the head, knocking him senseless. Bill Dunn's arrival on the scene unquestionably saved the man's life. Of course, Bill asked him why he hadn't fought back. " If I strike back I know they'll shoot me," the Chinese explained, "and nobody will care." About that same time a more terrible example of typical Burma Road lawlessness was witnessed by two American officers who were bringing a United States Navy supply truck up from Lashio. Just in front of them a truck was crashed into head-on by a Chinese army conveyance which was speeding on the wrong side of the highway. Out leapt a dozen Chinese soldiers. They hauled the driver out of the truck, knocked him down, and began kicking him fiercely from head to foot. Then the two Americans, so outnumbered they did not dare to intervene, saw one soldier grab a rock-crusher hammer from beside the road and literally bludgeon the brains out of their victim's head. Meanwhile other soldiers pulled a second man from the truck and knifed him to death. After that the murderers pushed the truck upside down into a ditch; then climbed back into their own lorry and rode away. For more than three years this kind of gangsterism had flourished, virtually without control and still without any attempt at effective police interference along the middle sector of the Burma Road, which we had just traversed with such relative ease and dispatch. Hold-ups and robbery were frequently part of the same pattern of mob beatings, shootings, and murder. That explained why Englishmen and Americans in Burma, men who knew the road well, had said: "Take a gun with you, if you go over the road." But I had never fired a revolver in my life and nourished an acute distaste for firearms; and beside that, I was pretty much of a fatalist. You needed to be a fatalist if you were going to travel the Burma Road at all, but especially so if you traveled it as we had, unarmed and comforted only by the massiveness of our ignorance.

So we were in Kunming at last and at the wonderfully clean and civilized Hotel de l'Europe a good friend awaited me. I had never met him, but I knew he was a good friend simply because he was a Greek. Ever since the Italo-Greek war any Greek anywhere in the world, regardless of his circumstances or condition and wherever I might meet him, had proved himself a warm-hearted and generous friend of mine. His dark eyes sparkling, Dimitri Kominatos grabbed my hand and pumped it.

"You were in Greece in the war? You were with the Greek Army? How did they fight? . . . Good soldiers, eh? . . . But you must tell us all about it. You must have dinner with us. . . . Sure, I can fix you a room. Sure you can have a bath. . . . And then we'll have dinner."

It was too bad that Peter Rowland had gone off to his Red Cross headquarters. What stuffed peppers and peas and roast chicken! And with them Mr. Kominatos opened up the last two bottles of Aloxe-Corton that he had in his cellar. For those few hours it did not seem at all that I was in China, nor that Kunming could possibly be so far from Athens and the Acropolis — so far from what most of us still thought of as another war.

I must get on to Chungking by the first plane, I told him; and then learned all the reasons (special priorities and permits and all sorts of red tape) which would make such a thing impossible. But my new Greek friend provided me with that most prized luxury in wartime China, an automobile; and three kind Britishers who were staying at the hotel put themselves out to get me in touch with the proper Chinese officials. Thanks solely to their combined aid, I crawled aboard a CNAC (Chinese National Airways) plane the following afternoon, with the echo of one old China hand's remark: "I'll bet it's the first time anybody ever arrived in Kunming one evening and got on a Chungking plane the next day." Well, they did take off most of my luggage and my bedding roll at the last moment, but they left me aboard. I was figuring fearfully all the while how many more days it would take to cover the 711 miles by road from Kunming to Chungking. Just then I felt that I knew enough about the Burma Road without pursuing it the hard way any farther.

Oh yes. When I tried to pay my bill at the Hotel de l'Europe that noon the answer was very firm — and very Greek.

"There is no bill," said Dimitri Kominatos. "If you want a bill, then you come back again. Sure thing. Don't worry. We'll always find a room for you."

Chapter II

CHUNGKING – CITADEL OF CHINA'S RESISTANCE

If you continually grind a bar of iron,
you can make a needle of it.
Chinese proverb

Between the thumb of the Yangtze and the forefinger of the Chialing River the many-headed bluff rises hundreds of feet above the yellow waters which meet and mingle at its base. The bluff is scarred by innumerable ravines and gullies, and its limestone cliffs and hillsides sheer off and fall with startling sharpness. Yet on all sides and in every crevice drab dwellings, some with dull slate roofs and others of new or fading thatched straw, cling to the sudden slopes like colonies of swallows' nests.

From across the Yangtze, when the sun is bright and pitiless, the city looks surprisingly like a large Pennsylvania mining town, transplanted and stuck hit-or-miss upon a half-crumbling section of the Hudson River's Palisades. But when the morning mists cloak the Szechuan Hills with filmy veils of mysterious gray, the great bluff loses all its scars and wrinkles and ugly warts. Both the bluff and the city become a faint and hovering silhouette, shrouded in the fog-born drift and uncertainty of some undecipherable never-never land. At such times Chungking is a fortress, straight out of the tales of King Arthur and his knights.

The Chialing House is an oversized swallows' nest glued high up on one of Chungking's steepest palisades. It's the only hotel in China's capital that Jap bombers failed to destroy in three seasons of raids. Its windowpanes have all been blown out long since and shell craters pock the slopes around it, but the long ramshackle building remains intact on its shaken foundations — an outstanding target which hundreds of Jap planes have bombed and missed. So you can still look down with wonder and delight from the outer balconies of the Chialing House upon something that is part of the eternal China. Several miles up the valley the

Chialing River sweeps out of the mountains and swings downstream in a wide majestic curve. On this side the hills stand stubbornly close, but on the opposite shore the land spreads out in gentler undulations. In some places it is richly green. In others lie red geometric patterns cut by peasants' plows. The river lies between, but it never seems to move. Its broad, curving surface lies motionless, a liquid brown of a strange and glazed and silent beauty. In October, when the river falls lower every day and its red-brown flats grow wider and wider and the thrifty Chinese begin to plant their low-tide crops on its newly exposed flats across the way, there are no waves or ripples on the river's surface. The river lies dead, yet it is full of life. Directly below the hotel balconies you look almost straight down upon it and there, more than four hundred feet below, the sampans poke their way upstream. They are always coming or going and the long oars of Chinese junks shatter the illusion. This polished and luminescent brown floor in the valley is really water. The sampans and the junks churn up tiny wakes that swell rhythmically behind them. Here China moves with the slow and toilsome pace of her long centuries. But on many days the mists seize the fields and peasants' huts, the river and junks and creeping sampans in their close embrace, and then the Chialing becomes its true self—the soft breath of an intangible and indefinable beauty; something uncapturable and indescribable, now approaching and now retreating, yet forever lost in the unfathomable.

From the Chialing House a rutted lane, usually thick with mud from October into May, winds back around the cliffs into the main road. This main road coils upward until it tops the summit of the bluff and reaches the rolling uplands of the plateau beyond; and it also twists downward crazily and laboriously, backtracking around hills and through business districts of Chungking, until it reaches the first street level at the head of the three hundred and seven stone steps which descend to the Yangtze ferry. Turning down the road from Chialing Lane, you walk nearly a mile to the corner known as Liang Loo Kow. Every day I passed this way once or several times, and every day, regardless of rain or the depth of slithery ooze upon the roadbed, I met them coming up. That first morning in Chungking they happened to be hidden by an elbow bend, so I heard them first.

"Hai-*toh!* Hai-*tah!* . . . Hai-*toh!* Hai-*tah!* . . . Hai-*toh!* Hai-*tah!*"

It was a rhythmic chant; really just a series of two-toned gasps. It sounded like — and it was — a Chinese version of the Volga Boatmen's Song, only much less melodious and even sadder and much more monotonous. Rounding the bend, I came upon them before I had figured out what this gasping chorus could be. There they were, three men and two small boys. Sometimes there are only three. Sometimes as many as six. Otherwise it is always the same; as it has always been, I suppose, for hundreds or thousands of years.

They are hitched to a massive two-wheeled cart, and this morning the cart is filled with baskets of crushed rock. The leader's place is between the shafts. He has a rope slung over one shoulder and down around his chest; then the rope goes back to where it is tied on the cart. The other two men, and the boys on either side, wear the same rope harness, and the ropes cut deeply into their knotted shoulders and narrow chests. The boys are about as tall as the average ten-year-olds in America, but much more slender. The men are equally small and slight and perhaps do not weigh more than 115 pounds. They are human horses. Have you ever seen human horses? Would you like to be a human horse? Would you like to be a human horse from the age of ten or twelve until you die?

"Hai-*toh!* Hai-*tah!* . . . Hai-*toh!* Hai-*tah!*"

The sound comes out of their throats, out of their very bellies, with a tearing sound. The load, cart and all, must be half a ton or possibly much more than that. In any case, it is so cruelly heavy and the road is so steep that the coolies, men and boys, are compelled to lean far forward so that the upper halves of their bodies are almost parallel with the highway. They lean forward digging their toes into the slimy clay, straining so that their muscles bulge and quiver on their thin legs and taut shoulders. They are naked to the waist and their brown skin is tight over their ribs, and the ropes tear against their shoulder bones. They cannot move the cart unless all are pulling together with every ounce in their frail, lacerated bodies. So they strain and strain — "Hai-*toh!* Hai-*tah!*" — and the big rubber-tired cart wheels just barely roll forward and upward. With all their combined effort the wheels roll slowly up the brutally steep slope; more slowly and painfully than you have ever seen anything drawn in your life. But the weight of the last gut and intestine of these little Chinese men and boys pushes into the harness and pulls on the ropes. Somehow they keep the wheels turning, over ruts and rocks, while the sweat beads their faces and half blinds their eyes and pours in rivulets down their incredible bodies of iron and bone.

I turn and watch them, and I watch with my stomach caught in a cramped vise, as they toil up and ever upward on this killing mud-greased cliffside. The sweat keeps rolling into their eyes. Each coolie carries a dirty rag in one hand. As he leans forward, digging his toes into the wet slime, he wipes the sweat out of his eyes again and again. But they do not stop, these human horses, not for several hundreds of yards. And the harsh gasp of their co-ordinated breathing continues unbroken. It is a chant that goes on day after day, year after year, century after century. "Hai-*toh!*" chants the leader between the shafts, the man whose pitifully thin, undernourished body is already breaking with age. "Hai-*tah!*" gasp the others in response. "Hai-*toh!* . . . Hai-*tah!* . . . Hai-*toh!* . . . Hai-*tah!*" It is as if they were saying: "It can — be done! . . . We've got — to live! . . . It can — be done! . . . We've got — to live." It is half a moan and half a challenge. It is half despair and half triumph. It is half an appeal to courage and half a cry of hopelessness from burning veins and tortured trembling flesh. "It must — be done! . . . It can — be done!" Slowly, ever slowly. Through how many hundreds of years gone by? Through how many hundreds of years to come?

Now I am aware that there are other carts and other human horses, above me on the heights and beside me around the bulges of cliffs and hillsides and below me in the tortuous labyrinth of Chungking. But everywhere the chant is the same. "Hai-*toh!* . . . Hai-*tah!*" It begins far down, miles below, where the Yangtze junks unload their cargoes. It continues miles upward from here, to the crest of Chungking's highest summit and beyond. It begins at daybreak and it echoes until night settles mercifully at last. I wonder what this kind of excruciating labor does to men's souls. What kind of will-powers are these which drain the last trembling drop of strength out of fragile bodies and flagellated flesh? What do we know of the indomitable spirit of man? These are men built like children. What manner of men are these? Ah, but these are the scores and hundreds of millions of China's people. These are the most important people of China. How many foreigners have come and gone, still come and go, and look once or twice when at first they hear that terrible endless chant — "Hai-*toh!* Hai-*tah!*" — and then look away and soon do not hear them any more, nor see them again? How many of us have done so, but how little we know! And how wrong we have been! You, too, have wondered at the strength of China? It is in the crushing of the rock that made the Burma Road. It crawls daily around and up the palisades of Chungking. It is in thousands of unknown towns and cities. It is in millions of acres of stubbornly tended soil. It lies within the harness and the hearts of millions of China's coolies.

2

No photograph or motion picture, even in technicolor, will ever give you the Orient. You cannot smell a picture. But without smells there is no East. Someone has laughingly told me that Shanghai (or maybe it's Hangkow) "is a city of a thousand smells — and all different." All the Orient, I've been discovering, is a conglomeration of the most amazing smells, and a great many of them are by no means pleasant. Chungking, too, is a city of mud and guts; of tawdriness and ugliness; sometimes of a rare and startling beauty — and also, inevitably, a metropolis of smells. In Chungking you can smell enough smells to last you a lifetime, and you can do the same in any city or town in China, or in Indo-China or Thailand or in how many other Oriental lands! Old Marco Polo was a remarkably talented reporter, but he had one great liability. Apparently he had no sense of smell whatsoever. In all his famous pages of documentation he fails to make the slightest mention of the unbelievable and fantastic olfactory diversity of the East. Marco Polo was the Middle Ages' first and greatest tourist-trade promoter, so he left the smells out. Anywhere in the Orient there are pleasant odors, intriguing odors, annoying odors — and revolting odors. Chungking, of course, has its full share.

Even so, on that first morning I thought Chungking's streets were exceptionally clean; especially for those of a bombed city and especially for China. That impression was chiefly due to the fact that I was in a rickshaw rolling down the main thoroughfares from Liang Loo Kow and so missing the side alleys and shortcuts, and missing those ravines and gullies where pigs live in the same huts with their owners and where cesspools, overflowing with human excrement, lie open so close to bypaths that you could walk into them in the dark. But the principal streets seemed clean enough and were crowded with bustling, unperturbed Chinese. Some of the shops were of new bamboo, rebuilt on the ashes of those which had been burned out a month or two previously. Some were old wrecks, with daylight showing through their cracked roofs and sides, but they were still open for business. Tiny tots, attractive and lively, toddled around everywhere. They were bright and astonishingly strong and many of them looked surprisingly well fed, perhaps because survival burned so fiercely in their small bodies. One little codger of no more than four, his head completely shaved, was carrying a baby in a basket on his back. I marveled again at the self-reliance which is imposed by necessity upon the Chinese while they are still babies. I met a man with a small dry-goods store on his back. He was pounding a leather gong, using a tom-tom to peddle his wares. Another man, loaded down with buttons of all kinds, swung a metallic clapper to lure customers. There were open shops with tanned hides hanging flapping outside. There were all kinds of shops as the road curved around the hillsides; then came some large buildings, half-wrecked by the bombs, and then more shops which were still untouched.

In our descent to the Yangtze, curving and twisting around in most confusing fashion, we struck ten or a dozen different levels of this palisade city. Each level constituted another section of Chungking and frequently, in between, we passed high reaches of limestone cliff. The base of every such cliff was perforated by dark doorways, entrances to the caves which had been blasted out to make the bomb-shelters which had proved the salvation of China's capital. Everywhere the hillsides and cliffs were excavated. All that previous spring and summer of 1941 the people of Chungking had lived in these hundreds of caves a great portion of the time. I didn't like the idea of using a human horse for locomotion, but Chungking's streets are a baffling rabbit warren when first you meet them. Without a rickshaw I had small chance of finding the Yangtze ferry, so scruples had bowed to urgency: Down the sharp slopes the rickshaw boys gallop wildly, letting the wheeled weight behind push them recklessly around the curves; and after one such mad dash we came out on another level stretch where a group of soldiers were just falling in to resume their march. Here, almost head-on, we ran straight into it — a second sight which I had seen nowhere else in the world and which I must ever after associate with China.

The soldiers wore shirts and shorts of a faded yellow cotton and they were very young — anywhere from seventeen to twenty, it seemed. Some walked stooped-over under great iron kettles and other cooking utensils, but most of the soldiers lugged two huge bundles of hay which were suspended from a pole slung across their shoulders. All were under way except one boy soldier. His body was terribly emaciated; really nothing more than skin and bones. His legs were so thin they looked like stilts. He had the pole over his shoulder and was trying to lift the two great bundles of hay off the ground. As we neared I saw him struggling and pulling. His face was ashen-white. With set teeth he tugged and tugged again, his entire body trembling violently from the effort. Once, and twice, and then a third time the young soldier with the toothpick legs tried — and failed. Probably he was newly released from a hospital — or perhaps he should have been in a hospital many days previously. His breath was coming in violent gasps when the sergeant stepped over. The sergeant lifted the pole with its double end-weights off the ground and slid it on the soldier's shoulder as he stood two-thirds erect. The boy staggered under the load, sticking his legs far apart. Then with an enormous effort he straightened up; slowly, stubbornly, silently. The sergeant stepped aside. The soldier staggered forward. Actually, he lurched, and as I watched him tottering I expected him to fall. His thin legs wobbled like those of a prizefighter who gropes blindly into the finishing knock-out punch. But no, he tottered forward doggedly. Somehow he kept his feet. My rickshaw boy started to run down the next incline. Looking back, I saw that horribly thin human wreck still staggering forward under his killing burden. Among the Chinese pedestrians no one had looked at him for more than a moment. These, after all, are sights which the Chinese have known all their lives.

When I came back that noon from the American Embassy across the Yangtze, I took another rickshaw. I was rereading my first letters from home in several weeks, so it was only of a sudden that I noticed what a terrific pull the rickshaw coolie was having up the formidable hills. I tried to make him stop for a rest, but he didn't understand any language I could speak and he paid no attention to my gestures. Nobody ever bothered to insist that he take time out to catch his breath. He would haul you for two miles up these sharp slopes for ten or twelve American cents at most, but when I gave him double what he had asked I still felt ashamed. Afterward, throughout most of my weeks in Chungking, I joined the Bill Dunn club. Bill, who was rather close to being a Mr. Six-by-Six, simply wouldn't fit into any ordinary rickshaw or sedan chair and he had a healthy humanitarian scorn of the contraptions anyway. So Bill hiked up and down the Chungking palisades, through the slime and the mud, some eight or ten miles every day — and growled about the lamentable fact that he still tipped the scales somewhere above two hundred and thirty and apparently hadn't lost a pound for all the sweat with which he larded the Chungking landscape. When Bill had mail at our Embassy, all he had to do was walk down some four or five miles to the Yangtze, and climb down 308 stone steps on one side and up 361 stone steps to the Embassy on the other side (the exact number, if you please, because we counted them any number of times). Then Bill reversed the process to get back up to the Chialing House. Most of the time we all did the same. It only used up two thirds of a day to make that one trek, but of course you slogged around for several more miles in the mud in order to see government officials in the different ministries. There are no automobiles for commonplace civilians. Chungking, journalistically speaking, is the greatest "leg work" capital in the world.

One day, without Bill's extraordinary energy to bolster my good intentions, I weakened and took a rickshaw. I asked Dr. Chi, the press bureau's interpreter, to tell the boy that I'd only take the rickshaw to the foot of the first big hill. I thought the boy looked much too weak to climb the hills, and I couldn't feel right riding up them anyway. But the boy refused categorically to take me at all unless he took me all the way. Reluctantly I relented, yet long before we reached the first stiff climb my rickshaw boy fell into a paroxysm of coughing. He was spitting blood and then more blood, but still tried to lope along. I jumped out and gave him some paper currency. But not enough — not nearly as much as I wish I had given him. It was the kind of charity that you hate yourself for; the kind of giving that is generosity to the recipient, but not to you. He was a fine slender youth. His face was sensitive and his smile extremely attractive. "He'll die in a few weeks," Mr. Chi said. "He can't do that kind of work." It was all too evident. Tuberculosis would yield him only a little more time. Yet I did not go back and empty my pockets. It was easier to give myself the poor excuse that I was afraid he would know that I knew.

At that time the press hostel was in the process of being rebuilt for the third or fourth occasion after being leveled by Jap bombs. Consequently the American and British correspondents who were resident in Chungking also lived in the Chialing House, where temporary visitors like Bill Dunn and Dave Woodward of the London *News Chronicle* and I were installed. The hostel was almost completed now, however, and its low mud-walled, straw-roofed sheds looked like a misplaced African kraal. It stood close to the battered and half-wrecked building which housed the Chinese bureau of information. There Dr. Hollington Tong, the bureau's energetic chief, and Jimmy Wei and many other Chinese men and women worked with great fervor and patriotism seven days a week without thought of anything but their country's cause.

When we went back to Chialing after dark we took the back-lots short cut; down a slippery embankment into a narrow gully, along the top of a stone wall, through a defile of huts where women worked by candlelight near the doorways and pigs grunted complacently on the board floors and babies laughed or cried. Then we took a sharp right turn, down a few more steps, to cross a dike which helped to irrigate some gardens in that little valley. Beyond the dike we climbed up toward the main road and right there the smell was horrendous, because that's where scores of pails of excrement were dumped — not very carefully

— every day. Human fertilizer is almost the only fertilizer that most of China knows. But when the ground was muddy (meaning most of the time) a slight slip could precipitate you into a disaster such as you would never forget if you lived for three centuries. Open cesspools like this were scattered around on all sides of Chungking's slopes and gulleys, even close to the central arteries of this city of more than 800,000 wartime inhabitants. I do not think it is in any sense derogatory of Chungking to mention their presence. Without its dirt and filth and squalor and poverty, without its disease and its lack of sanitation and its primitiveness, no picture of China can pretend to be true. Nor can the heroic dimensions of China's struggle for freedom and for modernization be understood without these uglier, ever present, and unavoidable elements. Any visitor to Chungking should walk the city's alleys and back lots day after day and should pick his way gingerly past that reeking pit on the Chialing short cut several times a week. Of course, that's no place for the squeamish-minded. But neither is China. Rather quickly the visitor will learn that he's got to take China as it lives and suffers and half-starves, and somehow continues to exist — in the rough. See China without smells, without filth, and without man's inhumanity to man? Once you might have been able to think you were seeing such a China in some small section of the International Settlement in Shanghai or in the luxurious hotels built by foreign devils in Hong Kong. I don't know. All I know is that Marco Polo played an unforgivable trick on all of us. There is no China without smells. There is no China without coolies racked by labor which ravages and tears their guts to the breaking-point. There is no China without toothpick-legged soldiers with hearts of iron. There is no China without rickshaw boys spitting blood.

3

One day, several weeks later, I went across the Chialing river with an American army officer of General Magruder's mission, to visit a Chinese hospital. Surgeon-General Li of the Chinese Army, an alert and intelligent man, accompanied us. This was November 1941, and the Sino-Japanese struggle was well into its fifth year. China needed 22,000 doctors, the surgeon-general told us, but she had only managed to produce about 6,000 over the last thirty years. What was an army doctor paid? From 60 to 250 Chinese dollars a month. Under the present runaway inflation this amounted to less than eight American dollars per month for the highest-paid doctors in the Chinese Army, yet even these top surgeons had to pay one and one half months' salary to buy a pair of shoes. Chinese public-health doctors received salaries twice or three times as high as the army physicians. That was one reason there were only 1,200 qualified doctors for the millions of Chinese troops. In this hospital only five out of twenty-three on its medical staff were qualified doctors. Perhaps that was why we saw an orderly dressing ugly open wounds with his own left hand encased in a dirty bandage. He was doing the best he could do under the circumstances, and he worked gently.

The building resembled an abandoned factory. Its windows were long and narrow, without panes. It stood but a short distance up the bank, so the damp and chilling air from the river swept into the dormitory rooms upon the wounded day and night. The cots were covered with sheets or cotton-stuffed quilts. We did not see a single woolen blanket in the hospital; and the soldiers lay huddled on their beds, clothed in the same soiled field uniforms in which they had fought. They lay very still, row upon row, and by their postures you knew they were cold. They watched us curiously, but few of them spoke or smiled. They had been brought hundreds of miles, over the mountains and down the river. Now they were in a hospital at last — but they had no blankets. They uttered no word of complaint. "Theirs not to reason why, Theirs but to do and die," was more true of the lot of Chinese soldiers than of almost any other army in the world. So they lay, scores and scores of these wounded men, with no kind of bed covering at all, with their knees pulled up toward their chests, scarcely moving; and the raw air poured in from the fog-bound river, chilling them to their marrows. What a pity, we thought, that even here in Chungking there were no blankets for the wounded! When I returned to Rangoon an American official said to me: "Blankets? Just come with me. Down near the docks I can show you several hundred thousand blankets for China. They've been there for months — they're eaten through with white ants. Never been moved, and now nearly every Lend-Lease ship brings more blankets. Probably the ants will get them, too." On that morning in the hospital across the Chialing, however, I was in one respect very fortunate. I did not know about the great piles of blankets rotting in Rangoon and I did not then begin to realize the amount of merchandise and private profiteering contraband that had been loaded into scores and hundreds of supposedly "war supply" trucks while the blankets for China's soldiers were left behind for the ants in Burma. In any case it was theirs not to reason why. They were used to that. But come to think of it, Marco Polo was guilty of another grave omission. He neglected to give any indication of the scope and infinite variety of "squeeze" and its traditional role in the vast empire known as Cathay. Squeeze, which is a disarmingly polite Oriental synonym for graft, must have flourished in China in those days, too, since authorities seem agreed that "squeeze" and the East have always been inseparable.

The contrast between the miserableness of the many and the privileges and immunities of a select few is glaringly great in every Oriental country, as it is also in the Near East and most of Latin America. But inevitably the tremendous strain of the long war had accentuated the extremes between the have-nots and the haves in China. Probably even the most efficient and most honest governing class in the world could have done no more than retard somewhat that process of accentuation. For by the autumn of 1941 inflation was already rampant. Chinese coolies were not the only ones who suffered from it. Chinese intellectuals — professors, scientists, engineers, and others in the small upper middle class — were often hit even more cruelly than peasants or coolies.

It came as something of a shock to meet a professor, a man distinguished in his field, and learn that his income represented only twelve or thirteen American dollars a month; and that those iron-willed little human horses who gasped "hai-*toh,* hai-*tah*" on Chungking's hillsides all day long actually earned nearly twice as much per month as this professor. One day we went outside the city to a remarkable cave, blasted out beneath forty feet of solid granite, where the Chinese government's wireless operated beyond the reach of any Jap bomber. Here teletype machines clicked as smoothly as in New York or London, behind walls of rock four feet thick. Some 13,000 telegrams a day were received or transmitted from this cave and there were direct communications with Shanghai, Hong Kong, Manila, Hanoi (Indo-China), and Moscow. It was a magnificent job, this snug underground telegraph center from which our press messages went ticking around half the world. The director in charge was an engineer who had taken advanced training in both England and the United States. He was a most capable man, an expert in his profession, but his salary amounted to twenty American dollars a month. In Chungking a pair of leather shoes would cost at least half that amount. You wondered how these Chinese professional leaders managed to keep themselves clothed and fed; and you marveled at their cheery faces and their deep patriotism.

At this season Szechuan produced great quantities of superb oranges and tangerines. They were heaped up in the markets daily and I thought what a godsend they were to an embattled people whose diet was far too little and seriously lacking in vitamins. At four or five Chinese dollars these oranges were not terribly expensive for us foreigners. But when the war began, more than three years ago, you could have bought fifty oranges for one Chinese dollar. It was as if you used to get apples for a penny apiece and now they cost more than a dollar. This was but a single illustration of a skyrocketing inflation which Clarence E. Gauss, the American Ambassador, assured me was "getting to be terrific." When the war started in July 1937, China's banknote circulation had been less than three billions. By the autumn of 1941 this circulation had more than trebled, or perhaps quadrupled. Nobody seemed to have exact figures, but the government's presses were printing handsomely designed five-, ten-, and hundred-dollar bills at the rate of nearly 800,000,000 dollars' worth per month. That was one of the most thriving businesses that some American middlemen were doing with the Chinese government, and the representatives of two of these banknote firms lived at the Chialing House. William Hunt, an enterprising American go-getter who typified the completely modern-age "Young China Hands," who were rolling up fortunes in the Orient, had a nice slice of this banknote business. There was one cement building, always guarded by soldiers, where the presses roared all day and all night. They were printing money, great heaps of paper money that could never overtake the country's soaring prices. In wartime China the cost of living had increased twelve times over within three years, and in some categories as much as fifteen times over. To understand what this means multiply the cost of everything you buy today, from a cup of coffee to a movie ticket to a suit of clothes, by twelve — and multiply by only four or five the amount of your present income.

In the Chialing House living-conditions were luxurious compared with the horribly cramped, hastily rebuilt quarters in which most of bombed-out Chungking had to exist. The Chialing's cracked walls and sagging doors let the damp gnawing air sweep through at will. The plaster was cracked. The upstairs rooms had no ceiling, only tattered strips of matting which partially shut off the barnlike garret. One morning I had cause to insert this item in my journal: "Add social notes: A rat fell through the ceiling on Mrs. Stein's face last night. That explains the screams which woke us up about three this morning." (Mrs. Stein is the wife of the *Christian Science Monitor's* hard-working Chungking correspondent.) Life at the Chialing was a trifle primitive, it must be admitted. There were no reading-lamps in our rooms and sometimes electricity in our section of the city was cut off for several nights in succession. Reading or typing by candlelight was hard on the eyes; and of course there was no heating — except open charcoal braziers. They ate up all the oxygen in the room, so you had to choose between headaches and constant shivering. The Chialing possessed a community washroom — or rather one for men and another for the women — and a community bathtub, which it required great courage to enter. It was a rickety-legged old tub, stained and overworked. All the water we used had to be carried from the river, a formidable half-mile climb for the unfortunate coolies. So of course the water was yellow. Water was precious and that probably explained why the Chinese boy never rinsed out the tub. Unless you superintended the job yourself, he just wiped the tub with a dirty cloth. When you felt so grimy you could take anything, you stepped into bath water so stained with silt that you couldn't see the bottom of the tub. Yet all this was comparatively soft living in Chungking. As usual, transient journalists had an easy time, and compared with most Chinese households we had virtual luxury.

4

In November, when the permanent newspaper correspondents moved back to the latest version of an African kraal, the mud-walled press hostel, I gained a new and abiding respect for the little group of men and women who cover the news from Chungking. Tucked on the knob of another big hill, the hostel was a long L-shaped series of sheds, facing a barren yard which turned to mud with the rain. The yard boasted of two bedraggled half-dead banana trees and on its lower corner stood a two-story building that had somehow survived the bombs sufficiently to be patched together again. The sheds were cut into small rooms, with cement floors, paneless windows and only plain wooden desks, washstands, chairs, and beds. The entire quarters were so narrow that you couldn't walk the thin ledge outside without seeing into each room. At the kraal privacy was well-nigh impossible. When you bathed, you donned a robe or coat and puddle-hopped across the sloppy courtyard to reach the community tub-room. The correspondents also had a community dining-room. In fact, almost everything was community except that Spencer Moosa of the Associated Press and Jim Stewart, then of *Time*, had wives to share their monotonous and trying existence. Mrs. Stewart, Nina Moosa, and Betty Graham (who had just returned from seven months of incredible wandering across the interior of China) provided a touch of feminine variety which the press hostel sadly needed, and which its male occupants usually appreciated — but sometimes didn't. It was a cramped goldfish-like existence with very little to relieve its dreariness; and for my tastes, its most objectionable feature was provided by the armed soldiers or policemen who stood guard day and night at one side of the courtyard or the other, apparently under orders to watch every move the correspondents made. Why that should have been necessary I could never figure out. These journalists, American and British, had proved themselves staunch friends of China and her cause. Yet even in this miserable little spot they couldn't share their lack of privacy with themselves alone. To me this was all the more surprising because the Chinese can be extraordinarily considerate about little things.

Sometimes we played hearts at night in Chialing House and sometimes Bill Dunn and I joined the gang over at the kraal, where we could count on the support of Mac Fisher, veteran correspondent of the UP, and Jack Belden of INS, or Spencer and Nina Moosa and occasionally of the self-assured young Australian whom I dubbed (to avoid confusion with McDonald of the London *Times*) " the Sidney Morning MacDonald." For some curious reason the Sidney Morning MacDonald possessed a super-British accent and a stilted phraseology which was really an achievement. When he announced he was "covered with confusion" it sounded like all of that. But he provided his share of jests and so did big, burly Harrison Forman of NBC, and Jack Belden, who was as unpredictably neurotic as he was extremely well informed on everything that had to do with the Chinese Army and the war. These and a few others were the regular Chungking correspondents. Their life was drab and hard and brightened by little more than a bit of local vodka now and then, or a most dubious concoction which an Old China Hand turned out under the label of "Chungking gin." They were a brave and warm-hearted group of men and women, these Chungking correspondents, and I came to have a great admiration for them; particularly because theirs is a tougher existence and a much less spectacular, much more thankless job than that of journalists I have known in any other wartime capital from London to China, including Moscow. Many of them are still there, living in the same mud-walled sheds and rounding out their fourth or fifth straight year of the same uninterrupted grind — undoubtedly with the same rifled gendarmes standing guard near their doorsteps.

Chapter III

CHINA INCHES TOWARD DEMOCRACY

To know the truth is easy. But, ah, how difficult to follow it!

Chinese proverb

One of the first things I learned as a newcomer to the Orient was that the attitude of the average American toward China is recklessly romantic; almost hopelessly so. In part this is undoubtedly due to that misleading phrase: "the lure of the Orient." But it is chiefly caused, I believe, by the American people's intense admiration for China's gallant and magnificent resistance to Japan. Because Americans feel a strong sympathy for the under-dog, they are in love with the Chinese. Perhaps, too, our enthusiasm for all things Chinese is fanned higher by a secret feeling of guilt for having made their sufferings so much greater through our prolonged shipments of scrap iron, gasoline, and other materials to the Japanese.

I came to China with a typically American romantic attitude; without any faint conception of the oppressive poverty and squalor which eats the flesh of China's "one fifth of humanity," and with only a vague idea of the great complexity of the Orient's problems and of Oriental character. But I came with a reporter's job to do and with journalistic tools which at least had been considerably sharpened by fifteen years of contacts with foreign peoples, their psychologies, and their politics. The tools, at any rate, had received plenty of realistic treatment in various parts of the world. Even so I found the East more confusing and confounding than any place in which I had ever sought to grasp facts and to achieve some measure of understanding. To get even a little way beneath the surface of China I should have to work very hard, and I worked hard.

Accordingly, during my first weeks in Chungking I saw and had long talks with a large number of Cabinet ministers and outstanding leaders of the Kuomintang, the one party which controls and governs wartime China. I found these Chinese dignitaries infallibly intelligent and unfailingly courteous, although they differed strikingly in their personalities and their social outlook. There was Dr. Quo Tai-chi, then Foreign Minister, a scholarly man with a broad world outlook, of definite democratic convictions and instincts. There was huge and burly General Wu Te-chen, a Chinese Jim Farley, who as secretary-general of the Kuomintang unquestionably ranked high as a manipulator of machine politics. There was China's long-term Minister of War, General Ho Yieng-chien, keen-faced, in every gesture a coldly efficient military man, who was disarmingly frank when he unrolled his maps, yet obviously kept a large proportion of his thoughts to himself. Among numerous others were the affable Minister of Communications, Chang Kia-ngau; the young and clever Mayor of Chungking, Dr. Wu, a Princeton graduate; and Ku Cheng-king, Minister of Social Affairs, who had studied economics at the University of Berlin and gave the feeling, as he talked, that his totalitarian inclinations were rather pronounced. Nor could one forget that portly and smooth-tongued riddle Dr. H. H. Kung, the king of China's uncertain finances, who is married to the former Ai-ling Soong, the sister of Madame Chiang Kai-shek. From a round of consultations with men like these, one begins to comprehend something of the enormous size and intricacy of the Generalissimo's task in keeping China welded and fighting, year after year.

While I was trying to get myself thus grounded, a double-headed typhoon struck Chungking in the shapes of Vincent Sheean and Edgar Ansel Mowrer, who had been traveling together from Manila, through Java, Malaya, and Burma. We soon got the impression that Jimmy's and Edgar's joint arrival had shaken Chungking almost as much as a cluster of Jap bombs. In the process they precipitated the first general press conference that the Generalissimo had given in more than two years and also a most interesting informal evening with the first lady of China. After individual interviews with Edgar, Jimmy, and one or two others, the Generalissimo received the foreign correspondents in the salon of his home. Holly Tong and Madame Chiang acted as interpreters when Marshal Chiang Kai-shek began to read a prepared statement.

China's famous war leader gives an immediate impression of strength and tenacity and great reserves of will-power. He is slightly above average height and stands very straight. As he shook hands with us he shot a swift piercing look into every face. His figure was wiry and tough-muscled and vigorous; it also revealed no sign of fatigue or strain. The Generalissimo laughed easily and often. But when he was not speaking, his face wore a lean mask, almost hard save for the brightness of his eyes. It was the face of a man who knows exactly what he wants and is in the habit of commanding and being obeyed. Above all I felt that here was a will, an exceptional will, rather than an intellectual force. If this had not been true, surely China would not still be fighting on, alone. With this intense will it seemed there was also a hint of ruthlessness, or perhaps it was merely an exceptional integration of character. Marshal Chiang elaborated on the prepared text of his statement as Holly Tong or Madame translated; and afterward I was interested to note that one of his insertions had been a phrase about "love and faith." It was the sort of improvisation which one would not have expected from this austere personality. The conference took place exactly one month to the day before Pearl Harbor, and it is curious today to observe the one quotation from the Generalissimo's statement which I recopied into my journal. After stressing the unity of the Axis aggressors Chiang Kai-shek said: "The initiative is almost within our grasp. In the very near future I believe you will find my words proved true by events." It would seem from these words that the Generalissimo was no more expectant of the terrific Japanese blow across the Pacific than were our own naval and army commanders in Honolulu. Or perhaps he greatly overestimated the capacity of the United States and Great Britain to take the initiative. It remains for me a puzzlingly optimistic declaration. Why did Chiang Kai-shek commit himself that far? It is difficult to hazard an answer.

That evening Edgar, Jimmy, and I received a sudden and gracious invitation to dine informally with Madame Chiang, together with Royal Arch Gunnison and Annalee Whitmore who was leaving in a few days for her marriage with Melville Jacoby in Manila. The exceptional good looks of Mei-ling Soong are justly renowned. Someone has said that she resembles a brilliant diamond, and I think this is true. You are prepared for her penetrating mind and for her impeccably harmonious taste in clothes. Perhaps one cannot quite be fully prepared for the scope of Madame's charm, or the swift byplay of her wit, or the facility of her poise. At any rate Mei-ling Soong is not only a remarkable diplomat, she is also a most natural and therefore excellent hostess. Beside her open fireside we enjoyed a simple and delightful meal of half a dozen different Chinese dishes and some three hours of engaging conversation.

Madame Chiang Kai-shek is an artist at repartee and innuendo. I remember that she commented on a magazine article which Martha Gellhorn had written about her; and I knew she was aiming a neat little dart at Jimmy Sheean (whose views about China have not always spared Kuomintang policies or personalities) when she remarked: "You journalists are among the bravest persons in the world. I admire your temerity. You see a person only once, and then sit down and say he is like this and that." It was such a skillful little rebuke, tossed off with seeming innocence but carefully implied, that I couldn't resist replying: "But, madame, after you've met someone for the first time I'm sure you do much the same thing. I'd really like to hear your comments. I suspect they're very much to the point."

In the course of the evening there was a good deal of light dueling of this sort, for Madame Chiang is nothing if not a calculatedly provocative woman of intelligence and wit. But she is also a woman who knows when to ask advice, which may be useful as well as flattering. Very modestly she sought our opinions about a broadcast she had just written for America. She read the text in her full and lovely voice. Most definitely it was so effective, as prepared, as to forbid any tampering suggestions on our part. Then she spoke with marked fervor about "my orphans," the child victims of the war for whom she has done so much. Then again, and as suddenly, Mei-ling Soong was playing deftly, lightly, and surely with words; with the same spirit and élan of a Comtesse de Noailles in France or a Margot Asquith. Once I left myself wide open for one of her characteristically barbed sallies by remarking it had just cost me $11.76 to obtain a copy of my own book by airmail from America. "Is it worth that much?" asked Madame Chiang. That was a fair question. But I'm sure that Madame got an impish pleasure in asking it. In every sense this was an enjoyable and instructive evening, and after these few hours I could understand perfectly how China's first lady was also China's irreplaceable first liaison with the rest of the world — and how perfectly designed she was to take the American public by storm. Madame Chiang is like a perfectly balanced and beautifully executed blade of Toledo steel. A dazzling array of sparks may fly from that slender flashing blade, but it is still steel. Perhaps this is how or why Mei-ling Soong is Madame Chiang Kai-shek, an incomparable foil for the stern and unostentatious Generalissimo of Free China.

2

It seems almost impossible for Occidentals who have never visited the Orient to understand the enormousness of the Generalissimo's task in striving to unite China; and just as difficult undoubtedly to comprehend the nature of China's feudalism, and what a long painful path Chinese democracy must travel to reach fruition. We do not think of China as a totalitarian state, yet the Kuomintang regime is a one-party dictatorship. Most of us do not think of Chinese army officers as predominantly antiliberal, yet the teachings of General Alexander von Falkenhausen and his military mission of more than a hundred officers * have left a distinctly Prussianistic imprint upon a great many of Chiang Kai-shek's generals and colonels. We do not wonder particularly about how much free speech and freedom of the press exists in China. Yet these and many equally vital matters inevitably command attention if you would get something like a rounded and realistic picture of China's struggle. Not that we should expect too much from a vast people just emerging from a semi-darkness of many centuries. Rather that we may better understand what a long road the Chinese still must travel.

The sincerity of Madame Chiang Kai-shek could not be doubted when, in a broadcast to America, she declared that "the democracy toward which we have been struggling through these bitter days of war is a modern democracy." Yet at best the China which I was discovering was only inching along toward this remote goal. It is true that the Kuomintang has a kind of party

* Cf. Edgar Snow: *The Battle for Asia.*

congress called the People's Political Council. At the time of its November session a Cabinet minister assured one of our press conferences that the PPC contained "members of all political parties, representing all shades of political opinions." Upon closer examination this statement was misleading. The government's rebuff to a new political movement called the Democratic Federation revealed what a wide gap separated fine words from actuality.

The Democratic Federation was a kind of united front of China's minority political groups founded in February and March 1941. It included leaders of China's Youth Party, largest of the minority groups; the so-called Third Party, and the National Socialist Party, which has no ideological relationship with the Nazi Party in Germany. It is perhaps significant that the Democratic Federation was founded secretly and only became publicly known when it published a manifesto — or a "bill for democracy" — on Double Ten (October 10, 1941), the anniversary of the Chinese Republic. Among the ten points in the Federation's bill for democracy the following were notable:

1. A demand that one-party rule should be ended in Free China.

2. A demand that the government should cease giving financial support to the Kuomintang Party.

3. A demand that the government should stop using its political power to recruit members for the Kuomintang, and that educational organizations should stop forcing teachers and students to join the Kuomintang.

4. The abolition of concentration camps.

5. The abolition of party organizations within the army.

6. Establishment of freedom of thought and freedom of the press, including freedom of newspaper circulation.

7. A clean-up of the government which would "remedy the inequality of war economics by which profiteers are becoming fantastically rich and the poor become poorer."

It will be noted that many of the practices which the Democratic Federation demanded should be eliminated from the Kuomintang regime are practices which have long been part of the machinery of Fascist states' one-party systems. The authors of this bill for Chinese democracy concluded their manifesto by declaring: "These things must be effected before there is the realization of democracy in China and a safe foundation for New China can be established." In fact, many Chinese regarded the formation of the Democratic Federation and its manifesto as an extremely significant step toward the development of democracy in China. It seemed to mark the emergence of a Popular Front dedicated to the creation of multi-party procedure and relaxation of the Kuomintang's one-party dictatorship. Some twenty-odd members of the People's Political Council signed this "bill for democracy" and it was handed to the secretary of the PPC on November 20, 1941, just half an hour before the time-limit for submitting bills was reached. According to information which I believe thoroughly reliable, the PPC secretary showed the proposed bill to Chiang Kai-shek and he forbade that it be presented before the Council for discussion. "Since the Kuomintang has such a vast majority it was impossible for us to do anything about it," said one of the Democratic Federation's members.

This development, of course, was not reported in the Chungking press; nor to my knowledge has any mention of it ever been contained in messages sent from China. Nevertheless, only three days before the Kuomintang's party machinery quashed the "bill for democracy" a Cabinet minister had assured foreign correspondents that the PPC provided an "auspicious opportunity for introducing democratic institutions in wartime. . . . The government," he said, "is fully ready to hear criticisms." But in actual practice the Kuomintang government immediately proceeded to reject this courageous effort of patriotic minority leaders to liberalize China by "introducing democratic institutions in wartime."

If one is romantic about China one can ignore the fact that there is still no room there for a forthright "bill for democracy." But a reporter cannot ignore facts like this, and that is how I became interested in the forgotten fate of Professor Ma Ying-chu. Until December 1940 Professor Ma (Yale University, 1910) was dean of the College of Commerce in Chungking University. He was one of China's most prominent economists, a former tutor of the Generalissimo, and greatly revered by his students. The professor saw China's fighting strength seriously undermined by war profiteering and corruption. He spoke out boldly — something, I am told, that very few people in Free China have dared to do. Demanding that the Kuomintang government clean house, Professor Ma declared: "What right have capitalists and high officials to profit while soldiers are dying and refugees are homeless? A capital levy should be imposed on all wealthy officials." The powerful secret police, which some observers call China's Gestapo, arrested the professor and held him incommunicado. His students launched a protest meeting, but were muzzled. Several weeks later Professor Ma, escorted by four soldiers, was marched before an assembly of Chungking University students. An officer said the professor had an announcement to make. He did — but not quite what the authorities had expected. Professor Ma rose to his feet and told his former students: "I hold the same beliefs I have always held. War profiteering must be stopped if we are to defeat Japan — " Brusquely the police bustled the professor out of the auditorium, and he hasn't been seen since. It is assumed that he is either in jail or in one of China's labor concentration camps. Professor Ma had no political affiliations. He is still revered by his former students as a Chinese patriot.

In Chungking I learned that a friend of China is supposed to close his eyes to the presence of concentration camps under the Kuomintang regime. Vincent Sheean had too great a sense of integrity for that, and he was bitterly criticized for telling abroad several things which most people conveniently overlook. Even so there remain some irregularities, widely talked about inside China as factual, which no foreign writer ever puts into print — nor shall I venture into that realm of popular gossip. The Russians have a saying which I suspect Oriental peoples are too sensitive to understand. "Love us black," say the Russians. "When we are white everybody loves us." There are some of us, then, who will continue to like and admire the remarkably human Chinese people without being able to maintain they are "all white." Certainly no conscientious observer could quite give that unrealistic rating to the Kuomintang regime. From a democratic viewpoint the maintenance of a considerable number of labor or concentration camps must be listed among its liabilities. Thousands of Chinese Communists are locked up in these camps. They also contain thousands of Chinese students and intellectuals who are as patriotic and democratic as Professor Ma. In the autumn of 1941 some of these camps were located in Chengtu, Loyang, Sian, Lanchow, En Tze, and Kweiyang; and one at Ching Hua (Chekiang) was said to contain more than 4,000 persons. It was estimated that no more than one fifth of these prisoners were Communists, and a large percentage of the camps' total inhabitants (estimated by some as approximately 50,000 persons) had been confined for criticizing the uncontrolled war profiteering and other abuses tolerated by the Kuomintang government. In any case, most occupants of China's concentration camps (as is true in Germany, Italy, Soviet Russia, and Spain today) were arrested without warrants, held without charges being preferred against them, and had never been granted the elemental justice of a court trial. These are matters, of course, which visitors to China may not hear about — or, if tactful, do not inquire about.

3

One of the two or three most powerful men in China and probably the most feared is a man of whom the outside world has never heard, whose name has been printed only a few times in the English language.* Once at Meiktila, on the far-away Mandalay road, I walked into a Chinese shop which bore the same name above its door and hazarded a meaningful jest with the lean Chinese at the counter. I wanted to find out if that name, nearly 2,000 miles from Chungking and outside of China, still meant the same thing to a Chinese. It did. I saw it in the eyes of the fellow at the counter. Obviously he had heard plenty about Tai Li.

Tai Li (pronounced Dye Lee) is a name which you rarely hear uttered, much above a whisper at any rate, even in Chungking. Actually Tai Li's title doesn't sound very important. He is the director of the Kuomintang government's Bureau of Investigation and Statistics. But that beautiful example of Oriental phraseology really means that Tai Li is chief of the secret police, or rather of the largest of three separate Kuomintang secret-

* It occurs only once in Edgar Snow's large and authoritative volume, *The Battle for Asia;* only once in John Gunther's *Inside Asia;* and several times in Agnes Smedley's *Battle Hymn of China.*

police organizations. The great mass of the Chinese do not joke about Tai Li, and those who are careful not to joke about him say that the Bureau of Investigation and Statistics is the Gestapo, or the NKVD, of China. Whether they mean that its methods are as brutal I do not know, but certainly Tai Li's power over civilians and even inside the armed forces is very great. Tai Li headed the secret organization of the Blue Shirts, which waged ruthless warfare against Chinese Communist leaders and other Chinese who opposed the Kuomintang and the Generalissimo. That was years ago when Chiang Kai-shek's movement is said to have required muscle men and most drastic measures in order to survive. Apparently Tai Li is quite as indispensable today, and certainly he exercises an extraordinary power. Yet a photograph of Tai Li (whom some of his enemies go so far as to call "the Himmler of the Kuomintang") is never seen in China. The man himself rarely appears at any public function. He is a former Whampoa cadet, which explains his lifelong devotion to Chiang Kai-shek, and is described as in his early fifties, very keen-eyed and flamboyant in his mannerisms. Some Chinese say that his life-story, if ever it could be unraveled, would make one of the most fascinating and revealing biographies to come out of modern China. "But," they add, "it will never be written."

Naturally I became interested in Tai Li as any reporter would be intrigued by a mysterious and virtually unknown personality who wields enormous power and has become a legend, living in the shadows; but in reality it was thanks to the careful attentions which some of Tai Li's plain-clothes men persistently revealed in the casual comings and goings of newspaper correspondents while I was in Chungking. It seemed to us a great waste of their time, yet it did serve to remind me that the Kuomintang regime is quite as much a police state as Nazi Germany or Soviet Russia. This fact, too, fell into the general pattern of popular American misconceptions about Free China. For "Free China" is still a misleading phrase. China is called "Free China" because she fights with inspiring heroism to be free from foreign domination. But perhaps we should not overlook the fact that in present-day China not even the first of President Roosevelt's Four Freedoms — freedom of speech — exists in real measure. It seemed to me that those who write and speak about

China all too rarely fail to point out such an elemental fact as this.

Dr. Quo Tai-chi was being absolutely honest when he said to us one day: "We are fully aware that China is not yet a democracy in the American or British form. Nor do we claim it is functioning to our friends' or our own satisfaction. But the important fact is that China has chosen to travel on the road toward modern democracy."

How long and how meandering can we expect China's road toward democracy to be?

How can the United States government and the American people best help China to make swifter progress on this difficult road?

Will the hundreds of millions of dollars already provided — and the billions of Lend-Lease dollars likely to follow — strengthen China's struggle toward internal freedom as well as toward armed victory? Or would the accompanying industrialization of China, financed in large measure by America, possibly serve to enthrone a select group of Chinese capitalists and to perpetuate the Kuomintang's one-party dictatorship?

Perhaps that would depend chiefly upon how realistically Americans understood China's political set-up and her problems.

At any rate I felt compelled to ask myself these questions, and in trying to find the answers I discovered a number of factors — usually ignored or glossed over — which could scarcely be reconciled with Americans' wide-eyed and romantic attitude toward China. If most Americans must insist upon being severely realistic toward the Soviet Union (and that undoubtedly was a sound idea, if one would also make an effort to be fair), then why would it not be equally commendable to be realistic in assessing the Chinese equation? One American who had lived many years in China replied in this fashion: "You see," he said, "most Americans have always had a missionary complex about China. The Chinese are small and very attractive and exceptionally bright, so we think we should treat them like children. It's a great mistake. The Chinese are the most grown-up children in the world." Level-headed Mac Fisher, after some ten years in the Orient, expressed it another way: "The Chinese are simply the world's greatest realists," he remarked. . . . Well, they are extremely likable people, and a long and hungering history has taught them that they need to be realists. Maybe we Americans need to be realists, too.

But what about democratic hopes or trends in this baffling New China?

In Chungking the Generalissimo has established a Central Training Corps school, which, in the autumn of 1941, was said to have given intensive one-month courses to approximately 15,000 army officers, Kuomintang provincial officials, school-teachers, bankers, and others of a sifted élite. Although there was no publicity about the Central Training Corps curriculum, it is known that strict military discipline prevails and applies to civilians as well as the military. Kuomintang party tracts are used in the school and there are many lectures, including some by the Generalissimo himself. I was reliably informed that this in reality is a party training institution, that secret pamphlets are used for instruction, and that special emphasis is placed upon the following: (1) the idea of a supreme leader; (2) elimination of individual concepts; (3) implicit obedience to the supreme leader under a slogan curiously like that of the Nazis — "one nation, one party, one leader." All this clearly seemed to add up, not to the gradual inauguration of democratic privileges and practices, but to an anticipated maintenance of a strict and highly disciplined one-party system in China for many years to come — in any case, it would appear, throughout the lifetime of Chiang Kai-shek. If the instruction courses at the Central Training Corps school followed lines as here outlined, it was most difficult to conceive that Chinese army officers (with their great power and influence over the coming postwar development of their country) would throw their weight toward anything except reactionary and anti-democratic principles.

These were among the contradictions and paradoxes of the Kuomintang regime and therefore, so long as the Kuomintang remains unreformed, they will constitute the contradictions and paradoxes of Free China. Many of them were things which I hadn't expected to find in my journalistic researches in Chungking. But if you wanted to believe, as Madame Chiang did, that China was struggling toward "a modern democracy," you could not afford to ignore these enormous and little-publicized obstacles which still block China's path to partnership in free speech, a free press, and a multi-party governmental structure. When could some of China's most patriotic and selfless citizens raise their voices against flagrant war profiteering and against corruption high up in the Kuomintang ranks without disappearing into a jail or a concentration camp? When would the People's Political Council (or perhaps the Generalissimo himself) permit the Democratic Federation or other minority groups to present publicly and debate a "bill for democracy"? Of course all of China's primary efforts were needed now to hold off the Japanese invaders. The burdens upon Chiang Kai-shek were staggeringly immense and the number of men upon whose loyalty and personal integrity he could count unreservedly was reputed to be pitifully small. Nevertheless, would a few concessions, a few feeble steps toward establishment of democratic liberties, have been utterly impossible? Indeed, did there exist a genuine *will* for democracy among many of the key leaders in the Kuomintang? If so it was not the opinion of many foreign observers who had known China intimately over a long period. Those public-spirited Chinese who had a pronounced will for democracy were too seldom to be found among the most successful politicians of the Kuomintang Party. Head and shoulders above all his contemporaries stood the oaklike figure of the Generalissimo, universally respected and universally hailed as an honest man. Whatever the commonplace gossip about self-seekers, fixers, and "squeeze" artists in the ranks of the Kuomintang (and such gossip is dishearteningly common to any newcomer to the Orient), Chiang Kai-shek was untouched and untarred by those who most abused their opportunities in his one-party system. It seemed generally conceded that he had won the moral right to lead his country toward unification. Yet some best-informed observers also held that the one-party system deprived the Generalissimo of the services of a great many upright and honest men whom China sorely needed at this moment.

4

I thought I had read enough about China to be somewhat prepared for her complexities and problems. Once in the East, however, I soon discovered that words on paper cannot convey the pitiless poverty, the animal-like existence, and the seeming hopelessness of nearly one billion human beings in India, Burma, Malaya, Thailand, Indo-China, and China. I discovered also that my vision, like that of almost all Americans, had been seriously blurred by my enthusiasm for the Chinese people's magnificent and incredible resistance to Japan. Somehow you did not pause to reflect that people who fought on and on so marvelously could still be handicapped and betrayed by corruption, selfishness, or indifference among a considerable portion of their governing class. Somehow I had not grasped the medieval feudalism of China any more than I had grasped the medieval feudalism of Spain before I had gone to Spain and seen it with my own eyes. Because my eyes were blurred in these respects, and because I could not smell the Orient from its photographs, the colossal dimensions of Chiang Kai-shek's task had escaped me.

As these realities hammered themselves upon the retinas of my eyes and into my consciousness, and as I segregated facts which were often jarring and unpleasant, I sometimes fell into moods of deep depression. After all, what hope could there be for Greater China's 450,000,000 submerged people? After centuries of stagnation and exploitation from above, could we expect the Chinese to move forward and upward more than a quarter of an inch, or possibly an inch, in a lifetime? Was this possibly nothing more than a horrible, vicious, unbeatable squirrel cage into which this gigantic mass of tortured human beings had been dumped thousands of years ago? But this was defeatism and it had always run counter to all my instincts to think, or to admit, that humanity over the long term could fail to progress. Those who had lived in the Orient long enough to take its filth and its faults for granted — some of these, the ones who in spite of all had kept the calluses off their hearts — could still harbor a calm but realistic hope for China. Theirs was no sloppy sentimentalism, nor a romanticism built on the sands of make-believe. They recognized a New China even while realizing that its birth pangs were still proceeding and that it might well be merely a New China in another hundred years. In this China now a-borning there was the stirring of nationhood and the slow awakening of conscience, as well as the eternally unleashed rapacity of greedy individuals and the cheap ambitions of those who coveted nothing but power. Here, too, although dim and too often betrayed or repudiated, there burned a thin high flame of aspiration and of hope. Would it survive? Or would it be snuffed out in another few years? Would *we,* by any chance, help to snuff it out?

Along the Burma Road, in towns and villages of China's hinterland, and in Chungking one learns that the Chinese can only travel the road toward democracy painfully and haltingly, at a snail's pace. Simultaneously one learns that the splendid picture of China's great war for independence has its black blotches and its darker side. If I have dwelt at some length on some of the aspects of this darker side, it is simply because it seems to me that China's English-speaking allies have given them, and still tend to give them, too little consideration. To achieve even a small measure of democracy in our time the Chinese people will need more than the cheers or the rapturous sighs of Great Britain and the United States. They will need our clear-sighted recognition of the obstacles which compel them to inch their way toward a democratic goal which is still remote. With that, and most of all, the Chinese will need an enlightened British and American statesmanship which works with, *and for,* the weak and fragile democratic forces which are striving to keep alive in China.

Is it too much to expect that we shall give the Chinese people that kind of statesmanship?

Probably so.

But in any event we can scarcely hope to provide that statesmanship in the next decade without a realistic conception of the dimensions of the job ahead.

Chapter IV

THE JAPS RIDE THE TIGER

A man riding on a tiger's back can't get off.
Chinese proverb

Even in Chungking we were all wrong about what the Japs would do next. My journal covering the three weeks previous to December 7, 1941 reminds me that the American naval and army forces which were caught flat-footed at Pearl Harbor had lots of company. While Hirohito's fleet was sneaking across the southern Pacific, members of the Chinese government expressed doubt that Tokyo was yet in a position to strike a major blow in any direction; or were convinced, if a blow was struck, that probably it would be launched from northern Indo-China in an effort to pierce the mountains and cut the Burma Road at Kunming. American and British diplomats and military observers with whom I talked during these three weeks also had their eyes focused on the Laokay-Kunming sector or speculated whether the Japs might knife the embattled Russians in the back by striking at the trans-Siberian railroad and Vladivostok. Those were the days when one still wondered in Chungking whether the Red Army had yet saved, or could save, Moscow. The temptation to the Japs must be great, we thought. So we were all watching for a Jap move "some time before long" and looking in the obvious — completely wrong — places.

Early in November Chiang Kai-shek told Brigadier General John Magruder, chief of our American military mission in Chungking, that if the Japanese were able to take Kunming China's jig would be up. According to Chinese intelligence reports, their enemy was moving tens of thousands of reinforcements into Indo-China. Of course there was always the possibility they might be used to occupy Thailand. But the Chinese were chiefly worried about an imminent Jap offensive toward Kunming. Would those mysterious American fliers, secretly training in Burma as recruits for China's air force, be sufficiently strong to give Chinese troops the necessary support along the Indo-Chinese border? There were only three squadrons of the Americans. Would Washington rush more of our army planes to China? The British, it was said, wouldn't promise to send planes unless the Americans did. Chinese government spokesmen admitted their anxiety about a Jap drive to sever the Burma Road in Yunnan, and on November 10 one of them told us that the Japs now had 120,000 troops in Indo-China. Judging by what I had seen and learned in Saigon just two months before, I thought that estimate rather exaggerated — and was wrong again. But as my journal confirms, I had plenty of company. Even the Generalissimo had said: "The initiative is almost within our grasp" and had used the baffling phrase: "in the very near future."

Then came the Kurusu mission to Washington and the formation of a government by General Tojo in Tokyo. At a press conference on November 17 Dr. Quo Tai-chi, the Foreign Minister, discussed these developments. When we asked if they might precipitate some Jap move, Dr. Quo said: "It would seem Japan is bound to do something. But I don't think she herself knows just what." There was also one school of thought in Chungking which insisted that some kind of temporary expedient or a compromise must emerge from the Nipponese-American negotiations in Washington. Some people even feared that the United States government might, with British support, yield to making a "deal" with Kurusu and enter an arrangement which would slowly strangle Chinese resistance. This was based on the knowledge that American defenses on Wake and Guam islands and in the Philippines would not be "adequate" for another five or six months. In fact, by November 21 Chinese concern over possible American concessions to Japan became so great as to prompt Chiang Kai-shek to send a secret and personal appeal to President Roosevelt. This could not be reported, but I learned it to be a fact. Optimism over the Washington conversations had suddenly come to an end. Chungking's fear of a compromise which would hamstring China nevertheless lasted for several more days. The war-weary Chinese were now extremely worried, and in their position one could not blame them for that.

On December 1, however, the attitude in Chungking changed strikingly. Tsiang Ting-fu, secretary-general of the Executive

Yuan, revealed indisputably that his government had been assured there would be no American "deal" with the Japs when he told our group of foreign correspondents that Washington's negotiations "have justified the faith we have had here in President Roosevelt and Mr. Hull." But Mr. Tsiang, as spokesman for the Chinese government, went on to make a statement which soon proved to be remarkable. This was only six days before Pearl Harbor.

"Certain misinformed writers have feared that American firmness would lead immediately to hostilities," Mr. Tsiang said. "That is not our opinion. After four and one half years of war the Japanese are not in a position to undertake new adventures. Firmness can do more for the prevention of war than weakness. So, although Washington has reaffirmed her policies, we do not expect any immediate breaking out of hostilities."

Ironically enough, as these words were spoken Jap warships and aircraft carriers were far on their way toward Wake, Midway, and Hawaii and the bulk of Nipponese troops in Indo-China were massed, not in the north as a spear against Kunming, but in the south, a javelin poised toward Bangkok and the Malay Peninsula. In reply to one of our questions Mr. Tsiang said: "I don't think the Japanese have enough resources to undertake any new aggressions. If there is more fighting it is more likely to be directed against us. I don't see how they can attack elsewhere. They must continue their attack in China."

Six days before Pearl Harbor this was the officially stated view of the Chungking government, astonishing as it may seem today. This fact may be taken as a measure of the extraordinary skill with which the Japanese concealed their plans for a quadruple dagger-thrust, delivered simultaneously against Pearl Harbor, Manila, Hong Kong, and the approaches to Singapore. Nevertheless, upon reflection, it is surprising that some inkling of a portion of Tokyo's blitzkrieg plan had not reached Chinese ears. For the Chinese were intimately acquainted with the methods and mentality of their Nipponese adversaries; they had legions of patriots operating behind the Jap lines; and the Chinese had the only military intelligence in the Orient which had operated with some real effectiveness in uncovering Japanese moves. Therefore, both on the mainland opposite Hong Kong and inside Indo-China, one might have expected that Chinese agents would get some direct hints of the Jap blows being planned in these two areas. Apparently they did not. Chungking seemed to anticipate nothing more unusual than an eventual Jap thrust toward Kunming.

On December 2 I had a talk with General Chou En-lai (Joe En-lie), representative in Chungking of the Chinese Communists' 18th Group Army. General Chou is a quiet-voiced, extremely intelligent man who — like all of China's Reds — is above everything else a Chinese patriot. "Japan must center her attack upon China," he said. "But I believe the Japs will also compel the British to intervene in Thailand." In this latter respect he was a little closer to the truth than the government's press spokesman; a shade closer, but that was all. On another point General Chou surprised me. "The Generalissimo was right to send a warning to President Roosevelt," he remarked. "But China can only keep fighting and win the war if democratic reforms are introduced here while the war is on, not afterward. I believe the Generalissimo will be forced to grant freedom of action to all the minority parties, and with this more and more democratic processes. Otherwise he cannot keep the support of the people behind the war."

"Don't you think he will be more apt to wait, or to wait too long?" I asked.

"He can't be too late," said the calm voice of the calm little man.

I thought General Chou was sadly mistaken; he was too trusting or he was indulging in wishful thinking. As this is written, twenty months have passed and the war continues unabated in China, but the Chungking government is still a strictly one-party affair. And in this long interim there have been no dispatches out of China announcing greater freedom of action for her minority parties or other innovations which could be described as "more democratic processes."

2

Spy stories are things that people like to read but usually take with several grains of salt. This was certainly the fate of a book called *Secret Agent of Japan*. It was written by Amleto Vespa, an

Italian who spent several years in the employ of the Japanese secret service in Manchuria, and was published in London in 1938. By chance a friend lent me this book in Moscow, nine months after Pearl Harbor. If I had found it in Saigon a year earlier, I should have been even more concerned than I was then about getting back across the Siamese border before things began to pop. Yet even today Vespa's book carries its moral on the blindness of governments and nations. Longer than he could stomach it, but until he could escape with a whole skin, Vespa performed all sorts of jobs under the personal direction of a man whose name he never knew — the chief of Japan's secret intelligence in Manchukuo. In February *1932* this very influential Jap undercover man exploded to Vespa in these terms:

"The Koreans will be eaten with vices," declared the Jap intelligence chief. "The Chinese will be the victims of opium. The Russians will be ruined by vodka. They will all be annihilated. . . . This is but the first part of the tasks which the gods have given our people. The second phase of the program calls for the conquest of India and of all the islands of the Pacific; also of Siberia as far as the Urals. Don't smile at these declarations. . . . Nothing can stop Japan from becoming the greatest empire on earth. . . . Why should the world raise so much fuss over Manchuria? They are a bunch of fools. What are they going to say when we occupy China, Siberia, the Philippines and Indo-China? They will see how Japan will surprise them. A nice surprise for everybody. For Russia — for America — for France — for Holland — and for our dear old lady England."

By the time I reached Manila and Singapore in August 1941 and had traveled through Thailand to Saigon and back through Bangkok to Burma, this amazingly ambitious program of the Japanese militarists had become reasonably clear to most responsible Allied officials. As the Japs took over southern Indo-China that August, their ultimate intentions stood plainly revealed. But could the Japs move fast enough to catch the British, Dutch, and Americans unprepared? Were they not still too heavily involved in China? Would they conceivably dare, in any case, to take on the British, Dutch, and Americans all at the same time? Representatives of these three Western nations all wanted to believe that they would have another autumn and winter in which to gird their possessions; that the Japs must still proceed piecemeal along their road of conquest. It was also very easy to think up plausible reasons in support of this comforting thesis. You heard these reasons in Manila, Singapore, Bangkok, Rangoon; even in Chungking.

We used to discuss what Japan would do, or could do, with the American army officers of the Magruder mission in Chungking; with General Magruder and his chief of staff, Colonel MacMoreland; with Colonel Ross Hoyt, Colonel Walter Soderholm, Colonel Sutherland, Major George, Major Merrill, and a number of others. They were keen officers and they were also most generous in inviting correspondents in to share their mess. I'm afraid we always stuffed ourselves shamelessly with the real American food which our hosts heaped on our plates, and were certainly a strain on their liquid reserves as well. In fact, it was thanks solely to the officers of the Magruder mission that we all had a Thanksgiving dinner that year; not turkey or pumpkin pie, but the essence of Thanksgiving, for all that. In the course of these pleasant visits I learned enough to know that the number of American troops and planes in the Philippines was still pitifully small, but that "things were building up all the time." It was the general belief that the defense of the Philippines should be in pretty good shape — if we could get through to April without fireworks. So the sudden, though unexplained, tone of optimism on the part of Chinese officials made one wonder whether Washington's equally sudden shift to pessimism over the Kurusu negotiations might be exaggerated.

Before this happened I had already planned to continue my exploratory round of the East by going on to Hong Kong early in December. In fact, I had a reservation to fly to Hong Kong on December 5. Then I began to get the same kind of uneasy feeling that I once experienced in Stockholm on April 5, 1940, when I held a plane reservation for Riga. I had postponed Riga in favor of Oslo and got there in time to watch the Germans march in. Now I was terribly impatient to get to Hong Kong and at last see one Chinese city that was peaceful, normal, and comfortable. But supposing the Kurusu negotiations broke down abruptly? Well, I ought to be where I could cover the Chinese government's reaction. Maybe I'd better wait a few more days and see. So I followed the hunch and common sense — things which, after all, are pretty much the same — and postponed my Hong Kong reservation until December 9. I'd fly on the 9th and get to Hong Kong that night in time to celebrate my son Bruce's birthday with a wonderful dinner. That decision saved me from sharing a Jap prison camp with Joe Alsop for the next six months or more.

Late on Sunday afternoon, December 7, Betty Graham and I dropped in on the *Tutuila*, the U. S. Navy's gunboat, on the other shore of the Yangtze. The *Tutuila* was always open house for newspaper correspondents, and its radio kept its officers better informed on outside events than anyone else in Chungking. When we left, Skeeter (a jovial young officer whose family name I never could remember) and the *Tutuila's* naval doctor accompanied us along the muddy riverbank as far as the ferry.

"It's going to happen tonight," popped Skeeter, all of a sudden and with a knowing air.

"What's going to happen?" chorused Betty and I.

"Just wait awhile and you'll find out," Skeeter promised.

"What are the Japs up to? Have you got news from Washington?"

But Skeeter wasn't giving any more.

"You'll know before Tuesday anyway," Doc Grace assured us.

Betty and I were convinced something big was in the air, but we couldn't figure out what it might be. At the press hostel the news from Washington remained the same: pessimistic speculation.

It was about six in the evening, Chungking time, when Skeeter told us: "It's going to happen tonight." That meant it was early morning in Honolulu. Next morning Marty Gold rushed into my room at the Chialing House shouting: "The Japs have bombed Pearl Harbor!" After that, during the few days that I remained in Chungking, we all lived in a madhouse of excitement. I never found time to go down to the *Tutuila* to ask Skeeter how much he had really known that Sunday evening of December 7. I don't think he could possibly have known about Pearl Harbor. Probably the *Tutuila* had received a message from Washington warning that war was possible; perhaps the same warning that was ignored at such enormous cost in Honolulu. But I don't know. I wish Skeeter would write and tell me some day.

3

When the United States was blitzed into the war some things were plain to American officers and correspondents in Chungking which could scarcely be imagined by the average American at home. We knew there were only about 8,000 American troops and only a few squadrons of bombers and pursuit planes on the Philippines. Within a few days we were stunned by the information that most of these planes had been destroyed with the Japs' first blow. Some of us also knew that British troops in Malaya were dangerously small in number and that in the air they were facing invasion, at the outset, with a handful of completely outclassed Brewster Buffaloes. The faces of our officers on the Magruder mission were grave when I talked with them. They knew, and I knew, that either Manila or Singapore was bound to fall — possibly both Singapore and the Philippines — within three months. Fortunately we did not dream what terrific losses our Pacific fleet had suffered at Pearl Harbor. It was fortunate because things looked plenty black as they were.

But you couldn't write much of all this without giving folks at home an awful jolt. "It's going to be hellishly tough going for the next five or six months," growled that fighting man's man, Colonel Soderholm. Sody and every officer on the mission were cursing their luck. If only they were in Manila right then — but they said that knowing full well that little less than a miracle would save the Philippines. Maybe if our navy could take back Wake and Guam and restore the line to Manila within three months. But, of course, they didn't know how little there was left of our navy in the Pacific.

Anyway, I would write as much as I thought it safe to say. On December 10 the Chinese censorship was realistic enough to pass a dispatch containing such statements as these: "The development of the Far Eastern conflict is already much more serious than most Americans may realize. . . . If the Japanese capture Singapore it seems certain the Oriental war will be prolonged unpredictably, perhaps by one or two years. . . . Still graver, if Singapore falls, Burma would probably be rendered untenable and aid to China would be definitely doomed. . . . In any case it's certain the Far Eastern war must be long." Four days later I wrote: "The question whether the Americans and the British can reinforce the Philippines and Malaya in time to hold both places becomes increasingly debatable. . . . It is possible that the Allied powers may shortly be compelled to choose between fighting to retain the Philippines *or* Singapore . . . . which is an indispensable keystone to future Allied offensives in the eastern Pacific." I thought then — and still wonder — if a draconian decision could have been taken in the first two weeks of our war, if shipping could have been found and MacArthur and his troops transferred to Singapore, then that Malayan bastion and Burma and the Burma Road might well have been saved. But probably it was politically impossible. It would have looked like the betrayal and abandonment of the Philippine people, even if eventually it might have shortened their period of subjugation by many months. At any rate the sole advantage of being in Chungking at that moment lay in the fact that it was the only place from which some of the bad news ahead could be broken to the American public. The Chinese didn't mind anyone pointing out that the outlook was black. Shocked as they were by the weakness and lack of foresight of the Americans and British, they *knew* how black the outlook was.

But the nearest big story would be in Singapore. I cabled Carroll Binder suggesting that I go there. He replied that George Weller of the *Chicago Daily News* foreign staff was already on his way to Singapore and added: "Want you remain cover Chinese sector." That was based upon the assumption that the Chinese armies would probably be striking somewhere soon — something which we in Chungking knew could not happen for a long time. Well, there was still Rangoon. The Japs were bound to bomb those huge piles of Lend-Lease materials on Rangoon's docks almost any day, and when they did, the only American fighter squadrons left intact in the Orient would go into action. I must get to Rangoon before it was bombed. I had promised myself I'd be the first to see those grousing, unorthodox AVG (American Volunteer Group) pilots in action. But my orders read: "Remain in China sector."

In my desperate mood I was in no mind to take this literally. "China sector"? Well, the China sector certainly included the

Burma Road — and where did the Burma Road begin, if not in Rangoon? If Chicago knew that part of the AVG squadrons were still down in Burma, and that that was where the first real test of American pilots and planes against the Japs would be fought out, then Carroll and Paul Mowrer, I knew, would give me the green light.

The CNAC (Chinese National Airways) had lost most of its planes in Hong Kong. As a result there was no plane available to renew the air service from Chungking to Burma for several days. On December 15 Bondy, the high-powered manager of CNAC, kept his vow to get me on the first plane bound for Kunming, Lashio, and Rangoon. Thanks to Bondy, I was in Rangoon exactly four days in advance of the Jap bombs. It seemed just as well that I had postponed that reservation to Hong Kong.

Chapter V

THE BURMA ROAD RACKET

Do not thrust your finger through your own paper lantern.

Chinese proverb

Long before my out-bound flight from Kunming, I was ready to subscribe wholeheartedly to the contention that there cannot exist a people, anywhere on this broad earth, more intelligent and hard-working, more charming and subtle *and* disarming, than the Chinese. I could not recall ever having seen a truly stupid-looking Chinese. I had never known a people who smiled so engagingly, yet wore such an aura of illusiveness. The Chinese fascinated me for all these reasons and most of all perhaps because, for all their grace and suavity, I could never quite be sure what they were thinking. At one and the same time they seemed remarkably friendly yet inwardly aloof. I could grasp the essential psychology of European or Latin-American peoples after a few weeks of contact and study. For a Westerner, for myself at any rate, the Orientals constituted a psychology infinitely more complex. How could Americans best seek an understanding of the Chinese mind and Chinese character?

One day I heard a remark which struck me as the truest synthesis I had ever heard or read about the intriguing character of the Chinese. The observation was originally made by Putnam Weale, who lived a great many years in the Orient. Commenting on why Americans and Englishmen so commonly misunderstood completely the Chinese psychology, Mr. Weale said:

"You must think of the Chinese as a nation of women."

I'm afraid most Chinese men wouldn't like that remark, yet the more I looked around me in China, the more profoundly accurate I felt it to be. It seems to me that the average Chinese is as sharply intelligent as a woman; as highly intuitive; as instinctively definite in knowing what he wants, and as naturally guileful in going about getting it; perhaps as ruthless in protecting his own interests; certainly as charming and certainly as sensitive as the female of the species is renowned for being. Turning these things over in my mind and observing the variety of Chinese with whom I had daily contact, I was forced to conclude that Mr. Weale had provided an invaluable key for an Occidental approach to Oriental psychology.

"You must think of the Chinese as a nation of women."

When I quoted Mr. Weale's maxim to another American (I think it was in Chungking), he immediately replied:

"That's damned sound, all right. But I'd like to make just one little amendment. You must think of the Chinese as a blonde in a night club."

That was rather extreme, and perhaps a little unfair. But I knew why this particular American insisted upon his "blonde in a night club." He had seen too much of the Burma Road scandal and of a certain type of Chinese, the war profiteers and "squeeze" artists, whose last interest seemed to be either the welfare of their country or the winning of the war. I am reporting this disillusioned American's comment because it seems an appropriate introduction to the story of the racketeers' stranglehold on the Burma Road; the story which, to my surprise, I found had never been reported in anything faintly resembling its factual nakedness throughout more than three long years of the road's checkered operation. From Rangoon to Chungking and back again I had spent more than three months studying the Burma Road and everything connected with its insufficient and seriously mismanaged traffic. I didn't want to think of the Chinese as "blondes in a night club"; but the evidence which piled up and up in my notebooks compelled me to realize that some Chinese, including some who were highly placed in government organizations, used China's lifeline chiefly for what they could get out of it.

The Burma Road was the greatest racket in the Far East. Yet unless all the tonnage that could be transported over the Burma Road *was* transported over it — unless its abuses were eradicated — the Chinese armies could never stage a large-scale offensive against the Japanese. Such an offensive would only be possible with vast quantities of Lend-Lease materials from America. For these reasons the Burma Road, its status and its operation and potential development considered as a whole, was of simply inestimable importance to the Allied cause. So I had plunged myself into a fact-finding expedition which soon proved to be the most discouraging and depressing experience I had had anywhere, in dozens of countries, since the second World War began. I shall not recount it all here, but merely try to give a summary which may provide some constructive signposts for the future.

2

Some time in the spring of 1941 the U. S. Congress made its first Lend-Lease appropriation of nearly $500,000,000 for aid to China. In September I spent two weeks in Rangoon, where tens of thousands of tons of Lend-Lease materials were already accumulating. Then I went north and spent another week in Lashio, where the Southwest Transportation Company and other Chinese government agencies organized their caravans and sent them up over the Burma Road. In Rangoon and Lashio I learned enough surprising things to keep my eyes and ears wide open when I traveled the road itself; and later on in Kunming and Chungking. Returning by air in mid-December, I stopped again at Lashio.

One of the important things I first learned was that our Lend-Lease had been improvised under the spur of necessity. We were not yet in the war and China was hard-pressed, so the materials which Chinese representatives in Washington declared to be needed most urgently were shipped as quickly as possible. Perhaps this was the only way the matter could have been handled under the great time-pressure which existed. At any rate the American military mission under General John Magruder did not arrive in Chungking until early September — as one observer remarked, "only three or four months late." That was not the fault of General Magruder and his very efficient staff. But their job was to find out what weapons China's armies most needed and what materials should be shipped to increase China's own limited war production. By the time the Magruder mission's first reports were completed, in mid-autumn, scores of millions of dollars in Lend-Lease materials had already been allocated in the United States — and much of it shipped. Whether American military experts on the spot in China were agreed with Chinese authorities that these were the arms and goods most immediately essential could only be known in Washington after decisions affecting a large slice of Lend-Lease had already been taken there.

In China I learned that Chungking's first requests under Lend-Lease fell into two categories. The first included trucks, gasoline, airplanes, anti-aircraft guns, artillery, and other arms. The second concerned machine tools, mining apparatus, blast furnaces, and a great variety of industrial equipment which could not contribute to the prosecution of the war within from one to three years *after* this equipment was delivered over the Burma Road. This latter category of Lend-Lease requests included such items as the following:

A rolling mill to be constructed at a cost of $1,000,000 — estimated to be capable of production only after approximately two years.

A large steel and iron works with a forging mill, conveyors, and a water-supply system; to cost $4,500,000.

A steam power plant to supplement the steel works — cost estimated at $1,500,000.

A blast furnace, to cost $737,000.

Pumps, hoists, and modernizing equipment for the Nantung coal mine; $500,000.

Machinery and installations for the Ki-kang iron mines; also $500,000.

More than twelve hydroelectric plants of various sizes, most of which would require from eighteen months to three years to build and install *after* they had been transported over China's lifeline.

These were only a few of scores of equipment projects for Chinese industries. But if you had learned even a handful of elemental facts about the Burma Road you would immediately wonder how many hundreds of thousands of tons this equipment would total. The Chinese government had handed in its applications for most of this equipment long before October 1. But how much tonnage of all kinds of materials (much of which was not war matériel) had been carried over the road to Kunming in September? According to the figures of Dr. John Earl Baker, then an executive assistant of Chungking's Burma Road organization, exactly 14,700 tons. The road's transport companies had never yet delivered 20,000 tons of cargo (including gasoline) to Kunming in a single month. Even the Arnstein committee of traffic experts, with its suggested physical reforms, which did not touch the vital question of graft on the Burma Road, had not dared to estimate that, given such partial reforms, as much as 30,000 tons of war materials could be transported over the highway per month. How, then, could this huge mass of industrial equipment, or even a considerable proportion of it, reach Kunming in less than a year or eighteen months? In fact, could China hope to transport more than a fraction of the most urgently needed armaments which were now piling up in Rangoon?

This was one aspect of the Lend-Lease tangle just before and at the time of Pearl Harbor. Under the pressure of Chungking's demands for help there had apparently been little, if any, selection between what was most essential and what was obviously only of secondary and long-term value. When I checked with officials who were in a position to judge, I obtained such opinions as this: "The Chinese have handed in pages of lists of machinery and machine tools to furnish plants which do not exist. It would take two or three years to put some of these plants into operation. But when they were ready China still wouldn't have enough engineers to direct them. She would still have to train her own men to operate them. There's no dodging the fact that a great many of these Lend-Lease bids have nothing whatever to do with resistance to Japan — not while the issue will be decided. The Chinese are simply asking us to underwrite the industrialization of China."

In any case this impression gained ground through the attitude taken by many Chinese capitalists at that time. When an American officer visited a privately owned textile plant in Yunnan, its proprietor proudly showed some American machinery which he had bought several years previously, and then inquired frankly: "Can you tell me how I can get the materials I need through Lend-Lease?" Obviously the textile-plant owner was not thinking of Lend-Lease in terms of an immediate strengthening of China's armament. One day I attended the opening of the China Industrial Development Company's new blast furnace outside Chungking. An executive of the company remarked to a Magruder mission officer: "You see, we need machinery." The officer had heard this viewpoint of Lend-Lease so much stressed that he pulled out a box of Chinese matches. "Look how poor these matches are," he said. "We can supply you with first-class matches from America. What about a few trade concessions in return for our machinery?" The Chinese businessman made no answer.

Much against their desires, many Americans in Chungking reached the conclusion that the emphasis on Lend-Lease had been misplaced by a good many Chinese officials. They felt that our shipments should provide an affirmative answer to the question: Is this helping China to prosecute the war? But even in the matter of weapons for the army the Chinese government's requests sometimes struck our military experts as impractical. One of them gave me a typical analysis in these terms:

"The Chinese have obtained an order for six hundred armored cars from the United States. Both the British and the Russians have far greater need for them and much better facilities for using them. Anyway the Chinese have the order, but when you take a look at China's war zones what do you find? Armored cars in this terrain would be useless. Besides, the Chinese haven't any men here who are trained to operate them. It's the same thing with the light tanks they've ordered. Who in hell can operate these seven-ton tanks when they get here? And how many Chinese army officers know how to use them? It would take at least six or eight months to train Chinese crews to operate those tanks — well, judging by the way they abuse trucks on the Burma Road it would probably take longer than that. God knows we want to help the Chinese to the limit, but why not help them with weapons they can use?"

Despite great handicaps the Chinese were doing a remarkable job at turning out small arms and munitions in their small and somewhat primitive factories. Government arsenals, however, often ran short of the necessary raw materials and they were also continually losing some of their best skilled workmen, who were hired away from them, at higher wages, by private industries. In Rangoon large stocks of these raw materials had been lying and rusting for more than a year. If a considerable portion of these raw materials were moved over the Burma Road, China's small-arms and munitions output could have been doubled or tripled, for the government arsenals were running then at one fourth of capacity. But for the past ten months, inquiry revealed, an average of only 200 tons per month of raw materials for the arms and munition plants had been transported over the Road. The amount of private contraband being smuggled from Lashio to Kunming at that time was easily eight or ten times that tonnage per month. Everything came back to the Burma Road racketeering, which reduced the contribution China's lifeline was making to waging the war to at least one third what it should have been. One extremely well-informed Allied official in Lashio could see no real prospect of improvement. He remarked bitterly: "If the Chinese can't or won't clean up the road themselves and move up the supplies they've already got waiting for them, what good does it do to keep pouring shiploads of American supplies into Rangoon? Unless somebody takes a firm hand here, most of that stuff is only going to be wasted."

Wherever I turned, in regard to the problem of Lend-Lease and American aid to China the needle always pointed back to the virtually unknown and unpublicized scandal of the Burma Road racket. Pearl Harbor came, but the Burma Road was still as lawless and untamed as ever.

3

In Kunming, while I was there, a new Buick car was delivered over China's war-purpose lifeline and sold for six thousand American dollars to a wealthy Chinese. The owner would buy black-market gasoline, stolen from Chinese government trucks by Burma Road drivers (or officials), for $1.50 a gallon. Along the road there were scores of government-owned Dodge trucks standing idle, rusting in the rain, because no spare parts were available for them. But in private-owned accessory shops in Kunming anyone could purchase parts for Dodge trucks or cars. They had simply been lifted off the stranded trucks down the road, the trucks which should have been busy carrying war materials up into China.

When I asked why some seventy or eighty per cent of the tonnage which came over the Burma Road was gasoline, somebody laughed and said: "Well, petrol is a splendid commercial commodity, isn't it?" Admittedly, one third of every truck's cargo had to be gasoline to be used as fuel for its round-trip journey; and high-octane gas was indispensable for the Chinese air force. But Kunming showed a great number of private cars in circulation. Black-market gasoline could always be found.

In Rangoon, when I arrived there ten days after Pearl Harbor, the docks and warehouses were bulging with some 85,000 tons of American Lend-Lease supplies — a simply tremendous haul for the Japs if they broke through from near-by Thailand soon. David Ladin, the extremely efficient director of General Motors' new assembly plant for Lend-Lease motor vehicles, informed me that 2,000 trucks and cars were now waiting to be uncrated and assembled. Another 200 crated vehicles would be unloaded in the next two days and hundreds more were on the way around Africa. The value of General Motors vehicles already in Rangoon alone was more than $8,000,000. How much the whole 85,000 tons of Lend-Lease goods was worth was anybody's guess; maybe $30,000,000, possibly much more. If the Japs were kind enough not to invade Burma, how long would it take to transport this 85,000 tons over the Burma Road? General Magruder had estimated that 15,000 tons of war materials *could* be transported per month up to Kunming. Nothing like 15,000 tons of bona fide war materials had ever been moved over the road in one month during its three years of operation; and to many closely acquainted with the problem General Magruder's estimate seemed over-optimistic. Actually, unless some miraculously rigid reforms were enforced, it would require at least six, and probably eight months to clear Rangoon of the 85,000 tons already accumulated there. But more Lend-Lease ships were coming into port all the time. What a temptation to the knowing and hungry Japs Rangoon was!

The enlarged and global war was now twelve days old, but no emergency measures of any kind had been taken to hasten the clearing of this enormous treasure from Rangoon's docks.

In Burma the British, too, were in a frightening predicament. For the defense of Burma they did not have enough of anything, not even of trucks or radios or telephone wire; and of much they had nothing at all. Yet here on the quays lay vast quantities of materials, absolutely indispensable to the small British forces, which could not conceivably be moved into China for many months. If the Chinese would turn over some of these weapons and supplies to the British for the defense of Burma — and of the one seaport which poured blood into China's lifeline — perhaps Rangoon could be saved from the Japanese thrust which inevitably must start almost any day. That would seem a common-sense arrangement. But what was happening when I reached Rangoon?

Among the first things the British asked for were short-wheeled trucks, blankets for their troops, and gas masks. At that time and for weeks afterward hundreds of new Lend-Lease trucks were parked in fields and along the roads outside Rangoon for lack of drivers to take them up to Lashio. "The Chinese have nearly four thousand lorries piled up around here, and we needed three hundred urgently," an Englishman said. "Finally they offered us some of the oldest lorries they had — battered wrecks a lot of them — at a price about three times their market value. The Chinese have hundreds of thousands of ant-eaten blankets that have been here for months. They offered us some of those blankets and some rotted-out gas masks."

Since Singapore was more exposed and had to come first, the British in Burma were short of munitions and very short of machine guns and some other weapons. Nevertheless American officials assured me that Lieutenant General McLeod, commander of Britain's few battalions in Burma, had been extremely moderate in requesting material from the Chinese. One of our Lend-Lease ships tied up at the docks contained a heavy consignment of Bren guns, reputedly 3,000, and Bren guns were almost nonexistent along the Burmese-Thailand frontier where the Japs would strike.

"I'd give my soul for eighteen Bren guns," exclaimed a major of the Burma Rifles.

The British asked for a small number. An officer who should have known told me the Chinese refused, and cleared the Bren guns out of Rangoon the next day. Considerably later this situation improved somewhat. There was plenty of room for improvement, for at this stage there was a great deal of bitterness and resentment among British and Americans toward Chinese representatives in Rangoon. One began to fear that that "blonde in a night club" simile might be more than a wisecrack. I was reminded of it because some incidents occurred which were hard to take. The Generalissimo had pledged "all that we have and all we are" — and had meant what he said. But some people seemed never to have heard his words.

There was the item of spare radios for the P-40 Tomahawks which two of the three American Volunteer Group squadrons would soon be flying from their Kunming headquarters. (The third AVG squadron was now stationed at Mingaladon outside Rangoon. Together with one RAF squadron of old Brewster Buffaloes, that was all the aerial protection Rangoon had.) The spare radios were shipped over the Burma Road. Like all Lend-Lease materials, their crates bore the initials "CDS," meaning China Defense Supplies. Crates bearing this label were not normally opened and inspected by the British Burma Road control officer in Lashio — a fact which made smuggling easy for certain people in the Chinese transportation agencies. It was rather difficult for a British official to challenge the authenticity of that magic label. Recently, I learned, an Allied officer had got the feeling that a certain caravan smelled rather too fishy. So he opened up the crates, which supposedly contained spare radios for the AVG planes, and found them stuffed — with perfume and women's toilet articles. Such things bring a very fancy price in Kunming or Chungking. The radio sets were gone. Undoubtedly they had been sold at a pleasant profit, either in Rangoon or Mandalay. This was the Burma Road functioning in its accustomed fashion. But the officer who discovered this slight error was fuming mad. You wondered how many Chinese air force planes — and American pilots — might be grounded during a crucial dogfight in a couple of months' time because of this neat little bit of brigandage. Perhaps it was high time to come down to cases about the Burma Road. Its corruption and racketeering had been a most costly luxury for China's cause for more than three years. Now its war-profiteering abuses and its lawlessness jeopardized the continuance of Chinese armies in the field, and jeopardized British and American as well as Chinese lives.

In Rangoon and Lashio I had learned a good deal of this sordid record even before going up the road itself; and inside China the evidence had simply accumulated in snowball fashion. After all, everyone in Burma and China knew that the Burma Road was a scandal; but it had been the Orient's greatest scandal for so long now that most people, including foreign correspondents, took it for granted. In the spring of 1941 Chiang Kai-shek had made a new effort to get China's lifeline organized on a sound basis. Old China Hands always insisted the road would never be cleaned up until some American or Britisher took over its management — and then, they added, "whoever gets the job will find his hands tied; he won't have any police force, and he won't have the authority." This was exactly what happened to Dr. John Earl Baker, a former American Red Cross executive with long experience in China, who in April 1941 was appointed to administer the Burma Road. After he resigned in October, Dr. Baker confessed to me that he had been promised executive control of the road under the chairman of its commission; "but the chairman vetoed my plans for hiring China-experienced foreigners and cut short negotiations I had started for a traffic patrol on the road." Afterward Dr. Baker found himself in a side alley and eventually he was transferred out of Kunming, where he was rather too close to Burma Road developments and doings. When he got back to Chungking Dr. Baker said: "I'm out of the Burma Road — fired."

That same summer Daniel G. Arnstein headed a group of American transportation experts on an inspection tour of the road for the Chinese government. After the Arnstein committee made its report another American, Lieutenant Colonel James Wilson, was given an administrative position with the Yunnan-Burma Highway Commission. General Yu Fei-peng, a close friend or relative of the Generalissimo, became chief administrator of the Burma Road. But most of the personnel in the highway commission and the Chinese transportation agencies remained unchanged. So did the practices along the road. Before Pearl Harbor the principal Chinese government agency was known under the name of the Southwest Transportation Company, with main offices in Kunming, Lashio, and Rangoon. In December I found its name had been changed, but not much else. China Defense Supplies and the rechristened Southwest

Transportation were responsible for Lend-Lease supplies from their unloading in Rangoon up the Burma Road.

Until the Burma government protested emphatically, Southwest Transportation used to charge fifteen per cent on all cargoes, including war materials, which it moved from Rangoon to Lashio. British authorities said this cozy profit was ended in time to save most Lend-Lease materials from being charged with this extra levy. But they said the Southwest's executives had other devices. One of these, as I confirmed in Lashio, was the subcontracting of Burma Road business to private trucking companies. Southwest's transportation rates had been fixed, but by turning over huge quantities of cargo to private "contractors" these energetic capitalists were free to charge double or triple tonnage rates on the cargoes their trucks carried. Cases verified by Burma control officials showed that profits of thirty American dollars per ton were often made on a three-day haul over one portion of the highway — as much as $1,000 on 36 tons. Did any of this juicy gravy find its way into the plates of certain Southwest representatives? Well, those British and American citizens who had watched the Burma Road closely for months or years merely said: "What do you think they're here for? Didn't you ever hear of Chinese squeeze?"

"I can tell you things that I know for a fact," one Burma control officer told me. "In October a Chinese government official in Lashio was promising to fix the delivery of a shipment of *commercial* goods to Kunming, and he was offering to pay nearly four times the regular tonnage rates. Why would he pay any such price as that if the goods weren't contraband? I've personally turned back enough stuff being smuggled under the label of 'Defense Supplies' not to have any doubts."

These were but a few of the ingenious devices, sometimes altered and frequently improved upon, by which racketeering had flourished virtually unimpeded since the Burma Road first opened. The road had made a good many millionaires in its tawdry history, and was still making Chinese millionaires as the Japs prepared to strike at Rangoon — and its 85,000 tons of Lend-Lease supplies — from Thailand. In September an openly classified 1,400 tons of commercial goods had been taken over the road. The amount classified officially as "war materials" had been 5,600 tons (the remaining tonnage having been gasoline). But any Britisher or American who knew the Burma Roadsters' system would seriously question whether as much as half of that 5,600 tons had really been war materials. Almost certainly, they said, more than half of it had been contraband, carried in Chinese government trucks — the rake-off of the war profiteers. If you still could not count on a maximum of more than 6,000 or 7,000 tons of Lend-Lease supplies being transported over the Yunnan highway in a single month, how long might it take to clear that 85,000 tons out of Rangoon? "They'll always give you a plausible story," a Burma control officer said. "They always have some impressive figures to show you — but the figures don't mean anything. I can take you to a Southwest godown where they've got a lot of contraband automobile tires hidden away right now. They're just waiting until my back is turned. Then they'll sneak them through. There's only one way to stop it. That's for British or American army forces to take over, manage, and police the road. That way we can deliver the supplies to the Chinese Army — and know that they get there. But I don't suppose we'll ever do it. You can bet we'll never be given the chance as long as some Chinese with a big pull in the Chungking government can prevent it."

4

From the time I went up the Burma Road in early October until the end of November I debated the question as to how much of the truth should be told. If the scope of the Burma Road racket was reported, I knew it would come as a tremendous shock to an American public which had come to look upon all Chinese as Sir Galahads and patriots. I knew that other correspondents in the Far East had remained silent — and perhaps rightly so at a time when American scrap iron was going to Japan — because they believed that the brave and self-sacrificing Chinese people desperately needed all the help and sympathy they could get from the United States. But now America was committed to giving China at least half a billion dollars' worth of war materials, and the American people confidently expected that this aid would be transported into China swiftly and efficiently. Unless the Burma Road was drastically reformed, this could never be done. This was not the fault of the Generalissimo. He was occupied by a thousand responsibilities and it appeared that he simply could not find enough competent and reliable men for all the jobs that had to be done. Would anything short of the sharp prod of publicity abroad precipitate a clean-up of the Burma Road? Nothing else had done it and this seemed to be one of the few expedients that had never been tried. Perhaps the one thing the Chungking government needed was a compelling reason for drastic action. Certainly with the Japs less than 250 miles from Rangoon the reasons were compelling enough, now in December. But even in November, if Lend-Lease were to reach China in any quantities, the only solution was clear.

The more fully I amassed the facts and the more familiar I became with the mute and humble heroism of China's soldiers and her poverty-ridden patriotic common people, the more clear it seemed to me that only the truth would serve China in the end. We, Americans and Englishmen, owed the Chinese people an inestimable debt for their long unwavering resistance to Japan. But we could scarcely repay any portion of that debt by letting them bleed and die in still greater numbers because of an untouched, and unmentioned, orgy of racketeering along the Burma Road. Of course, if I wrote about this I would be blamed and perhaps never forgiven by some of my Chinese friends. But if a newspaper correspondent has kept any kind of a conscience intact through a long succession of disillusionments, it is he who must live with that conscience. Few disillusionments of mine had ever been greater or more acid than this which I had suffered behind China's front. At the end of weeks of painstaking work and self-debate there was only one thing that I could do. I had decided that before the closing days of November. I would leave China and write the story. After that the responsibility would no longer be mine. It couldn't possibly make the Burma Road racket any worse. Conceivably it might save millions of dollars' worth of Lend-Lease supplies for the Chinese people, who so richly deserved it. When Pearl Harbor came, the fact that the United States was in the war did not change any of these fundamental issues in any particular. If anything, they were simply more urgent than ever, for America's ultimate victory now quite as much as for China's.

So, once back in Rangoon, I pulled out my notebooks and kept punching the keys until I had completed a series of seven articles for the *Chicago Daily News* and the fifty-odd American and Canadian newspapers which subscribe to its foreign service. The following excerpt, I think, is an accurate illustration of my approach to a highly unpleasant task:

"The whole of eastern Asia has suddenly been enveloped by war while the chief artery for making an offensive force of the great Chinese army remains in a deplorable condition, crippled by inefficiency, politics, lawlessness, racketeering and other abuses. The responsibility unfortunately must rest chiefly with the Kuomintang dictatorship which has tolerated these abuses for years; and likewise upon the profit-seeking appetites of a lamentably large number of Chinese businessmen, politicians or governmental officials and employees. When one has seen the fortitude and selfless courage of Chinese soldiers and the hunger and poverty of China's common people, the record of the Burma Road racket seems shameful beyond words. To all who have admired and been inspired by the wonderful resistance of the Chinese people this other, and sordid, side of the truth about China can only come — as it has come to me — as a bitter deception. The critical exigencies of the ABCD Allies' present war efforts throughout the Far East command that recriminations should be ruled out. They do not command that the American and British governments or peoples should remain uninformed about the truth regarding the Burma Road."

When the old-style British civil servant who was press censor read the first three of my Burma Road series he looked definitely upset. But at last he found reason to relent and reluctantly pass the articles. "Well, I suppose they must be passed," he sighed. "But I really can't take any responsibility for them, you understand." Before I could file the remainder of the series Rangoon received its first two terrific bombings. Transmission was so chaotic it was certain the dispatches would be greatly delayed in reaching America. Finally, early in January, a cablegram from Chicago got through. "Burma Roadsters causing sensation," it said; and added that publication had started with number four because the first three (filed two days before the others) had not yet been received. I suspected they had been held up in India, and filed them over again. But it was bad luck that Chicago had had to begin with number four. That dispatch contained the unvarnished picture of the Burma Road racket, and I had tried to put the subject in balance with my opening articles. A few days later another cable from Carroll Binder informed me: "On urgent suggestion higher-ups publication remainder China series suspended pending upclearing present crucial situation stop heavily upplayed fourth fifth third which provoked bitter criticism threats reprisals stop personally appreciate your courageous coverage." *

That was the kind of support Carroll would always give a foreign staff which he had carefully selected and in whom he had complete confidence. But the fat was clearly in the fire and unquestionably my half-published series was giving my editors some bad headaches at a difficult moment. Well, perhaps enough had been published to give greater headaches to some other people who were in a position to do something about the Burma Road. I showed Carroll's message to Darrel Berrigan of the United Press and O. D. Gallagher of the London *Daily Express*. "Chalk up another score for Stowe and his scorched-ass policy," chortled Gallagher. "If you will go around lighting fires under people's bottoms — "

When I thought of the wounded Chinese soldiers lying in their dirty uniforms and without blankets in the hospital across the Chialing River, and of the radio-set cases filled with perfume and lipsticks, I must admit to a certain inner satisfaction. Of course, as had happened a good many times before — especially in the case of my April 1940 dispatches about the Trojan Horse in Oslo and how the Nazis seized Norway's capital — I would be attacked and denounced. I knew from experience that it isn't pleasant to have your professional integrity the object of revenge, or even to have your journalistic standing attacked by an understandable but misguided wounded national pride. But a reporter is supposed to be first of all a reporter, even when it hurts. When

* The "higher-ups," as I suspected, were in no way connected with my newspaper.

governments are involved, particularly Allied governments in the midst of a war, facts sometimes have a way of colliding too sharply with national or international policies. In this instance we saw the reactions almost overnight in Rangoon; first of all among the representatives of the Chinese Burma Road and Lend-Lease agencies, but also among American and British officials.

On January 11 (1942) I was surprised to receive an urgent message asking me to call upon Sir Reginald Dorman-Smith, the British Governor of Burma, at the Governor's mansion. Sir Reginald, a tall and handsome man in his mid-forties, fully appreciated the importance of his position, but he was also possessed of great affability and all the measured charm of a Tory-born British gentleman. He received me in a most gracious manner and made me at ease with a Scotch and soda, whisked expertly to my side by a perfect Indian servant. Eventually, without undue haste, His Excellency revealed what was on his mind.

"It appears, Stowe, that your articles about the Burma Road have provoked a rather violent controversy," Sir Reginald began.

"Yes, Your Excellency, I'm afraid they have."

Sir Reginald cleared his throat and took another sip of Scotch. "I've just received a message about them from my Secretary of State in London. It says something like this, in effect: '. . . Stowe's reports are undoubtedly justified, but can't you persuade him to discontinue a pursuance of the subject? It would make co-operation with the Chinese much easier. . . .' I imagine you understand how things are."

I told Sir Reginald I thought I understood that only too clearly, and in any case messages I had received from America indicated that it would be a waste of time for me to file any more dispatches about the Burma Road — at least for some time to come.

"Well, I've been up against the same sort of thing," confessed the Governor. "I was even criticized for insisting that the AVG pilots should be given the use of the airfield at Toungoo for their training. I know you're right about this, but — "

"That's quite all right, Your Excellency. I'm glad to have the opportunity of knowing what you think about it."

5

The reaction of Chinese officials in Rangoon to the half-published Burma Road exposé was remarkably swift. There were immediate conferences between the Chinese and American officers of the Magruder mission. General Yu Fei-peng, chief administrator of the road, went to Lashio to confer with other American officers there. By January 15 the American colonel whom General Magruder had just placed in charge at Rangoon told Darrel Berrigan that the Burma Road was going to be militarized from Rangoon to Paoshan and that "the bottleneck is going to be cleared up." The colonel said the American mission would establish priorities, that commercial traffic over the Yunnan highway would be subordinated and military cargoes would go first. This was more action than the Burma Road problem had excited in many long months and it sounded encouraging. But like so many things in the Orient it sounded much better than it actually was. Berrigan got the impression at first that the road's traffic would at last be under American military control. When we investigated, however, this was still not the case. In fact the Americans still did not have the authority — or the machinery and the men — to prevent contraband from being smuggled over the highway. Without rigid police control along the entire 1,500 miles of the road they simply could not do that. The great loophole in the colonel's optimistic statements was lack of provision for a large Burma Road police force. Nevertheless Chinese representatives at last gave evidence that they were genuinely concerned about what the outside world might read or think about the dubious functioning of China's lifeline.

For the first time in my experience the Chinese officials called a press conference for all American and British correspondents in Rangoon. This was on January 16, when our numbers had grown from an original three to eight or ten. Mr. R. C. Chen, Rangoon director of China Defense Supplies, and a Mr. Shen, who was assistant to General Yu, presided at the conference. Mr. Shen stated that 20,000 tons had been delivered over the road in December while about 17,000 tons had been transported in November. Some sixty per cent of December's tonnage had been motor and high-octane gasoline, he said. But Mr. Shen did not provide a breakdown of the figures to show how much cargo had been war materials and how much commercial goods. The Chinese now had about six hundred laborers to load Lend-Lease goods on trains for Lashio and we were informed they could load sixty cars a day. It was estimated that the January average would be fifty-three cars per day, or a total of 16,430 tons sent to Lashio by rail. As for the unloading of some twenty to thirty Lend-Lease ships now hung up in Rangoon's port (being bombed by the Japs every two or three days), Mr. Shen justly pointed out that unloading was not a responsibility of the Chinese. That was the job of the British port commissioner, most of whose Indian laborers had fled the city with its first bombing on December 23. The Chinese officials did not give us the detailed figures on how much Lend-Lease supplies had been sent by rail, by trucks, and by Irrawaddy River boats from Rangoon in December. Instead, they provided a detailed forecast of the China-Burma Transportation Administration for the month of January. I found this estimate of exceptional interest. It read as follows:

By rail — 53 cars per day at 10 tons per car	16,430 tons
By river — 10 ships a month, at 300 tons each	3,000 tons
By road — (a) if 1,000 GM trucks are assembled in January, carrying 1 ton each	1,000 tons
(b) 275 trucks which departed between Jan. 1 and 10, each with 3 tons	825 tons
(c) 300 Chinese govt. trucks, to leave between Jan. 11 and 30, each with 3 tons	900 tons
Estimated total to be cleared from Rangoon in Jan.	22,155 tons

If you glanced at these figures hastily they looked extremely encouraging. But what struck me about them was the fact that they had singularly little relation to the chaotic conditions prevailing in Rangoon at that time. They failed completely to take into consideration the thousands of coolies who had vanished from the city, the paralysis of the port, and the certainty of increased paralysis from Japanese bombings, which were bound to be accelerated. The Rangoon port commissioner was still unable to unload nearly thirty ships which were now in the harbor or at the quays. If he did not have the labor to unload even three of these floating bomb targets, where would the labor be found to load ten Irrawaddy River boats in the next fifteen days? Even if the Chinese could load fifty-three railroad cars per day, how could the Rangoon-Lashio line (already seriously overtaxed by transportation and equipment urgently required for the defense of Burma) handle this many freight cars per day? Mr. Shen had said that Dave Ladin's General Motors plant was assembling fifty trucks a day — at the rate of 1,300 a month. But Ladin had lost three fourths of his trained workmen when they vamoosed after the first Jap raid, just as the Burma Road organizations had lost nearly 500 out of 750 chauffeurs. Since the Japs were bombing steadily, the truly heroic efforts of Dave Ladin, Wally Thorensen, Alec Gardiner, Bill Whitelaw, and Charley Hogg — a group of first-class and hard-working American engineers if ever there was one — could well be stymied at any moment. Let the Japs paste Rangoon heavily for two days in a row and Dave and his staff might have to perform wonders in order to assemble an average of only thirty trucks a day for the next month.

I asked a number of such practical questions and then said to Mr. Shen: "It seems to me that this January estimate, under present conditions, is excessively optimistic." We had each been handed typewritten copies of the January estimate. After I had pointed out a number of the most obvious loopholes in its figures, Mr. Chen announced that he thought perhaps it might be better not to publish these figures, since it might not be wise to mention the number of ships that were counted on being used. Then why had the January estimate of 22,155 tons of Lend-Lease goods *to be* moved out of Rangoon been prepared and distributed to the British and American correspondents? Some of us could scarcely avoid the conclusion that it had been hoped to get some reassuring figures about Burma Road traffic into the world's press. But the figures would scarcely be impressive if a correspondent analyzed them in the light of existing conditions in Rangoon. Like all people, the Chinese have their failings. One of their failings, old-timers in Chungking had insisted, is a pronounced weakness for drawing up "beautiful plans." Old-timers said, "The Chinese simply love to put things on paper. You should see the railroads and highways that are on paper in the government files." I remembered that when I examined the January estimate.

But the Chinese, I had soon learned, also have qualities which are quite as great as any of their faults. I was reminded of this a few days later when Mr. Chen invited me to a dinner given by the Chinese Lend-Lease and Burma Road officials for an officer of the Magruder mission, Squadron Leader Jack Newkirk of the AVG, and me. My dispatches had caused these Chinese representatives a tremendous amount of work and inconvenience. I couldn't have blamed them if they had greeted me with stony silence whenever they met me — not because any of my essential facts were wrong, but simply because it would have been a perfectly natural reaction. The Chinese, however, are much too civilized and much too wise to reveal annoyance or a grudge, whatever their inner feelings may be. We were served a magnificent Chinese dinner that evening, and the lovely and charming Mrs. Chen, sitting at my left, was particularly gracious in seeing to it that my plate was heaped with the choicest morsels. I wanted these Chinese officials to know that nothing I had reported had been written in a spirit of animosity, so I was glad of this opportunity to share a social evening with them — oddly enough, in the attractive house of General Yu himself. Of course, there was plenty to drink as well as to eat and hospitality was poured overflowingly into my glass, as upon my plate. Not being any too sure that I could hold the pace well into the morning hours with my genial hosts, I had taken the precaution of agreeing to meet Berry and Gallagher at the Silver Grill shortly after midnight. I met that deadline with several more highballs under the belt than I would normally have consumed, for the Chinese are masters at the art of showering one with kindness. Yet throughout that most enjoyable and rather unusual evening not a single reference was made by any of the Chinese officials to the embarrassing publicity which I had given the Burma Road. They bade me good-night warmly and graciously. This entire occasion had been a triumph for Chinese intelligence and Chinese manners. What other people in the world could have handled a situation like this with such delicacy and diplomacy and tact?

Of course, I could still ask myself whether reporting the facts of the Burma Road racket had been justified and whether it would serve any constructive purpose. I still believed it had been justified and in Rangoon I thought I saw indications that a considerable amount of good might result. Several months later two different officers of General Magruder's mission assured me that in their opinion my Burma Road series had done a lot of good. Nearly eighteen months afterward I met another of these officers, a man who had been closely connected with the Burma-China problems until long after Burma fell. "Your stories were the one thing that got immediate action out of the Chinese," he said. "Do you know that more Lend-Lease tonnage was transported over the road during the next two months than at any time in its history?" Well, I suspected that the Japanese troops' approach to Rangoon had probably been the chief factor in regard to that. But it was rather gratifying when this American officer, who had been where he could observe developments closely, insisted: "I think most Chinese are intelligent enough to know that you rendered a real service to the Chinese people." Whether or not my friend was correct about a service rendered, it certainly wasn't the kind of service that ever brings many citations. But I had been more than amply rewarded — by a magnificent Chinese dinner and a memorable example of the nuances and depth of Chinese psychology.

6

This has not been intended as a mere recital of a world scoop that was prematurely drowned by the exigencies of national policies in wartime. Rather, I have tried to give the background of the Burma Road's abuses which weakened the fighting strength of the Chinese armies, because it should now be possible — many long months after the Japs have taken over the lower half of the road — for all parties and governments concerned to face the indisputable facts of the past, to face the future and to profit from past mistakes. Upon the courage and the realism with which this is done, once Burma has been reconquered, will depend the lives of countless thousands of Chinese, American, and British soldiers or airmen. For the Burma Road must be reopened if Japan is to be defeated and all Chinese soil is to be cleared of the invaders. At the moment when I now write, it is impossible to prophesy just when the Allies' great Burma offensive will be launched. If enough force has been built up in India, the drive to recover the Burma Road should surely get well under way during the winter and spring of 1944. If that does not happen before the Burmese heavy rains start in May, then it would probably have to be postponed until the following November. But the Chinese must not be kept waiting for another long and agonizing year if that can possibly be avoided.

In any case we know that Burma will be won back for the Allies, primarily and overwhelmingly because Burma and the Burma Road are keystones to Allied victory in the Far East. China's lifeline must be restored because it is her only operable and available overland highway of supply. Thanks to the Japanese military, the Burma Road racket finally died an appropriately ignoble death, by strangulation. Thanks to the Japs, too, it would seem that the road can only be reopened under complete and strict control of Allied armed forces. If the lessons of a shabby and excessively costly past are learned, this is the sole manner in which the Yunnan-Burma highway can function efficiently, at least so long as the war endures. If military men drive the trucks on the road, police it, and administer it, there can be no opportunity for the racketeers and war profiteers to resume their old practices. American Lend-Lease materials will be delivered to the Chinese forces and to Chinese hospitals, and to such war plants as require vital materials, under military supervision. Common sense would seem to dictate that this supervision will be a joint affair between the British, American, and Chinese military authorities. The one object of this chapter and the preceding first chapter has been to make clear what the new status of a reopened Burma Road must be and why abolishing its past abuses has become as inevitable as it is imperative.

Some correspondents will have the joy of riding up and down the Yunnan Mountains, through the great and magnificent Salween and Mekong gorges, and on to Kunming with the first Allied cargoes that come through from recaptured Rangoon. They will see China's lifeline functioning as it never has functioned before. Undoubtedly they will be thrilled by a piece of highway transportation such as China has never seen in its thousands of years. I wonder if they will quite be able to imagine that this fabulous highway was first constructed by incredible toil and perseverance, without a single rock-crusher or tractor or steam shovel? I hope they will not fail to see the thousands of Chinese men and women, in their cheap and dirty jackets and trousers of blue denim, who dig the earth and smash the stones and fill in the ruts on this serpentining back-breaking highway which was built—first of all—by some of the simplest and poorest and greatest-hearted people of our modern world.

PART II — THE WAR IN BURMA

Chapter VI

SLEEPWALKERS AMONG THE BOMBS

Two days before Christmas the Japs hit Rangoon — on schedule.

There was scarcely a minute's warning. Suddenly dozens of bombs tore into the heart of the city, a city without cellars and without air-raid shelters worthy of the name. Our hotel rocked from the explosion of three or four hits near by. Big fires raged on the docks just across the street. Lend-Lease munitions, piled on the quays, made a fearful din as they went up in smoke. On all sides buildings blazed and were still flaming fiercely when a second wave of thirty Japanese bombers came over. Rangoon's central streets were now littered with bodies, guts, brains and blood. Between 600 and 800 persons were killed — most of them standing in the open or cringing helplessly against walls as the raiders released their bombs.

The moment we could find an automobile Gallagher and I made a dash for Mingaladon airfield, twelve miles out. We knew there was only one RAF squadron and another AVG squadron at Mingaladon, and they must have had a tough fight. Several of the hangars and administration buildings were a smoking shambles. Jap machine-gunners had riddled the barracks and operations huts, killing several RAF ground-crew men. We rushed to the pilots' mess shack because everything depended on what kind of showing the Americans had made. The shack was an astonishing sight — like a locker room when an under-dog football team has knocked over the champions. The AVG with only fourteen P-40's and the RAF with but ten old Brewster Buffaloes in the air had taken on some eighty Jap bombers and pursuit planes. G. B. MacMillan of Winter Park, Florida, led the AVG. We talked with Mac and R. T. Smith of Lincoln, Nebraska, and the others as they came in flushed from the fight. They were both jubilant and fighting mad — the first fighting-mad Americans I had seen since meeting the boys of the Abraham Lincoln Battalion in Spain.

"The bastards got Gilbert — and Martin, too," Mac said grimly.

I scribbled down their names — Henry G. Gilbert of Wyoming and Neil G. Martin of Texarkana, Arkansas — the first American airmen to die in combat in Burma.

"But we made the sons of bitches pay for it," Smitty was saying. "We got eight or ten of them, and the Brewsters got seven more."

"If only those yellow bastards come back tomorrow," somebody else was saying.

It was a great change from the beefing, undisciplined crew I had met at Toungoo in September. Their tails were up. Against five-to-one odds they had punished the Japs plenty and American prestige in the Orient had been saved. I knew then that the AVG was going to make us proud of being Americans. Gallagher and I rode back to Rangoon and its sudden desolation. We passed thousands of Indians and Burmese — in cars and carts, in rickshaws and on foot. Loaded down with bags, bundles, and children, they flooded every highway as they fled from the city. By the next noon fully half of Rangoon's 500,000 inhabitants had vanished, leaving the city deserted, without automobiles or rickshaws, its hotels denuded, its shops shut. The palsy and panic of death gripped Rangoon.

At the Strand Hotel John Drysdale told us that Harry Pope, the manager of Watson's large garage, and his wife had both been killed by the first stick of bombs. Their nineteen-year-old daughter was acting as a volunteer nurse in a hospital, helping unload victims from stretchers. "Here comes another," she said. Then she lifted the sheet and cried: "Mother!" In hundreds of such tragedies the war spread its first woe in Rangoon.

That night we encountered Captain Bobby MacLean Brown and his stout-hearted wife, Mara. Captain Brown was a British sailor of the old school and had something to do with shipping in the port. Another ship, the *Étoile du Jour,* had come up the river in the middle of the raid, Captain Bobby said. "She's loaded with more Lend-Lease stuff — airplanes and guns," he added. "But I'll bet you lads they'll never unload that ship. Those blokes at the top won't do anything about it. They don't know what to do in a tight spot, and they don't know how to handle the natives. These Indians and Burmese, they're all right if you handle 'em right. All you've got to do is stay with them. If the commissioner would give me authority, I'd get those ships unloaded. My crew were all waiting this morning. Give them cigarettes and stay with 'em and they'll stick. But what can you expect from the officers of the Burma Navy?"

"What about the Burma Navy?"

"Sure there's a Burma Navy," guffawed Bobby. "It's got about a hundred and fifty officers, but only two of them are regular Royal Navy men. Most of the others were signed on from important families here in Rangoon. You never saw such a lot. They've got lieutenant commanders who've never been to sea — not once in their lives. One of them has just been appointed assistant director of the port. What do you expect those blokes to do? They don't know a bloody thing about ships. I've spent my whole life at sea — and I have to take orders from blokes like that. Just look around this town. They still don't know there's a war on."

The next morning was Christmas and it proved to be a strange sort of Christmas. Before Darrel Berrigan, Gallagher, and I could scrape together some kind of breakfast in the deserted Strand, another raid was on. The AVG and RAF took on terrific odds that day; more than a hundred Jap bombers and fighters against their twenty-two planes. Once more we dashed out to Mingaladon and once more we found the battered mess shack a scene of American jubilation. The RAF had lost three pilots and the AVG had two pilots missing. But together this single combined Anglo-American squadron had shot down no less than twenty-eight Japs. "Just like shooting fish in a barrel," one Yank declared. Duke Hedman, a blond farm boy from South Dakota, had accounted for five Jap bombers. Olson, the squadron leader, confessed that the AVG only possessed enough munition for one more fight. "Lucky the Japs didn't send over a third wave today," he remarked. "But we're getting 70,000 rounds flown down from Toungoo tonight."

Even so the AVG's planes had been whittled down to fourteen and many of these were badly shot up. The RAF was also down to about eight Brewsters in condition to fly. If the Japs raided as heavily as this for four or five days in a row, we all knew the answer. Rangoon's air protection would be wiped out. Maybe the Japs had been so badly hurt today they wouldn't dare try bombing every day. That seemed to be the only chance for the boys at Mingaladon. But what a Christmas for this little group of British and American airmen! They had fought all day on empty stomachs. For some reason somebody had failed to get food out to them since the first raid two days before. And there were still no anti-aircraft guns around the field. The Chinese had a hundred ack-ack guns on the Rangoon docks, but they had refused to lend any to the British a few days previously. It was now exactly eighteen days since the Japanese struck at Pearl Harbor, Manila, and Hong Kong, but this was the state of British Burma's defenses.

The Strand that night was a shabby-looking mess of dirt and broken glass, without a servant left in the place. About eight o'clock two Englishmen, attired immaculately in dress shirts and black ties, walked in with a woman who was togged out in a sweeping evening gown. They were bound for a chota-peg in the bar, according to a ritual which was undoubtedly of many years' standing. They did not seem remotely aware that Rangoon's fires were still smoldering or that parts of the city were a shambles or that its hospitals were overcrowded with some two thousand wounded. It seemed that these three hadn't seen a thing all day — perhaps not for years and years. This was my introduction to the sleepwalkers among the bombs.

2

Berry, Gallagher, and I had moved out to the Rangoon golf club in order to be close to Mingaladon, which was less than three miles away. This was the only way we could keep in contact with the air battles, but transportation was a serious problem. Lieutenant Colonel Joseph Twitty of the Magruder mission literally saved our journalistic lives by signing over one of the mission's extra trucks to me, and later on we swapped it for a jeep. It seemed fantastic, yet was none the less true, that Rangoon was flooded with idle Lend-Lease motor vehicles, but the British were having a fearful time trying to pry some of them loose from the Chinese. There was also the great problem of getting trucks assembled. Alec Gardiner of the General Motors assembly plant, which was operating for China's Lend-Lease, told us they had one thousand six-wheel-drive trucks but almost no labor to assemble them. "The Tokyo radio keeps saying Rangoon will be wiped off the map," an American business man said. "It's just propaganda to paralyze the city. But it's succeeding beautifully. The Governor won't declare martial law. There's plenty of food in Rangoon but no distribution for it. The damnedest case of municipal sabotage I've ever seen."

William D. Pawley, president of Camco (Central Aircraft Manufacturing Company), was paymaster of the AVG and in charge of all their supplies. Bill needed a lot of material for three new Burma airfields and the material was all bogged down on the Rangoon docks. I accompanied Bill when he went to appeal to Group Captain Manning of the RAF. "The Governor has had the authority to conscript labor for the past ten days," Manning said. "The city council voted him that authority." It was now one week since the Japs' first bombing and the quays were heaped with millions of dollars' worth of Lend-Lease stuff which had not been touched. Pawley took matters into his own hands. The first materials which were moved from the docks were not moved by the Chinese or the British, but by a handful of Americans in Pawley's organization. Meanwhile the British appealed to the Chinese to release certain weapons and equipment for which they had desperate need. But their requests were met only partially and after dangerous delays.

By the first week of January the Chinese had turned over to the British 250 out of an estimated minimum of more than 2,000 trucks which they had parked around Rangoon. According to an official admission, the Chinese also supplied the British with 300 Bren guns, of an odd caliber for which they no longer produced ammunition in China. The British obtained from the Chinese about one quarter of the signal equipment they asked for, and their request for copper wire was cut down to almost nothing. (The British in Burma were perilously short of radio and telephone equipment, copper wire, and a great variety of materials which clogged the Rangoon docks, marked for China.) As of early January some 600 jeeps — ideal for Burma's defense — were in running order, but the British got none of these and did not obtain any jeeps until weeks later. Washington had instructed the U. S. military mission to let the British negotiate directly with the Chinese about sharing Lend-Lease material.

The result was a prolonged and costly Chinese-British negotiation, which dragged on while the Japs were bombing Rangoon almost daily. It seemed the Japanese would be pounding at Rangoon's gates before Allied representatives had decided what and how much could be spared for the defense of Burma and its indispensable Burma Road.

One night Captain Harry Stott of the Royal Army Service Corps dined with us at the club and we learned just how close the Japs had come to scoring a knock-out in their first raid on Rangoon. Harry, a big and burly Yorkshireman with a wonderful Yorkshire accent, is one of those rare men for whom wars seem to have been made. He looks, talks, and acts like a charter member of the Three Musketeers. Major Melloy and Harry, in the face of the Nazis' break-through in Belgium and northern France, had blown up gasoline dumps all the way back to Dunkirk. We only had to see a little of the major and Stott to under stand how the Dunkirk miracle happened. Give us fifty Stotts, I thought, and even Rangoon might be saved.

"The Japs could 'ave landed on Mingaladon an' captured it," exploded Harry. "Our chaps only had six rifles an' three Bren guns on the whole bloody field. Not one f— piece of ack-ack. Not one, mind you. The ground crews got into a bloody flap and beat it up Prome Road in their bloody lorries. They left their oil tankers on the field, they did. There was nobody to defend the place. Next day the wing commander gave 'em a dressing down an' one of the lads says: 'What would you 'ave done, sir, against machine guns without even a rifle?' Of all the damned bloody inefficiency — not even rifles for the ground-crew men on the airfield. I went out to see if I could 'elp an' they said they needed petrol. Maybe you lads wouldn't believe it, but I'm tellin' you. I saw it myself. I went to *five* petrol dumps on Mingaladon before I could find *one* drum containin' one yard of 80-octane. Four dumps were clean dry of petrol — an' the bloody Japs 'ad been at war with us for sixteen days. The RAF 'ad no checking system on their petrol supplies. They 'ad no wire fence around the field to guard it. They were ordered last April to build sixteen airfields in Burma an' they still 'ad no more than six ready."

Stott said he managed to get twenty trucks to move a thousand tons of high-octane gasoline from a ship at the docks on December 27. The ship's officers and crew agreed to help unload, without pay, so as to clear it before it could be bombed. He went to get authorization from one of the Burma army colonels. The colonel said: "This is Saturday. We can't interfere with the week-end amenities." Stott couldn't get the proper port passes; the colonel went out for his Saturday afternoon round of golf (Rangoon had already suffered two heavy Jap bombings); and the gasoline couldn't be moved until Monday. Rifles were finally issued to the RAF ground crews the day *after* the Japs first strafed the field mercilessly.

"Just bloody colonial rot," said Harry. "If our lads 'ad only a few Bren guns they could 'ave shot down five or six Japs that first raid. One of these Burma lieutenants, just commissioned from an insurance salesman, comes into our office an' says: 'Is Melloy here?' Did I lay that bloke out. Talking like that to a major who's commanded twelve thousand men at Dunkirk — an' got the bloody lot out, too. I told 'im. I says: 'Look 'ere, if you're lookin' for 'im he's Major Melloy to you, and you call 'im sir. An' if you come into this f— office, you call 'im sir an' you call me sir. An' you salute every time you come into this bloody place.'

"That's what we regular army men get. They pay us Imperial rates — fourteen rupees a week [less than five dollars]. An' they pay these bloody Burma army blokes colonial rates — twice as much — an' most of them don't know what the bloody 'ell they're doing most of the time." We asked Harry where he got his cars for his motor repair staff. "Swiped 'em," said Harry. "I got all my transport by swiping it. The Chinese wouldn't give us any of the lorries they got parked all over town, so I swiped my car from a Chink. He claimed it belonged to the Chinese government. I told 'im: 'No, you're mistaken, my friend. This car damn well belongs to the British Army now.' He didn't make any argument. I guess 'e was right about that."

The first weeks of the Burma war clearly foreshadowed everything that happened afterward; so much so that those of us on the spot knew from the beginning what the inevitable end must be.

With the swelling moon we expected the Japs back early, and

they obliged as usual. The Blenheim boys rushed out on the first green in front of the clubhouse to see the show. As Berry, O. D. (Gallagher), and I joined them, Sidney Lee, the handsome Australian, gave us the tip. "Old Stone is up with a Hurricane tonight. He's bloody good at night fighting — had lots of it in England, you know."

We could hear a couple of Jap bombers off to one side of Mingaladon and we could hear the Hurricane feeling around up above. The tropical sky seemed luminously clear until you tried to locate a darting dark speck in it. Then, even with the moon, it looked hopeless. We were all straining our eyes and the Japs now sounded no more than a mile away, but we still couldn't catch their silhouettes for as much as two seconds. We stood out in the open before the big sombrero-topped kokobin trees, staring and staring. A million stars winked beyond thin wisps of cloud. We could hear the Hurricane buzzing, but it was still invisible. The Japs had faded away again. Stone had lost them — or rather he was still reaching for them, half-blindfolded.

"Wait! There he comes," said Hookey Russell. "It's a twin."

Bomber boys can always spot a bimotored hum. Maybe the first Japs were coming back or maybe these were new ones. But the clouds were getting broader and fuzzier now. Would the Hurri's pilot be able to make a contact? He'd have to have eyes like an owl to do it. We strained our ears to the double hums which were coming straight in and we strained our eyes for that other waspish buzz burrowing around up there. It seemed that one buzz would never catch up with the other. Awfully tough hunting up there, even for a night fighter who is a veteran of the Battle of Britain. Buzz, buzz to the north of us — and buzz-buzz, faster and sharper, but well to the east of us. Then everybody was yelling at once.

"He's on her! . . . Tracers! . . . He's pourin' it in! . . . Bloody fine going! . . . Look — look! "

A long train of red lights shot diagonally up into the dim reaches of the night. Hundreds of crimson dashes chased one another in a straight line up and up. The twin and single buzzes were all mixed up now. Would the flames burst out? Would it happen? Even as we held our breaths the stabbing dashes vanished. They left a darker blur against the fuzzy cloud layers. They left nothing at all. We were all babbling. "He was too far. . . . No, he missed her. . . . Wait a minute. Give the blighter a chance. . . ." Then once more that slender, stabbing chain of red dashes, and we were all yelling like madmen as the chain thrust on and on. This time the tracers slashed diagonally earthward. They were like a synchronized, perfectly segmented flash of lightning. The Hurricane was on top now. The javelins of red dashes thrust down and down. Then a single white light broke suddenly at their tips and we were all shrieking at once.

"He's got her! He's got her!"

But the red javelins and the white light had both gone. The sky was blank. It seemed he had missed the Jap again. We were still staring, blinking with the effort of sight, at that darkened spot in the sky where the machine-gun bursts had been blotted out. Then a great flame rent the darkness. It flashed out and out. Cheers roared from our throats as the spot of flame widened, hovered — and then plunged earthward like a flaming arrow. We danced and pounded one another's shoulders as the slender mass of fire shot down toward the dark tree-line to the north of us. It plunged into the black horizon and almost simultaneously a series of huge and blinding flashes illuminated the flatlands a mile or more away. We were dancing and yelling more wildly than ever now. A night fighter had shot down a Jap bomber for the first time in Burma. Probably this was the first night-fighter victory of the Allies anywhere in the East. Beside me stood one of the Gloucesters, the British troops which guarded the approaches to the airdromes.

"That'll teach 'em," chirped the Gloucester corporal contentedly. "But did you see 'im? When 'e dropped 'is flare, that was 'is bloody undoings."

3

The air battles over Rangoon were the only aspect of the Burma war that gave us anything to cheer over. The mystery of the swift fall of Tavoy was cleared up by an Englishman who managed to escape through the jungles. Tavoy had been taken by less than one hundred Japs, he reported. The Burmese troops had dropped their guns and run. A young lieutenant informed the British colonel of the Burma Rifles battalion that everything was in readiness to blow up the gasoline dumps on the airfield. "No. I can't take the responsibility of ordering you to dynamite the dumps," he quoted the colonel as saying. So the Japs had captured many tons of high-octane gasoline at Tavoy.

Crews of the Blenheim bombers now slept in the rubdown room as well as the veranda of the Rangoon golf club. They were steady and fine and somehow amazingly resigned to indifferent treatment. The club was British and had plenty of beer, yet for some time the club would not sell any beer to these young fliers who risked their lives every night in the defense of Burma. Their food was inexcusably bad, although Rangoon was plentifully supplied with provisions of all sorts. Finally an RAF officer was sent to look into the situation and we heard one of the Blenheim pilots say: "At lunch we had no bread, no butter, and no cheese. We have had no tea or jam." Truckloads of such things could be bought in Rangoon, only twelve miles away. The bomber boys never had eggs for breakfast. One night O. D. bought three dozen eggs and asked the club cook to serve the RAF crews omelets for breakfast. The cook misunderstood and prepared the omelets right away. Although the Blenheim boys had finished their supper only an hour earlier, they finished off the omelets with great gusto. Half the time they were hungry — because of inefficiency and lack of organization, nothing else.

"Oh, we're just the ——," one of them said bitterly.

"Yes," said another. "Nobody gives a —— about us."

Wherever we turned it seemed the tropical rot of colonial Burma hopelessly bogged down the efforts of brave men who were anxious to fight. More than a month after the first Jap bombings of Mingaladon, four out of seven Hurricanes, recklessly left on the airfield instead of being dispersed for the night, were knocked out in a night raid. These Hurricanes were almost invaluable, the first we had in Burma. Not to disperse them amounted to criminal negligence — as had also been true of American planes in Hawaii and the Philippines — but the lesson once more had to be learned the hard way. Sometimes it seemed there was a deadly resignation among the British soldiers and fliers; that they had come to expect inefficiency and bungling at the top.

There was an enormous difference between the young soldiers

and airmen who had recently come from England or Egypt and most of the British who had lived a long time in Burma. The newly-arrived Britishers had not acquired any of the slothfulness of the colonial East, nor were they nearly so intolerant toward the natives.

Little by little we became acquainted with the Burmese. Many of them were attractive characters, while many more appeared truly difficult. The little head waiter at the club was called Maung Meng. He had been brought up in a Baptist school and would quote Biblical phrases in a pious voice which his mischievous eyes completely belied. One of the waiters had the face of a natural-born pirate, and with his yellow skirt and saucy red turban he looked the part. His name, appropriately enough, meant Red Rat. But the Burmese boys were all willing workers. They were shrewd, clever fellows who loved to laugh and always responded to friendly treatment. We soon learned they had names for all of us. Because of his unquenchable gaiety Berrigan was called Lubyo (pronounced Loo-bee-oh), meaning The Young One. Because of my white hair (I hope it was nothing more) they referred to me as Ahphogyi (Ah-foe-gee) — The Old One. Gallagher was known as Myey Khwé (Mee-ay Gway), otherwise The Fox. That seemed to be as pat as anyone could make it.

Under the stress and dislocation caused by Rangoon bombings it was difficult to become acquainted with many Burmese. But the few upper-class Burmese we met were charming and cultured people. If they permitted themselves to talk frankly they revealed a strong anti-British sentiment, which had grown with the long years of British rule. Somehow the average Burmese gave one the impression of being tricky and often unreliable, and I must confess, the more I saw of the run-of-the-mill Burmese, the less attractive I found them. Foreigners who had lived long in Burma had little that was good to say about them — probably without complete justification. Nevertheless, it was a fact that thievery and murder had been extraordinarily prevalent in Burma for many decades. The murder rate in Burma was said to be the highest of any country in the world. I saw figures for one rather small district near Rangoon. January over a period of five years had averaged something like 360 murders committed in this one district. Poverty explained that to some extent, but the Burmese were generally credited with being excessively quick with a knife. We were warned never to show any money wherever we went because you could be killed as quickly for a five-dollar bill as for a purse containing five hundred. Along with all this, most Burmese politicians were described as expert grafters who waxed fat on their machinations. Most foreigners would not admit the Burmese could ever govern themselves. Yet few foreigners could pretend they had ever made a genuine effort to make friends of the Burmese.

As a consequence of these various factors all Burma was a hotbed of actual or potential Japanese agents. It was hardly fair to call these scores of thousands of Burmese "fifth-columnists" simply because they were so fiercely anti-British. Obviously a great proportion of these people regarded the British as exploiters of their country and therefore believed that patriotism compelled them to assist any outside force that promised to bring an end to British domination. Did the British governing authorities offer any new inducements to create loyalty and a desire to cooperate among the Burmese? His Excellency the Governor was silent. So were the other British authorities. Instead of an offer of a greater degree of home rule for the Burmese after the war, the British Burma government merely adopted the official attitude that the great majority of Burmese were loyal (which everyone knew was not the case), and that the continuous incidents of Burmese sabotage must be hush-hushed.

After the first bombing of Rangoon the charred remains of oil trucks were found in streets where not a single bomb had fallen. In the confusion of the raid they had been fired by saboteurs. One night O. D. drove home very late from the Silver Grill. The main Prome Road passes directly along the lower side of Mingaladon field and Gallagher noticed a car, parked without headlights, only a hundred yards from some of the airport buildings. O. D. drove straight at the car. A Burmese, with a white scared face, threw the car into gear and raced down the road. It looked as though there were gasoline tins in the back of the car. A bonfire on the field had been prevented by mere chance. But the natives kept other bonfires burning night after night, all the way across country, to guide the Jap bombers coming in. During one of these raids signals from a flashlight were spotted by a Gloucester sentinel. They were being flashed from an upper window of the Burma Rifles' administration building, a few hundred yards above the field. The Gloucester fired, but the Jap agent got away. Incidents of this kind happened continually. Usually the civil censors cut out all mention of them from our dispatches. Apparently the civil censors had orders from the local British government; one must not risk offending the Burmese (as if many of them would have been offended). The Japanese must not be given the impression that their fifth-column allies were giving considerable trouble (as if the Japs, who paid them, did not know perfectly well everything their agents were doing so successfully in Burma). So the official British policy resolved itself into make-believe just as the September publicity about "hundreds of Brewster Buffaloes in the skies over Burma" had been make-believe. It didn't fool the Japs and it certainly didn't fool the Burmese. It merely helped to mislead the home publics in Britain and the United States. And while the Governor and other British authorities in Rangoon were maintaining that the members of the Burma government were reliable and pro-Ally, the premier of Burma's local government, U Saw, was arrested abroad for connivance with the Japs. Thus the British policy toward the Burmese was utterly unrealistic. It did not offer the Burmese the slightest hope for greater independence in the future, nor did it dare to take a strong hand toward those who were enemies of the British and active at sabotaging for the Japs.

The Gloucester enlisted men, guarding the cut-across highway from Mingaladon to the club, always greeted us with humorous gestures and jokes. And they always queried: "What's the news?" They were the last to get any news, but they knew full well that most of it was bound to be bad. They didn't grumble. They lived in tents in the dust-covered, insect-infested bushes. They knew the Japs might land parachutists behind them any night, and they knew they'd be the last to get orders to leave when the evacuation came. They did their jobs humbly and earnestly. They were good soldiers, these homesick sons of Britain. We found them better men than most of their officers deserved; certainly much better than they ever had a chance of demonstrating to the outside world that they were.

4

On January 31, 1942 we learned that British forces had withdrawn across the Johore causeway and the siege of Singapore had begun. On that day, too, the capture of Moulmein by the Japanese was announced. So now the Japs were at the mouth of the Salween River, and only about one hundred miles straight east from Rangoon. The battle for the Burma Road was on in earnest. Two days after the fall of Moulmein the British high command appealed to Generalissimo Chiang Kai-shek to send Chinese troops to help defend Burma. At this crucial juncture what were the relations between the Allies in the Burma theater? In most respects they still served as a striking example of how not to co-operate.

The Rangoon docks were still clogged with scores of thousands of tons of Lend-Lease materials. At the lower end of the city hundreds of General Motors trucks still lay in huge crates near the Monkey Point assembling plant, despite the remarkable efforts of Dave Ladin, Wally Thorensen, and the other GM engineers. After losing more than half of their workmen in the general panic flight from the bombings, these men had somehow fought back until they were assembling from sixty to eighty trucks a day — a truly extraordinary achievement under existing conditions. Did they get the wholehearted support of General Yu Fei-peng, chief administrator of the Burma Road, and of other Chinese government officials? If this is to be an honest report I can only quote an American officer who shared a seemingly hopeless task with the American civilian engineers.

"I'm afraid the Chinese officials here have no use for me," he confessed. "Perhaps I should be more diplomatic. But I tell you frankly some of the Chinese authorities I've met here are just about the rottenest people I've ever known. Every time General Yu visits the assembly plant he upsets everything for several days. He talks with our Chinese laborers in Chinese. One day, just when we were taking over the handling of trucks from the Southwest Transportation Company, General Yu told them: 'You ought to be paid higher wages here.' Then he came two days after the Christmas raid and in a loud voice declared: 'In my opinion the chief executive should be here whenever there's a raid.' Well,

Dave Ladin is here practically all the time. The reason he wasn't here at noon on Christmas was that he went to the Strand to keep a luncheon date with R. C. Chen — and Chen didn't show up. You'd think it would be to General Yu's interest to urge our Chinese workers to keep plugging. After all, this stuff is for China. A hell of a lot of thanks we get trying to get it clear for them."

The British had had a difficult time persuading the Chinese to release materials that they urgently needed for the defense of Burma. But the British high command had also committed the capital error of refusing the aid of Chinese troops at the outset. When General Wavell and Major General Brett went to Chungking at the end of December, the Generalissimo had offered to send his Chinese Fifth or Sixth army into Burma. We were informed, and it was confirmed to me later on unimpeachable authority, that General Wavell told Chiang Kai-shek he did not need Chinese troops, as sufficient British Empire reinforcements would soon be on the way. One could only deduce that this rejection was prompted by political considerations: if the Chinese helped to save Burma, how could the British be sure they would be willing to leave after the war? So one whole month had been lost — the month which might possibly have saved Rangoon, providing Chinese troops had come down from Yunnan early in January.

At a press conference on February 7 General Hutton, the recently appointed British commander-in-chief in Burma, told us the Chinese were going to assume entire responsibility "for certain sectors of the front." He said they were assured of a warm welcome from their British, Indian, "and Burmese" comrades. (Most of the Burmese actually felt anything but comradely toward the Chinese, for in all business affairs the Chinese offer the toughest kind of competition throughout the Orient and there were already far too many Chinese in Burma to suit the natives.)

"Have we accepted all the aid offered by the Generalissimo?" someone asked.

General Hutton paused very noticeably and finally said: "I would prefer not to answer, but I believe so." The pause made one wonder. At any rate the general, a tall and very thin man who had looked extremely tired when he assumed command in Burma, appeared somewhat encouraged that day. He explained that Moulmein had not been a place in which to lock up a large number of troops. There was now a prospect of a much stronger line along the Salween. "We are in a far stronger position to cry halt to the Japs than we were a few weeks ago. Having seen the Japs cleverly landing small parties of troops down the Malayan coast, we must be prepared for similar attempts here. But we should profit by our experience elsewhere."

In the next three weeks we saw the Japs continue their infiltration tactics with unchecked success as they pushed steadily through the jungles toward the Sittang and Pegu, the last defense point of outflanked Rangoon. Shortly after our press conference with General Hutton, Sir Reginald Dorman-Smith, the Governor, made a public declaration to the effect that Burma would never fall and that Rangoon would be another Moscow or Tobruk. This, on February 9, was the first public appeal that the Governor had made since war came to Burma with the first Jap raid on December 23. We were told His Excellency only spoke now upon the insistence of the British military command. But to the great majority of people in Burma anything the Governor might say now sounded only like whistling in the dark. Which, of course was exactly what it was.

Even two days before General Hutton made his statement to us about being "in a far stronger position" something extremely disturbing happened. Press Relations at GHQ admitted that "a few Jap patrols have crossed the Salween." If the Japs could get parties across the Salween so quickly, where could the British hope to stop them? The Salween was the broadest river in Burma. The vital section of its western bank extended from Martaban, opposite Moulmein, northward some fifty or sixty miles. The British Empire troops in Burma were a typically mixed assortment. There were two or three British battalions made up of Gloucesters, Cameronians, Koylies (King's Own Yorkshire Light Infantry), and others; there were some excellent Indian troops, including Gurkhas, Pathans, and Sikhs; and a few battalions of Burma Rifles, who were native troops and undependable for any hot spot. All together General Hutton possessed the First Burma and the 17th divisions, indifferently armed and poorly equipped troops — whereas they could have been immeasurably strengthened in the previous month by at least three or four Chinese divisions if General Wavell (or the London government) had not ruled against it. Even so, the Japs were still tied up before Singapore and there was no indication that they were yet using more than one division, or two at the very most, in their invasion of Lower Burma. With the two-mile width of the Salween as a shield, it had seemed that a well-planned disposition of British Imperial troops should make it possible to hold that sixty miles or more of the river line. But by February 11 the Japanese had struck straight across the mouth of the Salween and had taken Martaban, which should have been a well-fortified position.

Between Martaban and Rangoon the Gulf of Martaban drives a deep triangular wedge into the southern Burma coast. This meant that the Japs must first thrust straight north along the railroad from Martaban, then break across the Sittang River above the head of the gulf and converge on Pegu. From Pegu the main Mandalay highway ran across open rice-fields and flat wooded country — an easy fifty-four mile roll, southward again, into Rangoon. Once Pegu was lost, there was only one other more westerly escape road running out of Rangoon: the highway to Prome, which could be cut in a few hours once the enemy crossed the Sittang. So Pegu was absolutely the last defense point for Rangoon, and already the Japs were within seventy-five miles of it. In other words, the battle for all of southern Burma — meaning also the battle for the Burma Road — would be decided between Martaban and the Sittang Bridge opposite Pegu. In this narrow, elongated sector — where, between troops of approximately equal strength, the advantages would seem to be definitely with the defense — it was decided, and in the incredibly short time of twelve or fourteen days.

When Martaban fell we dashed north to Pegu in our jeep, the Flying 69, and talked with wounded men just brought back from the front. We knew these men would probably give us a more accurate picture of what was happening than higher officers were likely to do. We had, in fact, become highly skeptical of the official line of optimism. One Burma Rifles officer, a Rangoon businessman without military experience until a few weeks previously, told us how his armored car had been ambushed and most of his companions killed. That occurred on the main road several miles behind the front. "The Japs keep cutting around behind us. You can't see them in the jungles. They always move at night.' Where were the British troops posted? Apparently most of them kept close to the one and only main road. Chinese officers whose troops took over in the Shan mountain sector farther north later told me the same thing. "We don't understand why the British don't put outposts on the bypaths and trails." Here on the southern front Japanese officers were leading forward their men by night and resting them by day. What were the British doing? At this crucial moment Eve Curie, en route to China for the *New York Herald Tribune,* reached Rangoon and showed a characteristic amount of intelligence and initiative. Somehow Mlle Curie dynamited official Rangoon into swift action — something which definitely seemed to prove that an attractive and clear-headed Frenchwoman was far more effective than Jap bombs. Mlle Curie was off the very next morning to visit General Smythe's advanced headquarters near Bilin, on the other side of the Gulf of Martaban. As she relates in her book *Journey among Warriors,* she found the British general's staff officers observing their accustomed hour for tea — and actually changing to full dress for dinner. So the battle for Rangoon and the Burma Road was being fought by the British commanders according to the orthodox and Kiplingesque ritual of an old-fashioned campaign in northern India. The aggressive, cunning, highly organized, and perfectly equipped Japanese veterans were being countered with tactics and habits that had proved sufficient for decades against the poorly armed, untrained tribes of the northwest frontier.

Upon our return from Pegu a wide-awake British friend gave us a confidential warning. "The situation is bad. You'd better be prepared for the worst." That night we also learned the RAF had only two Blenheim bombers left at Mingaladon in condition to fly. And the next morning's Rangoon *Gazette* carried one of the delightfully misleading effusions of Major Cook, the director of the Burma news service. The major, as son-in-law of the Governor, Sir Reginald Dorman-Smith, had risen from the rank of lieutenant to that of major in about six months. And as director of the Burma news service, designed for information and propaganda by radio and press inside Burma, he had confessed to correspondents that he didn't exactly know what to do. At any rate Major Cook's home-consumption release that morning contained this statement: "The widespread offensive activity of RAF bombers reported in Wednesday night's communiqué is a significant feature of recent operations which, as these increase, will render Japanese communications more and more precarious." As civilians in Burma were reading this, exactly two RAF bombers remained in condition to undertake a mission from Mingaladon field. If there was no good news, as certainly there was none these days, you invented it.

The next day, February 14, six Blenheims arrived from India as if in answer to prayer. Unless we had bomber protection the Japs — if they knew it, and probably they would — could land barges of troops unmolested at the mouth of the Irrawaddy just below Rangoon. By night, for that matter, the Japs undoubtedly could do that almost any time they wished. But even six new bombers were a help. Thanks to them, we learned that same night that our troops had lost Thaton, only twenty-five miles south of General Smythe's GHQ at Bilin. It was announced that the RAF had bombed Thaton — so the Japs must have it. But there had been no mention of this latest withdrawal in the army communiqué. For one thing this meant the Japanese were now advancing just as rapidly toward the last-ditch Sittang River line as they had previously advanced across the mountains to Moulmein. For another thing it meant that British Empire troops were withdrawing as steadily as ever. For a third thing this indicated clearly that the Japs' infiltration tactics, which General Hutton had hoped would be mastered as a result of British experience on the Malayan peninsula, were still working as efficiently and devastatingly as ever.

The night that we knew Thaton was gone and also knew that Rangoon's days were numbered I happened to be thumbing through an old copy of the *American Magazine* in our cabin at the club. I stumbled upon an article written by Lieutenant Colonel Howard Neville Stent of the U. S. Marine Corps. In the article, which was in the issue of May 1941 (seven months before Pearl Harbor), I read these cheering words:

"No foreign observer in Asia believes Japan could win a war with any major power without outside help. . . . The reason is principally psychological. It is not because the Japanese are atrocious marksmen, nor because Japan's military forces are indifferently organized, nor because the Jap soldier lacks intelligent fighting spirit, although all this is true. It is rather the fact that the Japanese have demonstrated themselves to be incapable of ingenuity or initiative. They are copyists, rather than creators, and thus are doomed always to be a step behind the progressive nations."

So these "atrocious marksmen, indifferently organized, lacking intelligent fighting spirit, and incapable of ingenuity or initiative " had now pushed MacArthur's little Filipino-American army back on Bataan and by some inexplicable circumstance were besieging the island of Singapore — and were far on the way toward seizing Rangoon and cutting the Burma Road.

It seemed only fair that some American specialists had been just as wrong as the British. After all, a great many United States senators and congressmen had voted against the fortification of Wake and Guam islands. Were the bungling defense tactics of British officers on the southern Burma front much different from the bungling of American navy and army commanders at Honolulu? I had reported the errors of the Norwegians when Oslo fell. Since then Pearl Harbor had in many respects exceeded the shortcomings in Oslo. We were all — British and Americans, Norwegians and French, Chinese and Poles and numerous others — in the same terrible, unescapable mess. Could I contend that we Americans had been more far-sighted, or militarily more efficient at the outset, or more prudent than our Allies? On the record, much as I might wish the contrary, I couldn't. So, in the midst of a ghastly muddle where British disintegration and lack of leadership were rapidly losing a great and vital battleground of the world conflict, perhaps it was well to try to remember this humbling fact.

5

On Sunday, February 15, we learned that the "fortress" of Singapore had fallen. That night about thirty RAF bombers flew in from the Near East in time for their pilots to get the news. If this was bitter medicine for civilians and such privileged persons as war correspondents, it was infinitely darker hemlock for boys who had seen the tides of battle turn against them again and again in Libya for over two years. They talked that night as they always do, as Bish's bomber crews and the pilots of the RAF's great and gallant 80 squadron had talked in Greece—from their hearts, looking at facts as they daily looked at death, straight in the face. If sometimes they were bitter, what fighting airmen anywhere around the globe had carried the unequal load so long, or had a better right to be? They were with us today, and some of them tomorrow were gone forever. It is a humbling thing to live with young men like these.

I remember one tousle-haired youngster from Essex, England. "It's just that we're always being let down from above," he said with unusual intensity for a Britisher. "It's lack of organization far more than lack of strength. We didn't have to withdraw from Bengazi. It was a retreat. We didn't fight. Our troops set fire to 130,000 gallons of high-octane petrol at Derna. Don't tell me that was a prepared withdrawal. And it wasn't for lack of planes either."

"What we need is younger generals," said the Australian who looked like a Greek god. "We've got too many old generals. They can't adjust themselves. They're too orthodox and old-fashioned for this war. But nobody will put them on the shelf. So we pay and pay."

What the RAF boys said that night was what we all knew. When I summarized it in my notebook it didn't take much space to cover a great deal of ground so far as the Burma picture was concerned: "A deep-ingrained British tolerance of mediocrity . . . lack of leaders our biggest danger . . . the Nazis and the Japs have no 'political' generals. . . . British carelessness and slowness . . . lack of punch and audacity . . . inefficiency . . . creeping paralysis . . . everything that the Japs are not."

In Rangoon these things were realized quite as clearly by the RAF pilots and crews and the ordinary Tommies in the Glouces-ters and by a few of the younger British Burma residents as by correspondents or other observers. They were also admitted in-wardly, if seldom outwardly, by a good many British officials. Among British, Americans, and Chinese as well as among Burmese the general assumption ruled that of course Rangoon would not be held. Not necessarily that it could not be held, but that it *would* not be held. By early February it was commonplace, upon meeting civilians or soldiers, to be hailed with the query: "When are you getting out? When do we leave?" Defeatism was rampant and the transparently pollyanna tenor of army and civil government communiqués merely fed this resignation to impending collapse.

Was this defeatism completely justified? In regard to the chaotic situation in Rangoon, the strangling red tape of the Indian Civil Service and the persistent failure of the Governor to act decisively about anything — in these respects it was more than justified. Militarily, however, there had seemed some reason for hope until the latter part of January. British Empire forces might be small, but they were not yet outnumbered. Admittedly they had dangerously few tommyguns, but reinforcements from India had brought field guns and some howitzers. It appeared there should be a fair chance of holding the comparatively short line along the broad lower Salween. Then, with two Chinese armies on the way in early February, it seemed at the very least that the Japanese should be held there for a considerable time. One Allied officer expressed his opinion in this way: "If they have the will to hold on the Salween, they should be able to do so until the Chinese take over their sectors in Burma. Once the Chinese are in position, we should then have a good chance." But the Salween line had crumbled so fast it was apparent there had been no real line — and no real will. Something was radically wrong militarily. It went far beyond relative strength in tommyguns. It concerned even more the method of combat and the will to yield no terrain without exacting a severe price from the enemy. This was shown by one small but most revealing incident. Two days after the British withdrew from Thaton a British train chugged into Bilin and then on down to Thaton because somebody forgot to tell the station-master that Thaton had been evacuated. General Smythe's GHQ expected the train to come back loaded with Japs and had the railroad line mined for protection. But a few hours later the train chugged back again, crammed with refugees instead of Hirohito's soldiers. The Japs had not yet occupied Thaton on the second day *after* the British withdrew.

On the basis of such a remarkable development as this it was difficult for correspondents to find fault with Rangoon's widespread defeatism. The Jap invaders had been on their way from the Thailand border for more than three weeks now — they were at last striking straight for Pegu — and as yet we could gather no evidence to indicate that a real battle had been fought in defense of southern Burma. The Japs sneaked through the jungles and around the flanks. They ambushed a few troops here or there. They fired great salvos and made a terrific hubbub at night, and sometimes used their mortars with terrifying effect. Another British withdrawal followed. Was there any indication of a real will to fight? If so I never encountered it anywhere outside of Major Cook's "news" commentaries. On February 17 I wrote in my journal: "There's no 'Stand here and die here,' like the Finns and the Greeks. No will to fight to the last ditch. It's impossible to expect anything better than withdrawal and another evacuation, or surrender."

The next day British banks closed down in Rangoon, preparatory to transferring their quarters to Mandalay, 430 miles to the north. At Mingaladon we stopped just in time to drop into the middle of a council of war of AVG pilots. They were lounging on the steps and porch of their operations hut. Squadron Leader Bob Neale, tall and angular and as Far-Westernly solid as a State of Washington spruce, was talking straight from the shoulder when we came up. "You fellows all know we're in a tough spot," Bob was saying. "Every man has got to accept full responsibility. It's not enough just to fly a plane. I've got to depend on you. If you don't come through — well, it will have to come out in the wash, that's all. Everything we've got must be evacuated or destroyed. Bartling will carry the squadron's papers. The ground crews will go by road to Prome. The plan to evacuate our air forces from here counts on twelve hours' notice. But you guys know as well as I do that we'll probably never get anything like that."

"We should be able to evacuate on three hours' notice," Charlie Bond of Dallas, Texas, said.

"When the RAF can't give us air-raid warnings," Bob said, "I won't keep the men here. Whenever the air warnings stop we get going. We'll fight as long as we have a chance to fight. But every man has got to do his full job. It's up to you."

So everything pointed to the early end of Rangoon at the very moment that Major Cook's bulletin advised the city's populace: "Well-informed quarters are not inclined to admit any question of an immediate, or even distant, threat to Rangoon at present. . . . Our forces are in very good heart and are only anxious in so far as they are counting the days until the time comes for an advance." We were all counting the days, but not quite that way. Gallagher knew from experience during the fall of France and I from experience in Norway that a newspaperman should never count upon anyone but himself in time of a military disaster. Fortunately for the other correspondents, anyone could get a jeep now because the Chinese couldn't begin to find drivers for the hundreds of jeeps that were parked about. As a result Darrel Berrigan, Dan DeLuce, and the others all had their own jeeps now. The one trouble with the jeeps was that their tanks held only ten gallons of gasoline. That meant you had to carry all the gas you could load in back for a long trip, and that left almost no room for personal belonging and kits. O. D. and I thought the evacuation might not come for another week or ten days, so it might be wise to take our bags and bedding rolls up north somewhere; find a place to live wherever army GHQ would be, and then come back traveling light to cover the evacuation. The government had still not made any orderly plans for evacuation, because the government still would not admit that such a thing as evacuation might be unavoidable. Therefore we all knew that the exodus from Rangoon would be a flight, with hundreds of trucks and cars dashing madly up the roads to Mandalay or Prome and with wild Burmese and Chinese drivers smashing into vehicles right and left. In such conditions you would have to ride with thirty or forty gallons of inflammable gas behind your back.

On the misty, murky morning of February 19 O. D. and I set out over the Prome Road. In the big, crowded, and tawdry city of Prome during nearly one hundred years British rule had not gone so far as to construct one modern hotel. So we rode on until we reached Yenangyaung and its rich oilfields, where the Burma

Oil Company had built a splendid clubhouse and swimming-pool for its British employees. A most hospitable Scot from Loch Lomond, MacGowen by name, put us up in his home for the night. In the railroad-station restaurant at Prome a burly English businessman, who was not very different from many American go-getters I have encountered in South America and the Orient, gave us some tips about the art of survival in Burma.

"It's bloody dangerous to travel at night in this country," he warned. "Murder is as common in Burma as drunkenness in Glasgow on a Saturday night. Don't you chaps ever show any money. You're askin' for a knife in your back if you do. And if anybody ever gets messin' around you — don't talk! Hit first! I never carry a gun. I always carry a chopper — a bloody axe, you know. Even in a railroad compartment at night you're not safe. The Burmese will open the window and pull out your bag or your clothes while the train's stopped. When a thief puts 'is 'and on my windowsill, I chop 'im. That's the only thing to do. If you chaps are going to ride across country in that open jeep, you'd better get yourselves a chopper — an' maybe a couple of guns."

Gallagher, who was much more practical-minded about carrying firearms than I was, had been trying for weeks to get a carbine or revolver in Rangoon. There were thousands of weapons in Lend-Lease cases on the docks, but they were still there, waiting for the Japs. O. D. hadn't been able to find even a small revolver. There were many nights later on when we both had cause to regret our scruples. We should have raided the docks and equipped ourselves with a small arsenal. But until the end of the Burma nightmare the only weapon we had was a piece of lead pipe which lay at our feet in the jeep.

After the monotonous paddy-fields of the south the trip from Yenangyaung to Mandalay over green and hilly country was a great relief to the eyes, despite dust and heat. The only European-style restaurant that we could find in Mandalay, under British occupation since 1854, was located in the railroad station. But there was not a soul in the station because Mandalay had had its first bombing the day before. Mandalay was the kind of place that made you wish Rudyard Kipling had had to eat his poem for breakfast every day of his life. Just a sprawling monstrosity of shacks and shanties and miserable sheds of bamboo or other wood, built upon four-foot or six-foot stilts; and a very few European structures near the center. The only attractive buildings in Mandalay were inside the fort on the island, and the British Upper Burma Club, someone had told us, was one of these. The dull brick walls of the old fort, topped with Burmese pagoda-like towers of red and gilt, came as a startling contrast, like finding a jewel-encrusted case in a garbage heap. Standing serenely above the moat which surrounds it, this old palace of the Burmese kings — or rather its shell — suddenly spoke with a voice of delicacy, beauty, and peace. But that illusion, too, was swiftly shattered. The British Upper Burma Club was only a mass of black cinders and smoking ruins. It had had a direct hit and several persons had been killed there the day before. It was just as well we hadn't left Rangoon a day earlier.

"We'd better go up to Maymyo," I said. "There's no place in Mandalay that the British can set up headquarters. Maymyo's the hill town — the summer residence of the Governor. They've got a swell club there, too. If we can get a room in the club before the mob piles in from Rangoon we'll be all set."

So we drove up the twisting, climbing forty-two miles; up out of the dry, dust-laden caldron of the Irrawaddy Valley and into the wonderfully cool and green and unbelievably European little town of Maymyo. It was the last haven and refuge for Europeans in the whole of Burma. Like everything else in this land where empire was falling to pieces, its days were numbered.

6

At Maymyo we learned the evacuation of Rangoon had been ordered that very morning. Before our Flying 69 had bounced into Mandalay the unorganized and uncontrolled exodus was on. All civilians had been ordered to leave. The seat of government was being transferred to Maymyo. The evacuation order had come without warning and urgently. Something must have gone radically wrong at the Sittang front. Thousands of trucks and vehicles of every description were pushing, dodging, racing up the Prome and Mandalay roads. By sheer accident we had missed that wild four-wheeled flood, and the next day the refugees began pouring in with their stories of Rangoon's last hours.

Colonel Miller, the Governor's aide-de-camp, was among the first to arrive — perhaps because the government had made no preparations for the housing of hundreds of British civil servants and civilians who were now fleeing northward; but almost certainly not for that reason. Matters had simply been allowed to disintegrate completely. It was every dog for himself.

Colonel Miller told everybody emphatically that His Excellency the Governor would remain in Rangoon until the last. It seemed that Sir Reginald Dorman-Smith hoped to compensate for his manifold sins of omission and inaction by setting an example of personal courage. So he remained behind with the British military and the picked demolition squads which must destroy the great oil refineries at Syriam across from Monkey Point. By so doing the Governor at least escaped some of the bitterest criticism that long-suffering Britishers are ever likely to heap upon a titled member of their most immaculate upper class. Yet that great empty shell of glittering Victorian imperialism the Governor's mansion in Rangoon must have been a comfortless and ghostly mausoleum in which to stay. In those ornate but deserted halls moved phantoms of blindness, smugness, and snobbishness, but also of British doggedness and British courage. Somehow it was utterly fitting that Sir Reginald retained those latter qualities.

New arrivals brought fantastic details of Rangoon's last days. British police were so few that they were helpless; and the ARP, which might have been invaluable for maintaining order, had dissolved because the government would not pay its loyal Indians a living wage. Burmese thieves and hoodlums and pro-Japanese saboteurs roamed the city day and night. All the large English department stores and luxury shops — Rowe's, Watson's, Barnett's, Orr & Sons — were sacked by roving bands. Burmese smashed in the doors of the large villas, which were the homes of well-to-do or wealthy British colonials, and plundered them of everything that caught their fancy. The evacuation order had come so suddenly, and with such lack of preparation, the owners had been compelled to leave virtually all their possessions behind. These included sets of family silverware, fine radio sets, priceless collections of Oriental jades and embroideries — a fabulous haul for natives whose fingers had itched all their lives.

Some British families left an extra automobile sitting in their garages. Some hurried away without bothering to lock their doors. What was the use? They knew what would happen.

Fires were set by fifth-columnists in all parts of the city. The big Scott Market, with its scores of shops crammed with all kinds of supplies, food and clothing, was burned to the ground. In a city of a normal half-million population there remained not a single restaurant open, nor a single European bar or coffee shop. Day and night the burning and the plundering continued unchecked. British officers and the few American or Chinese Lend-Lease officials who remained did not dare to walk the streets alone. All of them carried carbines or revolvers and kept them ready to use. Burmese looters fled at the sight of jeeps or military cars, but they ruled the side streets, and their feverish plundering and destruction could not be checked. This was a moment of supreme revenge such as they had never dreamed would come to them. So they ransacked Rangoon, piling the mockery of brigandage upon the humiliation of governmental collapse and military defeat. The hopelessly outnumbered police shot looters wherever they found them. For days bodies lay on the streets where they fell. But machine guns were too few and too scattered. The looting went wildly on.

While chaos and plunder were at their height in Rangoon, an amazing thing happened. On the outskirts of the city there was a jail, crowded with several hundreds of Burma's most hardened criminals — mostly murderers. There was also an insane asylum and a detention camp filled with lepers. An Englishman, who had been steeped all his life in the red tape of the Indian Civil Service, was in charge of these institutions. He didn't see how he could arrange to feed the occupants. All civilians had been ordered to leave. The panicky flight was on. But how could you leave people locked up, probably to starve? Apparently the English director didn't think of appointing a Burmese assistant to take over; or perhaps he didn't trust anyone. So he ordered the cells of the jail and the doors of the asylums unlocked. Out rushed more than seven hundred murderers, lunatics, and lepers, mad with joy at their incredible freedom. From that moment Rangoon was a nightmare surpassing anything the war has unleashed from Barcelona or Warsaw to Hong Kong. Between its burning buildings and down smoke-filled streets, regardless of the occasional crack of policemen's rifles, murderers joined forces with the looters. Lunatics ran leaping and laughing incoherently. Lepers wandered about aimlessly. The ICS official whose curious action released this additional terror finally found a revolver and committed suicide.

"We went down to the docks to get some guns," Bob King, an AVG ground-crew man, told me. "You should have seen those docks. Cases and cases of guns and munitions torn open. The British officers were handing out revolvers and brand-new Enfield rifles to any European or American who wanted them. But the stuff was all over the place. They couldn't begin to guard all that stuff at night. Burmese looters stole plenty of guns. There's shooting all over the city and bodies in the street everywhere. Nobody can control it. Believe me, Rangoon's a place to get out of fast. Why, there's millions and millions of dollars' worth of guns and everything else just lying there for anybody who wants it.

"We went on the docks looking for batteries. We found a Britisher and asked: 'Who's in charge here?' 'That's what I'd like to know,' he says. 'Come on in and help yourself.' . . . Well, that was it, believe me. Hundreds of natives scrambling and pawing over everything. They'd smash open huge cases of medical supplies — there was a fortune in medical stuff for China. The natives would pick up a bottle of this, look at it, then smash it and turn another case upside down. It made you sick to your stomach to watch the way all those medical supplies were being destroyed — and people dying for lack of medicine in China. Do you know the British or Chinese — I don't know which — didn't even start to try to move any of that stuff until three days ago. There's thousands of tons of it left. Now the looters have ruined most of it. And you should see the lunatics. Out Prome Road there were dozens of nuts dancing on the road. Some even sitting in the middle of the road and waving their hands at you. I never saw such a hell of a mess in my life."

This was the end of empire in Rangoon. It did not end in a manner to suggest that empire had quite succeeded there or had by any means justified itself. Would empire return there after the war? If so, one could only conclude that it could only presume to return with a much broader vision and with younger men, equipped with far greater capacity for hard work and organization — and also equipped with a far greater degree of democratic instincts and of understanding. Providing, of course, that imperialists are capable of that kind of psychological and spiritual progress. At any rate, who could deny there had been a certain grim and appropriate consistency about the last days of Rangoon? Through all of these events ran the cruelly cold and impervious steel cord of inevitability, as in a drama which could not possibly finish any other way.

The Burma Road, too, had remained unreformed and unregenerate to the last. Very close to 70,000 tons of American Lend-Lease materials — some of it destroyed, some of it stolen, and some of it untouched — remained behind in Rangoon. Approximately 1,100 GM trucks and jeeps were splashed with gasoline and burned. A great many of these had been assembled, regardless of all obstacles, under the dynamic persistence of Dave Leiden and his American engineers. But for months there had not been enough drivers, and for months the Allied authorities had failed to find any means of obtaining more drivers. So the trucks and jeeps went up in smoke. Most of a superimposed European existence and most that was important to pursuance of the war also went up in smoke in Rangoon. So did one kind of British Empire, whether or not Winston Churchill is yet ready to recognize that fact.

Chapter VII

THE ROAD FROM MANDALAY

Maymyo is the one and only town I found in the Orient which might have been transplanted bodily from somewhere in England or America. This was because it was built by the British for the British as a refuge from the summer heat and humidity of Rangoon. Maymyo nestles on a high upland plateau of the Shan Mountains, perhaps 2,000 feet above Mandalay. Its streets are of glistening macadam and most of them are lined with great elms. Shade trees and broad lawns surround the comfortable frame houses and bungalows. Everything is green and spacious and lazily restful, like a slumbersome village in Kent or Connecticut. Some of the main-street shops and the small Burmese and Indian sections provide the only touch of the Far East. As for the Maymyo club, its big rambling bungalow-style building faces hundreds of acres of rolling countryside dotted with clumps of huge oaks and elms. From an easy chair on the club veranda I could easily imagine I had dropped in at a country estate on Long Island.

That illusion was swiftly destroyed, those first days in Maymyo, whenever I entered the big club lounge or the bar. The British men and women who congregated there, including many young officers of the Burma Army, were quite naturally obsessed by the fiasco of Rangoon. For the first time in my life I met Englishmen who were in a mood for revolt. Mrs. S., whose husband was an officer, exploded:

"Our men are all right but we have no leaders. Most of those who are supposed to lead are terrible, simply terrible. I don't understand the things they do. A friend of ours has been in officers' training camp less than three months. Now he's sent here to be an instructor of other candidates for officers — and he's never had any experience as an officer himself. What's the matter with us out here? Really, sometimes I could go Bolshevist."

"And what has the Governor done?" demanded Mrs. M., the lustiest and prettiest young matron in the place. "He never conscripted labor. He didn't even start a women's auxiliary until Rangoon was falling. His Excellency — my bottom!"

"Well, what has he ever done?" said Mrs. M.'s Irish husband. "He was given a place in the Chamberlain Cabinet because he was a Tory and had a title. You remember that story about Dorman-Smith when he was Minister of Agriculture? Well, personally I believe it really happened. It could have, anyway. He went out to a meeting where the farmers were in a terrible huff about something. They spoke right out and he couldn't shut them up. So finally His Ex remonstrates a bit. 'After all,' he says, 'if you turn a bull loose in a pasture with fifty cows you don't expect fifty calves the next morning, do you?' And one farmer yells back: 'No, Mr. Minister. But you do expect to see some contented faces.' . . . Well, there you are. Don't talk to me about the Governor. All he's been doing is living in hope of getting back in the Cabinet again. They shunted him off to Burma — so we foot the bill."

There were women at the club whose husbands had stayed behind in Rangoon with the demolition squads. They were under a great strain because the chances of these men getting caught by the Japs was certainly more than ninety per cent. Nearly beside herself with worry, one of these women walked up to towering and super-British Colonel Miller, the Governor's aide, and demanded:

"What's your stupid fool of a Governor going to do?"

"I resent that, madame. As an officer on His Excellency's staff I cannot tolerate such language."

Colonel Miller barked on and on with all the excessive dignity of the Kipling-India tradition until the harassed woman burst into tears. Later, wiping her eyes, she said one of the truest things I heard uttered during more than four months in Burma:

"I don't trust them. I simply don't trust them."

A roly-poly air-raid warden was ranting about the government's failure to provide an advance machinery for evacuating Rangoon. "What good is an E-card to you or me?" he asked. "Sure they fix it so all the big bugs get out first. That's just it — the big bugs! They're the ones that got us into all this mess." Then turning to me: "I could tell you plenty, but I'll keep still. You've been in Burma long enough. You've seen it."

We had to drive down to Mandalay to file our stories — about the evacuation of course, not about these revealing conversations. First we had to get gasoline. The captain in charge of the army's transportation urged us to try to buy gasoline in Mandalay. "We've only got about 1,600 gallons of petrol up in Lashio and we're running fearfully short here. Now these hundreds of cars of evacuees are coming. I don't know what we'll do. I've ordered our stations to refuse supplies to all civilians." (Burma, it should be remembered, had been producing oil since 1888. The Yenang-yaung fields, which were now producing 28,000 gallons per day and could produce 1,000,000 gallons a month, were 225 miles from Maymyo. In two and a half months of war no oil reserves had been built up in Maymyo or Lashio by the British Army or the British-Burma government.)

"I'm in charge of transport here," the captain sighed. "And I haven't even got one truck or car for my own use. For weeks we've had to rely on twenty bullock-carts to move petrol here in Maymyo. Oh well. I can't do anything about the higher-ups."

What was it the RAF bomber boys had said? — "We're always being let down from the top." . . . An army transport director without an automobile. What was it that fine patriotic English girl had told us the previous night at the club? — "I volunteered as a chauffeur and typist at GHQ in Rangoon. I had my own Chevrolet and offered it to headquarters, but they didn't want to take it. They gave me an Oldsmobile instead. I only drove it once a day or not at all. I just sat around the office and maybe typed one letter a day. There were three other girls in my office doing the same thing. GHQ finally got half a dozen jeeps from the Chinese. The officers used them to drive to lunch and back. I'm going to India. What's the use of staying on here?" . . . You heard such things day after day, and always the same sort of thing. You heard them so much that you couldn't remember to write down more than a fraction of them in your notebook.

"Can you beat it?" O. D. said. "A country that produces millions of gallons of oil — and we'll be damned lucky if we can get enough petrol to get out of here. God, what a bloody mess!"

While we were in Mandalay that day the Japs bombed Maymyo for the first time. They straddled the Burma Rifle barracks without hitting them, but three persons were killed and a number of others injured. Now the war had come to northern Burma as well. That night the air-raid control officer was in high dudgeon. "We never got any warning at all," he fumed. "I was just going to sound the alarm when the bombs dropped. Half an hour later I got the warning from Rangoon. You see, everything has been centralized in Rangoon. Burma's bloody close to a thousand miles long, but the air-alarm system has never been split up into districts. How can we hope to protect people here from raids? Sure, I'm responsible. But what can I do?"

That same evening I picked up an October 1941 issue of the *Asiatic Review* in the club library. In it was an article entitled: "Burma — A New Strategical Position," by B. F. Burton-Leach, C.I.E. Among other things the author said: "The Japanese have published fantastic stories of 50,000 Chinese troops having been brought in to defend the frontiers of Burma. The Empire is fortunately able to defend its own frontiers without such assistance and British, Indian and Australian forces have been sent both to Malaya and Burma in large numbers."

It was now February 22, 1942. The Empire forces hadn't proved to be very large. More than 50,000 Chinese troops were now hurrying down through Lashio and Mandalay to take over the defense of Toungoo, far down the Irrawaddy Valley — at the urgent invitation of General Wavell, who had refused to accept them weeks earlier.

Another article in the *Asiatic Review* was written by the Hon. Commander Sir Archibald Cochrane, recent Governor of Burma. "What is the conclusion about Burma in wartime?" I read, wondering what indeed it would prove to be. "As I see the picture it discloses a determination throughout the country that nothing shall be left undone the doing of which might increase Burma's ability to assist in the defeat of Nazi Germany. At the same time there is a growing sense of responsibility and of the gravity of the issues that have to be faced by a Burma separated from India."

More make-believe. And more Dr. Coué. "Every day in every way we're getting stronger and stronger."

2

The army's new Press Relations chief was a lawyer and a writer of detective stories, so he had been commissioned a lieutenant colonel and placed in charge of the war correspondents. I suppose we provided him at least with a variety of villains for his future fiction. The lieutenant colonel was rather peeved at O. D. and me for having filed dispatches from Mandalay before the evacuation, and the press department caught up with us. That had made it difficult at first to get permission to go down to Pegu. We had to try to get to Pegu. No one yet had a clear understanding of what had happened on that front to provoke the pell-mell exodus from Rangoon.

By chance I met General John Magruder, down on a brief inspection tour from Chungking, and he gave me the first inkling of the disaster. On or about February 20 two and one half British-Indian brigades — most of the 17th division — had been ambushed on the eastern side of the Sittang River just a few miles beyond Pegu. The British had been compelled to blow up the bridge over the Sittang, while most of their troops were still cut off. Losses had been very heavy. A British tank battalion had just disembarked in Rangoon. It raced to Pegu just in time to prevent a general collapse. of General Smythe's line. All remaining British forces were now behind the Sittang, with Pegu, Rangoon's last defense point, only twenty-five miles in their rear.

General Magruder did not divulge any details, but his gravity was eloquent enough in itself. Later I learned that General Hutton, the commander-in-chief in Burma, had frankly described the situation as "desperate." A majority of British troops had been cut off. This was the fatal battle of Mokpalin, beyond the Sittang Bridge. It was never reported from Burma because it was one of those costly reverses which couldn't be reported. Eventually we met a Scot lieutenant who escaped from Mokpalin. He estimated that a thousand men had been killed there, and anything like that loss was a major catastrophe to Hutton's small defending forces.

"We had crossed the bridge and were packed in tight on the road leading south toward Bilin," the lieutenant said. "Burmese traitors had led the Japs around through the jungles and the Japs had their mortars with them. They cut loose from behind us with their mortars and machine guns. We were caught flat-footed. The ambush worked perfectly. The Japs travel twice as fast as we do, you know. They move through the jungles like greased lightning. Wherever we turn we find machine guns and mortars ahead of us. We didn't even have a chance of operating a field gun at Mokpalin. It was a death trap. Our brigades were ordered to get back as best they could. It was a bloody business. Hundreds of our chaps tried to swim the river. The Japs sprinkled us with machine-gun bullets and dropped mortar shells right among us. I don't know how any of us got across. Hundreds were left behind, and at least five hundred were captured. Many fought in small groups and were wiped out. Others wandered around in the jungle without food for three or four days, and some of those managed to get back.

"But you should have seen the Gurkhas. Whenever there's an ambush they always call on the Gurkhas. Every time they call for the Gurkhas. Those Indian troops are wonderful. They grab their knives and wade right in. Really, they were bloody wonderful at Mokpalin. Before we blew up the Sittang Bridge the general tried to keep the bridge open so we could get back. Those Gurkhas had already been through hell, but they were ordered to go back and hold the bridgehead. I talked with chaps who saw them do it. They said you should have seen the Gurkhas. They formed up, just like on parade — and they marched back across the bridge right in the face of the Jap fire. They held the bridgehead for several hours, but we couldn't get out that way. I tell you those Indian troops are bloody wonderful. Our lads always say they'll go anywhere with Gurkhas alongside them."

One day Gallagher and I picked up an Anglo-Indian civilian in our jeep.

"Bloody fine show you people are putting up," O. D. said.

"We get no credit for it," replied the Anglo-Indian bitterly. "We got no credit for it in the last war, and of course we won't get any after this war. That doesn't matter. We expect it. But we resent being told we didn't contribute anything."

Well, it was easier somehow for British authorities to pay occasional tribute to Indian fighting troops — much easier — than to give public recognition to those humble civilians whose race was half-Indian as well as half-British. At that moment the British radio station was still functioning, from the midst of chaos, in Rangoon. All the East heard "the voice of Rangoon" nightly. But the voice of Rangoon was not British. It was the voice of one of two Anglo-Indian employees in the radio station; one by the name of Acosta and the other named Lazaro. The Governor's son-in-law, who was in charge of Rangoon news-casts, was somewhere else. These Anglo-Indians were paid all of 150 rupees (about $30) a month for their services. Until the Japs walked in they continued their broadcasts. It is probable that they had never been invited to a British home in Rangoon in their lives. That, at any rate, would have been quite normal.

At Mandalay we swapped the Flying 69 for a jeep with a livelier motor. From Maymyo we had dropped suddenly out of a cool and springlike paradise into a blistering inferno of blinding sun and choking dust. We turned down the valley from Mandalay, racing for Pegu, nearly 400 miles to the south. Past the slim and needle-pointed white pagodas which border the highway; through Meiktila, until we put up for the night in the upper story of a wooden municipal building in Pyinmana. Next morning we passed dozens of burned trucks. They had been fired by an American who was in charge of a motor-repair station for the Burma Road. He had got panicky and ordered them destroyed. Another bit of inexcusable wastage. Approaching Toungoo we passed through a bombed-out Burmese village, whose ruins were still smoking. But the road was virtually empty all the way until, well below Toungoo, we found our way almost completely blocked by a bewildered horde of nearly 4,000 Indian refugees. They were traveling on foot and in hundreds of bullock-carts heaped high with their household belongings. They said they traveled at night because the Burmese attacked them with knives if they tried to rest after dark. They were helpless and pitiful beyond words. They had never fought anyone in their lives. They didn't know how to protect themselves. They asked if they could still get to Mandalay, and how long it would take them to reach India. We hadn't the heart to tell these lost souls the terrible truth: that there were roads only part of the way, then jungles and mountains, cholera and malaria.

We located a British battalion GHQ at Nyaunglebin, forty miles north of Pegu. The Japs had had patrols across the highway during the night, and at three in the afternoon the British brigadier still didn't know whether the road was open. "I can't let you go on until I get a definite report," he said. This was the tight stretch just behind the Sittang line. Why didn't we have motor patrols operating up and down the road? Why were these few British troops here so uninformed about the situation in Pegu? The Japs were also reported to be trying to cut the road we had just come down from Toungoo, yet along these 125 miles we had seen no sentinels of our own. At night the Japs could walk across, anywhere they took a notion. Here the British were groping in the dark exactly as I had seen two other British battalions groping and hugging the main road north of Trondheim in Norway. Late that afternoon the brigadier still had no idea whether the lower lap to Pegu was open, so we had to return to Toungoo.

A large slice of Toungoo, a big town, was in flames as we arrived. Thirty Jap planes had heavily bombed the area around the railroad station. Once more we had missed the raid, this time by only an hour. Five full blocks of tinder-dry wooden dwellings and the city's markets were blazing like cardboard. A handful of British and Burmese battled desperately to save the rest of Toungoo. The flames roared savagely and every flimsy house was kindling-wood. This, I thought, is what can and will be done to Tokyo and Yokohama. Tongues of fire ran swiftly up the trunks of tall leaning palm trees, a weird yet beautiful sight.

The meaning of this destruction was plain. The Japs were now systematically bombing every town on the Burma Road from Pegu north to Lashio, some 600 miles away. The wounded in the Toungoo hospital had to be evacuated at once. A train was ordered for them and hundreds of men, mostly on stretchers, were laid out near the tracks. Then the train went by without stopping. Somebody had slipped up again — the old, old story. So the wounded had to lie there all night, wondering if the bombers would be back.

That night we also learned why there were no motor patrols below Nyaunglebin. The British commander in Toungoo received an important order to send a patrol across the Sittang near Nyaunglebin before daybreak. But GHQ at Toungoo did not have a single automobile to transmit this order — not for all the hundreds of Chinese Lend-Lease trucks which had been parked in Rangoon for weeks, nor for all the British civilian cars which had not been mobilized. O. D. offered the use of our jeep and spent the night taking an officer to deliver this operational order. When such things were happening right and left, how long could one expect Burma to last?

3

The Chinese Fifth Army, consisting of three light divisions, was being rushed down from the Shan Mountains in central-eastern Burma to take over the Toungoo front. No correspondents had yet spent any time with the Chinese troops in Burma; that was why we took the road south from Mandalay again. Eventually we reached the sprawling town of Pyinmana, seventy miles above Toungoo.

The streets were crowded with slight, boyish soldiers in faded shirts and shorts of yellow denim. Their visored caps made them look like child coal-miners and they were loaded down with heavy packs and equipment. Pyinmana, where we had spent the night on several previous trips, had become the temporary headquarters of the Chinese Fifth Army. As O. D. remarked, these were China's first expeditionary forces since Genghis Khan. The soldiers were setting up field kitchens, carrying huge sacks of rice, and toting buckets of water on their shoulder-slung poles. They were the same tough and wiry men, built like boys but strong as iron, that I had seen in China. They had marched nearly eight hundred miles from the Yunnan Mountains to fight in Burma. Some of these amazing little Chinese had carried a 104-pound mortar, slung on a pole, a full pack, and an eight-pound rifle and had marched twenty miles a day with that load. I wondered how many American football players could do that. The Chinese troops moved methodically and steadily about their tasks. Somehow you got a long-forgotten feeling of confidence as you watched them.

"Look at the soldier with bobbed hair," I said. And then: "My God, it's a woman!"

She wore the same Chinese army uniform as the men, and she,

too, was carrying two big pails of water, slung from a shoulder pole. When we found GHQ and a keen, smiling young captain, he explained: "Oh yes. We have about a hundred Chinese girls here. They're part of the army, so they came with us. They help with the kitchens. They do political work and they make propaganda plays. Sometimes they sew, or they nurse the wounded. They are very patriotic — and very good for the soldiers' fighting spirit. Sure you can talk with them."

These, then, were the WAC's of China. We talked with a group of about a dozen of these girl soldiers — and they were girls, for their ages averaged from eighteen to twenty-one. Several of them were definitely pretty and all had the grace and delicacy of Chinese women. They lived the life of common soldiers, yet their faces bloomed with health and their tiny muscles were indubitably hard as nails. "We like it here," one of the Chinese girl soldiers said. "It is much better than school. When your country is invaded you must do something for the war." I wished that we had a camera. I saw much in the attitude of the young Chinese staff captain. He was proud that Chinese girls would come to a far-off unknown land with Chinese soldiers. They made him prouder than ever of being Chinese. I had a strong feeling that their very presence made better soldiers of him and his comrades.

We were taken finally to a one-room basket-woven house on stilts, a typical Burmese dwelling. The general was squatting on his haunches pointing at the map he had spread on the floor. Outside, the sun thrust down a million stabbing invisible bayonet blades upon the lifeless palms and withered banana leaves heavy with dust. It was unmercifully hot, probably much more than 100 degrees, with not a quiver of life in the air. As he pointed, the general's forefinger, as slender and tapering as a woman's, rested first upon India. You'd never have guessed he was a general. He wore the same faded denim uniform which all Chinese soldiers wear, with no insignia of rank on the shoulders or collar. He looked extraordinarily young, and in fact he was only thirty-seven. But he had been wounded four times and was commander of one of Chiang Kai-shek's hand-picked armies.

"This is what is most important," the general said, his finger moving back and forth above the outlines of India. "The Germans must never be permitted to come through this way; the Japanese must never be allowed to go across here. So long as the Germans and Japanese cannot meet in India we shall surely defeat them."

Beads of sweat rolled down our faces as we bent over the map and General Cheng-ting Che (the name means Good Boy of the Family) gave a quick command. A soldier brought us steaming hot towels with which to wipe our faces and hands. We sighed with relief. The general continued to indicate the war zones for Britain, for Russia, for America and China.

"But the Japanese control all of the South Pacific. How can they be defeated?" I asked.

The general's wonderfully expressive fingers darted down again on Tokyo's bull's-eye. "Let the American bombers strike Tokyo from here, and from here" (from Hawaii and Dutch Harbor). "We must hit the Japanese at home; we must wipe out their bases of supply. Once that has been done, all their forces in Indo-China, Malaya, the Philippines, everywhere will be doomed. We must simply cut off the Japanese Army from Japan."

"What about Vladivostok?"

"No, we must not ask too much of the Russians. They have a a very big fight and they're doing very big things. Against Japan we must count on Chinese soldiers, chiefly, on land; and we must count on the Americans by air and by sea. Everything must be aimed first at Japan, at home."

"What about the present outlook in Burma?"

"Our Chinese troops are now at Toungoo," General Cheng-ting Che replied. He smiled confidently and the elegant gold caps on two of his upper front teeth gleamed beneath his clipped, dark mustache. "I don't think the Japanese will ever reach Pyinmana."

"But if they should?" I persisted.

The general launched into an explanation of time-tested Chinese tactics, illustrating their functioning on the map. "If the Japanese do this, we do this. Then we fight, fight, fight."

The Cantonese captain grinned happily as he translated these words. It had been a long time since we had encountered such serene sureness as this. The Spanish Republicans, the Finns, and the Greeks all had it; but this was the first time I had found it anywhere in Burma. Could the commander of the Chinese Fifth Army be correct? We knew what had happened to the British 17th division beyond the Sittang Bridge. We knew what we had seen down the road below Toungoo — and what we hadn't found there. Had the Chinese come in time? Or through no fault of their own were they one month too late? We were very much afraid the Chinese had arrived too late, but we wanted to believe the contrary.

"What are Japanese soldiers like? What do you think of them?"

"They're not as brave as people think," said General Cheng-ting Che. "They fight very hard when they have the advantage in guns and planes. When they do not have more and better weapons, the Japanese are not especially brave. Our soldiers have better hearts. I know."

"And the Jap officers?"

This was later, when we were sitting around a foot-high circular table, out in the dusty yard at sundown, plying chopsticks into an assortment of good Chinese food. The general was sitting on the lowest stool. He had donned a smart officer's uniform in our honor, but still wore no markings of his rank. Common soldiers, passing in and out of the gate, addressed him freely. Republican Spain was the only other place where I had ever seen generals living on such intimate terms with their men. The general put down his rice bowl to reply:

"Japanese officers are too ambitious." Then with a smile: "They try to eat too much. Now they have reached the dangerous stage because things have gone too well. Now they think they can eat everything. Soon they'll have to take a purgative. That's sure to happen. For us it is very good."

4

Seeing the Chinese troops and their calm, intelligent commander almost made us feel there might be some hope for Burma yet. In Pyinmana that night we were taken in by Breedom Case, the American Baptist missionary, at the compound of the American agricultural school. Another missionary, named Cummings, had just come down from Loilem to get seeds with which to grow vegetables to feed the Chinese forces in the Shan States.

"The British haven't learned a thing," Cummings said dejectedly. "Washington once said if you fight Indians you must fight as the Indians do. The British lost Malaya trying to hold the main roads, with the Japs cutting around behind them. Now they've lost Moulmein, Martaban, and Bilin the same way — and they won't post patrols on the side roads up on the Shan front either."

Mr. Case had been born in Burma and had labored there all his life. He knew British and Burmese from one end of the country to the other. "I talked with B—," Mr. Case said. "He's the district police commissioner. He's much incensed over the way the defense of southern Burma has been mishandled. The leadership, he says, has been terrible. The general down there is jittery as can be. He keeps withdrawing his troops before there's any real fighting. B— says it's inexcusable. He was an officer in the last war and he ought to be able to judge."

"Up at Loilem the British officers are in a rotten state of mind," Cummings reported. "Many of them are humiliated because they feel no real fight has been made in the south. It's not the fault of the British troops. They seem perfectly all right. But their leadership is appalling. By the way, did you hear that Nyaunglebin is finished? Jap bombers practically wiped it off the map yesterday. I don't know where the front is now. I suppose close to Toungoo."

We returned to Maymyo to learn that Pegu had fallen and Rangoon was also in the hands of the Japs. The great Syriam oil refineries had been completely demolished — that was one job which the British had done well. Major General Joseph W. Stilwell, for some time in China, had been appointed commander of the Chinese armies in Burma. And General Sir Harold Alexander, at this late date, had been named to succeed General Hutton as GOC (General Officer Commanding) of the British Burma forces. This step, it seemed to me, was about three months too late. The battle for Burma was already lost. The little four-page *Burma News Sheet,* which was the only English-language substitute for a newspaper left in Burma, carried a magnificently ironic statement that 9th of March from

His Excellency Sir Reginald Dorman-Smith, the Governor.

"At this stage of the war," solemnly proclaimed His Excellency, "there is only one unforgiveable sin, which is the failure to take decisions and to carry them out. . . . If you are close to the front or in other vital positions do not worry about referring to anyone. Act! Provided your decision is one calculated to embarrass the enemy and to contribute to our war effort, I will back you — right or wrong."

British officers and civilians in the Maymyo club lounge thought if anyone in Burma should understand the "one unforgiveable sin" that man was the Governor. In the north the shortage of gasoline and food was already serious. Salt — an urgent necessity in tropical climates — was nearly impossible to find, yet southern Burma itself produced great quantities of salt. The government, with months of time at its disposal, had failed to create stores of even the most indispensable materials either in Mandalay or farther north. So the Allied retreat must be toward near-famine as well as almost impassable jungles and mountains. Maymyo was now saturated with confusion, defeatism, and bitterness. When an American officer mentioned the Governor to one live-wire British general he exploded: "I wish somebody would shoot the Governor. That would be one of the biggest possible improvements that could happen." The British military, it appeared, were still having a hopeless time trying to persuade His Excellency to take decisions. "Another blow-up with the Governor last night," a colonel said to me gloomily.

"I'm afraid perhaps His Excellency is too much of a politician," I ventured.

"You're the third person who has used those exact words to me today," burst out the colonel.

More and more it looked to be less and less of the slightest chance of saving Burma. And of course the Burmese fifth-columnists were now increasingly active. On the road from Mandalay we had passed their brush fires night after night. We knew that Burmese had led the Japs through the jungles to ambush the 17th division at Sittang Bridge, and again had shown the Japs where to cut off the Prome Road below Pegu. A Burmese with a heavy stick tried to knock out Gallagher in the jeep on one of the central streets of Mandalay in broad daylight. We wrote about these and other fifth-column activities, but the government's civil censors suppressed all such items. Colonel Raymond informed us: "I always ask myself if my dear devoted daughter in England would be alarmed by this." No one in Britain must be permitted to get alarmed about the situation in Burma. The great make-believe policy held firm to the end.

And to the end the British command in Burma was immersed in a fog about the size of the Jap forces and where they were. At the time of the fall of Pegu a United States Army major went to British GHQ in Maymyo to check some information about the Japanese Army. He wasn't optimistic, because he had found the British officers in Burma were usually indefinite; frequently as if they hesitated to take the responsibility for stating a definite fact; sometimes as if they sought to conceal the simple truth that they did not know the answer.

"What divisions do the Japanese have in Burma?" the American major asked.

"Well," began a headquarters staff officer, "that's rather obscure. You see —"

"I don't want anything obscure," snapped the major, who had heard the same language too often. "Do you know, or don't you?"

"Well — I'm afraid not."

"Then I'll tell you," said the major. "The Japs have their —— division and their —— division" (giving the numbers).

"How do you know that?" asked the British staff officer.

"I got it from the Chinese. They've known it for the past month at least. Why didn't you ask them? They know more about the Japs than anyone else does."

The major was telling me about it afterward. "They're just too damned proud to ask the Chinese for information. But that'll give you an idea of what the British Army's intelligence service is like in Burma. Imagine fighting for two months without having the foggiest notion of how many divisions are against you, or what their identity is."

So the Japs had only needed two divisions to take Rangoon and doom all of central-southern Burma. Rather too cheap, that. But it had happened; and there was still no place in sight where you could expect the British forces to make and hold a line. The British way of retreat lay by the more westerly highway out of Rangoon, northward to Prome and Magwé. The latter must be held if the indispensable Yenangyaung oilfields were to be saved, and the Magwé-Yenangyaung district enjoyed much higher and more open terrain, which seemed favorable to defense. Directly east of Prome, on the main Mandalay road, the Chinese had taken positions at Toungoo. Both Prome and Toungoo were about 175 miles north of Rangoon, but the British Imperial brigades — disorganized and demoralized after the 17th division's disaster at Mokpalin and their crushing defeat at Pegu — were falling back rapidly toward Prome. If they failed to dig in solidly well in advance of the RAF's last good Burma airfield at Magwé, then the Chinese Fifth Army would be outflanked. The Chinese, too, would have to fall back on Mandalay. Already, and only three days after Jap units entered Rangoon, it appeared virtually certain that our allies would save little or nothing south of Mandalay. Not until now were many hundreds of British women ordered out of Burma. But how could they get out? A thousand or more persons were actually clamoring to get on a CNAC plane from Lashio, but that was hopeless. The evacuees — women and children as well as elderly civilians — would have to go far up the Chindwin River, several days by boat, and then through wild jungles. Finally they would take to trails and at last must spend several terrible days climbing over steep mountain ranges into India. Thousands of poverty-stricken Indian families were fleeing by this route and many were dying from cholera or malaria en route. Because the British marine navigation companies had for years blocked the construction of a highway between Burma and the adjacent Indian provinces all of central and northern Burma had become a desolate and disease-sown trap. This was probably the most terrible trek that refugees have had to endure in any country in the global war. Those who reached India in three weeks were fortunate, regardless of their condition upon arrival.

For several reasons I did not intend to take the overland route out of Burma. First of all, it would not provide a newspaper dispatch of particular value. Even though this was the world's most formidable mass flight, by the time it could be written it would make stale reading for daily newspapers and might be lucky if it got printed on page seven. The thing to do was to manage somehow to get on a plane and so get to Calcutta fast and write as much about the reasons for Burma's fall as the censors would permit. That would be mighty little, of course, but a few hints at the true explanation might at least throw a ray of light. Aside from all this, however, I could not afford to lose the time of a long trek out of Burma, nor could I wait around for the last skirmishes and the inevitable collapse. I couldn't do that because I was under orders to get to Moscow in time for the Germans' spring offensive. Pearl Harbor had first delayed my departure. Late in January, when the *Chicago Daily News* again queried me about my Russian visa, I had cabled back that I thought I should remain in Burma for about another month. I couldn't say so, but I knew Rangoon was going to fall and I wanted to see that decisive episode through.

Well, Rangoon was gone and a lot more was going fast; I now had seen enough — more than enough. I had seen enough bungling, red tape, inefficiency, and creeping paralysis to last me for a lifetime. The Orient, from the inexpressible poverty of its masses to the Chinese racketeers of the Burma Road to the dry rot of British Burma, had afflicted me with about as much depression and despair and disillusionment as the spirit can absorb in heavy doses in a short period and under exceptionally trying circumstances. For weeks my one hope had been to live to get out of the East. There are parts of the world, like Spain or Greece in my own experience, where one could almost be contented to die. But death in these particular paddy-fields and tropical jungles was somehow a repugnant thought. Those who had conquered them or misruled them had shorn these lowlands of whatever natural dignity they once had possessed. Today the land of Russia must be an entirely different thing. Neither hardship nor death is nearly so difficult upon soil which men's valor has made proud. Some time, much later, I could think back and realize where there had been a soft luster or a sharp beauty in Burma's landscapes. Eventually I could also realize that it would be interesting and perhaps even pleasant to return there. But not now. There was no time now to linger if I were to reach Russia by the month of May. Already I had risked being late. The thought of starting westward — westward toward Europe and an utterly different civilization — was as welcome as the first whiff of an oasis well to the nostrils of a camel. And in any case what was the good of prolonging the spiritual torment here any longer? We already knew the end of Burma. In the beginning and middle of the Burma campaign we had seen its end.

Gallagher had reached the same conclusion, so we set out on our last jeep ride down the road from Mandalay on March 11. Frank Merrill had given us an invaluable tip. We might be able to get a ride in an RAF plane from Magwé across to Calcutta. In a few days that chance would be gone.

The next morning, before reaching Yenangyaung, we met a truck full of British soldiers and a British tank corps captain in a car. They had been in the battle of Pegu, the only engagement that could honestly be described as a battle anywhere in southern Burma. They were headed north toward Mandalay, and they were just as confused and disheartened as the officers and men of the defeated Koylies' battalion whom I had encountered fleeing north from Steinkjer in the Namsos sector of Norway almost two years before. I talked with the tank corps captain. He had commanded some of the tanks which had chiefly been responsible for making Pegu a battle — of sorts anyway. What he revealed bore the authority of a brave Britisher whose pride had been deeply wounded.

"I'm fed up to the teeth," the captain said. "I wish somebody on the ground would decide to stand and fight. If a rifle is fired from the bushes they think they're surrounded. The trouble is most of our officers here are inexperienced. They only try to fight in the open and on the main roads. No, I don't know who's in command below Prome. Our tanks are patrolling the road near Tharrawaddy, but they can't do much. It's just a bloody mess. The 17th division is unfit for service. It's got to be reorganized. No one seems to be in charge. They're just washed up and anxious to get out."

"Haven't the losses been pretty heavy?"

"I think the losses may be exaggerated. There's simply been too much flap.* We had 114 tanks and we only lost nine. We got many Jap tanks and we killed off a bloody lot of the bastards.

* British army slang for "panic."

Yes, we have American thirteen-tonners. They've done a grand job. We never had a single one go out of commission for any mechanical fault."

"We heard a rumor that General Hutton had been captured."

"I haven't heard, but it's not much loss if he has," said the captain curtly.

At a gasoline station in Yenangyaung the attendant told us: "We've been ordered to be ready to get out any time." So it looked as if these oil wells and refineries would not or could not be defended for long. Virtually no oil reserves had been stored at Mandalay or farther north. Without gasoline how could northern Burma be held? But these hills around Yenangyaung were rough and mostly barren. They seemed to offer by far the best defensive possibilities of any terrain the British forces had yet fallen upon in their repeated withdrawals.

"Looks like our chaps won't be here long," O. D. muttered grimly. "We aren't getting to Magwé a day too soon. If we can't get on a plane today, it's the bloody jungles for us."

At Magwé field we found Bob Neale and a small group of AVG boys and also a considerable body of RAF fliers. We lunched with the American pilots. They doubted that Magwé would hold very long, but their fighting spirit was still fine. A DC-3 belonging to the RAF was taking off with a few Anglo-Indian and Anglo-Burmese evacuees, women and children, at two thirty. The RAF officer in charge said there weren't many refugees left here; probably he could get us on.

It was 450 miles and a three-hour flight to Dum-Dum airport outside Calcutta. Only three hours, and the Burma nightmare lay far behind in another world. I had never been quite so glad to leave a place in my life. But was India really such a totally different world? In a short time I discovered that in many ways we had only made a flight — into the familiar.

5

The collapse of Burma was one of those experiences which you hope and pray you will never go through again. It does not quite seem that the mind and heart could stand a repetition of that kind of nightmare. It is something you wish to cast behind you and forget, like a foul deed or the stench of rotting corpses.

Yet there it is, etched indelibly inside you. You cannot erase it. You cannot escape either its ugliness or its connotations. You can only conquer it by building something better in its place. To return to yesterday will not work. The "damned spot" of Lady Macbeth is always there. You can only face forward because things can and must never be the same.

If any people have learned this truth in the world conflict I believe the British people — and the French — must have learned it. And provided they are sufficiently informed of the details of Burma's debacle, the British people will not be satisfied with a return to the past in Britain's colonial policy, any more than they would now tolerate a return to Baldwinism and Chamberlainism in England. Winston Churchill's background is generally described as incorrigibly imperialistic; but Britain's incomparable wartime leader is also a great realist. When he swears that he did not become Prime Minister to liquidate the British Empire, Mr. Churchill, in part, is speaking after the fact. In any event, it's most unlikely that he pictures himself as another King Canute bidding the tides of the revolutionary twentieth century to move forward no more. These tides have already swept across Hong Kong, Malaya, and Burma as well as Indo-China and the East Indies. None of these places will be the same when the whirlpools of Hirohito recede.

What to do about Burma?

Yesterday's sole value lies in the extraordinary degree in which it points out what not to do.

The British in Burma did not disintegrate shockingly and tragically because their original capacities were lower than those of a similar group of run-of-the-mill upper-class and middle-class Americans or Frenchmen or Germans. The Burma-British disintegrated because they were products of a system — an exploitative and standstill, anti-progressive system. The system destroyed initiative because it was both narrow and anachronistic. The system destroyed self-respect because it was built upon the enrichment of a very few at the expense of a great mass of helpless human beings. The system spawned hatred because it denied the equality of races and placed greed above elementary human rights. Of course the men who were born in this system and devoted their lives to serving it did not clearly see what the system did to them — and they had unconsciously trained themselves not to see what it did to others. They didn't really *see* the system. They merely had, deep within themselves, an uneasy feeling that something was wrong. It was human to blame the natives, or any outside element, for this. But even while they did this, the uneasiness and lack of certitude would not be stilled. They could not act or meet a completely new and terribly unexpected situation because the colonial imperialist system — ever since 1826 in Burma — had trained them not to act boldly; not to improvise; not to accept responsibility. The system had trained them to keep things as they were. The Burma-British had long since wound up by being crippled, spiritually as well as in physical habits. They were prisoners of their own domination. In the matchless words of Clemenceau: "the victors became the victims of their conquest."

Of course this has happened to every empire in the history of the world. There was a time when Americans in the Philippines went a considerable way along the path the British traveled in Burma and elsewhere. That we did not go the whole way seems little more than a providential accident. If, however, we had governed the Philippines for more than a century, who would presume to say that we would have ended very differently? Had our treatment of the American Indians and the Hawaiians been any more enlightened? Has anything the British have done in India been more violent, brutal, and shameful than the race riots against Negroes and Mexicans in the United States today? When Americans continue to betray such colossal and perilous intolerance at home, can we rightly assume that we would not have made the same grave mistakes in conduct if it had been our lot to govern — and exploit — Burma?

But another and perhaps greater economic imperialism beckons to many Americans, as well as to many British, once this present World War has been won. We shall all need world trade, but how to develop it without building up another world imperialism will be a delicate navigational problem indeed. Perhaps Americans, no less than the British, will need to understand and remember Burma's all-important lesson — *how to lose an empire*. For systems of some kind will be established or re-established in Malaya and the Solomon Islands, in the Dutch

East Indies and Burma and elsewhere. In form of rule and administration they may be outright colonies, or they may be mandates held in trusteeship under a new League of Nations or World Council, or they may take new aspects. In whatever shape they assume, the fundamental test must inevitably remain the same. Will the form of control and of government simply be a remodeled cloak to dress up the same system of exploitation by white men? If the system remains essentially unreformed, how can one expect its product, in another generation or two, to be any different? War and fifth columns, paralysis and collapse—the victors once more the victims of their conquest.

During more than one hundred years enormous fortunes were reaped in Burma by the British. Burma has produced and still produces a fabulous wealth in oil, teakwood, tin, silver, rubber, and rice. It is extremely difficult to find traces of this great native Burman wealth in the lot and the lives of more than 14,000,000 Burmese natives. You do not find well-built and attractive schools in Burma's towns and villages. You do not find many hospitals or clinics. You do not find anything much that is halfway modern except what has been built for the use of white men, with the exception of a few missionary schools, mostly financed by American church groups. The vast natural wealth of Burma, like a large part of the natural wealth of Mexico and the Central and South American countries, has been drawn out of the country for the enrichment of a small band of foreign capitalists who have no other interest in the land and the people who are the source of their fortunes.

Some say the world has always been like this, so it always will be. There was a time when the world had always been flat; and a time when the plague, malaria, and syphilis were incurable or uncontrollable. There was a time, ranging over an almost inconceivable number of centuries, when China was nothing but an incoherent mass of conflicting kingdoms, provinces, and peoples. There was a time when no one had heard the words "Asia for the Asiatics"; when Hindus and Moslems in India had never associated in a single political movement and had never dreamed of resisting even by passive resistance. But the times are now changing with every week. In Soviet Russia, covering one sixth of the earth's surface, the gold and silver and tin mines, coal and minerals and oilfields, the forests and railroads and factories of production, all belong to the state. This new kind of state may develop and exploit these great basic riches well or badly. Nevertheless the people hold the title of ownership. No small group of individuals may stake out and own any of these things. The people's title of ownership may be partly on paper as yet. But the people of the Soviet Union have got an idea. The idea is not on paper. It is in a much more fertile spot. It is in their heads. The world of the Russians didn't use to be like this at all. The world of the Chinese and of India, too, quivers in an unprecedented ferment. In each of these great crowded lands the ferment has produced an idea — nationalism. The idea is in the heads and the hearts of hundreds of millions — nearly 800,000,000 human beings. You cannot kill and you cannot forever deny an idea like that. It is stronger and more powerful than all the bombs the world can produce. In fact, bombs have served tremendously to make the idea grow.

So Burma is just a test-tube for those who used to carry Mr. Kipling's "white man's burden." And Malaya and the Dutch East Indies and the Philippines — how many places on this restless, tormented, impatient globe! — are all test-tubes. Not for the yellow or the brown or the black races, but for the whites. Not test-tubes for the have-nots, but for the haves. Shall we return to a system that poisons the spirit and paralyzes the will? Or shall we devise a system that gives hope and health to native populations? Perhaps such a system need not be out-and-out socialism. Perhaps you and I can't tell just what it will be. But perhaps we ought to know enough by now to know that it cannot be a system of uncurbed exploitation; that it must have within it a new freedom and the prospect of greater growth for the voiceless masses in lands which have so long been regarded and treated as mere colonial reserves. If we do not allot to them their rightful share, if we do not work *with* them instead of *upon* them, eventually these masses will revolt. In the slow remorseless turn of the wheel of justice the day will surely come when they will accumulate the power to show us that we have, in fact, become their inferiors.

If I saw anything in Burma, I saw retribution — and a warning.

Have Winston Churchill, the members of the British government, and the men of London's money marts seen it? Have President Roosevelt and those Americans who must shape and approve the peace seen it? Before long we shall know. Meanwhile perhaps we should ask ourselves whether the formula of the Four Freedoms can have any real substance anywhere in the world unless it is implemented by the clean tools of economic liberation and bold forward steps toward political democracy for all.

There remains only one more thing which I want very much to say about the awful Burma fiasco. Bravery was not enough, but, for all that, the British soldiers and the Indian troops fought in Burma with great courage whenever their leaders gave them an opportunity to fight. The men of the Gloucesters, Cameronians, and Koylies, the Gurkhas, Sikhs, and Pathans did not fear the Japs nor wince at their thankless, hopeless task. They did not fear to die and they were worthy of the finest and best in Britain's and India's military traditions. When they lost confidence in their commanders it was only long after most soldiers would have lost all faith. They lie in a lost land in forgotten places, and the graves of most of them will never be known. They, the common soldiers, and also a good many boys of the RAF and some American airmen and a great many Chinese.

Chapter VIII

THE FLYING TIGERS IN BURMA

"What kind of bonuses do you war correspondents get?" asked the lanky pilot from Seattle.

"Bonuses? Don't kid me."

I laughed and couldn't help it. In exactly twenty years of reporting I had never encountered such a thing as a bonus. Sometimes, when newspapermen won a Pulitzer prize, they received a bonus. When mine came along, the newspaper on which I then worked not only forgot all about a bonus; it even overlooked such an obvious gesture as a small increase in salary. I could understand a bonus for winning a Pulitzer prize for an outstanding job of reporting, or for hard work. But what reporter had ever asked for a bonus for covering a war? . . . And what publisher had ever thought of giving bonuses for covering a war?

"You mean to say you don't get any bonus?" exclaimed the dark lynx-eyed flier from Spokane. "What in hell do you go to places like Burma and China for?"

"You fellows have got queer ideas. Listen. If you're a foreign correspondent it's your job. Well, if war comes, then it's more than ever your job. Sure I'd like a bonus. Anybody would. But you don't go to a war to get bonuses. I suppose some fellows have got them, but so far I never happen to have known a war correspondent who did — and I know quite a lot of them."

"Well, I'll be God-damned!" drawled the pilot from Seattle.

"You wouldn't catch me going to a war in China for a straight salary," said the slender dark one. "You don't have to. It sounds cockeyed to me."

"Maybe you go to cover a war in China or Greece — anywhere — because it's important that people at home should know something about it," I explained. "Or maybe you go to China to try to understand what's happening to the Chinese, and what's happening to us."

They didn't seem to get the idea, these two young Americans.

They seemed to have the notion that shooting down Japs would be duck soup. But they didn't want to shoot Japs because Jap armies had been plundering, raping, drug-addicting, and murdering millions of helpless Chinese for years. You couldn't quite tell whether they even wanted to shoot down Jap planes for the adventure of it. Yes, they wanted to see China, but the thing that interested them most of all was being the world's highest-paid combat fliers. They were counting on that $500 for each Jap plane shot down. They were like the handful of French and American mercenaries who flew for the Loyalists in Spain. What had happened to the sense of adventure and the idealism of American youth? Twenty-five years ago you would never have had to scrape around to find one hundred American boys who would fight as genuine volunteers for China. These were attractive and lusty fellows, all right. But somehow they threw you off a bit. They didn't seem to realize that Hitler and the Nazis were out to conquer the world and had been blowing people to bits and exterminating them like rats for years now. They didn't seem to realize the same thing about Japan. Yet they did seem to be typical Americans — and that was what disturbed me and made me wonder when I first met a sampling of the AVG in Rangoon's Silver Grill. That was in September 1941.

These young Americans were the first military "tourists" the United States, unofficially and surreptitiously, had sent to the second World War. They had been smuggled out of the U. S. Army and Navy air forces and smuggled across the Pacific, so that the champions of America's anti-war — and anti-freedom — Neutrality Act wouldn't get upset. It had taken a great deal of careful connivance. Why the connivance? Because there were higher-ups in Washington who had intelligence enough to know that the Chinese, while fighting for themselves, were buying time for us. The United States was still woefully unarmed and weak in the Pacific. So China must be kept fighting. It was worth approximately $585,000,000 to us, our initial Lend-Lease appropriation, to try to keep China holding the dike. But these materials still might be too late. China's handful of obsolescent aircraft was almost gone. Against Japan's hundreds of planes the Chinese could not put up a single fighter squadron. They had no adequately trained and equipped pursuit pilots. That was why these American pilots and ground-crew men were now here in Burma, but very much incognito. On the Clipper, flying out from San Francisco, I had met William D. Pawley and from him had learned a good deal of the story of the original conception and formation of the AVG.

Bill Pawley, a trap-jawed and hustling American businessman, liked the Chinese and liked profits, too. Early in the Sino-Japanese War he had got some of the first planes to China; he had also built one or more airplane factories there and had lost them. As Bill told me the story, he and a former U. S. Navy commander, B. G. Leighton, first convinced the Chinese government of the necessity of getting American fliers with American planes into China. Colonel Claire Chennault, retired from the U. S. Army air force because (like Billy Mitchell) he had too many "unorthodox" ideas, for several years had held a nondescript Chinese air force together on a shoestring and a few outmoded kites. Chennault had been nursing the same hope as Pawley for a long time. Pawley went to Washington and found that some Roosevelt administration leaders and Secretary of War Stimson and Secretary of the Navy Knox could see beyond the end of their noses. So the vanguard of some four hundred Americans, less than one-fourth of them pilots, reached Rangoon on August 21, 1941. It had taken some very fat greenback inducements to get them there. For instance, pilots who had received $175 a month in our own armed services were being paid $600 a month or more by the Chinese. Radio specialists, mechanics, and all other ground-crew men had their incomes doubled or tripled. They were a part of the Chinese air force — in fact, they were almost all there was of China's air force. They were named the American Volunteer Group (the AVG), but none of these men were volunteers in a true sense. They were mercenaries. That was the only way China could get them, except for a very few idealists who had a genuine interest in China's cause. And that was the only way China could get them even six months before Pearl Harbor — and if any American can feel tremendously proud about that he probably won't have much company.

Bill Pawley gave me the general outline in strict confidence. I couldn't write about the AVG now, but some day there'd be a real story there for America. In three or four months the AVG would go into action from Kunming, China, with their three squadrons. When they did they would be the first American-trained and American-manned fighter squadrons to match skill and courage with the Japs. If they met the test they might go far toward saving China. If they failed it would be a disastrous blow to the white man's prestige in the Orient. Such failure would probably even be interpreted by the Japs as an invitation to clean up the sissified Americans. When I first talked with these boys I saw no sign that they had begun to understand the far-reaching and incalculable responsibilities that rested on their shoulders. They were typical devil-may-care Americans, keen and energetic and rather too cocky, who had been toughened in our armed services but had chafed at the discipline and wanted to get away from it all — and lay up a fat bankroll in the process. There were a few notable exceptions, but most of them were like that.

A great deal of tommyrot has been written about the AVG, some of it by members of the AVG.* Some members who never flew a plane in Burma posed as aces when they came home, and one or two of these made a killing in the magazines or around Hollywood. I've also seen at least one book advertised whose author, to my knowledge, was never in or near Burma although nine tenths of the AVG's fighting was done in Burma. It hardly seems surprising that so many fairy-tales about the AVG have found print, as this group of adventurers had a fair quota of amateur Baron Munchausens scattered through the ranks.

In Burma I never heard the American Volunteer Group called the "Flying Tigers." I never even heard that name until long after I had left Burma. I suspect that some clever Chinese up in Kunming had that inspiration. Anyway it's a wonderful name and a natural, given the tiger shark's teeth which they had painted under the noses of their P-40 Tomahawks. But in Burma they were simply the AVG or "those AVG's" or "those Americans."

That September I went to Toungoo to see how the AVG's were getting on with their training. I met a dark leather-faced man with piercing eyes and a fighter's jaw. He had the quiet way

* The one notable exception that I have seen to date is Olga Greenlaw's book *The Lady and the Tigers* — an authoritative, gusty, and true-to-life story of the AVG.

of a man who knows exactly what he's about. He had no military frills whatever. Although he himself was slightly deaf, he spoke with a soft Southern drawl. He seemed to be in his middle fifties, but was sturdy as an oak. The two things that I felt in him most sharply were thinking capacity and decision. This was Claire Chennault, U. S. Army, retired; the man who knew more about Japanese aviators and combat tactics than any other officer in the world. Chennault only had the rank of colonel then. The American command has since then given an example of fine judgment by promoting him to the rank of major general and naming him commander of the 14th U. S. air force in China. I believe every man who has ever fought under Chennault, and a vast number of others, will insist that he should wear the stars of a lieutenant general long before the war is over — at least that.

Joseph Alsop, who had quit a most profitable position as one of Washington's ablest columnists to get into the war before the U. S. A. was in it, had met Colonel Chennault in China. The man and his tough task were enough for Joe. He joined Chennault's staff as an aide. Joe Alsop had been born with a silver spoon in his mouth and had also accumulated an almost super-Harvard accent; not exactly an ideal preparation for making good with the AVG gang. But here was Joe, pouring out sweat and tearing around from daylight until long after dark and getting things done. I took my hat off to him. It was a cruel trick of chance that he was caught in Hong Kong and missed out on the triumph of Colonel Chennault and the AVG.

I found Colonel Chennault and others of his Old China Hands, like Skip Adaire and Harvey Greenlaw, somewhat concerned about the "volunteers." Every AVG candidate had been given $100 for spending money upon going aboard ship in California, yet a great many of them ended the voyage with big bar bills which they couldn't pay. Now, one of the first reactions of these young Americans was to bellyache about everything. They were spoiled, and most of them thought you should be able to go to war and still have all the luxuries. They grumbled about their food, which, after two years of covering the war, I knew was exceptionally good and, for the Orient, wonderful. They were really merely like most Americans when they go abroad for the first time — annoyed that the whole world isn't brought up on ham and eggs and hamburgers. But these recruits to China's air force did not seem to have any real conception of the seriousness of their job. One of the pilots was offered a chance to go to Singapore on a special mission. "Is there any extra money in it?" he asked, and then refused to go. When I heard things like that I was disgusted. Was much of young America like this? If so they needed a war.

A good many of the AVG boys had joined up for easy money, thinking they'd have planes twice as good as the Japs and they could shoot down an occasional $500 worth as easy as shooting gray squirrels. Colonel Chennault had quickly disillusioned them on that score. In his first lectures he told the American pilots that the Japs Zero had very great advantages over the P-40 Tomahawk. The Zero was much more maneuverable, could turn much faster, and could outclimb their Tomahawk by five hundred feet per minute at least. There was no "duck soup" in that set-up. So within the first month half a dozen pilots came to Chennault and asked to go home. Some of them admitted they hadn't thought they'd have any real fighting to do. They had had their fare paid all the way from the States. Now they wanted it paid back home again. They weren't bothered by any feeling of obligation to the hard-pressed Chinese or to the reputation of Americans. Colonel Chennault wisely let them go.

While I was at Toungoo someone came around with tickets for a benefit for the British bomber fund. Only a handful out of four hundred Americans bought tickets. "Any girls?" many of them asked. "No thanks." The tickets cost only sixty cents and these boys were the highest-paid air-force men anywhere in the world. They happened to be training on an RAF airdrome, the best in Burma, and living in wonderfully clean cement-floored barracks which had been built for the RAF. Even so, the vast majority of the AVG boys felt not the slightest sense of gratitude to the British, nor any sense of ordinary social obligation. Later on, most of them were heroes, but in little things many of them were also cads. During my stay in Toungoo I heard many things which made me ashamed of them as Americans; and they made it worse by ignorantly assuming they were unquestionably better fliers than the RAF.

"Stowe, you've seen something of the war in Europe," Colonel Chennault drawled. "Quite a good deal, I understand. Most of these boys here haven't yet got the idea. I wish you'd give them a little talk."

Well, that was one talk I was delighted to give. There were several things these thoughtless, over-cocky and intolerant young Americans obviously needed to be told; and a few of these things any war correspondent could rub home, by indirection. "You fellows think you're good, and maybe you are," I remember saying. "But as far as any newspaperman is concerned, you're not good until you've shown it in combat. Whether you're an American or a Hottentot doesn't make any difference to a reporter. It's only how you perform." I told them about what I had seen British pilots do in Greece — about the RAF's magnificent 80 Squadron — flying planes as outclassed as their Tomahawks would be against Jap Zeros, or more so. "You fellows may be hot stuff. I hope you are. But you can't possibly be better than some RAF fighter pilots I've known. Nobody in the war can be better than they were. All I hope is that you'll be as good — and if you are, every American will be proud of you." They listened with serious faces. But their salvation — and we all knew it — lay in the knowledge and personality of their commander. Colonel Chennault didn't give a damn whether they saluted properly, or at all. But Chennault knew his stuff and he had great powers of leadership. Any ordinary American army officer would have lost patience with the bellyaching, spoiled AVG boys, burned them up with curses, and lost all chance of controlling them in the first three weeks. Colonel Chennault not only knew what to teach them; he knew how to get the best out of men. He took a bunch of unruly and hard-headed young anarchists and made a truly great fighting team out of them. Everybody knows something about the incredible record of the AVG. Very few people have any conception of the impossible psychological start of a great portion of the AVG men. Having seen them all the way through, I am ready to insist that Major General Chennault is one of the few outstanding military leaders that America possesses anywhere in this war.

I must confess, however, that the AVG boys at their Toungoo training field almost convinced me that Chennault faced a hopeless task. As I took the train up to Mandalay, bound for China, I scratched down in my notebook: "Most of them are 100 per cent mercenaries . . . over-cocky and know-it-all . . . very critical and intolerant . . . a pretty lousy impression of America, if you judge by them . . . but a few are tops . . . and lots of good material, if they're given the works."

2

The bombs were falling all around the Strand Hotel when I heard an AVG pilot say: "Where in hell is a car? I've got to get out to the field." That sounded a lot different from Toungoo in September. This was the show-down at last. It was the first test of the AVG against the Japs — December 23, 1941 — and it was repeated on the same walloping scale on Christmas Day.

The moment I found Mac Macmillan and Smitty and Duke Hedman, fresh in from the fight, I knew everything was going to be all right. They were excited. Their faces were flushed. They were talking like mad. They were saying: "Just give me another crack at those dirty yellow bastards." They were cursing and they were happy. Everything was all right. I didn't know the score, but I knew already that America's honor had been saved. That meant the faith of General Chennault and the faith of the Chinese had been justified. It meant some Japanese airmen had learned that American pilots can fight. This, in all truth, was one of the happiest moments I've ever had as a war correspondent. Nobody talked about having made $500. (I never thereafter heard an AVG pilot so much as mention the size of his bonus bag.) The only thing they talked about was shooting down Japs. These American boys were still cocksure and still far too intolerant of other nationalities and foreign customs — that seems to be an inborn, almost universal, and almost incurable American fault. But they were fighters. You could see it. And they had forgotten all about the heavy odds against them. How they reveled in the fight!

In those two Christmas-time combats above Rangoon, one of the most significant chapters in the entire air war of the East was written by the AVG's machine guns. There was only a single American squadron, the 3rd AVG, at Mingaladon then; and the RAF's one squadron of Brewster Buffaloes. In these two combats, the first and most crucial, a maximum of 22 American and British planes took on somewhere between 100 and 130 Jap bombers and fighters. They fought against odds of more than five to one, and they seldom fought with odds of less than that at any time during the next three months. This, too, was the first time during this World War that American and British squadrons flew together and fought together in battle. Rangoon was the place where Yankee and British pilots blazed the trail toward complete collaboration of our two great English-speaking air forces and proved what was later established with such extraordinary success over Tunisia, Sicily, and Italy.

On December 23 and 25, 1941 the AVG was able to put a maximum of fourteen planes (only half a squadron) into the air. The Americans shot down thirty-six Jap planes, sixty per cent of them bombers. Against that score they lost five planes and two pilots. The percentage losses were: more than seven Jap planes for each AVG plane lost; approximately 190 Japanese flying personnel killed, against the death of two AVG fliers. This was accomplished by a single American squadron, equipped with outclassed P-40 Tomahawks; by pilots who had never faced an enemy's machine gun before. I do not think it can be described as anything less than a notable achievement, and as a most remarkable tribute to the training and leadership of General Chennault. Some of the men who did this were already saying: "I'd rather fight those yellow bastards than eat."

From then on, the only thing that curbed the AVG was lack of planes and a serious shortage of mechanics and repair men. Day after day the Tomahawks had the hell shot out of them. If these old-type P-40's had not been amazingly sturdy, like the aged Gladiators that the RAF's 80 squadron flew in Greece and Albania, they'd have been washed out very fast. Even so, the AVG could never get more than twelve or fourteen planes in the air at once at Rangoon, and sometimes they were down to eight or ten. By January 4 the shoestring was already that thin. Then the 3rd squadron was called back to Kunming for repairs, and Squadron Leader Jack Newkirk's 2nd squadron replaced it. Later on, the 1st squadron, led by Squadron Leader R. J. Sandell, took its turn. But the first heavy Jap blow was taken by

Number 3 under Squadron Leader Arvid E. Olsen, Jr. Once parts of the 2nd and 1st squadrons overlapped, but there was never more than one full AVG squadron at Mingaladon from beginning to end.

It was Scarsdale Jack Newkirk, tall and keen-faced and dynamic, who led the 2nd AVG boys on their first ground-strafing raids over Jap fields in Thailand. On their first try they bagged eight Jap fighters out of nine. When they went back for more, they ripped up another enemy base. That was the day that Alan Christman brought his plane home with twenty-seven holes in it and one tire shot through. They were deadly serious at their work, these high-spirited Americans from all corners of the U. S. A. It was fun to drop in at their operations tent and listen to their ragging and grouching. The ground-crew boys were a great lot, too. They lived in burning heat and dust and dirt, and they had to dive into slit trenches continually when the raids came. But their tails were always up, and the more wrecked Mingaladon's buildings became, the more the landscape seemed to match their appearance. Here, day after day, we heard authentic Americanese. That was music to the ears of one who had been with almost everybody else's army and had begun to wonder if ever he would get with Americans.

The ground-crew men and boys constituted the least publicized cog in the AVG machine, but one of the most extraordinary. Characteristically it was Jack Newkirk, a real leader with a sense of fairness, who first pointed out to me just how amazing a job the ground crews were doing. "Those boys are doing a wonderful job," Jack said. "We'd be sunk without them. They deserve a story if anyone around here does. Listen, they have guys doing things with a pair of pliers and a screwdriver that would be done in a machine shop back home. That's the truth, literally. We've got twenty-four men here doing work that it takes nearly 150 men to do at any army airfield in the U. S. A. They could never do it if it weren't for the older enlisted men who joined the AVG. Fellows like Jimmy Fox and Micky Mihalka — you know. Fellows who are old-time army sergeants or were chief gunners or chief machinist's mates in the navy. Ten out of our twenty-four are men like that. Watch Jimmy Fox. There never was a sweeter line chief on an airfield. And watch some of our crew chiefs. Those guys keep us in the air. I'm telling you."

Newkirk gave me some figures that were astonishing. The one AVG squadron at Mingaladon had only two radiomen, four armorers and twelve mechanics with which to try to keep thirty planes in condition. It simply couldn't be done at the unrelaxed tempo of air battles and damage, but they performed near-miracles for all that. At an army airfield at home, Jack pointed out, a pursuit squadron would have twenty-eight crew chiefs, one for each plane, plus fifty-six mechanics. The AVG had only twelve mechanics, including its line chief; four armorers instead of eighteen; two radiomen instead of ten. Jimmy Fox, of course, did the work of five mechanics in anybody's air force; and the inimitable Micky Mihalka, with some twenty years in the U. S. Navy behind him, was easily equivalent to four or five radiomen. I suppose that one or two ground crews on Guadalcanal may have performed similar prodigies. But certainly the AVG ground crew at Mingaladon did the greatest job of its kind that I have ever witnessed or heard of. If they were mercenaries they had long since forgotten it. In any case they earned five or ten times any amount they were paid. And like all the AVG men, at that crucial moment when these American fliers and ground crews were providing the only victorious news in the entire Pacific war, what they were worth to the Allied cause could not be computed in dollars and cents. They had saved the name of American aviators throughout the entire East; and for many weeks, with a little band of British Buffalo boys contributing all that their planes would let them, they alone saved Rangoon.

One day twenty-five Jap fighters strafed the field at Mingaladon. AVG mechanics were working on a shot-up P-40 that was badly needed. They dove into their trenches, then leapt back to their jobs the moment the last Zero had passed. They put the plane back into commission while the battle was being fought out over their heads. Things like this happened many times. The ground-crew boys simply took it as part of their job. They were the same boys who had bellyached so foolishly about food and almost everything else when they first reached Burma. Could it, by any chance, be that most Americans had need of hard living and dangerous days to discover the stuff that was in them?

On January 23 and 24 the AVG had two more big days above Rangoon. Led by Squadron Leader Sandy Sandell, one of the very few absolutely superlative fighter pilots I have known, the Americans shot down a confirmed total of thirty-seven Jap planes in two days against a loss of four of their own P-40's and one pilot killed. He was the 1st squadron's Flight Leader Louis Hoffman of San Diego, a brave man. Probably he was killed because of his thirty-two years. For fighting combat that is much too old. The reflexes can rarely stand the pace. But this score of thirty-seven Japs against four planes and one pilot was truly remarkable. Again the Japs had paid an excessive price. This time it was so excessive they never tried another full-scale daylight assault on Mingaladon until Pegu was falling and Rangoon was doomed. Nevertheless, in any war a price must be paid on both sides, and although they were comparatively few as yet, we felt this price in the gaps which gradually grew in the roll of the AVG.

I think that no loss was so great and irreplaceable as that of Sandy Sandell. Sandy was a born flier; a potential peer of Pat Pattle (Thomas Marmaduke St. John Pattle, squadron leader of RAF 80 squadron), who was the RAF's highest-scoring ace when he was shot down over Athens in the last air fight of the Greek war. Sandy reminded me of Pat, that South African flier among fliers and gentleman among gentlemen; the same knife-edged mind, the same quietness, and the same sureness. That was why I liked him so much from the first. The greatest flier I have ever known, and one of the finest men, was Pat Pattle. Sandy had many of his flying and fighting qualities and also his essential shyness. The way it happened was as if it had been in the cards all along.

There was another dogfight and the score was all our way. Sandy got two Japs before he was forced back to Mingaladon out of ammunition. A Jap chased him home and swooped on the field just after Sandy stepped out of his plane. There were no other Japs anywhere around. This one, for some reason of fury or suicidal madness, let go with his machine guns at some ground-crew men and then swerved around and dove straight at Sandy's P-40. He plunged his plane straight into the ground and demolished the tail of the Tomahawk. We had our pictures taken with Sandy beside the wreckage a few minutes later. Well, the Jap was crazy, we thought. He didn't get much for wiping himself out.

Ten days later George Burgard of the 1st Pursuit came over to the club before breakfast.

"Sandy's gone," said George in a voice that told everything.

"My God, no. It's impossible. Not Sandy!"

"Yes, Sandy. He had the new tail assembly on his plane. Took it up to test it out an hour and a half ago. He was doing a few rolls only a thousand feet up. The controls must have jammed, or something went wrong with the tail action. We saw him go into a spin. He went straight in. Couldn't get out of it. What a wonderful fellow! . . . Those stinking sons of bitches. We'll smear them for this. . . ."

So the Jap madman had much more than evened the score by his suicide dive. His revenge came ten days later, but it came.

3

A great many wild figures about the number of planes shot down by the AVG have been published. Undoubtedly a few of the least prominent and least combative of the Flying Tigers contributed to this. In any war zone it's naturally difficult to maintain an absolutely accurate score, especially where air battles are over jungles and open sea. Another confusing factor was Chungking's weakness for propaganda headlines, a fact which has long been known by all correspondents and diplomats in the East. Here is a typical example of how this works out.

As director of the organization (Central Aircraft Manufacturing Company) which had to pay out $500 per Jap plane destroyed, Bill Pawley had enlisted RAF officers and one or two others to keep the most accurate account possible of the AVG score in Burma. This score certainly leaned to the conservative side, but it was valuable as the official minimum count. Also the RAF totals served as the basis on which the fliers' bonuses were paid. The RAF's list credited "Buster" Keaton, a former football fullback from Colorado Springs, with shooting down the AVG's hundredth plane in Burma on February 3. Most of us were convinced the actual count was at least twenty more than that, but for five weeks even one hundred planes made a fine record. Two weeks before the RAF recognized the Mingaladon boys' bag as at the century mark, however, Chungking announced "that AVG operations against the Japanese air force since the outbreak of the Pacific war have accounted for 108 Jap planes in China." The catch in this Chinese press release lay in the words "in China." At least ninety per cent of AVG combats during this period had been in Burma, nowhere near Kunming. AVG pilots at Mingaladon had been fighting ten or twelve air battles to one fought by AVG units at Kunming, which was then a quiet sector where the Japs scarcely ever attacked. When the boys at Mingaladon read the Chungking story about 108 Jap planes downed "in China," they laughed out loud. They knew it was simply impossible; that an accurate Kunming count was certainly no more than one fourth of that figure, if that. But of course Chungking had beaten Rangoon to the world headlines with a round and impressive figure.*

Sandy had told about escorting Chinese bombers on a raid into northern Indo-China and at first missing the target by sixty miles because "Chinese bomber pilots made no allowance for wind drift. Jack and I went down four times and brought them back on the course. Then we gave it up." Sandy added: "We hit near Haiphong finally by sheer luck. The Jap ack-ack came up through heavy clouds, so the bombers dumped everything they had. I guess they hit the field, but we couldn't see anything at all." The Chungking propaganda release had said the bombers "unloaded twenty tons of bombs on the Japanese airfield and barracks, while fighters strafed grounded aircraft and Japanese troops." Sandy led that particular fighter escort, but reported he hadn't even been able to see the field. While we were discussing this with an

* Hanson W. Baldwin, authoritative military columnist of the *New York Times,* in a "Review of the Chinese Situation" of July 20, 1943, wrote: "These [Japanese] forays are rarely, if ever, intended to seize and hold more ground; they are forays and nothing more. . . . The Japanese suffer casualties in these operations and sometimes are badly mauled, *but the Chinese communiqués have too often magnified skirmishes into battles and the usual Japanese retirement to their original positions into major strategic 'retreats'!*

"Foreign military attachés who have tried to find some of the 'battles' reported in Chinese communiqués have sometimes been puzzled to discover that the area in which the 'battle' was reported was peaceful and quiet."

Mr. Baldwin's statement is obviously based upon the testimony of foreign military attachés who have served in China and have a long acquaintance with Chungking's communiqués.

American officer who worked closely with the Chinese, he remarked: "I don't think they mean to misrepresent. They just feel they'll lose face with you if they admit that they didn't do this or that, or can't do it." That seemed perfectly logical. It was difficult for Chungking to admit that the AVG, which was being paid with Chinese money after all, was doing virtually all of its fighting in Burma.

This same American army officer was later involved in the preparatory arrangements when it was decided that the AVG would function best by being reinstated in the United States armed forces. "The Chinese didn't make any protests about money arrangements," he said, "or against the AVG joining the American army, as we expected. The only thing they were most anxious about was to have the AVG stationed in China, so that the publicity announcements would come from Chungking." That statement seemed sufficiently revealing. Everyone in the Orient knows that the Chinese are experts at handling their war propaganda and that figures in communiqués must usually be read in that light.

In any case, it was perfectly clear at that time that the real record of the AVG was being hung up in Burma, and that Burma was the place where these fliers could best serve the interests of China. I talked with the pilots after every air battle in Rangoon and was in constant contact with RAF officers. I do not think that any score card, under the circumstances, could be strictly accurate. Nevertheless I checked as closely as possible and I'm confident that my unofficial score for the first six weeks of AVG fighting near Mingaladon is sufficiently reliable to be worth recording. Between December 23, 1941 and February 7, 1942 the AVG shot down approximately 130 Jap planes, of which at least half were bombers which averaged crews of eight men. In this same period the Americans lost 25 planes, six pilots killed in action, and one taken prisoner.

This meant that the Japs lost better than five planes for every P-40 they shot down. In these six weeks the Japanese personnel loss in air crews amounted to nearly 585 against a loss of 7 for the single AVG squadron which opposed them, usually with ten or twelve planes. By March 12, when I left Burma, I know the AVG's score had passed the 200 mark and the Japs' loss of personnel had reached approximately 850. At that time, incredible as it may seem, the Americans had lost only seven pilots killed in action, two who died in accidents, and three who were prisoners or missing. I believe this is one of the most extraordinary records made anywhere in the global war by any fighter-plane unit of such small size. It is one of the truly great aerial combat records of the entire war. The AVG's score would unquestionably have been larger still if many Jap planes had not fallen into deep jungles or the sea where their destruction could not be confirmed.

How did the AVG do it?

First and by all means most important, they did it on the specific instructions of General Claire Chennault. Pilots of the American Volunteer Group were the only Allied pilots, anywhere from Hawaii to Kunming, who were trained long and carefully in Japanese combat tactics and how they could defeat the Jap Zero plane. They were the only American or British pursuit-ship squadrons — and they were only three — who were instructed by a brilliant aviation commander who had actually studied Japanese air tactics at close hand for nearly four years. General Chennault had had three precious months in which to drill methods and warnings into their heads. Beyond that, and never to be overlooked or underestimated, they had had the full benefit of Chennault's brain — and it is a great strategic brain. All through the air battles of Burma the AVG had nothing but the first and oldest model P-40, the Tomahawk. They did not receive a single Kittyhawk, which is a much better plane, until their last Burma airfield was lost. But Chennault had shown them exactly how the old Tomahawk could be used to outsmart the Japs' Zero, and from the first combat they flew and fought as he had taught them to do.

"Get in and get out fast! Hit them and run! Never stay in and fight with a Zero. He can turn in on you, outmaneuver you every time. But you've got more fire power than he has. The Zero can outclimb you, but you can dive faster than he can and stick with him on the level. Give him all the fire power you can, then get out and come back on your own terms."

The whole tactic was punch, speed, and fluidity — and it worked like a charm. But pilots must know the things they shouldn't do, right from the start. Thanks to Chennault, the AVG boys knew that, and that, more than anything else, I suspect, explained why the old American Tomahawks made a much better showing in Burma than the British Hurricanes which came in toward the end. The RAF pilots hadn't had General Chennault's training and they had no officers with sufficient knowledge of Japanese aerial tactics to give it to them. Nor, as far as I know—and the record seems to substantiate it—had any other American fliers at that stage of the war. At any rate the AVG men who fought the battles and took the risks, and thrilled every American and Britisher who knew what they were up against, gave complete credit to their shrewd and trigger-minded chief, Chennault.

"It's the old man," the AVG boys would say. "Everything works out exactly like he said it would. The colonel—say, he's a wonder."

The one thing they regretted was that Chennault, their leader and their idol, couldn't be with them during the air battles of Mingaladon. But because he was commander and AVG headquarters were in Kunming, and also because his presence close to the Chinese authorities was absolutely essential, Chennault had to remain up in Yunnan—and his boys had to meet their test completely on their own. That was another remarkable feature of the AVG record. They took orders for strafing missions from the RAF command. Otherwise their squadron leader had to carry the entire responsibility alone. He had to handle administration and ground crews, problems of morale and everything else, yet fly and fight at the same time. In this respect the performances of Sandell, Newkirk, and Neale were especially notable; the more so because these three placed themselves among the best of the AVG's aces despite their heavy additional responsibilities.

The last air battles over Rangoon occurred on the last days of February and at the beginning of March. Pegu was falling. Rangoon was doomed. The Japs struck in full fury. In their final two battles before evacuating Mingaladon the AVG's 1st squadron (the boys who had as the emblem on their planes an apple with a snake coiled around it and inside Eve chasing Adam, as a symbol of The *First* Pursuit) shot down more than forty

Japs. But the enemy caught ten Blenheims on the ground the second day and destroyed them. The airfield was almost unusable. Ed Lussier, a radio operator from Plymouth, Massachusetts, described those battles as something terrific.

"Bob Neale was up all night between those fights," Lussier said. "That last fight Snuffy Smith got three and in two days Bob shot down six or seven. You should have seen Bob when he came in. His windshield and his instrument board were shot to hell. He had seventeen bullets through the tail of his P-40. Both his tires were flat — and he landed the damned thing safely. God knows how he did it. He's a wild man in the air, Bob is."

And Bob was the fellow who had once asked me if war correspondents got bonuses. Bob could ask me any questions he wanted from now on.

"The RAF had twelve Hurricanes up the first day," Snuffy Smith told me later. "They had ten Hurries up the second. They got six Japs Thursday and two on Friday, and lost one each day themselves. We never had more than eight P-40's up at one time those last two days, but our final score was twenty-three and twenty. We really raised hell with them — and didn't lose a man."

That, in large measure, seemed to be the difference between having been trained by General Chennault to fight Jap Zeros, and never having been trained to fight Zeros.

Both Ed Lussier and Snuffy said that what the AVG had most feared would happen at the end had happened. The RDF (radio direction finder, upon which the squadrons depended entirely for warnings of Jap raiders approaching) had been removed without either the AVG or the RAF being notified in advance. The RDF, it appeared, was under the control of the British army. In the "flap" to evacuate Rangoon somebody apparently forgot to give a warning, the first elemental protection, to the fliers who had saved Rangoon and its occupants for more than two months.

"They didn't give us any warning about the RDF," Lussier said. "Bob Neale heard about it accidentally about midnight on Friday. The RAF were already leaving. Forty of our AVG ground crew and seven British mechanics and armorers who worked with us were the last to leave Mingaladon. Bob and

Snuffy stayed until the trucks were loaded and had started up Prome Road. Then they flew to give us aerial protection as much as they could. Bob and Snuffy were the last to leave Mingaladon—and they both had forced landings outside Magwé. Snuffy smashed up his plane. Landed in a dry riverbed somewhere. Hell, no. He didn't get hurt. You can't hurt that kid."

For about two more weeks, until the middle of March, the AVG kept a skeleton force at Magwé, north of Prome, with the RAF's Hurricane squadron. Then a big Jap bombing force came in before nine o'clock one morning without any warning. Either the RAF's radio detection finder was out of order, or a fifth-columnist had cut the telephone line back to the field. At any rate, most of the British and American planes were caught and destroyed on the field. The British decided it wasn't any use staying there any longer. The RAF withdrew to Calcutta, where many of its officers and bombers had already gone. The last of the battered AVG flew up to Kunming. The air battle of Burma was over. All that remained was the score card of the Flying Tigers—for fighter squadrons all around the global war to shoot at. Six months before—remembering Pat Pattle,* Sammy Cooper, Hickey, Ripley, Hugh Flower, the Keg, Waldo Price-Owen, John Lancaster, and others—I had told them the best they could possibly do was to be as good as the RAF's 80 squadron. Well, they had done it—and nobly so. No wonder General Chennault was proud of his boys.

4

You live with them. You drink with them and laugh and pull legs and tell stories with them. Then the planes take off again—and one by one they are gone. In the cities and towns where they came from a very few remember. For millions of others life goes on. They have never known, and they will never know. This is one of the great rebukes that war points at the conscience of mankind. But mankind is busy raking in big wartime profits. Man-

* Squadron Leader Thomas Marmaduke St. John Pattle, twenty-six years old, of Grahamstown, South Africa, was killed in the RAF's Battle of Athens on April 20, 1941. He had been awarded Britain's DFC and bar. His confirmed total of enemy planes shot down was thirty-four, at the time of his death the highest in the RAF. He died fighting high above the Acropolis, a place which is worthy of the man.

kind is feeling cheerful because the stock markets are going up again. Mankind is having a terrible tough time without beefsteak. Mankind knows all about suffering because taxes have become so high. Mankind is haggling and clawing to keep its comforts. Mankind is reading the headlines and saying: "It's in the bag. Our boys are doing fine. Say, did you notice? A. T. & T. has gone up again." You live with them. You drink and laugh with them. The planes take off once more — and one by one they do not come back.

Somehow it would be easier if you and I and humankind could deserve them.

I remember the lean and chiseled face of Alan Christman the day that a Jap bullet put a groove down his cheek, and how he needed steadying words, and how he went back and got the hell shot out of his plane a second time, and how he went back the third and the fourth and the fifth time — and then no more.

I remember the devil-may-care ease of Scarsdale Jack Newkirk and his joking manner with his men and the sharp alertness of his eyes and the sudden click of his jaw. It was as if this whole air-battle business was a game. He lived it day and night. On the ground he fought the incompetence and rot of British Burma, but he worked *with* the British and he won their confidence. In the air he was a fast, daring, and ruthless fighter. He led his fliers and he led them well. His fearlessness was perhaps his only weakness. He loved to ground-strafe the Japs. Diving into a hail of bullets; the swooping thrust, the straightening out, the swerving up and away — he loved all that. One day, up in China, General Chennault had to send Jack and two others on a particularly dangerous ground-strafing mission. Jack led them in, as always. He went in hard and very low. The Japs had too many machine guns there. It was hard to lose a man like that.

Bob Little of Spokane was much like Newkirk; not so tall, but dark and lean and clean-jawed, with a bit of acid in his humor. He had the same thrust and speed, the same swift reflexes of a born fighter pilot. He was Bob Neale's close friend and stand-by, flashier than Neale and more swift-spoken, but awfully sure and level-headed in a fight. They were both from Washington State and both courted the same girl, and the girl, just before they sailed for Burma, married Bob Neale. But the two Bobs stuck together. They were the first AVG pilots I met. They were always together. They were friends and they flew together and shot down Japs together. In the 1st Pursuit Bob Little's score stuck close to Bob Neale's. They were with the last of the AVG to leave Rangoon and to leave Burma. Somewhere over China Bob Little made his last flight and fought his last fight. I didn't hear about it until long afterward. You say: "Too bad." But it's no good. You know what you mean, but it won't come out.

There's something about the face of Sandy Sandell and something about his sureness and his quickness. You watch him with the men and with the planes and you know he has it, the thing only a few airmen ever have. He's a flier and a leader. He's got that eloquent quietness in his manner, but there's never any lost motion in his actions or in his words. His eyes are very straight and there's a sudden warmth when he smiles. Later one of the few persons who know tells you some girl back home turned him down and he still cares. God, but some women can be fools — or maybe they can't help it. On his second day Sandy shot down two Japs. When a fight was on he was everywhere in the air. In no time he had a score of five or six. Then that damned insane Jap dove into the ground and smashed the tail off Sandy's plane, and the new tail wasn't fixed right — probably because every ground-crew mechanic was trying to do the work of four men. So Sandy is gone, and it's like losing Pat Pattle over Athens. Beyond doubt he would have been the ace of all the AVG's aces. We had felt it in the man and we had seen it in the making. Were we mistaken? In Washington more than a year later I asked General Chennault about Sandy and his answer did not surprise me. "Sandy was the greatest fighting pilot I have ever known," General Chennault said. If ever R. J. Sandell has a tombstone, those are the words which should be engraved upon it. In Westchester County, New York, they say an airfield will be named for Jack Newkirk — and rightly so. San Antonio is a city of warmhearted people. There is need and room in San Antonio for Sandell airfield. If ever it happens there is one, I hope there will always be fighter planes on that field. It would be better yet if an old P-40 Tomahawk could be placed there permanently.

But when I think of the AVG's and their Tomahawks I also think of one unknown RAF squadron and its Brewster Buffaloes, and of RAF bomber boys who lived with us at the golf club near Mingaladon. We used to drop in at the operations huts of the Buffaloes' B and A flights on the other side of the field and we saw their numbers dwindle and dwindle. The AVG had much sturdier and faster planes. The AVG fliers also had another tremendous advantage. They had an average of about 800 flying hours apiece when the battle for Rangoon began. The Buffalo boys, British and New Zealanders, were much younger — mostly kids — and few of them had chalked up as much as 200 flying hours. Many of them had only been in training for a year. But they had to fly the old and slow Buffalo suicide crates — against Jap Zeros. They could only hope to bag a few bombers. They hadn't a chance of shooting down a Zero — against a Zero they had no chance at all. The victories always belonged to the AVG. The Americans got most of the planes and all the glory, and $500 per Jap plane shot down besides. The RAF's Brewster squadron ran infinitely greater risks. Its pilots were mowed down, one after another after another, yet even a share of the glory was denied them. They, in all rectitude, were the greatest heroes of the air war in Burma. They never faltered. They were badly fed and badly treated. Some of their own higher commanders sometimes forgot that they even existed. Yet their courage and their patriotism were superlative. Finally, and in the greatness of their hearts, these British and New Zealand lads were above envy. "Those AVG's are bloody wonderful," they'd say to us countless times. Sometimes I wished that their American comrades in the air would say as much or more about them.

While thinking this I was equally at fault. The AVG's achievements made Rangoon's air battles primarily an American news story and it seemed to take most of my time to keep up with what our own pilots were doing. So I failed to keep a record of the RAF Buffalo boys who were killed. It was an almost unforgivable omission, as I realize hunting through my notebooks today. For the list of the dead from that brave little band of RAF pilots belongs on this page. They rarely, if ever, made a headline in the world's press. There will be no airfields named for them. They belong to the unknown and the unsung. Yet no airmen more truly gallant will fight and die anywhere in this World War.

There was one slender and sensitive-faced lad named Wigglesworth. He had something of the playing fields of Eton about him; that blooded strain and that peculiarly winning youthfulness which Britain's best so often has. He was not above calling on an Anglo-Indian family and I doubt if he had ever seen Eton. He was that unspoiled. The last time I saw Wiggy he was at the home of this Anglo-Indian family. They liked him tremendously. There was no resisting his gaiety and his charm. But that night he could scarcely joke, even with our host's lovely daughter.

"They have us Buffaloes over at Satellite now," Wiggy said. "Usually when a raid's on they don't even bother to inform us. We're just left there on the ground — easy eating for the Japs if they ever come our way. Sometimes Freddy smells something's up. He phones GHQ and somebody says: 'Oh. Hadn't you been informed?' So we're sent up half an hour late — just when we wouldn't have a ghost of a chance if the Japs pounced on us. Headquarters doesn't really care whether we're in the fights or not. But we have to stay there, twelve pilots with only five or six planes, from daylight till eight at night. They won't give any of us a leave. We're doing nothing where we are, but none of us can get a leave — and our chaps have had it steady since the first day. We can't do our best. We're too tired. So we're at Satellite all day, and they don't send us a bite of food. The RAF delivers a mess to the ground crews, but we pilots have to bring our own. For three weeks now we've been bringing our own sandwiches."

"My God, you mean to say they can't organize luncheon for you?"

"Oh, you know how it is," said Wiggy wearily. "I've got to where I don't give a damn. They treat us bloody awful, and expect us to fight our guts out. Now they've got a few Hurricanes, so we're forgotten. What the hell? They want us to stick there, even when our planes need overhauling. Well, we'll stick."

A few days later somebody said: "Did you hear about Wiggy? . . . Yes, he's gone. Crashed in a paddy-field near Pegu on Saturday. Bad engine, or something." At that time out of twelve original pilots in the Buffaloes' B flight only one remained who was able to fly. Four were in the hospital. The seven others were dead. For more than six weeks they had flown and fought in their suicide crates against hopeless odds, without chance of victory or glory. They were not so cocky and self-confident and dashing as the Americans. They were more tolerant and softer-spoken than most of the Americans. They were as brave and gallant as it is possible for men to be. After you knew them and had seen them go, they left with you a deeper meaning of humility and a new comprehension of greatness.

Among the RAF bomber pilots who lived at the club we saw a great deal of Hookey Russell, a South African; Sidney Lee, a blond and fine-looking Australian; and big Jim Purvis from Nova Scotia. Hookey took Gallagher on a raid over Bangkok and they had a close call when his Blenheim ran amok on landing at Mingaladon. With close-cropped sandy hair and a hatchet face, Hookey was a tight bundle of muscles, a first-class pilot who rode into bad luck, it seemed. But it wasn't bad luck. It was bad management somewhere in the RAF ground staff or command (which, incidentally, was not nearly up to the standard of the RAF I had known in England and Greece, I suspect because some left-over officers were first shunted out to dead-end Burma and Air Vice Marshal Stevenson, when he arrived, couldn't replace some of the dead wood). Hookey Russell was quiet and solid, the kind of flier you'd gladly entrust your life to any day. About a month after the first Blenheim squadron arrived, Hookey had to make an emergency landing at Toungoo. A tire burst, the ship nosed over, and as Hookey jumped out a terrific burst of flames caught him. Bill Clearihue, a Canadian sergeant, found him staggering blindly and pulled him away. From the waist up Hookey was terribly burned. Fortunately there was a hospital in Toungoo and the doctors managed to save both his life and his eyesight. As the Japs struck north the British had to fly Hookey out and to India on a stretcher. He had months of hospitalization ahead of him, and was out of the war. The thing which made O. D. and me plenty angry was this: Hookey's plane, which had gone bad on him at least twice on landing, had been performing missions steadily, but we were told that it had not been inspected once in six weeks' time. That was entirely in harmony with the RAF-Burma picture (not to be likened in any sense to the RAF in other theaters) . So it was probably true.

Sidney Lee of the RAAF had the splendidly proportioned physique, the wavy blond hair, and the flawless profile which would have fluttered millions of feminine hearts if ever he had taken to the screen. You could have forgiven him if he had been a lady-killer or rather numb above the collar. Instead, Lee was modest and intelligent, a gay and good companion, and brave. I wished afterward that I had known him much better and longer. He never told us much, not even about his most dangerous missions. He was interested in a long view of the war, and after the war. The club was a much more pleasant place because he was there. Eventually it was a crash landing and the Japs came down and machine-gunned the Blenheim as Lee and his gunner were getting out. They sent a bullet through Lee's jaw and fired the bomber. Lee stumbled and collapsed among the flames. Before his gunner could fight his way to him, our Australian friend was gone. I remember his smile and his handsome presence and his quiet unassuming comradeship. I wish his people knew of the esteem which he won among us.

There were many others. Some of them were Americans and some were British. Some were South Africans, Canadians, Australians, or New Zealanders. You knew the names of some. You knew only the nicknames or the faces, or the pranks and jokes of others. You lived with them and then they were gone. They lived together and worked together, all speaking a wide variety of accents of one single mother tongue. Of America or of the British Commonwealth, they fought together and they died together. Their story is one story — of costly compromises and costlier blindness on the part of each of their governments — of a common sacrifice, a common courage, and a common glory. One cannot rightly do less than remember them — together.

PART III — INDIA

Chapter IX

THE BUS THE JAPS MISSED

We stepped out of the closing phase of one nightmare into what had every appearance of being the opening scenes of another. Calcutta in late March 1942 was frighteningly like Rangoon in the previous December. It offered the same pageant of folly and futility, simply staged on a grander scale and at far greater risks. You looked and scarcely could believe your eyes. The province of Bengal — and some insisted most of India — was merely Burma all over again.

Across only three hundred miles of water to the east the Japanese had taken Prome, British troops were falling back toward Mandalay, and one of the most humiliating and inglorious defeats in Britain's history was moving rapidly to its bitter culmination. In Calcutta more than 500,000 natives had fled the city for fear of Jap bombs, fifty-seven Allied ships were tied up down the river, and the port itself was almost paralyzed — yet thousands of persons, including many British officers, thronged Calcutta's racetrack every afternoon. In the lobbies and diningrooms of the Great Eastern and Grand hotels hundreds of army and RAF officers drank, chatted, and stuffed themselves as if all was for the best in the best of all possible worlds. I arrived just in time to witness the Belvedere ball at the Grand. The place was jammed with laughing women in evening gowns and feverishly gay men in uniform. I met a number of pilots and other British officers and civilians whom I had known in Rangoon. They were having a fling and drinking to forget. Everybody was having a fling, but very few seemed to appreciate exactly how much there was to forget. Later I was taken to Calcutta's superexclusive Saturday Club. From its founding decades ago the Saturday Club had prided itself upon its snobbishness. It had never accepted a member without first examining his family tree and social status most minutely. The Saturday Club, with its splendid cuisine and perfect decorum, was approximately as far from the war as Easter Island or the South Pole. The 300 Club was more crowded and much more riotous.

In the Great Eastern lobby I met some of the same fine and steady Norwegian skippers who had been grounded in Rangoon for weeks. Now they were stranded in Calcutta — seventeen Norwegian ships that were urgently needed on the seas. Some of them had been here now for a month. The American skipper of the *Cape Cod,* also a refugee from Rangoon, had had his ship held up down the river for eight days before a space could be cleared for it at Calcutta's disorganized docks. The *Silver Star,* loaded with Lend-Lease materials, which included forty-nine airplanes, had been waiting for four weeks to be unloaded. There was a terrific shortage of dock workers. Rangoon all over again. The director of the central telegraph office had not arrived for work at ten forty in the morning. Where had I heard this song before?

At six o'clock Monday evening an air alarm startled Calcutta. In a few seconds scores of thousands of natives vanished from the streets. Ack-ack guns started popping. Rumor said a Jap reconnaissance plane was over the city. Next morning the papers announced it had merely been a practice alarm. I walked into Cuthbertson & Harper's shoe store. "We used to have forty-six employees here," explained the elderly Englishman who finally waited on me. "Yesterday we still had four workmen, but two of these left this morning after last night's alarm. The others all fled from here when Rangoon was being raided." So Calcutta was crippled for lack of labor just as Rangoon had been crippled, but no workers had been impounded by the government. An enormous amount of shipping and cargo was immobilized in the port. Calcutta's races and night clubs were doing a capacity business. After Burma, the food was marvelous. The luncheon menu at the Great Eastern offered a choice of twenty-six different dishes.

Everyone seemed to have converged on Calcutta. Dave Ladin, Wally Thorensen, and the other General Motors engineers had a fantastic story of their trek overland from Upper Burma. Betty Graham was in from Chungking. Two British seamen told about terrible bungling during the last days of Singapore. Raymond Clapper was in from Washington. An American sailor, whose ship was starting home without a single gun on it for protection against submarines, demanded: "What's the matter with these guys? We're going to lose this war if they don't wake up damned soon."

Here was the wife of a Rangoon bank executive. On the way out she had lived for three weeks in one room with four men at Mandalay. She and her husband had lost everything they owned. "Idiotic — these people that say we can't lose the war because we're British," exclaimed the Englishwoman. "It's just our appalling incompetence. At Shwebo we met seven British soldiers. They said they had deserted — not because they didn't want to fight, but because their officers were hopeless — didn't know their jobs. They said they had demanded that they be brought back to India and put under officers capable of leading them. Can you blame them? Out here we British have been lolling in complacency for years and years."

Now the Japanese would soon be in Akyab (the British were reported to be evacuating it) and less than three hundred air miles from Calcutta. What were Bengal's chances of resisting an invasion? What kind of prize did Bengal offer the Japs?

When you investigated that matter it was rather frightening. Three fifths of all India's production of war materials was located within two hundred miles of Calcutta — yet India was one of the chief sources of supply for Egypt and Syria as well as for China. The great Tata iron and steel mills — the largest in the British Empire and the only place where armored vehicles were made in India — stood only 180 miles west of Calcutta. Burnpur, with its Steel Corporation of Bengal plants, was also near Jamshedpur, the Tata center. All these mills were based on the coal mines of eastern Bihar. "If Calcutta is bombed at all heavily," an expert on India's industry confessed, "the native coal-miners and the armaments workers will quit work by the thousands. The Japs can practically stop India's production of guns, munitions, mortars, and armored vehicles by bombing the Calcutta region. Do you realize that there's only enough coal surplus to keep India's railroads running for three months? A few Jap raids will make the port of Calcutta useless — for complete lack of labor if for nothing else. So if the coal-miners run home to their country districts, the railroads simply can't begin to serve eastern India. Calcutta is a bottleneck with only one railroad line running out of it — and only one bridge that needs to be knocked out. The city's water supply can be cut easily. This eastern coastline has hundreds of miles of beaches. The Japs can land almost wherever they choose. India is wide open for invasion — especially if the Japs hit it in the next two or three months."

I learned that the Indian steel kings at Jamshedpur had demanded anti-aircraft guns for protection of their plants, but the British had none to give them. At that moment there were only forty-six ack-ack guns for all of Calcutta, a city with a population of 1,500,000 in its metropolitan area. The vital industries at Jamshedpur and Burnpur could only be adequately defended by fighter planes based at Asansol, but the Asansol field was so small that a large force of pursuit ships could not operate there. Aside from that, the RAF had only a few squadrons in all of India, and a United States air base was just being built with utmost speed near Karachi. The British were so extended on other fronts they could not protect India from the air alone, nor could combined Anglo-American squadrons do more than an uncertain job for many weeks yet.

So Bengal was the ripest plum the Japanese could get in India, and its native population of more than fifty millions was bitterly anti-British. Many uprisings and much terrorism had occurred in Bengal in the past. In fact, Bengal was reliably described as "the most disaffected area anywhere in India." Long-time residents of Calcutta admitted chaotic conditions were certain if the Japs moved westward from Akyab into Bengal. Fifth-columnism would be rampant, they said. The natives were "very soft" for Japanese propaganda, and the followers of Subhas Chandra Bose, the Indian pro-fascist, were particularly strong in Bengal, ready to welcome the Japs with open arms.

It was most difficult to discover any reassuring circumstances in India's exposed condition in the spring of 1942. A friend told me: "I spent the week-end with some British military intelligence officers who really know what's going on. They not only see how bad things are; they're very defeatist. Nothing can be done, they say. We might as well admit that Bengal is lost. I had to spend my time bucking them up. Well, Burma was worse than

Malaya, but Bengal is infinitely worse than Burma." It all seemed to crystallize in a great and golden invitation to the Japs. Small wonder that the British government was rushing Sir Stafford Cripps to India with some kind of last-minute proposal for dominion status. But what could Cripps do? Even if he said: "Stretch out your arms and walk!" India would still be a cripple suffering from both physical and mental impediments of many years' malignancy.

2

Of course there was only a handful of British troops in India, and the best and most dependable Indian divisions had been sent to Burma, Malaya, Ethiopia, Palestine, Iran, and Egypt. The 4th Indian division, fighting in Libya, had suffered hundred-per-cent casualties (some 15,000 men). Large bodies of Indian troops remained at home, but it was said there was much more nationalism and discontent among them than had been the case in 1914–18. Indian officers (and splendid officers most of them are) were much dissatisfied because the pay and allowances of British officers of equal rank exceeded their own by approximately forty per cent. This inequality of long standing was a blow to morale and did not increase confidence in the outcome if the Japanese struck India with a strong invading force. Whatever happened, Calcutta and Bengal were most dangerously exposed and ripe for disintegration. An American consular official asked the chief secretary of the Bengal government what plans had been made for the evacuation of Calcutta (a most complicated problem owing to the one railroad bridge and the bottleneck terrain). "Oh, we don't like to think about that sort of thing," said the chief secretary of Bengal.

I learned a good deal about the palsy of civil government in India when, immediately upon my arrival, I tried to obtain authorization to file press messages collect. This was a purely routine matter. I had had press-collect privileges in Burma for more than six months, and all the dispatches I had sent in that period had been relayed through India. My name was registered at the cable and wireless company's main office in Bombay. I had also been a war correspondent officially accredited to the British forces for months now. In addition the Calcutta representative of the British Ministry of Information had vouched for me personally to the local director of Post and Telegraph. I had several messages about Burma which required urgent filing. Despite all these circumstances it required exactly fourteen days for me to obtain a "press collect" card in India. In that period the British army press-relations chief in Calcutta sent three telegrams to New Delhi on the subject, and two more telegrams to Bombay. I did not finally get the authorization until after I had reached New Delhi, where another press major remarked: "It's terrible, what's happened to you." In day-by-day detail the procedure was simply fantastic, far exceeding anything I have ever encountered anywhere else in the world. But when I told the story to an American of long residence in India, he replied without the slightest surprise:

"What's happened in your case happens in regard to everything in India. Yours isn't an exception, Stowe. It's merely the rule. Here in India every little matter has to be referred to Delhi, no matter what it is. Nothing can be decided outside of New Delhi. Usually it takes weeks to get a decision on a very minor question. Did you ever see the India Civil Service's two big volumes on procedure and etiquette? Well, you ought to read them some day. Hundreds of pages — mostly devoted to instructions on how *not* to do things."

Well, I had seen plenty of the India Civil Service's bureaucracy in Burma, and Burma had only been detached from British India by law in 1937. In spirit and method, I now discovered, Burma had never been detached from India.

On the train out of Calcutta a few days later I met a Britisher who was going to New Delhi on a business mission. He said, "My chief told me to stay there until I get this through, even if it takes three months." He laughed as if a three months' delay would be quite normal. In the morning I heard this envoy of commercial affairs shout: "Bearer!" I missed what he said to his Indian servant, but I saw the servant stoop down and pull the master's bag from beneath the master's chair. The servant took out a pair of spectacles, which the Britisher could have got by bending over, and handed them to his master. That, in a single flash, was what had happened to the British in India. You shouted: "Bearer!" because you had become too lazy to move and had formed the habit of showing your authority.

Were the British capable of defending India? Was India able to defend or help defend itself?

An affirmative answer was very dubious indeed, just as the answer had already been proved negative in Burma. India was lacking in many vital industries which were absolutely essential if she was to be self-supporting in war. The thousands of miles of sea voyage made it impossible to rush many necessary weapons to India in time to gird the country against an early Japanese attack. But Indian leaders and capitalists had been clamoring for these self-supporting industries for years — and for years the British government and British capitalists had blocked them. The critical lack of airplane factories in India — a lack which now threatened the Allied cause with the loss of both India and China — existed because of London's policy. British big business and finance had almost contrived to cut the jugular veins of the British Empire. It was enlightening, on March 25, to find such a time-serving voice of imperialism as the *Calcutta Statesman* suddenly calling spades by their right name in unfamiliar and unprecedented outspokenness.

"The future is indeed all-important," said the *Statesman*. "But what is of evil omen is the determination of the men who have failed to burke all responsibility for their failure and to retain power in their incompetent hands. They resisted from the outset all suggestions that the air arm should be developed on a large scale, that aircraft industries should be established, that new heavy industries should be created, and that power should be transferred from London to India; that a national government which should be a working model of a future federal government should be set up, and that the Indians should be rallied to the defense of their own country and armed for that defense. In September, 1939, the Defense Secretary of the Council of State [India's] refused a plane production proposal because it would mean 'an industrial revolution of the kind the world has never seen.'

"Not until June, 1940," continued the *Statesman*, "was there the beginning of a move to consider the possibility of assembling aircraft in India. When the Eastern Group Supply Council was formed there was, despite all warnings, no provision made for the possibility of Japan entering the war. . . . Ever since we've been told that India's war effort left nothing to be desired; that everything needed was being turned out on an ever-growing scale. Now we are told there is a desperate shortage of small arms and much else. We need indeed a political settlement. But above everything else we need a governmental machine more suited to waging the war — a clean sweep of the present bureaucratic methods."

That was a British judgment from a British editor most intimately informed about India. On the same day an Indian nationalist newspaper, the *Allahabad Leader,* declared: "India is militarily weak today, not because the authorities of the Defense department abided by the wishes of the Indian legislature, but because they did not. . . . Japan owes her victories on the Far Eastern front to a large extent to her supremacy in the air. The Indian legislature demanded that the government should take steps to establish an air industry in India. The government ignored the demand. . . . There is no lack of recruits for the army, but lack of equipment. Did not the legislature again and again say 'Industrialise or perish!'?"

In all of India, when Japan struck at the British Empire and the Philippines, there was only one small aircraft factory and that had been created — despite great obstructionism — through the initiative of an American. In December 1939 William D. Pawley signed a contract with some Indian capitalists to build this plant. From Manila Pawley telegraphed the British commander-in-chief (GOC) in India saying he would deliver planes nine months from the date that New Delhi gave its authorization for construction of the factory. Receiving no answer, Pawley cabled again from Hong Kong. Then he went to Calcutta and telegraphed again. Eventually, by ordinary post, he received a brief letter stating that the matter had been referred to the Commerce Department for its consideration. Later one British member of the New Delhi government described the idea as "fantastic." When Pawley finally got an appointment, the official concerned had forgotten to bring his files on the subject. Pawley could make no progress on his plan until after France had fallen. In the end this one plant was only a drop in the bucket. It couldn't begin to furnish India with the hundreds of fighter and bomber planes of latest design that were now so urgently needed.*

Prominent Indians more than confirmed the statements in the *Calcutta Statesman*. One of them told me: "During all these years the British government has deliberately prevented us from building up our industries. Although we wanted them for defense purposes, still they prevented it. We need especially automobile, airplane, and shipbuilding industries. We had the capital. We didn't need any outside money. We had the trained personnel and were prepared to start, but the British government always came in the way. Their policy was not to start industries which would lead to competition between British and Indian industry after the war. One British delegate at the Eastern Group conference said this frankly. This attitude has provoked great dissatisfaction among our capitalists and scientists, who are not politicians. Indian scientists' inventions have not been utilized here. They've been suppressed here and used abroad — and we get no benefit from them. But what we might have done two or two and one half years ago to prepare the country to defend itself cannot be done effectively now. India today is hardly defended. She has neither the planes nor the weapons nor the mechanized troops available. Today the problem is: what in thunder are we to do about it? How can we possibly put an adequate defense into effect in the short time at our disposal?"

* A pamphlet entitled *India's Third Year of the War,* distributed by the British Information Services in New York City in the early summer of 1943, says: "In 1941 a factory in India turned out its first aeroplane and thus marked the beginnings of an aircraft industry in India. The factory was a private enterprise but the Government of India and the Mysore government owned a large proportion of the shares. . . . Financial risks and administrative complications involved in the commercial operation of the company were found to be such that during the past year it was decided that the factory must be operated as a Government concern for the period of the war at least. The founder of the company and his associates accepted an offer from the Government for the purchase of their interests. . . . The company was engaged in the manufacture of aircraft to the order of the Government of India. This programme has been modified and tapered off in such a way as to give absolute priority to servicing. . . . During the last twelve months many aircraft have been repaired in the factory."

It would be interesting to know whether William D. Pawley, the American who founded India's first (and as yet only) aircraft plant, has obtained the right to resume private manufacturing operations in India after the war, if he so desires.

To all intents and purposes British imperialism had cut its own throat in India. Already the British were welcoming United States pilots and crews and American Flying Fortresses in Karachi and New Delhi. The British had only a handful of bombers and nothing comparable to the Fortresses in all India. Because the British government had refused to let Indians provide their country with a large and powerful aviation industry the whole Far Eastern war was denuded of Allied planes. Because of that particularly blind piece of imperialism the British now had to depend chiefly upon American bombers to keep Japanese ships away from India's shores. Raids upon Jap shipping in the Andaman Islands were being made by Americans. Even as I write, nearly eighteen months later, it is the 10th U. S. air force that is still bombing enemy bases all over Burma from bases in India. It did not have to be that way, and Americans did not ask for it to be that way. When I was in Calcutta and New Delhi, I used to wonder — and I still wonder — whether American pilots flying *from* Indian bases will impress Washington sufficiently so that the United States government will take a stand for the freedom of India after the war? I knew some of our fliers who died in India — and helped save India. Did they die for the preservation of the old British imperialism in India? They saw that the system could scarcely defend itself and had been rendered almost defenseless by those who ran the system. Was it a system that could possibly be made compatible with the Four Freedoms, or even one or two of them? Would the President of the United States and the American government conveniently remain mute about the future of India? I had only seen a little bit of India then, but enough to wonder.

3

Perhaps one of the most extraordinary things about India in the spring of 1942 was this. An outsider did not need to inquire what was wrong in India. All he needed to do was talk to British subjects and read the British-Indian press. The British themselves were so terribly concerned about the very grave and imminent peril to India that they had lost all pretense. Day after day remarkable self-portraits appeared in the British-edited newspapers. The *Bombay Standard* published a letter signed by "An Old Woman" in which this, in part, is what she said:

"In the past the man who was the life of the party, the good actor, the potential ADC, was considered the perfect type [for a British officer in the Indian army]. The ruthless man, however good at his job, was often dubbed a 'tactless fellow, he rubs people the wrong way.'" The writer urged that all officers over forty-five be given physical examinations by an impartial medical board. "It would be interesting to know the age and physical condition of all officers above the rank of acting lieutenant colonel . . . to know for how many years they have moved from office to office and job to job in Delhi and Simla; to know just how long it is since they had active experience of the matters they are supposed to control . . . and how much longer the physically unfit and the failures will be nursed." Commenting on the letter, the *Standard's* columnist wrote: "Is it not a fact that so many in the higher ranks of the army stick with the tenacity of leeches to their positions in spite of their obvious inability to live up to modern conditions? Social pull, indirect influence, family connections, nepotism, the old school tie — these place unsuitable men in responsible positions. These keep them there in spite of their ludicrous bunglings; these keep them there with exorbitant emoluments until at long last they are gracious enough to retire on a pension. By which time, time and opportunities for younger men with active experience are frittered away. Is it surprising that an old lady has seen it necessary to exhort the army in India to take thought on these matters? That an old lady should ask for more ruthlessness, energy and more drive? Surely conditions are grievously wrong when such things come to pass."

So in this, too, India was merely a duplicate of Burma on a much greater scale.

A few days later I chatted with an Indian girl who was manicuring my hands. This was in New Delhi. The manicurist had just been in the adjoining restaurant. "There's a British captain and six lieutenants in there. They've been sitting there drinking from luncheon until tea-time," she said indignantly. "They asked me to join them. I said: 'Some of us have work to do.' The captain said: 'So have we, but you must relax now and then, you know.' I told him: 'If you drank less and worked more maybe we wouldn't lose so many battles.' They just laughed. One of the lieutenants said: 'Oh, a little vixen!' Really, how can you expect people like that to keep the Japanese out of India?"

That same week General Molesworth, deputy chief of the British India General Staff, addressed the Delhi Rotary club. "This is the time at which we've got to put everything aside — political, communal, racial, or social squabbles," the general said. "We cannot arm everyone. On the other hand we can do a great deal to educate the masses to give the Japs a great deal of trouble. This must be done by people like you. People can work in bands and give trouble and delay and destroy the invaders. It may be there is no proper lead from the top and no proper leadership down below. Still, I feel the Japanese invasion can be beaten if we educate the people on the lines of 'They shall not pass' psychology. It can only be done by the intelligentsia working definitely shoulder to shoulder with the peasant. . . . We have to look both ways and from my own point of view the situation is gloomy — and I say gloomy because the more gloomy it is, the more the Commonwealth will rise to deal with it."

The general seemed to have an idea when he spoke about working shoulder to shoulder. But what was it the olive-skinned little manicurist had said? "There's a young American named Campbell. He's made many friends among the Indians. But the English people here say: 'Oh he's always going around with the Indians!' That's supposed to be a term of derogation, you know." . . . Now at the fifty-ninth minute of the eleventh hour a British staff general urgently recommended that the British work "shoulder to shoulder" with the Indians and "educate the masses" for resistance.

There was a sharp contrast — indeed, a complete contradiction — between General Molesworth's proffered solution and what one saw about one every day in India. In the most revealing columns of the *Calcutta Statesman* I read letters from anti-fascist Hindus. One declared it was sheer stupidity to claim there was no organized fifth column in India. "Those who can read facts know that certain determined political groups are feverishly active setting the stage for the final catastrophe. We have misgivings that in certain areas ARP and other organizations are being used for this purpose. It is high time that the authorities shook off their stupid complacency. There is something very rotten with the official administration of things. They simply won't understand the political implications of this war They are still suspicious of the genuine anti-fascists. We demand the removal of such men from positions of authority. The sands are fast running through the glass." Another letter from an Indian read: "As revealed by your article all is not well in Bengal. May I inform you that things are not well even elsewhere. In the streets, shops, cinema halls and even in educational circles I find a very strong pro-Japanese feeling. People are anti-British to the point of helping the enemy. If something is not immediately done to 'pump' this docile cynically indifferent public, all seems lost to me."

But the political implications of the war had an aspect entirely different for most Indians from what they had for General Molesworth and the British Raj. The *Amrita Bazar Patrika* expressed this very succinctly when it said: "The British ruling classes do not define their aims either because they have no clear idea about a new world order, or because the coming of a new order would challenge their vested interests or positions of privilege." How far did some of these privileges go? I was talking one day with an American army colonel who had visited the Indian coal mines. "Did you know those coal mines are paying about forty per cent dividends to the British shareholders?" he asked. "Well, I saw Indian women down there — some of them pregnant women — carrying baskets of coal on their heads all day. Do you know what they get paid? Four annas a day — just about *four American cents a day!* Do you think those people are going to be much worried about the Japs taking over India? Well, that's what we're up against."

Sometimes I met Indians who spoke bitterly of the "master folk." They were not talking about Hitler and his *Herrenvolk*. They were referring to those near at hand who treated almost all dark-skinned people as "bearers" and who owed their position and wealth to the exploitation of India's riches and her people. In Great Britain, too, the voices of intelligent and humanitarian men were still raised in favor of justice and a new deal for India; voices which found echo in such journals as the *Manchester Guardian* and the *New Statesman*. But they had little influence beyond recurrent protests, like the occasional murmur of an uneasy conscience, which, in truth, they symbolized. Britain

— and now to her great danger — still had not produced a Harriet Beecher Stowe for India. Yet for more than two centuries the system had eaten into the minds and souls of the "victors," slowly but devastatingly, as Burma had already revealed when the mask fell and the acquisitive masquerade ended. I have never seen such a clear and concise statement of how this happens as that given, with remarkable objectivity, by Jawaharlal Nehru in his autobiography, *Toward Freedom*. If Britishers or Americans would understand the bankruptcy of British rule in India or the revolution which this rule has engendered they cannot ignore these words of Nehru:

"The British regime in India has pushed up into prominence the official class, both British and Indian, and this class is most singularly dull and narrow-minded. Even a bright young Englishman on coming out to India will soon relapse into a kind of intellectual and cultural torpor and will get cut off from all live ideas and movements. . . . For this gradual deterioration of mind he will blame India, curse the climate and generally anathematize the tribe of agitators who add to his troubles, *not realizing that the cause of intellectual and cultural decay lies in the hidebound bureaucratic and despotic system of government which flourishes in India and of which he is a tiny part.*" (Italics mine.)

Was this, by any chance, an exaggeration? I could not dismiss it as such. It was an extraordinarily accurate portrayal of what I had just seen for many months in Burma and was now seeing all about me in the paralytic bureaucracy of India. This was what caused the *Calcutta Statesman* to demand "a clean sweep of bureaucratic methods." This was why "an Old Woman" insisted the Colonel Blimps of the Indian army should be thrown out before it was too late. This was why a fine New Zealand squadron leader, whom I met in the Allahabad Club, said to me: "I wish I could hop a boat for the United States or Australia. I'd like to get where I can do something. In Rangoon and here in India it's the same thing — just bloody inefficiency. I'm fed up to the teeth. What's the use? I want to get with people that are really interested in fighting this war."

I disagreed with the New Zealand pilot on that last point. Undoubtedly there were plenty of Britishers in India who were interested in fighting this war. For one thing, they had the most comfortable livelihoods imaginable at stake. But how many of them were mentally and morally equipped to fight this war? How many of these rulers of India were free from "torpor" and "decay"? If Americans or Frenchmen or Spaniards had been in India since the early 1600's, was it likely that the present inheritors of their age-old privileges would be much different today from the British occupants of a creaking imperialistic stagecoach? In an effort to be fair, this question had to be asked. It did not change the fact, however, that the system had made the product and that the product in general was woefully lacking in capacity to ward off the challenge of a very much younger and far more explosive Japanese imperialism. But one more question remained.

If, by some mercy of providence, India could yet be saved from the Japanese, *could the British in India still be saved from themselves?* Winston Churchill and Britain's Tories would insist that of course this was possible — or, perhaps more likely, they would insist that it simply wasn't necessary; the question did not exist. But every high American officer, either military or other, whom I met in India in these spring days of 1942 understood very clearly that the question did exist. That was the essence of the reason why no one dared say that India could be held against an early Japanese invasion — because no one quite dared hope that the British in India could be saved from themselves. This, too, was the essence of General Molesworth's fears when he made the astonishingly frank public confession: "It may be there is no proper lead from the top. . . . Still, I feel the Japanese invasion can be beaten *if* we educate the people on the lines of 'They shall not pass' psychology." No greater "if" had ever been dropped into the seething and antagonistic caldron of India's political awakening. The hour was very late indeed for the British Raj to become concerned about the "education" of India's 389,000,000 people. General Molesworth obviously was tormented by the realization that the British had probably waited much too long.

4

The façade of British India is indeed imposing, but what peeps out through the chinks and fissures of this grandiose façade completely belies the seeming quality of its marble.

Armaments, coal, gasoline, and railroads were four of the great vulnerable spots in India's armor (aside from the truly perilous psychological weakness). I had learned that India only had sufficient coal to keep her railroads operating for three months and also only a three months' supply of gasoline. If the Japanese successively bombed Calcutta's great industrial area, production of most arms industries and of coal would be cut down to a trickle. What would India do for gasoline, and where would she get it? I discussed these problems at length in Calcutta with George Merrill and Clayton Lane of the United States Consulate, and Lane most generously took time to put me in contact with an oil executive who had the facts at his fingertips. Eighty per cent of India's gasoline had come from Burma, and this supply was now cut off. Hereafter India would have to obtain virtually all of her petrol from the Anglo-Iranian refineries at Abadan in the Persian Gulf — but that would depend upon how many oil tankers the hard-pressed Allies could now divert to India.

"If the Japs make the east-coast ports of Calcutta, Madras, and Cocanada untenable," the oil man said, "then oil will have to be shipped to Bombay and delivered across India by rail. No, I don't know how the Indian railroads can handle that much more traffic. They're in a terrible jam as things are."

"And if the coal mines' production is cut down to one fourth or one fifth?" I asked.

"If that happens, God knows what India will do for oil in another three months," admitted the oil man. "Even if Calcutta and Madras remain open, it will now take a seven weeks' round trip to ship petrol from the Persian Gulf to the east coast of India. Losing Burma means that twice as many tankers will be needed for India. So far the over-all production of petrol has been reduced forty per cent. If we have to depend on the railroads, rationing will have to be very drastic. It may be that we'll come to no petrol for non-military purposes. In any case, with the Dutch Indies also gone, the only place the Allies can now get hundred-octane for the air forces here is Abadan. It's going to be a hell of a job to fly hundred-octane into China and keep India supplied as well."

And what about the functioning of India's railroads, upon

which the defensive strength of all India might soon depend? I found an illuminating letter in the columns of my helpful friend, the *Calcutta Statesman.*

"During my brief connection with the [Indian government's] Supply Department," the writer said, "I found the most appalling inefficiency, muddle, circumlocution and haphazardness. . . . I called on the Controller of Supplies at Lahore and mentioned the name of the firm I was going to visit. He said I need not waste my time as he knew that firm had an immense organization and could turn out 1,000 ambulance stretchers a day. The manager of the firm told me their maximum capacity was 100 a day — then he came down to 50 a day.

"It is this love of employing India Civil Service and provincial civil service men on business jobs that is wasting half the money and more than half the time of the nation. You would be astounded if I gave you details of the contortions through which a letter passes when it reaches the Supply Department. It takes an average of ten days to send a reply. . . . There is a chronic shortage of railroad wagons and daily appeals from the railways to the public to travel less and to clear wagons without loss of time. Yet it will be a surprise to many that Sunday is still sacrosanct in the goods section; that if a wagon reaches its destination on a Saturday it need not be cleared till the following Tuesday; that *the railroads are moving wagons at the average speed of forty miles per twenty-four hours* [my italics] and that wagons are still being sealed with only twenty per cent load of their capacity — i.e. a 600-maund wagon can be sealed with a load of only 120 maunds and hauled without carrying any other load. Yet I am told that the railroad problems are being efficiently handled by the Indian Railroad Board."

So if the Japs knocked out Calcutta and Madras, it scarcely seemed that the railroads of India could possibly keep the rest of India in the war for a very long time. Sometimes I used to wonder what the letters must be like that the *Statesman's* editor decided were too hot to print. It would surely have been instructive if one had the privilege of going through his wastepaper basket.

On March 26 he wrote: "In this hour when only truth will serve let us say also that if Indians were incapable of now uniting to take and guard their freedom, *we do not believe that it would be in the power of Britain to keep the enemy from coming in* [italics mine], or to hold India in trust for a period in the hope that some unity would be produced at a later date. *On the basis of Britain's war India is as good as lost.* She must make it her war and with Britain aiding her to the utmost she must save herself."

This was the psychology, the morale, and the conditions when Sir Stafford Cripps arrived in March 1942 with a British Draft Declaration for the establishment of "Indian Union" — an offer which both statesmanship and circumstance dictated should have been made, at the latest, in November 1939.

On the basis of Burma as I experienced it and India as I found it, the fact is irrefutable that the Allies control India today merely by a fluke, and little more. Allied representatives of important standing confessed to me in the spring of 1942 that 100,000 Japanese troops, if landed any time in the next few months, would "certainly take two thirds of India" without serious trouble. About all that the British could rely on was Sir Stafford Cripps, a prayer, and the good Lord. Or that the Japanese would strike farther toward Australia. By some incredible good fortune the Japs obliged and proceeded to get themselves bogged down in New Guinea and the Solomon Islands. This, I believe, was the first great strategic error of the Japanese in this war — and also their fatal error. To anyone familiar with the disintegration, paralysis, and weakness of Burma and India it remains incomprehensible that the Japanese failed to concentrate everything they had upon India in the summer of 1942.

In the South Pacific the Japanese could have safely contented themselves with a line from Timor north through the Celebes to the Philippines. Neither the Americans under MacArthur nor the Australians were in any condition to challenge that South Pacific line until 1943. Nothing in New Guinea or the Solomons was worth more than a counterfeit dollar compared to the vast resources, riches, and solid land base of India. In India the Japanese would gain two of the world's greatest seaports and possibly three. They would take over scores of air bases. They would have the inflamed masses of India's hundreds of millions with them at the start. Most important of all, for the first time they would have added huge steel and arms factories to their Asiatic empire — potentially one of the greatest sources of industrial development in the entire East.

It remains a mystery why Tokyo did not abandon the southern Pacific islands and Australia to go all-out against India. Had the Japs over-extended themselves? It scarcely seems they were short of ships, for they had seized roughly one million tons of shipping or more in their southward blitz. Were they short of airplanes? At that stage this, too, seems unlikely, for only a few hundred bombers and fighters would have sufficed to support an invading army along the Indian coast. The Japanese had everything in their favor and the plum overripe on the bough, yet they failed to strike. It was nothing less than a colossal and fatal error. At the very least, given the circumstances, the Japanese high command should have tried. Because the Japs failed to invade India in 1942, when that land lay exposed and its victors were clearly "the victims of their conquest," our war in the Far East will be several years shorter than it would have been. To this great and inestimable degree we are much more fortunate than we deserve.

Will India also be more fortunate tomorrow?

That's another question — and another story.

Chapter X

INDEPENDENCE? – TOO LATE AND TOO LITTLE

The fundamental fact of the world today as it is reshaping India and other countries is the conflict between the peoples and the "master folks," which is bound to solidify the people.

The Hindustan Standard

The Indians may be wrong, but they hate the devil they know more than the devil they don't know.

Mahatma Gandhi to Eve Curie

Japan has got a very powerful case based upon fundamental realities. She was quite right in acting with the object of creating peace and order in Manchuria and defending herself against the continual aggression of vigorous Chinese nationalism. Our whole policy in India, our whole policy in Egypt stand condemned if we condemn Japan.

Leopold S. Amery, present Secretary of State for India (February 27, 1933)

During these two and one-half years Britain has left nothing undone to anger or alienate the Indian people — especially in regard to Amery."

It was difficult for me to determine which was most exceptional about Jawaharlal Nehru: his striking features, the quality of his mind, or his extraordinary lack of bitterness. After more than eight years of imprisonment by the British, after centuries of exploitation of his country and centuries of humiliation of his people, he could discuss the British in India with no more emotion or resentment than you or I would discuss the ancient Egyptians. I listened to Nehru's softly modulated and ever reasonable voice and thought how differently we Americans react to British foibles or failings; how often we let something British rub us the wrong way and how many of us, knowing extremely little about the British, can scarcely discuss them without self-righteousness or recrimination. This slender yet resolute man, one of the two greatest leaders of Nationalist India, possesses two things (I thought) which America's melting-pot and the American climate seldom produce — objectivity and the capacity for compassion.

Betty Graham and I had already spent most of a day at Anand Bhawan, the spacious Nehru family mansion in Allahabad. We came as strangers but were received as friends, quite as if we had been expected all along for the marriage of Indira Nehru two days later. On the previous day Eve Curie had been a guest in this household, where aunts, nieces, and other kinfolk were already weaving intricate "jewelry" of tiny flowers for the wedding, which would be attended by more than a thousand persons. Because of the moral stature of Indira's father her wedding had already become a kind of public celebration of faith in the Indian Nationalist movement. Despite the manifold domestic activities, Nehru gave us several hours at a moment when he must most have longed for the company and privacy of his family. It was less than four months since he had last been released from jail, and it might not be many months before the British Raj would place him behind bars again. There was no hint of this in his manner.

As we conversed in that airy living-room of Anand Bhawan, I studied one of the most memorable faces I have ever seen. Jawaharlal Nehru springs from the aristocracy of Kashmir and that, I suppose, is why his features resemble a fusion of Roman patrician and Greek poet. His nose is long and slender. His eyes are a deep and brooding brown. His mouth, with its protruding lower lip, is at once strong and highly sensitive. There is great intelligence in this face, but above all there is the intangible aura of nobility — nobility in the spiritual sense. Although his hair was gray, he looked surprisingly young — not more than forty. It was difficult to believe he was actually fifty-two. Perhaps that was because of the quick boyishness of his smile, yet there was nothing youthful about the direct and ruthless logic of his speech. His English wore the immaculate inflections of Cambridge. Again and again his words and their context reminded us that in this son of Kashmir, who is second only to Mahatma Gandhi in power over India's millions, East and West had indeed met and mingled. But his grace and his graciousness bore the indefinable quality of the East even as his socialist philosophy was a clear product of European thought. I scarcely noticed the white tunic and tight trousers of the Indian Nationalists' costume at first. The man himself was infinitely more striking than his clothes.

"Even if the British did not want to change their policy toward India," Nehru was saying, "just keeping Amery on there as head of the India Office was a constant irritation to our people. We can only interpret that as meaning that the British government has no desire to grant independence. Whatever happens, the British won't give up their Empire in India. The average Indian feels this way. So if Britain wins the war what can we hope for then? . . . Immediately after France fell the [Indian National] Congress deliberately stopped our non-cooperation program. For eight or nine months after that we took no step. Finally Gandhiji started civil disobedience again, but on a small scale among selected persons. In all about 25,000 of our members went to prison — prime ministers of the provinces, members of our legislative assemblies, and Congress executives — all the top people. I was sentenced for four years at this time and served thirteen months. There are still about two thousand in prison now, some of them held in concentration camps without trial."

"Is it likely that you will go to prison again?" I asked.

"I should put it — a fifty-fifty chance either way," said Nehru with the curious laughter of a man whose spirit is free.

"Most of us are wholeheartedly anti-fascist. But conditions may arise" — Nehru was now speaking with great seriousness — "in which there is no wherewithal for effective armed resistance. Not enough weapons or sufficiently trained troops. In that case it's far better for us to resist, peacefully if you like, than to submit. It would be a dangerous thing to have ineffectual armies put up and create the impression among the people that we are trying to do something we can't do — and so create a very feeble Maginot Line which breaks down. It might almost be better for the people to be trained for some other form of resistance which cannot so easily break down."

"But if Sir Stafford Cripps brings an offer of real independence?"

"The Cripps proposal deals with transfer of political power in

India. If that transfer is complete it must be accepted, no matter how difficult the circumstances may be. But the British government, in tying us up, have tied themselves up in so many knots. Everything involves risks, whatever steps they might take or we might take. The question becomes which risks to accept. Which is the lesser risk and which is more in conformity with our objective?"

"Do you think progress can be made as a result of Cripps's visit?"

"It's a little difficult at this time to imagine anything good coming out of this," Nehru replied slowly. "It may happen. But the difficulties are much greater today than even one year ago. The difficulties are partly due to imminence of Japanese invasion, but they're partly due to the pronounced growth of anti-British sentiment in this country."

"Do you think the British in India are capable of organizing a defense against the Japanese?" I asked, and saw a cloud move across Nehru's extremely mobile features.

"I don't think you will find anybody in India who has any belief in British capacity to do anything. It's astonishing how their whole administration is going to pieces."

To this I could make no rebuttal. It was true that as yet I had not encountered a responsible person in India who believed the British could organize an effective defense against a Jap invasion.

"Suppose we came to an agreement with Cripps short of granting of independence," Nehru suggested. "Various groups in India would immediately exploit that — and the Japanese certainly would. They would say Congress is selling the very independence that Japan is offering us. No. We can only resist through creating a feeling that India is already free. If Bengal is invaded the Congress feeling all over India would be that we must resist. But how can it be done? Again, we can't resist without arms. But if present conditions continue there will be no acceptance of British leadership by India's masses. Promises for the future are not acceptable."

"Is a solution possible at all, then, or is it too late?"

"Everything except a single fact points to no solution," Nehru answered in his curiously measured manner. "The personalities and past records of Churchill and Amery offer no real hope of a solution. The one fact in favor of it is the fact that Sir Stafford Cripps has undertaken the mission."

"What would be satisfactory to the Indian National Congress?"

"The very first thing is recognition of India's independence," Nehru said decisively. "Secondly, giving effect to it in the largest possible measure. Naturally, that can't be done all in one step. But the point is this: *The control in India must shift hands. The change must come at the top.*" (Italics mine.)

"That means New Delhi?"

"That means New Delhi," repeated Nehru. "The only question is of having a national government in India and then backing that government's war effort. If it is a question of helping the British government in India, no help at all will be given them. The past position of Congress has been based on three things; first, India's freedom; second, democracy; third, unity. Give us these three things and any solution within them will be possible."

I asked about Mohamed Ali Jinnah and the Moslem League with its demand for Pakistan — the partition of India into Moslem and Hindu states. After all, the Moslems numbered about ninety millions, nearly one fourth of India's population, and Jinnah claimed a majority of them favored partition. Nehru's reply was that Jinnah, although undoubtedly an important person, had been "boomed up" by the British into an artificial importance. "We have said, let Pakistan be considered in a constituent assembly. The reasons for resisting a division of India would be far greater than they were in the United States during your Civil War. India is bound to be a federated country. Suppose British domination ends. We in India must come to agreement among ourselves or have a civil war. Now a third party keeps the communal problem alive without solving it. If it is left to the Indians the problem must be faced. Even Jinnah would not welcome a civil war to solve it."

"Then there's the problem of the native states with their maharajahs, and their private armies," Betty intervened. "Isn't that a major problem?"

"It's more than a major problem," Nehru declared. "These states came into existence about 135 years ago. The British *brought* them into existence, and now claim that their treaties with the native states (which they created) are sacred. Think of the countless principalities of feudal Europe, all of which vanished long ago. But the Indian states still remain because they have been protected from collapsing by British power. Out of 600 native states about 540 must be absorbed — simply because they cannot exist as economic units. Not much more than thirty of them can stand on their own feet economically."

"If the Cripps proposal isn't acceptable, will there be time for another proposition?" I queried finally.

Again Nehru's handsome face became extremely serious.

"No," he said in a low voice. "What will happen one doesn't know."

"Is it too late?"

Nehru paused and then answered, looking straight in my eyes:

"In my mind Britain has long ceased to count as an imperial power. They cannot be expected to control India. The one problem is this — how to control India when it cracks up. The threat of Japanese invasion complicates this very greatly. We are organizing committees in cities, towns, and villages. We hope that families can be grouped in units of three or four hundred, so they can be self-sustaining if possible and so they can organize non-co-operative resistance to the Japanese. If the railroads cease to function, people must somehow be able to eat and carry on. Our program is for self-sufficiency and self-protection. We must do what we can."

"Then you think it likely that there'll be a good deal of chaos?"

Suddenly a fatalistic resignation darkened the keen and thoughtful face before me.

"I suppose so," said Nehru wearily. "One doesn't like it, but —"

If the Japanese struck soon, Jawaharlal Nehru knew too well the exposed condition of India's 390,000,000 people and the disintegration inherent in the structure of British India. I have rarely talked with a man of equal intelligence and comparable comprehension, but never before with such a man — a superior human being — when his mind and spirit were torn by hopelessness and despair. In everything except the matter of Japanese invasion events justified his restrained but deep-felt gloom.

At this moment Sir Stafford Cripps reached New Delhi.

2

On the eve of the Cripps negotiations Victor Thompson of the London *Daily Herald* had a bright idea. He wrote a dispatch around excerpts from an article on the Indian problem which Sir Stafford Cripps had written six years previously. The excerpts included this quotation from Cripps: "I do not myself believe that any British government could, in fact, consent to Indian self-determination in the full sense of that word unless it was so consciously socialist that it was prepared for the break-up of the British Empire. That break-up would involve the most serious problem for internal British economy, a problem that could only be solved by a complete socialist program." Thompson thought this statement of Sir Stafford extremely interesting — and so, evidently, did the British-Indian censorship. The censors, rather significantly, refused to pass the dispatch on the ground that it did not represent Sir Stafford's current views. This seemed to indicate clearly that London's latest proposal, as yet unpublished, did not envisage anything which might disrupt India's Empire status for a long time yet.

Correspondents and diplomats converged on New Delhi as the torrid heat of spring was setting in. Those of us who had never been there before were almost lost in New Delhi's wide avenues, in the calculated and ostentatious grandeur of its massive red-granite government buildings and in the cold formality of the British-built capital's elaborateness. The Viceroy's palace was as vast and impersonal as another Versailles. Together with the huge secretariat and administration structures it occupied every square foot of a broad knoll with the lordly and slightly frowning air of a new Rome. In fact, all this carefully designed magnificence was a new Rome, constructed at a cost of some fifty million dollars, less than fifteen years ago. The main boulevard of approach to these temples of the British Raj extends at least twice as far as the distance from the Place de la Concorde in Paris to the Arc de Triomphe; and it, too, has its triumphal arch. Nowhere in the world has a modern imperialism endeavored so brashly to create an atmosphere of awesome power and might. You can look at this astonishing conglomeration of architectural effort and wonder if, when all its halls are empty some five or ten centuries from now, they may not somehow seem much warmer than they do today. I gazed at these proud columns and thought of Singapore and Rangoon and Calcutta, what I had seen there and what was happening there today. It was as if the palaces of New Delhi were a gigantic and preposterous joke which the Empire of Kipling — and of Baldwin, Chamberlain, and Churchill — had played upon itself. This grandeur and ostentation seemed to have so little to do with the harassed and puny men who were now striving frantically to hold India together. New Delhi and its palaces belonged to another world.

And in reality it was true that New Delhi was located in another world. We could drive six or seven miles across the sun-scorched plain to Old Delhi. There, suddenly, we were in India again. In Old Delhi were the crowded streets, the bazaars, the old great fortress, the mosques, the teeming thousands of India's humanity: all the dirt and squalor and poverty — India with its bated breath, its denied hopes, and its endless life. Beside these things New Delhi was an ornate and foreign element grafted onto the unwilling body of India. It could live on this body; at least it had done so for a long time now. But it could never synchronize or merge itself with the body of India. In its very construction and essence it could never be *of* India. New Delhi did not belong here. One had only to look to see that the grafting had been done with the wrong materials, by the wrong specialists, and in the wrong way. It seemed that New Delhi had been built merely to become a tourist curiosity a thousand years from now. Who had paid for its palaces? Had they been built chiefly out of taxes on the fat profits of British enterprises in India? Dividends which sometimes ran up to forty per cent scarcely made that seem likely. You could look about you in any Indian city or town and see who was bearing by far the greater part of the load. This somewhat arrogantly extravagant monument to imperialism had been built, in the fundamental sense, by the sweat — and the blood and the tears, Mr. Churchill — of the common people of India; by her helpless and hungering and illiterate hundreds of millions. I had seen them in Rangoon, Calcutta, and Allahabad — everywhere — sleeping in doorways and on dirty sidewalks night after night, like stray cats and dogs. I had walked around and over their prostrate, half-naked bodies. I had stepped across them where they lay. But I had *seen* them. This was why the blatant grandeur of New Delhi provoked a kind of lingering incurable nausea inside me.

At the Imperial Hotel I met Sam Brewer, Matt Halton, and other correspondents. I hadn't seen Matt since the night we kept each other from freezing on a forty-below-zero ride above the Arctic Circle in northern Finland, more than two years before.

"You look older, Lee," said Matt honestly.

"My God, I feel older. Nearly a hundred years older."

At such times the company of old friends is like cool water found unexpectedly in a vast desert. We dined and laughed together, helped greatly by Lee Spencer, Doris Jepson, and a few others who were attached to Major General Brereton's headquarters. But Sir Stafford Cripps was holding his first press conferences. The future of India would soon be decided, and where could one find a more complicated and crucial problem in all the Allied world? Anyone with but a brief acquaintance with India could not fail to feel ill-equipped to report the difficult Cripps negotiations and I felt all too aware of my own limitations. Perhaps the only slight advantage I possessed was a personal knowledge of how the London government had handled the India crisis at the outbreak of the war. I had followed this with keen interest in London at the time and had made a small beginning at trying to educate myself on the Indian problem. As I watched developments unfold in New Delhi in the spring of 1942, I was reminded of the opportunities which the British government had so curtly rejected in the autumn of 1939. As I write today I have beside me my London war diary, and perhaps one or two excerpts are needed here to put the picture in perspective.

On October 9, 1939 I wrote in my journal: "Six hundred delegates of the All-India Congress are meeting in India today to put British war aims on the spot — either England is fighting for democracy or for imperialism and her status quo. The Indians demand a free government, or will give no aid to fight Hitler. It sounds awfully logical — and is enough so to prevent any mention of the All-India Congress in today's London press, save in the *News Chronicle,* which honors itself by publishing Nehru's statement. But Britain's press just hasn't been carrying any news about India and has never printed the text of the Congress declaration, although it's of supreme importance to every British citizen. Unless this government is careful it's going to get into a jam over India." Again, on November 7 my diary reads: "The British are very badly on the spot in India. I think, if the war lasts, the Indians can scarcely fail to get dominion status or something closely approximating it. Britain will have to charge this up to war costs — or maybe to Munich costs."

My journal also reminds me of the details of a very unusual event which occurred in London on November 10, 1939. Lord Zetland, then the Secretary of State for India, called a press conference in the India Office — in itself a most exceptional development — uniquely for American correspondents. This step was obviously taken because the Indian situation was receiving considerable attention in American newspapers whereas the London press, possibly on instructions, was largely soft-pedalling or ignoring it. This press conference proved to be a curious affair. Lord Zetland's statement reviewed Britain's offer to bring representatives of India's political parties into the central government during the war "provided that the Indian National Congress and the Moslem League can compose their differences." At the end of the war, Lord Zetland said, Britain would willingly consult with India's parties and princes toward a co-operative effort to frame "such modifications of the constitution as may seem desirable." The fact that the Chamberlain government had taken India into the war without consulting the parliaments of the eleven provinces of British India was not mentioned. Lord Zetland, with his stiff gray mustache and haughty bearing, cut an icy figure as he read his statement, fumbling nervously with his watch-chain. He was flanked by eight assistants and secretaries of the India Office, and their faces fascinated me. They were distinctly not a study in frankness or democratic co-operation. They were hard and cold faces — civil-service imperialist faces which could not entirely conceal a secret irritation over the necessity of this contact with "pressmen." As he concluded his statement Lord Zetland suggested: "You may use this on your own responsibility." This evoked an immediate protest from the American correspondents. We saw no reason to put out the British government's official position on India as our own opinions. We finally extracted the concession that the statement could be ascribed anonymously to "official circles," but only after American news agency men had declared they could not file the statement at all on their own responsibility. After that we began to ask questions which proved to be surprisingly embarrassing. I asked one as a simple quest for facts:

"Could you tell us what percentage of the votes in India's 1937 provincial elections was cast for the India National Congress?"

"I really couldn't say at the moment," Lord Zetland replied. Then turning to his eight frozen-faced assistants, he asked: "Do any of you happen to have the figures available?"

There was silence. No one volunteered the information. It seemed strange, since the India Office was supposed to be documented on everything that happened in India. So I asked another and much more pertinent question.

"Would it be possible for you to give the majorities by which seven out of the eleven provincial Indian governments voted to resign a few weeks ago?" (In protest against India being taken into the war without an opportunity to vote on the matter.)

Lord Zetland said he did not know what the exact figures in these provincial parliament ballotings were, nor whether other parties had joined the followers of Gandhi in their protest votes. To many of us this seemed an almost inexplicable state of affairs: that Britain's Secretary of State for India should not know the exact size of the opposition majorities in seven of India's provincial parliaments. We did not get an impression of frankness. We did gain the impression of an effort to use the American press to present only one side of a grave Empire controversy. Perhaps our alertness rather annoyed the Secretary of State for India. At any rate he became sufficiently impatient to accuse the leaders of Gandhi's party of employing "purely totalitarian principles." In the hostile and autocratic atmosphere which dominated that press conference in the India Office on my fortieth birthday, that phrase sounded strange indeed, and troublingly contradictory.

When I wrote my dispatch to the *Chicago Daily News* that day, I began the lead by reporting that Lord Zetland "charged the working committee of the All-India Congress with talking much of democracy but acting upon 'purely totalitarian principles.' Since the followers of Mahatma Gandhi are still demanding a clear-cut declaration of British war aims and accuse the British government of pronouncing India at war without submitting the decision to a democratic vote of India's eleven provincial parliaments, observers here fear that the Indian Nationalists will greet Zetland's statement with counter-charges of totalitarianism." Under censorship, that was as far as one could go to point out a most striking discrepancy. Not long afterward Prime Minister Chamberlain made his first war-aims speech and promised each European country the "unfettered right to choose its own form of internal government." I linked this in my next dispatch with the fact that the India Congress working committee had just adopted a resolution charging the British with denying self-government to India. "The question now appears to be raised as to how the British government will be able to reconcile this pronouncement with refusal or reluctance to grant dominion status or independence to India." Already I had been informed privately that certain London authorities were watching my dispatches about the Indian situation with considerable displeasure.*

So my first lessons about the British-Indian controversy had been given me in London's India Office by Neville Chamberlain's Secretary of State for India. I had since learned that the contrast between Lord Zetland (or his successor Mr. Amery) and Jawaharlal Nehru was quite as great as the contrast between Hitler's Foreign Minister Baron von Ribbentrop and Thomas Mann, Germany's Nobel-prize winning novelist. Lord Zetland had used weasel words. Indian leaders might be taken into a

* Could that fact, by any chance, have had anything to do with the further fact – two and a half years later – that it had required fourteen days before I could obtain a press-collect authorization to file dispatches from India? Probably not; but if so, I was still trying to be a reporter.

central wartime government *provided* — provided what had always been impossible was achieved: namely, that Gandhi's Congress party and Jinnah's Moslem League composed their differences first. The only other noteworthy portion of Lord Zetland's statement read as follows:

"We are pledged under our treaties and engagements with the princes to afford them protection against aggression from without and rebellion from within. We cannot treat these pledges as scraps of paper and bring them to an end unilaterally, to meet our own convenience or that of anyone else. It is indeed against bad faith of that kind that we have taken up arms in Europe."

There were 562 princes and maharajahs of various categories controlling the lives of less than twenty-four per cent of India's population.* The British government could not revise its agreements with 562 princes to meet its "own convenience," but it had taken all the states and provinces of India and all of India's 390,000,000 people into the second World War without consultation or vote of any kind — to meet the convenience of whom? This was why, in the autumn of 1939, it was perfectly plain to almost everyone (except the dominant Tory leadership in the Chamberlain government) that London was courting grave trouble in its Indian policy of "Don't budge an inch." Lord Zetland had not so much as breathed the suggestion that dominion status should be granted India after the war. Nothing that resembled an advance over the existing deadlock was offered at that time — when both the British and the Indian parties had plenty of time in which to negotiate.

But there were Britishers with foresight and magnanimity who clamored for statesmanship rather than standpattism. One of these was Edward Thompson, an authority on India, who warned in the *Manchester Guardian:* "Civil disobedience [in India] is bound to come with fierce despair and resentment sustaining it. In the American revolution we had a strong case, but because taxation without representation is tyranny history and our after-judgement have condemned us. India has reached the Lexington stage: 'If there is to be a war, let it begin here!' The break has come over the right of one nation to commit another to war without bothering to consult its wishes and interests."

* Cf. *Inside Asia* by John Gunther.

Voices like Thompson's were Britain's voices of reasonableness and of realism. They passed unheeded by the Chamberlain government and again unheeded for almost two years by the Churchill government. Now it was late March 1942, and Sir Stafford Cripps had presented a proposal for "Indian Union," saying: "This scheme goes as a whole or is rejected as a whole." London was suddenly in a tremendous hurry. Sir Stafford had announced that things must be decided urgently as it was necessary for him to start back to London in another two weeks.

3

On Sunday, March 29, Sir Stafford Cripps read the text of Britain's proposal to a crowded audience in a regal hall of New Delhi's Secretariat Building. It was truly a breathless audience; press representatives of Hindus and Moslems, of the Indian National Congress, the Sikhs, and the princely states — men of all the diverse classes, races, and creeds of India — waiting for words which would spell so many different things to their conflicting hopes and prejudices. In the faces and eyes of many I saw a burning hunger for freedom. In their dark and expressive features I saw hope flame swiftly high at certain passages of Sir Stafford's; then saw it fade into sudden suspicion or be submerged by deception. And one man's elation was another man's despair. I have rarely witnessed a scene so dramatic and so intense in its shifting emotional registrations. The fate of 390,000,000 people for several years to come hung upon the contents of the brief paragraphs which Sir Stafford, with his fine voice and winning sincerity, was reading. Would their contents be sufficient to bring independence and a prospective end to India's age-old internal divisions? At this fifty-ninth minute of the eleventh hour that seemed too much to hope — and it was.

The so-called Cripps proposal was in reality a Churchill proposal. It began with a section about tomorrow, outlining the steps which, "immediately upon cessation of hostilities," might lead to realization of self-government through creation of "a new Indian Union which shall constitute a Dominion." It ended with a single paragraph dealing with what should be done today, "during the critical period which now faces India." Britain, at any rate, had at last committed herself to offering what should wisely have been offered at the outbreak of the war — dominion status for India.

The tomorrow section provided for the convening after hostilities ended of an assembly to draft a new constitution for India. The lower houses of the provincial legislatures would elect their delegates by the system of proportional representation, but the princes of the native states "shall be invited to appoint representatives in the same proportion to their total population." Thus nearly one fourth of the delegates to the constituent assembly would not be elected by some 80,000,000 Hindus and Moslems. They would be hand-picked by 562 Indian princes who owed their continued rule and privileges to Great Britain. The Churchill government's proposal granted the right of any of the eleven provinces of British India to refuse to accept the new Constitution and retain its present status. This amounted to the right to secede from the "Indian Union" even while it was in the process of being set up as an experiment. Britain also went so far as to offer such "non-acceding provinces . . . the same full status as Indian Union," should they so desire. This meant that the door was left wide open for the Moslem League's cardinal demand of Pakistan — a partition of Hindu and Moslem India. And that was precisely what India's largest and most representative political party, the Indian National Congress, had always declared they could never accept under any circumstances. In reserving the right of secession to separate Indian provinces the Churchill government had retained the very principle on which the American states had split irrevocably and had fought a bitter civil war in 1861–5.

But the possibility of dominion status and independence under whatever disputable procedure was at best several years removed. The today section, or paragraph, was the one decisive factor for the present. It provided that Britain must "retain control and direction of the defense of India" as part of her war effort. On the other hand, "the task of organizing to the full the military, moral and material resources of India must be the responsibility of the Government of India." The immediate participation of leaders "of the principal sections of the Indian people" in the counsels of their country would be invited. Much of the thorny negotiations which ensued in New Delhi centered upon the degree of responsibility which Indian representatives would be given in India's defense ministry.

In the course of animated meetings and debate seven statements were issued by the leading parties and groups in India. These came from the Indian National Congress, the Moslem League, Hindu Mahasabha, the Sikh All-Parties Committee, the Depressed Classes, the Non-Party group, and the Indian states. All but the two last named rejected the Churchill government's proposal, for reasons which differed very widely. The negotiations dragged painfully on, with Gandhi's Congress party most powerful of all in the opposition, and Sir Stafford Cripps finally adjourned his departure for several days. On the long-term procedure for establishment of some portion of India as a British dominion after the war there seemed no possibility of agreement. But Britain urgently needed to gain the collaboration of Indian leaders in the defense of India before Japan launched a seemingly imminent invasion. Here, too, Mahatma Gandhi and the working committee of the Nationalists' Congress remained adamant.

There seemed little hope of a compromise until Colonel Louis Johnson, who was present in New Delhi as President Roosevelt's personal representative, quietly intervened behind the scenes. Colonel Johnson had talks with Cripps, Nehru, and General Sir Archibald Wavell, who had the complete military responsibility for India's defense. At the moment that negotiations seemed doomed, Colonel Johnson had a frank talk with General Wavell and they then conferred with the Viceroy, Lord Linlithgow. When I attempted to report that Colonel Johnson had gone "to discuss the seemingly hopeless situation" with Wavell and had played the role "of an eleventh-hour mediator," the chief press adviser of the British-India government suppressed these facts. I was not permitted to describe Johnson as a mediator (which is precisely what he was) or to indicate that he had taken the initiative of going to see General Wavell. Well, it appeared for the next two days that the negotiations had been saved, and that was really all that mattered.

Then, out of a clearing sky, we learned on April 10 that the negotiations had broken down. It was all over and Sir Stafford was leaving in two days. Apparently the rupture had come on the question of India's defense. Rumors were legion, but no one was yet willing to tell exactly what had happened. I had to start for Russia immediately and I left New Delhi quite as confused as all the other correspondents I knew. As a matter of fact, a complete and reliable explanation did not reach print in the United States until nearly six months later. It was provided by Louis Fischer, author of *Men and Politics* and *A Week with Gandhi*. Writing in the *Nation's* issues of September 19 and 26, 1942, Fischer told at last "why Cripps failed." That, I think, is of much greater importance for the record than a host of the secondary details of the New Delhi negotiations which I have taken care to omit here. I have it on the authority of one who had close knowledge of the course and the denouement of the Cripps negotiations that "Fischer's article is an accurate piece of reporting . . . the only accurate one I have seen up to this time." I was told this near the end of 1942.

What Louis Fischer revealed by factual testimony was the fact "that the Cripps negotiations broke down when Cripps withdrew a promise he had made to the Indian leaders that India could have an immediate national government." They did not break down, then, on the issue of how much responsibility Indian representatives should have for India's defense. Failure came when the Churchill government insisted that the proposed and so-called national government in India, even if unanimous in its decisions, could still be overruled by the veto of one man — the Viceroy of India.

On April 11 the president of the Indian National Congress, Maulana Abul Azad, wrote Sir Stafford Cripps a letter in which he stated: "What we were told in our very first talk with you is now denied or explained away. You told me then that there would be a national government which would function as a Cabinet and that the position of the Viceroy would be analogous to that of the King in England vis-à-vis his Cabinet. In regard to the India Office (headed by Leopold S. Amery in London) you told me that you were surprised that no one had so far mentioned this important matter, and that the practical course was to have this attached or incorporated with the Dominions' Office. The whole of this picture which you sketched before us has now been completely shattered by what you told us during our last interview." When Sir Stafford Cripps sent Maulana Azad a five-line reply authorizing him to publish their correspondence, he failed most significantly to deny Azad's assertion, or even to mention it.

Louis Fischer continues: "I had the following conversation in New Delhi with the British official to whom Cripps reported late every evening during his negotiations. 'I did what I could,' the official said, 'to draft a formula for defense. But then they reverted to the question of the Viceroy's rights in relation to the Indian members of the government.' . . . 'Is that the issue on which the negotiations broke?' I asked. . . . 'Yes, quite definitely,' the official replied." Fischer continues: "Azad, Nehru and Rajagopalachari negotiated with Cripps on behalf of Congress. Each one of them separately gave me an account of the negotiations which coincided with the version of this British official."

This seems to establish, beyond fear of contradiction, why Cripps failed. I do not think there can be any question of this, since I have the further testimony of another extremely authoritative source — not that of Colonel Johnson, let me add for his peace of mind. But what does this extraordinary delay in getting at the key factor behind the breakdown of the British-Indian negotiations mean? It means that the exact cause of this most far-reaching rupture has never been published in detail in America's newspapers; that the overwhelming majority of Americans are still ill-informed or completely uninformed on the reasons which keep India's hundreds of millions from actively supporting the Allied cause in the war.

While I was flying to Karachi on April 12, the *Calcutta Statesman,* British-owned but clear-eyed, carried this editorial verdict: "It would be easy to blame Congress and the other parties for the failure . . . but the blame lies *with the India Office* and the official section of the Government of India" (italics mine). The *Statesman* continued: "The question therefore to be answered is, Was Sir Stafford Cripps empowered to offer a real national government or not? . . . It seemed to us that what was proposed was Dominion status in action now, but that the diehards were determined to pretend that it was not. Success, we wrote, would elude Sir Stafford unless he was empowered to use very different language, accompanied by striking changes that would make it clear that the old regime is ended. . . . Sir Stafford was not empowered to use such language. . . . The India Office, 'this undesirable relic of a past age,' is to remain, and with it the whole theory that the Government of India is responsible not to India but to the Parliament of Great Britain. . . . How can they know anything about governing India? How can they be anything but an incompetent and unpopular authority in a war? . . . Sir Stafford has been made a dupe."

As Louis Fischer reports, "while in India Cripps told members of his staff and non-Englishmen too that before he left England he had asked Winston Churchill to remove the Viceroy from office. . . . Cripps maintained that he had full authority to set up a real Cabinet government in India. On April 9th this authority was specifically withdrawn in new instructions to Cripps cabled from London. Cripps was therein told that he could not go beyond the text of the British government's draft declaration. . . . The same evening Cripps said his enemies had defeated him." It happened that I flew on the same plane with Sir Stafford Cripps from Karachi to Basra. At that time he was very careful not to give a plain statement of the cause for the failure of his mission.

So the Churchill government and the India Office had refused to "make it clear that the old regime is ended." But was Sir Stafford alone in having been made a dupe? Or was this also true of American public opinion?

4

It seems to me a most questionable procedure for a nation that has always been free, to leap to hasty conclusions about the attitude and decisions of a nation that has never been free.

Yet this, so far as one could judge by press reports which reached India, was precisely what a large proportion of vocal opinion in the United States was doing about the Churchill proposal. Undoubtedly British censorship carefully sifted out all the American comments which were most favorable to the British government's position, so as to create the impression among the Indian leaders and people that the United States had turned its back on them. But the American editorial reaction, which was republished from one end of India to the other, did include comment from many of our most influential newspapers from coast to coast and from a number of our most widely read columnists. Reading these comments in New Delhi the sum-total effect was one loud and impatient lecture delivered by the U. S. A. to the people of India: "You've been offered dominion status and independence. Why don't you take it? Don't you Indians realize that we Allies are at war and we haven't got time to discuss details? Why should you insist on a large share of responsibility for the defense of your own country? What's all the arguing about? The Japs may hit you at any moment. Don't you understand there's no time now to waste discussing mere details and ways and means?"

This was what American reaction sounded like; as petulant and childish and ill-informed as that. The Indians did not even have an opportunity to reply to our safe and secure editorial gods or their strangely undemocratic sermons. If so, they would have begun like this: "You Americans say there's no time for details. Ah, but these details will determine whether in actuality we ever get freedom and self-government. . . . You say there's no time — but whose fault is that? Didn't we pose this question frankly in the first weeks of the war in 1939? Who postponed even trying to do anything about it until March 1942? Not the people of India. . . . You Americans say we are endangering the democratic cause. Is it really we who endanger it? Or is it those who have waited so long before offering us even a portion of democratic self-government? All the rest of our lives and the lives of our children are involved, yet the voices of America's free press chide us for being unreasonable. . . . Were your Washington and Jefferson and the signers of your Declaration of Independence willing to wait until England's European wars had been settled? . . . What has happened to Americans? We thought that you believed in true democracy. We thought you were our friends."

As I read the rebukes which American editorialists and commentators addressed to India, it seemed to me that many influential people at home had swallowed British Empire propaganda hook, line, and sinker. There did not seem to be any effort to look at the Churchill government's proposal through neutral eyes, or to try to judge it from the viewpoint of those most intimately concerned — the Indians. We Americans were in the war, the war was going badly, and the Indians were blocking our recovery by "holding up an agreement." That was the American attitude, so far as it was portrayed to the Indian people, at any rate. In that form, even if deliberately one-sided as a result of British censorship, it reflected little credit upon American intelligence or fair play.

I do not think that any objective observer of the Cripps negotiations can absolve the British government (particularly the Churchill-Amery-Tory-imperialist dominant factors in London's government) from the major responsibility for its failure. One can grant that India constitutes just about the most complicated political-social-religious problem anywhere on earth. One can grant that the Indians, who have never known the responsibilities of freedom and self-government, are an excessively sensitive and often a difficult people for Westerners to deal with or understand. One may even grant that Mahatma Gandhi, for reasons with which I personally have very little sympathy, may have secretly wanted to prevent an agreement. Nevertheless the British government had all the physical power in India, and as a consequence it had the chief responsibility for offering a proposal which events proved was riddled by several most debatable loopholes.

Some of the principal errors or abuses which doomed the Churchill proposal from the outset were the following:

1. The maintenance in office of the two instruments of British Imperial domination who were most objectionable to the Indian people: namely, Secretary of State for India Leopold S. Amery at the head of India Office in London, and Great Britain's Viceroy of India, Lord Linlithgow. Whether justifiably or not, both these men had become a symbol to Indians of Britain's determination to retain a strong-arm control over India. India's leaders of whatever party could never forget that Amery had once declared: "Our whole policy in India, our whole policy in Egypt, stand condemned if we condemn Japan." Churchill asked the Indians to join in active defense against Japan while he retained in office, in direct control over any Indian government which might be formed, the man who had publicly white-

washed Japan's imperialism in Manchuria and had described the Japanese as defending themselves "against the continual aggression of vigorous Chinese nationalism." The British people had long forgotten Amery's words and ignored his mentality. India's leaders had neither forgotten nor ignored.

2. The Churchill proposal offered India dominion status, but continued in existence in London the vast and irreconcilable machinery of the India Office. The Indians could not fail to regard this as a complete contradiction between words and action. Why, indeed, had the *Calcutta Statesman's* British editor declared flatly that the blame for Cripps's failure "lies with the India Office" and why had he described it as "this undesirable relic of a past age"? Why, too, should the Churchill government propose dominion status for India, yet neglect most eloquently to transfer India's affairs to the Secretary of the Dominions? If India's aid was so urgently needed for prospective success of the Allied cause, this would have been in truth a small concession, but a mighty symbol of British sincerity to the Indian people. Instead of this the British government (in part over the apparent protest of Sir Stafford Cripps) kept the India Office, kept Amery, and kept Lord Linlithgow in the Viceroy's palace in New Delhi. More than a year later Linlithgow was replaced by General Wavell, a debatable choice so far as the Indian public is concerned. But since Lord Linlithgow's usefulness in India had about ended, a far more constructive move would have been for him to have been replaced before Cripps reached New Delhi.

3. The British government had two years and a half in which to put forward a proposal for India and did virtually nothing while time for genuine negotiations existed. The urgency for a settlement in India was evident to every thoughtful official or observer in London in October 1939. The delay was inexcusable and purely British by origin.

4. The Churchill proposal was finally put up to India's deeply divided parties and classes on something very close to "take it or leave it" terms. Sir Stafford Cripps announced at the beginning that he had only two weeks in which to discuss the project. This was only seven days longer than one of Hitler's ultimatums previous to Munich, yet this Indian matter was indescribably difficult and involved. Accordingly one can scarcely contend that

the question was approached by the British government in a statesmanlike manner, or in a manner which was fair to India's 390,000,000 people.

5. The people of India and their provincial parliaments were taken into the war without being consulted and without an opportunity being given for their representatives to vote on the matter. While the Cripps negotiations encountered difficulties and impatience mounted in the United States, most of the American public apparently had forgotten that India had been committed to war without consultation. Supposing, in the spring of 1941 — at the time of the Lend-Lease debate and some seven months before Pearl Harbor — President Roosevelt had tried to take the American people into war without presenting the question to Congress? Of course, that couldn't be done constitutionally. But the point is this: How would Americans react if they were ever plunged into a war, for which they had no hankering or desire and from which they apparently had nothing at all to gain — plunged into such a war without a vote by their elected representatives? This happened in India. But it has been convenient for most of us to overlook that fact.

As a consequence of these major errors on the part of the British government, the British people and their allies have lost the active support of India's enormous population for the duration of the war. Gandhi, Nehru, and tens of thousands of others — including some of the best brains and much of the finest talent in Indian leadership — are locked behind bars. The vast semicontinent of India smolders with resentment and unrest. All of the Asiatic peoples, approximating no less than one third of humanity, are asking themselves what the Anglo-American spokesmen mean when they talk of freedom and democracy. In Great Britain, in the Dominions, and in America we are all paying the price for a tragic and almost immeasurable blunder.

The 10th U. S. air force is in India, together with many thousands of American armed forces. The assault against Burma must be made from India and, at least in the air, Americans must play a considerable role in the reclaiming of Burma. America has a share in the holding of India and in India's defense. Will the United States government have any share in hastening the day of self-government in India? It is not primarily our responsibility, but there does exist very clearly a joint Anglo-American and United Nations responsibility for a new kind of colonial trusteeship throughout the post-war world. And there does remain the question whether Americans and British will help people on the road to self-government — or whether we shall seek excuses for delaying the day of trial and experiment.

The Chinese are rightly alive to this question. When Chiang Kai-shek visited India he threw a bombshell in the shape of a farewell statement which was utterly unexpected by the British officials. The Generalissimo urged the British to give the Indian people "real political power" as speedily as possible, so that they might "thus realize that their participation in the war is not merely an aid to the anti-aggression nations for the securing of victory but also a turning-point in their struggle for India's freedom."

The turning-point in India's struggle has been postponed. The American government and people may forget that fact. The Chinese, we may be sure, will never forget it.

5

The fiasco at New Delhi was over and I was at Karachi. Here was our old friend Wally, still smiling but still battling the immovable and the inexplicable.

"We're trying to dope out a way to move Lend-Lease stuff for China across northern India from Karachi in American trucks," Wally said. Then he laughed humorlessly. "My God, these people are incredible. They've been in India for a couple of hundred years, and they haven't produced a road map of Sind province — of this very province, mind you. Yesterday I went to British headquarters here. Would you believe it? Headquarters itself hasn't got a single road map of Sind province either. A fine mess they'll be in if the Japs ever get this far."

Karachi's Killarney Hotel was jammed with American officers of our air force and army supply service. I talked with the Indian manager of the hotel. "It's a pleasure to have the Americans here," he said. "We like them as clients and they're almost always friendly. You see, the trouble with the British is they don't know how to treat people as equals."

That seemed to be the last word to be said about India.

Part IV — Soviet Russia

Chapter XI

"NOBODY CAN FIGHT FOR ME"

Excepting the Chinese, I know of no other people who are so indifferent to death. . . . The Revolution, by infusing into youth a crusading spirit, has only intensified this indifference to death.

Maurice Hindus in *Hitler Cannot Conquer Russia*

War is bad, but it is better for self-respecting men to die while they still feel like men than to become cowards and hypocrites and the laughing stock of an unscrupulous enemy.

Ellict Paul in *The Last Time I Saw Paris*

I have never gloried quite so much in uplands and sharp, clear air and white mountain ranges as I did journeying across Iran, with the washed-out tiredness of nine months in the Orient and the tropics still hanging on inside me like a dull toothache. April in Iran bore the full promise of new life and new beginnings. I wanted very much to linger and forget the war for two or three weeks. Instead, I took the road north from Teheran and traveled another Lend-Lease route — the road over which Allied supplies were being taken up and through the Elburz Mountains and down to the Caspian for transshipment into Russia.

The flow of Anglo-American materials on this final 1,500-mile land lap of their 15,000-mile journey remained a small trickle as yet, but the contrast with the Burma Road was most striking. The Red Army men, who operated the few hundred trucks thus far available, drove with deadly earnestness and skill. They watered their vehicles' radiators at regular intervals. I did not see a single smashed or stalled truck anywhere and I got a long-forgotten feeling of organization, purpose, and efficiency. Thanks to this and the mountains, my spirits broke away from their prison of despond, even though the toothache of fatigue persisted for many weeks and nearly floored me on the trying six-day, ten-mile-an-hour crawl by train from Baku to Moscow. All the way from New Delhi to Teheran people had been asking: Can the Russians possibly hold through another summer and autumn? Even some of the highest American and British officers were beset by grave doubts. What would the attitude be in Moscow? In mid-May you reached Russia's capital with this question foremost in your mind.

May 17, 1942 fell on Sunday, and it was opening day at Moscow's big Park of Culture and Rest, which borders on the Moscow River. The sidewalks and bypaths were crowded with young Muscovites; laughing and chattering blonde girls and Red Army men in their trim smock blouses and office workers and a smattering of factory workers whose eleven-hour shift did not begin until seven at night. The Russian girls wore simple dresses — no one was really well dressed — but they looked neat and amazingly fresh. We didn't see many who could be called pretty, but almost all had sturdy, well-developed figures. They carried themselves straight and walked extremely well and they had the air of being on holiday, as if they had scarcely a care in the world. This, too, was the first real day of spring that Moscow had known. All these people had existed half-frozen and very poorly fed through the long six months of the wartime winter, but they seemed already to have forgotten all that.

Youngsters from eight to fourteen thronged the park's exhibition building and climbed in and out of battered German Heinkels, Junkers, and Messerschmitts which had been shot down by the Red air force. They examined every enemy machine and weapon with a keen and lingering interest. Others were riding the Ferris wheel, and just beyond was one of the most fantastic amusement contraptions I ever saw. I happened to look up — and there was a human figure describing a tremendous arc through the air on the end of a high pole. "For God's sake, what in the world is that?" I exclaimed. The device was like a clock's pendulum, weighted at its base and operating upside down. The pole-pendulum had a little seat on the end of it, and a girl of thirteen or fourteen was just being strapped in. She sat with her stomach against the pole's top, leaning forward, with her hands clutching her ankles. The operator released the pendulum and the girl shot up into the air like a stone out of a slingshot. At the peak of the arc she was suddenly level for a second and then plunged swiftly earthward — head down and bottom up. Just short of the ground the pendulum stopped and swung back up and over, then up and over and up and over again. I watched one Russian youngster after another clamber into this upside-down swing and ride it with unmistakable relish. These Russians certainly like their play on the strenuous side, I thought. And looking down toward the lower entrance of the park there was further evidence of this. Scores of young men and women were climbing the parachute-jump tower and blithely leaping off into one hundred feet of space. Suddenly I felt as if we Americans were a rather soft race, after all. Decidedly, these Russians practiced the strenuous life. Maybe that was one reason why they had astonished the world by stopping the Nazis' panzer divisions only twenty miles from Moscow.

This was my third day in Moscow. I had seen many people who looked pale and many who were thin and undernourished. But I hadn't yet seen anyone who looked worried about the war. Under the warm sun along the promenade of the park men, women, and children seemed almost as casual and quite as lighthearted as peacetime strollers in any park in America. While I was pondering about this, a band started playing and then — before you could say Hermann Göring — it happened. A towheaded Red Army boy grasped his bobbed-haired laughing companion around the waist, a dozen other couples followed suit, and there they were, swaying and swirling to the music. Soon many girls who had no escorts, pairing off by themselves, had joined in. It wasn't a scheduled outdoor dance. There were no public dances in Moscow. But the band had opened up with a catchy tune and this was the Muscovite's first day of escape from winter (and the war) — and when a Russian wants to dance, a table-top will do if nothing better is handy. The sinking sun threw a sharp light on their young faces and I noticed they danced as Americans dance, as if it had to come out — as if they had to let themselves go. I heard their shoes scraping on the rough asphalt, and to me it sounded like *sock, sock, sock* on Adolf Hitler's jaw. Just as if the front was a thousand miles away, instead of a mere hundred miles. Just as if Adolf didn't have another bombing plane to his name. As if the pride of the Nazis' Wehrmacht were nothing but tin soldiers. The Moscow sky is wide open and it's broad daylight and here are scores of young Russians dancing in the open air beside the Moscow River in the heart of the capital Hitler most detests. Where are the Heinkels and the Junkers? Where is Field Marshal Göring? And who, around here, seems to care? It's just as if the German Luftwaffe were a pipe dream out of the Führer's chimney in Berchtesgaden. What a sock on the jaw for Adolf Hitler! . . . And people in Britain and America, in India and Egypt, are still wondering whether the Russians will hold. Well, this wasn't military evidence, of course. But it was a revealing sidelight on the morale of a people who had had every right to become downhearted.

As spring waned into summer I took long walks about Moscow and found it a city with a curious mixture of attractiveness and ugliness. There were many drab streets and gray unpainted houses; but the main boulevards, like Gorki Street, were even wider than Fifth Avenue, and the streets themselves were the cleanest I have ever seen in any large city. You explored side alleys into drowsy old quarters where pre-Revolutionary cobblestones still served instead of pavements and little weather-stained churches had remained tucked away for generations. You discovered the circular inner boulevard, which once enclosed most of Moscow; and the circular outer boulevard, which now does not begin to encompass all of this great city of more than three millions. In Gorki, Sverdlosk Square, and the Kuznetsky Most you observed great modern office buildings which were constructed by the Soviets. But always you would return, as I returned, to the Red Square. At dawn or at dusk I watched the sky register its changing pastels behind the nine onion domes of St. Basil's Cathedral, or marveled before the superb simplicity of Lenin's modernistic tomb of magnificent red marble, or stood under a waning moon and saw the Kremlin's unique silhouette of high crenelated walls and ancient Russian churches and spaced turrets with their huge stars (no longer lighted) standing high up at their thin peaks. At first, in the course of these wanderings, I looked for the damages wrought by Nazi bombs; but these were so few that I never found more than half a dozen ruined or partially burned-out buildings.

During these first weeks in Moscow I made a particular effort to discover whether the Russians, with Hitler's formidable summer offensive due to be launched at any moment, secretly feared their capital could not be held. Curiously enough, I couldn't seem to find a Russian who was worried about Moscow being captured. On my first visit to the big Botkin Hospital I put this question frankly to several wounded men, but they all acted as if they had forgotten that such a possibility had ever existed. Finally I came to a Russian soldier whose leg had just been amputated.

"Do you think the Germans will take Moscow?"

The soldier's name was Peter and he had flashing dark eyes.

"Ho-ho-ho!" laughed Peter. "Take Moscow? Don't talk nonsense. They can't even think of it any more."

It seemed to me it might be worth while to point out to American readers that, whatever the Nazis' summer drives might accomplish elsewhere, the Russians were remarkably confident about holding Moscow. So I wrote a dispatch, but when I presented it to the handsome blond censor, he called me in and explained why he could not pass it. "But if we Russians are not worried about Moscow falling, then the question simply doesn't exist," he said. I remonstrated that, however the Russians might feel, the question did exist in the minds of a tremendous number of persons in the U. S. A. and Britain. But the censor — and throughout my stay in the Soviet Union I found the Russian censorship extremely reasonable and fair — had a Soviet bureaucrat's penchant for looking for hidden meanings. "I don't doubt the honesty of your motives," he said. "But if you write a story explaining why we Russians believe Moscow cannot be taken, what will be the reaction of some people abroad? They will say: 'Aha, why are the Soviets letting correspondents write about Moscow being strong? They must be worried about holding Moscow.' . . . No, I think there is no need to be concerned about Moscow. Therefore it is better not to write about it." I felt the censor's viewpoint was as sincere as my own. But whether I could write about it or not I had become convinced that Moscow, physically and in spirit, was much stronger than many

Anglo-Americans imagined. It was the spirit of Moscow that impressed me especially; perhaps because it had been so long since I had been where such a fighting spirit existed.

2

One of the things you soon learn in the Soviet Union is that Russian hospitality is as exuberant and wholehearted as American hospitality is. At official functions it's rather dangerous, for the Russians — like the Chinese — are inveterate toast-drinkers and vodka is one of the most potent forms of liquid dynamite ever invented. On an excursion to a Russian airfield outside Moscow it hadn't occurred to us that there would be a banquet, with the first potatoes most Moscow correspondents had tasted in seven or eight months. Nor did I then know that the Russians have their own system for dinner speeches. The system is quite logical. You simply propose a toast and talk your two or three minutes' worth whenever the mood strikes you, and so on all through the meal. I was trying to figure how many times I could safely drain my glass when another correspondent punched me.

"Come on. It's your turn. You've got to say something."

Which was all very fine, but what on earth should I say? Then I remembered lying on my back in a great field of snow near Elisenvaara, Finland, and watching six glistening oval objects drop from beneath seventeen big silver bombers with red stars painted on their sides, and lying there watching as those shiny bombs sped straight down toward me, and watching until I couldn't stand the agony of it another second — and then burying my face in the snow and thinking: "Oh God, it's yes or no." I remembered how the earth under me seemed to rise two feet or more with the first roaring explosion, and then again and again in swift succession — and when it was over I had paced through the snow to the first bomb crater, counting the yards, and counted forty-five of them, no more. If I ever remembered anything I'd remember that as long as I lived, and here we were having a wonderful time with a group of crack fliers in the Red air force. Would I give them a toast? You bet I'd give them a toast. Except for the essential part I can't say exactly how it went, but the essential part was easy enough.

"I've been bombed by Germans, by Italians, and by Japanese.

But I want you to know that the bombs which came closest to hitting me were dropped by members of the Russian air force. That's why I have the greatest respect in the world for the Red air force. I want you to know that I'll never forget Russian bombers and what they can do. Gentlemen, I drink to the success of the Red air force — and I feel much more comfortable being with it in front of me than being where it's coming at me."

The Russian pilots at the table burst into gales of laughter at the translation and applauded warmly. Some might have thought they would have resented the fact I had covered the Russo-Finnish war with the Finnish Army, but not these Russians. They know how to laugh and they like and appreciate frankness. One of the first things I observed in the Soviet Union was the fact that Russians and Americans have a surprising amount of common ground on which to meet; they get along well together; whenever they can use a common language they mix easily, and the Russian sense of humor has the same boyishness and robustness that American humor has. It's just about as difficult to dislike a Russian as it is to dislike a Chinese. I was continually wishing I had been born a linguist; for in Russia, as in the East, three European languages do not carry you very far. I should have liked to be able to chat with people in the streets, in the subway, and on buses; to have got much closer to the Russian people and Russian psychology. I envied Maurice Hindus and Henry Shapiro of the United Press their fluency in Russian, and the considerable progress other correspondents had made in one or two years. In Moscow, of course, you met many Russians who spoke English, French, or German — often with scarcely an accent — but you couldn't expect that to be true of ordinary workmen or soldiers.

Consequently I got my first picture of the thoroughness of Red Army training from a Red Army man who was a twenty-year-old Spaniard named Ramon. He was a refugee from Republican Spain and had volunteered in the Russian army as soon as Germany attacked. Ramon was a quiet unassuming boy, who had first gone to war as a mere youngster in defense of the Spanish Republic. He was one of several hundred young Spaniards who were fighting with the Red Army or air force, without any publicity, without thought of recognition, simply because they recognized fascism as the universal enemy. When he discussed the qualities of the Russian soldiers, Ramon spoke factually but with undisguised admiration.

"Yes, it's true," Ramon said. "After the Finnish war the Red Army was reorganized very intensively. The Soviets learn their lessons very fast. In the Red Army they don't make the same mistakes twice. And the training they give their men — really it's terrific. I think it must be about the toughest in the world. In Spain we are used to hardship, and we are a tough people, we Spaniards. But I'm often amazed at the endurance of the Russians. In the Red Army I have known them to march their training units twenty-three miles between eight at night and one in the morning, then let them sleep until five o'clock, and then march them another thirty miles with full packs. Russian soldiers will average two kilometers an hour more than our Spanish troops used to do — and our Spanish soldiers were strong men."

"They were fine soldiers," I said, thinking of the French, British, and American governmental policies which had killed them, and so had robbed us of Spain as an ally and a priceless land base on the European continent in this war.

"Bayonet drill and obstacle training, everything in the Red Army is the hardest kind of work," Ramon said. "Now most of the Red Army has been trained on skis. More and more ski divisions are being trained in Siberia. When next winter comes the Germans will learn a few lessons. But one of the most amazing things is the marksmanship of the Russians. The standards set by the Red Army command are terribly high. Imagine this: Using a rifle with a telescopic sight and shooting at 800 yards, a Russian soldier must hit a target the size of a man's head twice out of three times if he's to get a rating of good. One hit out of three only counts as average. That's true. And with ordinary rifles Red Army men must qualify shooting at 500 yards instead of 300 yards, which would be regulation in most armies. Yet even at that distance I've seen twenty per cent of the soldiers qualify as good or very good. Up to the rank of colonel Russian officers have to pass the same marksmanship tests as their troops.

"But I think Russian women are even stronger than their

men," Ramon continued. "I have been in arms plants where girls are working fourteen hours a day — and after that they would go out and play games and think nothing of it. Before the war my Russian fiancée had never done any hard work because her family was in better circumstances. Like all the other women she was called to do work on the fortifications of Moscow. At that time she worked from five in the morning until eight at night. One day I met her after work. She said: 'I'm tired, but let's go for a little walk.' She walked me for six and a half miles that evening. I don't know what I'd have done if she hadn't been tired."

Ramon smiled and his smile was very boyish and open. We had just finished a simple meal and suddenly he said: "Did you ever eat cat meat when you were in Madrid? . . . It's curious. A cat tastes just like a rabbit. Once I thought I was eating roast sheep — then afterward I learned it was a dog."

I saw Ramon only a few times. The last time we met by accident in the subway and he was leaving for the front. That was when things were very bad at Stalingrad and it seems most doubtful that Ramon may be alive today. Without revealing any secrets he gave me a first intimate picture of what makes the Red Army man a first-class soldier. When he did not come back I missed Ramon. He was what the Spaniards call a *verdadero* — which is more than "the real thing." I should translate it "a man of quality."

About the time I met Ramon the first wartime session of the Supreme Soviet of the USSR was held in the Kremlin to ratify the new Russo-British treaty. This was a notable event in itself, but especially so for me for three reasons: I saw Joseph Stalin for the first time, I saw how the Soviet government's parliamentary organization functions, and for the first time I got a vivid conception of the polyglot nature of the vast Soviet Union. We entered the Kremlin by the Borovitzkiya Gate, which adjoins a hoary structure built in 1473, and we had to pass five separate and very rigid inspections of our press credentials before we were admitted at last to the gallery of the Supreme Soviet hall on the top floor of the Great Palace. Under the czars part of this hall had been the Throne Room of St. Andrew, where Nicholas II and his predecessors had received the Romanovs' crown. Today the ornate blue and gold and pink and gold of czardom has been replaced by a subdued and strikingly simple decoration. At the front of the long hall, behind the platform and in a niche in the wall, stands an impressive statue of Lenin in pinkish-gray granite. More than twelve hundred members of the Supreme Soviet, representing sixteen Soviet Federated Socialist Republics and numerous autonomous regions, stretching from the Baltic Sea to the Pacific Ocean near Kamchatka, filled every seat in the auditorium below us. A. A. Andreyev, president of the Council of the Union of the Supreme Soviet, occupied the center chair directly behind the speaker's rostrum, and most of the benches farther back on the platform were empty.

Suddenly a great storm of applause broke out as a small group of men took their places on the two rear benches of the platform. These were the members of Soviet Russia's all-powerful Politburo * and the recently formed Supreme Council of Defense — the ten men who control the destinies of the USSR's 190,000,000 inhabitants. But the cheers were for one man, Stalin. He was dressed in a plain gray military tunic, or smock blouse, tight-fittting at the neck. He stood smiling for a moment and then sat down. The thing that struck me first was that he looked rather slight and shorter than most of the others. Stalin, although commander-in-chief and premier and chairman of the Supreme Council of Defense and of the Council of People's Commissars, took no active part in the proceedings. Sometimes he watched and listened with his chin resting on a raised palm. Sometimes he talked animatedly with Mikhail Kalinin on his right, or with Foreign Commissar Viacheslav Molotov or Lazar Kaganovich. When a speaker evoked pronounced applause, Stalin clapped his hands in a perfunctory fashion. He did not seem at all interested in playing the role of a powerful dictator, or to have any desire to take the spotlight. I was struck by the fact that, in this great and colorful assembly, Stalin resorted to no tricks in mannerisms or attire to attract attention. In his rear seat off to the back of the big stage he looked rather shy and almost wizened.

Meanwhile we looked down upon what is probably the most variegated and colorful political assembly anywhere in the world

* Political Bureau of the Central Committee of the Communist Party.

today. Hundreds of men and women sat quietly, almost motionlessly, with earphones pressed to their heads. But their features and their dress were in extraordinary contrast. There were Moslem features, Russian features, Armenian, Georgian, Mongoloid — and as I studied them I suddenly realized that this, whatever its political creed, is the only true league of nations left in our present world. These men and women represented more than fifty different races (almost as many as had ever sent delegates to Geneva), and they and their people spoke more than one hundred and thirty different languages and dialects. Suddenly the tremendous and incredible scope of the Soviet Union came home to me as it never had before. Nowhere else in the world was a reunion of representatives of so many completely different races and creeds and traditions possible under one roof. This was what the "ten days that shook the world" had finally accomplished. The rest of the world's nations might experiment with internationalism, bungle with internationalism, or balk at it and betray it. Here in the Great Palace of the Kremlin was the personification of an internationalism that already covered one sixth of the earth. Whether we liked either its ideology or some of its methods had nothing whatever to do with this fact. This internationalism was still holding itself together despite the most formidable armed assault — and as I looked down I saw one thing very clearly. Whatever the faults of the Soviet regime and system this internationalism drew no lines of creed or color. It had rejected the poison of racial discrimination. If Americans and Britishers and Germans and others of the white race continued to practice racial discrimination, what would they be doing? Eventually they would make the Kremlin and Communism the one refuge and hope of four fifths of the human race. Where else would Chinese and Japanese, Burmese and Indians, Jews and Arabs, Negroes and a vast legion of the white race's dispossessed be able to turn?

Here were burnished bronze faces of Buriat Mongols. Here were Tajiks and Turkomans from Asia's deep south, and here a row of dark-skinned Uzbeks, their heads crowned with small Moslem skullcaps embroidered in bright yellow, red, and green. Here were Tatars and Ukrainians and Yakuts and Samoyeds from far-northern Siberia. All were dressed in their native costumes and all were symbols of strange, far places and utterly different customs and traditions — yet all, or nearly all, understood and spoke Russian. To me this was a phenomenon which no amount of anti-Marxist sentiment or prejudice could ever touch. This was a kind of political assembly such as the world, until Lenin came and conquered, had never seen or ever dared to attempt to unite. I had seen and reported many sessions of the League of Nations Assembly, but in all the years at Geneva I had never witnessed anything so thought-provoking as this.

I do not intend to indulge in sentimental cheering. Perhaps it is simply an appropriate reminder — as it certainly was to me — that Americans and Britishers have still failed to consecrate themselves to an international society, and while we have been torn by dissensions and nationalistic greed another experiment in international society has been fast coming of age. As I watched the speakers who addressed the Supreme Soviet I observed that this international organization, in convention before me, still suffered from obvious lacks. I did not get the feeling that any of these delegates was likely to feel free to stand up and speak his mind. I noticed that virtually every speaker read his speech — it had obviously been written out carefully in advance. For me that very fact robbed the meeting of what would have been its greatest force. This body constituted a startling step toward internationalism, but it still had not reached the stage where democratic expression could reign. If that time ever came, with what arguments or protests could the democratic nations hope successfully to reply?

3

In Soviet Russia I learned, even more than in Republican Spain or Finland, what all-out war really means. Except for the aged and the infirm it seemed almost impossible to find a Russian, male or female, above the age of fourteen who was not contributing directly to the war effort. Everywhere women were doing the work of men; cleaning the streets, driving Moscow's buses, operating the subway trains, running boats on the Volga Canal, manning at least half of the city's very numerous anti-aircraft batteries, digging and reinforcing the fortifications, driving and unloading the trucks which brought Moscow its food and fuel. By mid-June almost all young women between the ages of sixteen and thirty (who were not employed at "must" jobs) had been sent off to the forests to chop down trees so that Moscow, having lost the rich coal production of the Donets Basin, might have a bare minimum of fuel for the winter. For five months these thousands of women worked ten or eleven hours a day, chopping and sawing wood in the forests, delivering it by truck, and piling it in the city's courtyards and cellars. In Russia's factories men and women workers also averaged an eleven-hour day. Whenever we went out into the country we saw the earth being plowed, or crops being planted, tended, or harvested — only by women and children. Once, near Volokolamsk, I saw a large group of children scouring the woods with big baskets. They were picking mushrooms, which alone might spell the difference between starvation and survival in January or February.

In Russia you had the feeling that this was everybody's war. You could see that virtually no one was spared from sacrifices and that virtually everyone was paying a real price for the arms and supplies which kept the Red Army fighting. In the first year of the war several millions of Russian soldiers and civilians had died. Perhaps six or eight million persons — at any rate, such a great number that already the overwhelming majority of Russian families had suffered at least one death in the family. People everywhere were wearing older and shabbier clothes than they had worn for many years, and everywhere people were poorly fed. Yet I never heard of a Russian suggesting that they might as well quit fighting. On the streets you saw many drawn faces and some which revealed pronounced suffering, but not so many as you would expect. It was the peasant strength and endurance of the Russians which kept them going, the dogged will by which they had survived centuries of serfdom. But while summer was still here, and we correspondents were enjoying potatoes, cucumbers, and tomatoes with our privileged rations at the Metropole, it came as a shock to encounter a Russian family which had nothing to eat for its principal meal that day but some coarse rice or barley. Most of the vegetables went to the army or the wounded and the factory workers. White-collar workers rated less food. Housewives, non-working dependents, and the aged rated progressively less than the others. In regard to food Russia's vast population was divided into categories strictly according to their active contributions to the war. The old and the crippled and the weak would gradually die of disease or hunger. But this was the only way the war could be fought.

In Russia during the summer and autumn of 1942 the official ration allowances (often unavailable in full in the lower categories) were as follows: *

	1st-Cl. Workers	*Office Workers*	*Dependents*
Bread	$1\frac{3}{5}$ lb.	1 lb.	$\frac{4}{5}$ lb.
Meat or eggs or lard	5 "	$2\frac{2}{5}$ "	$1\frac{1}{5}$ "
Cereals	5 "	3 "	2 "
Sugar or jam	$2\frac{2}{5}$ "	$\frac{3}{5}$ "	$\frac{2}{5}$ "
Butter or fat	2 "	$\frac{4}{5}$ "	$\frac{2}{5}$ "
Fish	3 "	$1\frac{3}{5}$ "	1 "
Food per month, exclusive of bread	$17\frac{2}{5}$ lb.	$8\frac{2}{5}$ lb.	5 lb.

For secretaries, clerks, and office workers of all kinds one pound of bread a day and 8 2/5 pounds of other food per month provides a diet not far above the subsistence level. Yet it was perfectly plain that there were millions of people in the USSR who were existing on much less than this. In Moscow and in other large cities, it is true, there were a few open markets where the collective farms were allowed to dump a small amount of surplus produce in the summer months — such things as cabbages, carrots, cucumbers, and the like. But the prices in these open markets were almost prohibitive for the ordinary worker. Whereas many workers earned no more than 500 rubles a month, two pounds of potatoes sold for 80 rubles and a quart of milk for 50 rubles. One Russian, who had three persons in his household, told me they had to spend about 100 rubles a day for extra food — very poor food, he said, but just enough to keep from being hungry. He had a better income than most and his mother was keeping alive by means of her dwindling savings, based upon small things she had salvaged during the Revolution.

Thus everywhere in Moscow, and probably everywhere in Russia, people who possessed any articles of value flocked to the

* Figures are per month except for bread, which is figured per day.

commission shops. They sold irreplaceable things — a coat or a sweater or a rug or furniture — for what they could get, usually no more than a few hundred rubles, and used the money for food. One day I watched an old woman offer a very good woolen blanket in a commission shop. It was a blanket which would be almost priceless in the fiercely cold winter, because blankets of any kind simply cannot be found in Moscow. The old woman received 450 rubles. She would probably eat that up in a few weeks, and then freeze to death when winter came. If the war lasted another year or two, I wondered how many millions of people in Russia must inevitably die of exposure and starvation. As they sold or bartered their humblest possessions, these people were using up the only reserves they had in the world. You could see women hungrily eyeing fresh tomatoes in the market in Arbat Square — but the tomatoes cost 100 rubles for two pounds, perhaps one fifth or one sixth of a month's income for an office worker. It was against the law to sell second-hand articles outside the government-controlled commission shops. Nevertheless people sidled around the alleys of the Arbat market with pitiful old belongings, looking for customers when the police were not in sight. One man had a tiny old electric plate, such as is used for heating water for tea. He asked 300 rubles for it, the equivalent of $25 at our "diplomatic" dollar-ruble exchange rate. There was one woman with an ivory comb and a pair of scissors; another with a dilapidated pair of shoes; and one man, with a watch that looked like a very cheap old-fashioned Ingersoll, was asking 1,000 rubles — what would equal about two months' income for most Russian workers. When you saw these things you wondered how people lived and what they could possibly have that they could turn into food in another year or two. One day on Sverdlosk Square a boy offered me a small cake of soap for 80 rubles — $6.66 at the rate at which we foreigners bought rubles. But in Russian terms this one cake of soap was worth approximately one full day's work for most people.

You could live in Moscow and not be conscious of the problems of existence which afflicted the average Russian family. Ever mounting privations were endured privately, behind apartment walls where people lived crowded three or four or more in single rooms. Now and then, however, the tragedies born of wartime suffering struck you in the face and without warning in the course of a walk through the streets. One day I met a ragged thin woman who was talking wildly to herself. It was plain that her reason had snapped under the strain of a cruel existence. This was probably happening to many elderly persons in the sprawling bypaths of Moscow. Another day, walking up the southern side of the Kremlin toward Mokavaya, I was mesmerized by a sickening sight. A bony barefooted woman, clad only in a single dirty garment, was standing on a corner across the street. She was standing still, staring vacantly into space, and urine trickled down her skinny legs, forming a pool around her naked feet. She did not move, nor did she seem to know what was happening. She would never know whether the war was won or lost.

"If it's like this after one year of the war, what will it be like after another year?" my companion asked.

It was easy to write dispatches about Russia's wonderful fight. But what did we who wrote them and those who read them comprehend about the cost of this wellnigh superhuman resistance?

One day I talked with a girl who worked as a volunteer in a Moscow hospital where the wounded were now so many they could scarcely be cared for. "I'm only supposed to wash the wounded and feed them," she said. "You see, I've never had any nurse's training. But now we have so many men, and so few doctors and nurses, they can't be treated properly. Yesterday I had to change bandages on some badly injured soldiers. Some of them had had the same bandages without any change for days. There was nobody else to do it, so I had to do it. One boy had a big hole in his head and it was covered with pus. I washed the hole with alcohol — I tried to keep it clean. Then I put on another bandage. That was all I could do."

"Have you been short of nurses for long?" I asked.

"They've always been badly overworked, and now many doctors and nurses have been sent to the front. What can one do? I try to comfort those who are hurt the worse. I talk to them, and often soldiers will hold my hand when they are dying. It's easier for them if they can hold a woman's hand. Yesterday there was one very young boy — really such a good face and such fine eyes. I knew he couldn't live long. He held my hand and said: 'Yes, I'm dying. But I can die happy. The fascists have killed me — but I killed many more fascists.' . . . Do you know, I can never forget how brave they are."

Another day several of us went for a hike in a lovely wood on the outskirts of Moscow. Before the Revolution this had been an estate belonging to some Russian nobleman. Its trees and lanes showed that the Soviets had given it expert care. In one of the lanes we encountered a very little, very old woman who was carrying a huge bundle of firewood on her back. She looked so extremely old to be carrying such a load that I prompted a friend to converse with her. We learned that the old woman was eighty-four, and with only one tooth in her head she looked all of that. She said she had a son who had been in the hospital, unconscious for weeks from a head wound; and that he had fought in the other war, too. As we were leaving her, sharp-eyed but bent and bowed under her great bundle of firewood, our translator made some such remark as: "Why work so much?" The little eighty-four-year-old Russian woman tossed her head and said: "Oh, I still have a lot of work to do."

These were the people whom Hitler thought he could shatter in a three-month blitzkrieg.

4

In the hospitals I met many soldiers who spoke simply but truly for the entire Russian people. One of these was a Red Army colonel, a keen-faced man in his forties, whose left leg had been amputated above the ankle. He talked of the fight for Stalingrad, but he did not even ask why the British and Americans were so slow in opening a second front. "We've got to finish them once for all," the colonel said. Then he bent over impatiently and made a swift gesture of tying something on the stump of his leg. "Give me another foot. I can still fight. We Russians will meet you in Germany." As I said good-by the colonel added: "Good luck to you and your people." That remark stayed with me. Under the circumstances it seemed one of the most magnanimous things anyone had ever said to me.

Another day we visited the Yauza Hospital, formerly a nobleman's home and the mansion in which Prince Murat had lived while he was with Napoleon in Moscow. Some of the wounded here had just been brought in from the central front, traveling two days and nights and going straight to the operating-table upon arrival. I didn't know this when I stopped beside the bed of a young boy, only eighteen. Thoughtlessly I began to question him about the battle. His face was pale and suddenly the tears started rolling down his cheeks and he broke into sobs. He could not bear the thought of the battle. I have seldom hated myself so much as at that moment.

My secretary introduced me to Anton Yakushev, in a corner cot. Anton was formerly a collective farmer in the Orel region south of Moscow. He had a face like an Iowa farmer's, seamy and gaunt, and he was thirty-seven. His left leg, broken in several places and torn with shrapnel, had just been placed in a cast and was suspended above his bed in one of those hanging devices which are weighted to keep the limb in a certain position. Anton had come from the operating-table only an hour before. Sweat stood out on his forehead as he started to tell me about the battle.

"Never mind," I said. "Don't tell me now. I'll come back another day."

But Anton would not be stopped. He told me how the attack was made, how the Russians gained only fifty yards in the first assault, how the Red Army's secret weapon Katusha was used, how they attacked again, how he was wounded and tried to crawl forward as his comrades captured the enemy strongpoint in the village. The sweat coursed down Anton's forehead and sometimes he paused slightly between phrases or sentences, but his brown eyes were steady. He talked simply, as a man from the land talks. At the end Anton managed a flickering smile and, as if apologizing, he said:

"They broke the bone in my leg this morning. Usually I'm cheerful."

I made some reply that could only have been idiotic. But Anton was lifting himself on one elbow again. With an effort he pointed at his leg in the sling.

"But it'll be better soon. It's got to get better. In a few weeks I must go back. You see, nobody can fight for me."

Chapter XII

BLACK SUMMER AND BLOOD-SOAKED EARTH

A Russian can endure anything and everything.
Russian proverb

First, and before everything, one saves a besieged city by swearing that the enemy will not get into it.
A Russian official to Eve Curie

Early in June, just as General von Mannstein was throwing ten divisions against Sevastopol, Alec Werth and Marjorie Shaw reached Moscow from Murmansk. The convoy with which these two British correspondents traveled had taken exactly thirty-three days from England to Russia's Arctic supply port. For six days German dive-bombers, operating from northern Norway and profiting by some twenty-two hours of daylight daily, had attacked the Allied convoy incessantly. Eight out of thirty-two ships, heavily laden with weapons for the Red Army, were sunk. Near the end of June another huge convoy of some forty vessels lost almost seventy-five per cent of its ships on the suicidal Murmansk run. After that no more convoys traversed the Arctic route until September.

These disastrous sinkings were chiefly due to the airfields which the Nazis held along the upper tip of Norway. There had been a time in the spring of 1940 when Allied troops held Narvik and the French general in command wanted to remain there, but somebody in London — with a lack of foresight already too familiar — had insisted upon withdrawal from northern Norway. That fatal decision was now costing the Allies hundreds of thousands of tons of shipping and considerably weakening Russia's power of resistance. For the northern sea route was by far the shortest and most important means of supplying Russia. Dozens of tons could be shipped to Murmansk and Archangel for every single ton transported some 15,000 miles by ship around Cape Town and then over the limited, laborious Iranian land artery. So Lend-Lease shipments to Russia received a grave setback just when Hitler launched his great 1942 summer offensive. We couldn't file dispatches about the crippling ship losses on the Murmansk run, but everyone in official Moscow knew that the black days which lay ahead for the Russians had been made considerably blacker. Contrary to popular opinion in the United States, and possibly in Britain, Lend-Lease weapons were not yet in Russia in sufficient strength to play a dominant part in the Red Army's second summer of battle for survival. As a matter of fact, Allied materials could not become of some decisive quantity in the Soviet Union until the end of 1942 — after the decision at Stalingrad had already been settled.

But this was June, Anglo-American aid was being choked off in the Arctic, and the Nazis were throwing against Sevastopol a mighty force of nearly 300,000 men, hundreds of tanks, and hundreds of planes.* For thirty days, outnumbering Sevastopol's defenders by four and five to one, the Germans and their satellite Rumanian divisions pounded the hills outside the old Crimean seaport and the historic approaches to Balaklava. The city itself was slowly blasted to pieces by thousands of bombing assaults and then by 24-inch German siege guns. Until this moment no modern city had suffered such an intense and ceaseless deluge of steel and fire, but the Russians fought on and on. In cellars and caves and holes in the ground Sevastopol's defenders somehow clung to life, although their numbers dwindled steadily and reinforcement from the Black Sea finally became impossible. It was a hopeless fight with only death and glory for an ending. The struggle, which began with heavy Nazi air raids on June 2, finally ceased when the Axis tide swept over the last numbed, half-starved remnants of Sevastopol's garrison on July 2. The Russians had achieved an epic of human valor, but they had lost the Crimea. In reality, however, the Red Army had gained thirty days. These thirty days had cost tens of thousands of lives — as well as several German-Rumanian divisions for the enemy — But Hitler's main summer drive for the Don River had been delayed most dangerously. Events were to show that the thirty days contributed by those who gave their lives at Sevastopol may well have saved Stalingrad — and with Stalingrad the lives of

* Cf. *Moscow Dateline* by Henry Cassidy, pages 234–6.

hundreds of thousands of American and British soldiers.

But the fall of Sevastopol, when it was officially confirmed by the Soviet high command on July 4, offered no hope of eventual compensation to the heartsick Russian people or to foreigners in Moscow. What made this blow all the more cruel for the Russians was the fact that some 20,000 Allied troops had surrendered Tobruk after only a few hours of resistance just a few days previously. Now Rommel was in Egypt, and as Sevastopol was falling Winston Churchill admitted to the House of Commons that the British had no more than 100,000 men in Egypt when Rommel started his offensive from Libya. It was more than two years after the capitulation of France and the perilous loss of the French army in Syria. Why, by this time, should there not have been at least 250,000 men in Egypt? These were things which it was extremely difficult to explain to people who had fought as the Russians were fighting. They were also difficult for many Englishmen to understand. I talked with a friend in the British Embassy who was saying what Britishers all over the world must have been saying:

"We had Crete for six months. General Sir John Dill inspected it and declared its defenses were excellent. Then Crete was a catastrophe. Its airfields hadn't even been mined. Then there was Singapore without a single big gun trained toward the mainland. . . . The *Prince of Wales* and the *Repulse*. . . . And now Tobruk. We've had it for months and months. They say it was chiefly defended by tanks. But why? Why hadn't we installed concrete fortifications and big guns. I don't understand how it could happen. It's just a bloody awful business."

As Russians fired their last rounds in the rubble of Sevastopol, Rommel's divisions were capturing El Alamein, the last British fortified spot still in front of Alexandria, less than seventy miles away. When Russians in Moscow heard this news, their eyes darkened with despair. According to their understanding of the June agreement, the British and Americans had promised to open a second front in Europe — by which they understood *on* European soil — some time in 1942. Now came this major disaster in Egypt. Now, suddenly and inexplicably, it appeared the Axis might conquer Egypt and sweep on into Palestine and Syria. Hitler's summer offensive, launched on June 28 from

Kursk when the fate of Sevastopol was sealed, had reached Voronezh, and the Nazis' armored spearhead had already penetrated southward along the Don as far as Boguchar. The battle for the great Don bend and for Stalingrad was in its opening phase and the Red Army, fighting bitterly, was being pushed backward despite all sacrifices. "If the British cannot even hold Egypt," the Russians were saying, "what help can we expect?" When little gray-haired Pasha came in to tidy my room her face wore an unaccustomed gloom. "The news is bad," she said. "Everywhere the news is bad. Do you think there will really be a second front?"

"Those British and Empire troops in Libya have put up a wonderful fight," a highly qualified American officer said to me. "They deserve plenty of credit. But the leadership and planning they've had has been simply atrocious. Twice Rommel should have been cut to pieces. If British commanders would only learn by past mistakes. The trouble is they've got too many lightweights at the top."

I talked with the wife of a young Red Army officer who had just been released from the hospital. He had only twenty-four hours of leave before returning to the front. His wife said: "Sacha was very nervous. Sometimes he would start to say something and then there would be tears in his eyes. I tried hard to make him forget, but I couldn't succeed. I wanted him to have pleasant things to remember, but he always thinks of his friends who have been killed. So many of them have been killed. Then he worries about leaving me in Moscow, in case the Germans should come back again. If he could have had seven days to rest, instead of one day — "

To foreigners the stoical Russians seldom revealed the torment of their doubts and fears, but in little things we saw how their anxiety mounted as the Nazis swept down the railroad to Millerovo and on toward Rostov and the news, through July and into August, always told of more reverses. The communiqués' set formula: "Our troops inflicted heavy losses on the enemy," could not conceal the truth. Among the wounded in the hospitals it was tremendously difficult for the authorities to maintain morale. The men who had just been brought in from the front, who knew how the supremest courage of the troops still did not suffice to halt the enemy, were subject to deepest gloom and sometimes outright despair. These were not things which foreigners heard much about, for the Soviet authorities rightly kept their morale problems to themselves. Even so, the Russian soldier, however magnificently brave, was also human. Among themselves many of the wounded questioned whether victory would ever come. They debated about the second front especially. Many of them scoffed: "There'll never be a second front. The British and the Americans don't want to lose their men. We'll be fools to count on them. We can only keep fighting as long as we can fight." And some, on the blackest days, asked: "What's the use?"

But when I talked with Brigadier General Philip Faymonville, chief of the U. S. Army mission in Moscow and one of the finest and most capable American officers I have met anywhere in the war, I got the long view of a man who really knows Russia and the Russians. General Faymonville, who had been completely right about the fighting capacity of the Red Army when most of the American General Staff was as completely mistaken, appreciated fully the terrific strain and the world-wide peril of the battle for the Don. But he understood the granite quality of the Russian character. "These people often get the blues and down in the mouth," said the general. "But they're not defeated and they're not rebellious. They've got remarkable leadership. It knows how to kindle and rekindle a great fighting spirit — and this leadership goes from the top all the way down. Their war commissars are playing a big role now in holding morale." . . . It was true that the commissars were doing a wonderful job at keeping the soldiers' fighting spirit at top pitch, but Russian civilians knew too well the terrific cost of this titanic struggle in the south. The whole rich Donets Basin was gone. On the Don steppes hundreds of thousands of acres of tall and ripening wheat — bread for millions of Russians — was being ravaged. The Germans had overrun the defenses of Rostov with startling swiftness and had crossed the Don's lower line to thrust southward into the Kuban. As the Red Army's finest divisions were rolled steadily back Russia's richest earth was soaked with Russian blood, ever deeper and always more red.

On such a day I met Ramon's young compatriot, the dark-eyed girl who had escaped the fascists on the last ship to leave Bilbao in June 1937. The other ship, crowded with hundreds of Basque and Spanish children, had been blown to pieces before her eyes — by Nazi bombers fighting for Franco through the permission of the British-French "non-intervention" policy. Juanita had ample reason to understand that this was all one fight. Since she was half-Basque and half-Spanish, her reaction was uncompromisingly direct.

"I'm going to the front," Juanita said. "I'll never sit in Moscow and wait for it to be starved out. I can't do it. *Yo no puedo.* If I die what difference does it make? I'm just a little person. Look at the big people who have died. I'll get all the grenades I can carry and go for the fascists' tanks. I'll kill some Nazis. That's all that matters. I can't stay in Moscow. I am Spanish. At least I'll avenge my father and mother. I'm not afraid to die. If God wants it, I'll live. If God doesn't wish me to live, then it makes no difference."

Juanita went to the proper commissariat and volunteered for the front. The Russian commissar listened carefully. At the end he told her: "If I have to stay up all night I'll fight the idea of sending you to the front now. You are young and you are Spanish. If things get worse, perhaps we shall need you. But you should wait until autumn and see how things are." This was at a time when it must have been difficult to refuse any volunteer, but the commissar's view prevailed.

2

From Tsimlianskaya, Field Marshal von Bock's panzer divisions had crossed the Lower Don elbow below Stalingrad and were fighting up the main railroad, northeastward through Kotelnikovo. The upper jaw of von Bock's pincers was threatening to cut the Don above Stalingrad. And the Berlin radio, on August 10, claimed that von Mannstein's spearhead had broken through to Piatigorsk, deep in the foothills of the Caucasus. I took out my map and measured the distance. The Nazis had already driven south and southeast 327 miles from Rostov. They were now only 170 miles from the great oilfields of Grozny, and the remaining route was barred by nothing more than low hills. In the seventh week of his offensive Hitler had the first rich oil prize of the Caucasus just beyond his reaching armored talons. Before August ended, it seemed most probable that the Germans would capture Grozny and break through to the Caspian above Baku. Even General Faymonville, always most careful and measured in his judgments, was doubtful whether the Russians would be able to hold Grozny — and everyone knew what it would mean to the entire war if the Nazis once struck Caucasian oil.

In these days of endless battle and unending retreats everything was black, black and red, for the Russian people. While the Red Army fought with desperate frenzy and scores of thousands of its men were being mowed down in unequal struggle, press reports from Allied countries daily reached Soviet officials in Moscow. One of these, from the *Chicago Tribune,* said: "The second front exists in the Pacific." Another, from the London *Daily Mail* openly hinted that the second front might be postponed until 1943. Observations of this sort from both the United States and Britain were not reprinted in the Soviet press, since they would have seriously damaged the Russian people's morale. But distrust of British-American intentions was steadily fanned among Soviet leaders by comments of this sort. Moscow was well informed about the speeches and policies of American senators, publishers, and other former isolationists who still revealed no desire to fight and defeat Nazism but limited their professions of patriotism to a clamor for vengeance on Japan. The Red Army was still the only Allied army that was really fighting the Germans and paying a very heavy price in bloodshed as it fought. With Colonel Robert McCormick's *Chicago Tribune,* Captain Patterson's *New York Daily News,* the Hearst press, and some others consistently flouting an anti-Soviet bias and a thinly disguised aversion to fighting it out with Nazi Germany, it was inevitable that Moscow, in these dark days, should question America's good faith. The British press was less offensive than the American in tone, but some Britishers privately made up for that.

At lunch at the Metropole one day the correspondent of the London *Daily Express* explained there would be no second front in 1942 because the Russians were not ready for it. "Of course, we can't open a second front in the west," he said, "until the Russians are able to take the offensive here in the east." It seemed a strange idea, when the second front was supposed to relieve the enormous pressure on the Soviet Union, that the Allies should wait until the Russians were strong enough to stage an offensive of their own. Such remarks, coming from a British correspondent, could merely heighten distrust of his government's intentions. The Russians had suffered something like 4,000,000 killed, wounded, and missing from their armed forces in the first year of their resistance. They were well aware that the combined British and American war losses were still not much more than one tenth of that figure. As the Don flowed red with Russian blood, the least that British and American representatives in Moscow could do was to be tactful and understanding — and also humble. But this was not always the case.

One night I dropped in on Alec Werth and found a member of the British mission, a naval officer, singing the praises of General Franco, the puppet of Hitler and Mussolini. He had been in Spanish ports during their war and all the "best people," he said, were for Franco. When I reminded the lieutenant commander that the Nazis' bombers had blasted the Basque town of Guernica to pieces as practice for London, Coventry, and Plymouth, he remonstrated: "But the Loyalists were aided by Russia."

"My God!" I exclaimed. "What are you British doing now? What are we Americans doing? We're being aided by the Russians. We're living on the Russians. If you detest the idea of Russian aid, why don't you go home? What in hell are you doing in Moscow?"

There were a few American officers, smart-alecky and glib, of whom one was tempted to ask the same question. Fortunately, among British and American official circles these were in a minority, but they contributed nothing to Allied solidarity and they served to increase the distrust which grew in Russian minds as their situation became more desperate. Sometimes little things happened which would make a normal person blush with shame. In mid-August a newly arrived Allied officer, visiting a war plant, made this remark to a Soviet woman engineer: "I've seen many old people, some of them begging for food. We take care of our old people. Why don't you take care of yours?" The Russian woman looked the officer straight in the eyes and replied with remarkable calm: "We hope to take better care of our old people after the war. But right now what are you doing to help us fight Germany?" A Russian told me of this incident with understandable indignation. It was an all too vivid demonstration of the failure of both British and American military commands to select every officer they sent into Russia with extreme care, laying particular stress upon intelligence, breadth of views, and adaptability. No American or Englishman who was not wholeheartedly anti-Nazi and anti-Fascist by conviction had any business representing our armed services in Soviet Russia; least of all when the Russians were still carrying virtually all of the punishment of Hitler's armies. In the absence of a second front, minor deficiencies and irritations from our side magnified themselves many times over in their contribution to lack of unity and confidence between the three great Allied powers.

I mention these incidents because they served to make Russia's black summer blacker still. Also because, in fairness, we must recognize that the rocky road to co-operation and understanding with Soviet Russia is a two-way affair. If the Soviets were secretive about their military weapons and plans, would you expect them to confide everything to Allied representatives with the mentality of the British naval officer? Winston Churchill came to Moscow, and later Wendell Willkie. I shall not discuss their visits in detail since Henry Cassidy, Larry Lesueur, James E. Brown, and one or two others have reported them at length in their books. It did not appear that the Churchill visit had done much to boost the Russians' confidence in the Anglo-American war program. "If it doesn't smell powder it smells bad," my Russian secretary remarked aptly. It did not appear that Mr. Churchill left Moscow in good humor. Stalin had apparently spoken with great bluntness and directness. Later Churchill told the House of Commons: "Stalin produced the impression of a man possessing a deep cold-blooded wisdom, with a full absence of any kind of illusions." He also called Stalin "a man of inexhaustible courage and will-power; a simple man, spontaneous and even rude in conversation . . . a man with a saving sense of humor." Most observers in Moscow at the time inclined to believe that the most important aspect of Winston

Churchill's visit might prove to be the resumption of his Russian education, together with a mutually realistic assessment of each other reached by the leaders of Britain and the Soviet Union. But Mr. Churchill had also made a disturbing revelation to our able American Ambassador, Admiral William H. Standley, when he declared himself "allergic to the press." There would come a day when peace must be negotiated for all of Europe and the Far East. Would a statesman who is "allergic" to the world's press be able to prove himself a reliable and staunch champion of a democratic peace settlement? As Mr. Churchill left Moscow one was compelled to wonder.

It is curious but true that Wendell Willkie's unofficial conversations in Moscow seemed to contribute more toward better Allied-Soviet understanding than the Churchill visit had done. Mr. Willkie, of course, was not in the position of having to explain why a second front would be delayed. Furthermore, the United States had not been in the war nearly so long as Britain and our army was still only in the process of formation. This made America's position vis-à-vis Russia considerably more favorable. Nevertheless Wendell Willkie unquestionably did much to convince the Soviet leadership of America's good faith. As yet America was not subject to popular Russian disillusionment nearly so much as Great Britain. A European communist who was close to the Soviet authorities expressed the difference in this fashion: "Here they used to count chiefly on Britain. Now things have changed and the Russians haven't much confidence in the British any more. They look to the United States. They feel the Americans may need a little time to get started, but if they start the job they will finish it." There existed, then, a real opportunity for the United States to win the goodwill of Soviet Russia — in the only place where it could be won, on the field of battle. When would we be strong enough to raise Russia's hope by our intervention? And when our armies did intervene in Europe, would we capitalize the opportunity for improved relations with Russia? That would depend on the Kremlin as well as Washington, of course. But the war had to be won and could only be won by combined military effort. Rommel had been stopped at last at El Alamein, but the Russians were still fighting virtually alone.

A Russian woman, emaciated and weak, had just reached Moscow from Leningrad. There wasn't much news about Leningrad because things were always the same there. Leningrad had now been under enemy shellfire and bombs for almost a year — probably the first prolonged siege that a city of three million inhabitants had ever endured. "Everyone is hungry in Leningrad," the woman said. "Bread is very scarce. The last dogs disappeared in the winter. People try to make soup out of grass. Nearly every day people drop dead in the streets. Somehow they get in enough food so the soldiers can fight and the workers can keep the factories going." No one knew the exact toll of life in Leningrad, but reports indicated that more than one million persons — approximately one out of every three persons in a city the size of Chicago — had died of starvation or exposure since the siege began. In the terrible winter months people had often lived with the corpses of mothers, sisters, or other relatives hidden in their rooms, hoping they could obtain the ration allowance of their dead for a few more days or weeks. Some of the stories which came out of Leningrad were too horrible to repeat. But Leningrad still stood. The Russians had said: "The fascists will never take Leningrad!" They had kept their word — at a price which the outside world could not possibly conceive.

Now the Germans were across the Don bend in great numbers and slashing close to Stalingrad from both above and below. Other Nazi divisions, although slowed down, were battling ever nearer to Grozny. August had gone and with September the mounting threat to Stalingrad weighed on every Russian's consciousness. If Stalingrad fell the Volga would be lost. Moscow could be cut off from behind. The war itself might well be lost, and the forewarnings of another fearful winter were already in the air.

What was winter like for the average family in Moscow? I knew one family which had lived through the first winter of the war in this fashion. Their apartment building had no heat and its water pipes were frozen. Part of the time there was no electricity. Bombs had destroyed the front windows, so seven persons lived and slept on the floor of the small kitchen. Most of the time they had no fire either for heat or for cooking, while temperatures ranged from fifteen above zero down to forty below outside. They lived on bread for the most part, with sometimes a little rice or barley and sometimes weak tea. It was so cold in their kitchen that they lived and slept in overcoats and all the clothes they possessed. As autumn came, this was the kind of winter which scores of millions of Russians saw looming before them once more. If some of them spoke bitterly about the continued absence of a second front in western Europe, they spoke with the justice of those who had suffered most and were still suffering far more than their British or American allies.

3

Hitler's commanders had told the German soldiers they would take Stalingrad on September 16. And on September 16, after a ten weeks' advance of nearly 400 miles, German divisions were fighting in the outer streets of Stalingrad. The bombing and shelling of the great Volga industrial city were already many times more intense than the holocaust which had smitten Sevastopol. In Moscow the most responsible Allied military observers did not dare to say that Stalingrad could stand for another three weeks. Yet they knew that if Stalingrad fell, the war against Germany at the very least would be prolonged for several years — if indeed it were not lost altogether.

On September 11 the Red Army's daily newspaper, *Krasnaya Zvezda* (*Red Star*), declared: "There is no way back from Stalingrad." So the greatest and most decisive battle of the entire war roared toward its zenith of destruction. German units penetrated into the streets of the city, into portions of the factory areas, even through narrow corridors to the banks of the Volga. Nazi bombers executed as many as one thousand flights over the city in a single day. The 62nd Red Army under Lieutenant General Vassily Chuikov, including Major General Rodimtsev's famous 13th Guards division, defended Stalingrad street by street and block by block, throughout September and all through October. While the earth trembled and was pulverized in Stalingrad, the Allied cause trembled with it. The Russian troops which were sent into this inferno of steel and flame and smoke were told: "You stay here. You fight here. You die here. But you must never leave. There is no land on the other side of the Volga." The Russians fought there and died there. From its early beginning the battle for Stalingrad is estimated to have cost the Russians close to 250,-000 in killed and wounded; in other words, more than three times the total American casualties in our first nineteen months of war.

While the gigantic struggle was getting under way at Stalingrad, I went with Ilya Ehrenburg, the foremost writer on the staff of the *Red Star,* to visit a convalescent home for Red Army officers. It was a big country house which had formerly belonged to Prince Troubetskoy and I wondered how many officers of the Czar had lounged in these same spacious rooms during the other war. Ehrenburg came to hold an open discussion with the wounded officers; to give them an up-to-date picture of the war, and to build their morale in the intelligent manner which the Soviets had perfected. The Russians, I observed, did not use their war correspondents simply as war correspondents. They were used for the education of troops and officers. They served as a psychological weapon for national defense. Listening to Ehrenburg and the extremely pertinent questions which the Russian officers fired at him, I wondered if meetings of this sort were a common thing in our army training camps at home.

After inquiring about the situations at Stalingrad and Rzhev, the wounded officers immediately asked about the second front. Ehrenburg, whose mane of disheveled gray hair makes him look like a cockatoo, answered something like this: "There's a political, a military, and a psychological angle to the question of a second front. On the political side there are circles in Britain and America who have never liked our country. There are other circles who want the invasion, but only under the best conditions. The British are slow. They are always used to walking — they never run about anything. Perhaps the real question is: shall we have a real second front, or only an ersatz second front? Will it be soon, or not until next spring? I think there are only a few men who know. We must hope for a second front — but it's safer to depend upon ourselves alone. It will be wiser not to risk deception by expecting too much."

Many of these wounded Russian officers were out of the war for good. All of them were torn by deep anxieties. As Ehrenburg talked, frankly and with a hard realism, I watched their faces. They were strong Slavic faces, but in many of them I saw the struggle to fight off gloom or outright despair. What is the meaning of Tojo as Foreign Minister in Japan? someone asked, revealing clearly that the Red Army's commanders were always thinking of the Japanese menace in the Far East. After the formal talk officers crowded around Ehrenburg, still plying him with questions, and on a certain point one of them definitely was not satisfied. The Nazis' superiority in matériel and numbers, he insisted, showed that Germany had the support of Europe. This was the precise kind of doubting mind that the Soviet war correspondent was working to quiet and clarify. The Soviet Russians understand that the place where wars are finally won is in the minds and hearts of the men who command and the men who fight.

As we rode back to Moscow late that night Ehrenburg urged me to remain in Russia until January. "I feel it's very important for you to stay until January," he said. "By that time the situation should be stabilized." Not until long afterward did I understand the full meaning behind those few words. Stalingrad's fate was hanging in the balance every day and almost every hour. Among the British and American observers in Moscow no one dreamed of looking so far ahead, beyond an autumn fraught with uncertainties and possible disaster, to conjecture about a Russian winter offensive.

In early October I spent seven days in the front sectors around Rzhev. This was the first time that any foreigner, either correspondent or Allied officer, had visited any war zone along the Russian front for more than two days. It was the longest period that any foreigner, traveling outside an organized press group and living with Red Army officers and men, had passed in Russian front sectors. The story of this trip is told in the next chapter in some detail.

Chapter XIII

WITH THE RED ARMY

U.S.S.R.	KRASNAYA ZVEZDA
Central Organ of the Peoples Commissariat for Defense of the USSR	*Editorial Office*
	September 27, 1942

CERTIFICATE

The correspondent of the American newspaper Chicago Daily News, *Leland Stowe, is being directed to the Regular Army together with the writer Ilya Ehrenburg.*

After the end of his trip Leland Stowe must return to Moscow, which is the place of his permanent work.

D. VADIMOV
Chief editor &
Division Commissar

In the flickering light of a kerosene lamp the wizened old woman suddenly pointed her finger straight at me and shrilled: "He's a German. Oh God! Why did I let you in? He must be a German. He doesn't speak Russian."

We were driving long and hard that night, still hoping to reach General Zigin's headquarters northwest of Rzhev before morning. The night was bitter cold and Major Arapov, scouring a lonely village for some hot tea, had piloted us into this peasant's log cabin. Now Ilya Ehrenburg, the Soviet war correspondent, tried to assure the excited peasant woman that I was harmless — and so save our cups of tea.

"He's not German. He's an American," Ehrenburg said.

The old woman peered at me skeptically through the dim lamplight. This village had long been occupied. She had seen many Germans in this same room. Maybe the fact that my hair wasn't close-cropped reassured her. Finally she declared: "Well, if he's an American, tell him they've talked a long time about

America helping us. If America really helps us it will be a great thing." She sighed and twisted her hands nervously as Ehrenburg translated.

"Tell her I hope America will be a real help to Russia very soon." And Ehrenburg told her. She was a frail and tired woman, and her thin shoulders lifted slightly, then drooped again.

"My God, my God! I hope so too," she exclaimed. *"We have waited too long."*

We had a devil's road all that night, from one quagmire into the next. It hadn't rained for days. This seemed to be merely permanent mud and the roadbed was so rough that riding in the rear seat was like being tied on the back of a mad billygoat. Every fifteen or twenty minutes we got stuck again. Sometimes the major's car pulled ours out; sometimes we pulled his out. The road was an endless succession of holes, bogs, and ditches, with pine logs tossed in haphazardly in an effort to offset the quagmires. Sometimes it took twenty minutes to pry the axles loose with logs. The drivers, the battalion commissar, and Arapov worked steadily in ten inches of mud, plunging their arms into the muck up to their elbows and heedless of the freezing cold. Sometimes our chauffeur, Ivan the Terrible, stumbled around in the headlights' glow with his head down like a bewildered bull, his prizefighter's mug screwed up fiercely as he tried to figure a way out.

These, in truth, were the worst roads I had encountered anywhere in the war. Compared to this the Burma Road had been a highway. Once in Norway, with deep snow thawing swiftly, I had experienced something almost as bad. But without any snow or rain the roads toward Rzhev were simply ghastly and unbelievable. All night and for twelve hours we averaged less than ten miles an hour.

"You see," Ehrenburg explained, "all this country, from here hundreds of miles north to Leningrad, is nothing but marshlands and forests. Actually it lies below sea level. You should see it in the spring. No wonder the Germans have trouble with their transport."

All night long our drivers battled with amazing patience and stubbornness and soon after daybreak we came to the edge of a pine-covered slope above the clear and swift-flowing Volga. We followed a path between the thick pines, passed several Russian sentries, and descended toward the riverbank until we stumbled upon tents carefully screened with pine boughs. Just below, the Volga, shallow and narrow at this point, splashed and murmured around projecting rocks. The sun was just beginning to sparkle on its dancing breast and the morning air was wonderfully pure and sharp. The tents were the headquarters of Major General Alexei Zigin's Thirtieth Army. The general was a heavy-set, strong-faced man of forty-four, and his army corps commissar, General-Polytruk* Vassily Boyko, was equally rugged, with quick brown eyes. They greeted us warmly; especially so, I knew, because Ehrenburg's daily column had made him known and respected by every man in the Red Army. Both these commanders wore decorations and I noticed that Boyko wore the Order of Lenin and the medal of a Hero of the Soviet Union. They ushered us into General Zigin's big tent. It was partitioned in two sections, had a large table and a stove, and its floor was covered with soft pine boughs. The general's daughter Elena, a dark-eyed, vivacious girl of seventeen, served us an enormous breakfast as we talked. There was caviar and cheese and cold fish; then a kind of Russian pancakes stuffed with chopped meat — a wonderful dish for wartime Russia — and finally, jam, tea, and cognac. We were still shivering from the night's ride, so we started with the cognac and ended with more.

"We've just routed the Germans' 87th division," General Zigin said. "The fascists held a bridgehead on the north bank of the Volga, and their artillery dominated one of our important communication lines. But we surprised them with a noon attack they didn't expect. We have cleaned them out."

At first it was difficult to get the general and his army corps commissar to talk about the Red Army's new blows against Rzhev from three sides, because they couldn't meet an American without speaking what was chiefly on their minds. Boyko, whose keen mind and exceptional ability had won him the reputation of being one of the best commissars in the Russian forces, plunged straight to the point. "Why don't you Americans take charge and make the British open a second front?" he asked. "Hesitation is what has put Britain in the mess it's in. If you

* *Polytruk* is the Russian abbreviation for political leader.

Americans do the same, where will you land?" I tried to explain the Allies' great shipping difficulties, the strain of the war in the Pacific, and the need of a far greater American air force in England. "Just the same, if you had the decision there would be no obstacle that couldn't be passed," Boyko insisted. "If you were really in the war a great country like the United States should be able to send a million men to Europe within a year." When I replied that our army was still only in the process of formation and that even most of our officers still had insufficient training, General Zigin said slowly: "The best education for officers in war is war itself.' These men were very friendly, but blunt and direct in expressing themselves. Above everything else I sensed in them a great earnestness about fighting the war. They were very determined men. Boyko ended the discussion of the second front by declaring: "But even if America should not march we would still fight on. We have the capacity to continue. History will judge."

By now I had remarked that General Zigin also wore the Order of Lenin, the Red Banner, and the Red Star. I asked how many wars he had fought in.

"This is my third major war — I don't count the little ones," the general laughed. Then refilling the cognac glasses: "Here's to victory for the Allies!"

Elena hovered near the table listening intently. Her father said she had been up to the front the other day. "I had never seen firing so close before," Elena said. "One shell fell only a few yards away, but I wasn't afraid. I went ahead with some of our troops. I wasn't afraid, except for the spiders. There were many spiders in the trenches. I hate spiders. My brother is an aviator. I wanted to join an anti-aircraft battery, but Papa won't let me. He says he needs me here."

Elena's face registered much annoyance, and the general laughed. She was a fine-looking girl and her cheeks were blooming from the outdoor life. As we chatted, guns rumbled fitfully farther down the Volga toward Rzhev, but in this pine forest all was snug and serene. We stepped out of the tent and the day was magnificently clear. General Zigin had arranged for a battalion commissar to take me to an advanced artillery post while Ehrenburg visited another sector. Before leaving, the general took my hand in one of those crushing Russian handshakes. "We must hit the Germans," he said emphatically. "We must do it before it is too late. We Russians shall fight anyway. But unless the British and Americans act soon, the war at best must be very long. Tell your people they must hit the Germans now."

2

"The German positions are over there, just across the Volga."

The battalion commissar pointed southward, but the expanse of wheatlands and occasional knots of trees revealed nothing, not even the river. Rzhev seemed lost in the prairie. Suddenly our chauffeur went berserk. We were driving across open fields and he stepped on the gas so sharply I was two feet off the seat before I could grab an anchor. Then our car was hurdling ruts and ditches like mad as we headed for a small group of peasants' cabins half a mile away. The major grinned and remarked: "They put five shells over here when I was coming for you half an hour ago." That greatly increased my interest in that invisible line along the Volga, but we reached the big knoll beyond the cabins without any music from singing explosives. The Russians' artillery batteries were firing steadily, however, from the lower end of the knoll. The ridge, with its sharp shoulder, gave them excellent protection and the Germans — answering back now — did not seem to have the range. The ridge had just enough shoulder to it and we were in the gully on its leeward side. On its steep slope a series of caves had been built deep into the earth. The commissar led me up steps which had been cut into the slope and then along a narrow passageway well into the bowels of the hillside. There were two rooms and the dugout walls were even whitewashed. This was the artillery battalion's headquarters and Lieutenant Colonel Anatole Alexandrovich Smirnov, its commander, joined us there. The lieutenant colonel almost needed a shoehorn to get into the place. When he straightened up I was looking at a Ukrainian Paul Bunyan — more than six feet of solid brawn crowned with a face like the map of the Ukraine, yet surprisingly similar to scores of Irish policemen whom you see in American cities.

"Horosho, horosho!" boomed Colonel Smirnov. In Russian *horosho* means "good," but when Smirnov uttered the word it

had the resonance of an organ chord with all the stops out. He had almost reduced the fingers on my right hand to the state of ground hamburger and he punctuated his remarks with laughter which nearly rivaled the voice of his guns. I had never met anyone who seemed to be having as good a time out of a war as this Ukrainian giant. The commissar and I followed Smirnov down into the gully, across the brook, and back toward the snug position where his batteries were concealed. All the time the colonel was talking, laughing, and gesticulating as if this particular war was one of the greatest holidays ever invented.

"It's too bad you didn't come two days sooner," he said. "We gave Fritz one hell of a smashing. Caught the whole 87th division half asleep. That's no joke. A lot of those fascists didn't even have their pants on when we hit them. They were scared out of their wits. Hundreds of them drowned trying to swim the Volga. We shot most of them to pieces before they could get back. We caught them with their pants off. Ho-ho-ho!"

Lieutenant Colonel Smirnov roared with laughter, and on we went. As we approached the first battery there was a lull and the guns were so well hidden I could scarcely see them. They were big ones, 155's, too. The battery's captain snapped to attention and in the Red Army this is always done with a precision that would satisfy a Prussian drill-sergeant. "Comrade Colonel," he barked, "we are awaiting the command to resume firing." Smirnov gave the order and the gun crew leapt back to their posts. They were bronzed, tough-muscled, and all in their twenties. "We'll give Fritz this round for you," laughed Smirnov. Properly spaced, the four gun barrels all stood at the same elevation. The captain shouted his command. The big shells were pushed swiftly into place. A soldier, holding the firing cord, leaned forward tensely with his eyes focused on the captain's lifted arm. The other gun-crew men stuffed their fingers in their ears and I followed suit. Then the captain's arm fell, the cord jerked, and the air rocked around us as the big guns bounced back on their recoils. "They'll feel it all right," grinned Smirnov as we went on to the next battery. Sometimes he got warnings of enemy planes. Then the entire battalion fell suddenly silent and additional branches were piled over the gun barrels. But usually these planes were Messerschmitts, in twos or threes, and going somewhere in a great hurry. The German guns were not answering very often and were not hitting near our knoll at all.

"Those Germans are no good with artillery," the lieutenant colonel said disdainfully. "Their gun personnel is second-rate and they can't shoot accurately. I still don't understand why, but the Germans simply don't know how to shoot. We can blow them out of the earth. It's the fault of their preparation or else they've got no real talent for artillery. But Fritz knows what Russian artillery is. He knows—and he'll never forget it."

Again Smirnov's laugh boomed like one of his 155's. We threaded our way back and around, then up the ridge and into a trench leading to the observation post. At its doorway another captain sprang to salute. *"Horosho,"* blasted Smirnov. Then he pointed to the two medals on the captain's chest and turning to me cried: "Another Ukrainian—see!" Then, shaking a clenched fist in the air he added: *"Horosho,* eh?" The captain grinned proudly as we ducked inside. Just below its ceiling a narrow two-inch slit ran around three sides of the tiny dugout. Underneath this slit was tacked a panoramic drawing of the terrain on all sides. Every grove, elevation, and other noteworthy feature was recorded. Smirnov swung the telescope around, focused it, and said: "Take a look at Rzhev." That was what I'd been longing to do for a long time, so I hopped to it. Exactly in the center of the lens lay Rzhev with its clustered roofs and steeples and the heavy smoke of battle around it.

"We've held the northwestern corner of Rzhev for several weeks now," Smirnov said. "Our troops are dug in on one side of the Volga where it goes through the city. It's like Stalingrad; bombings and street fighting. We shell them too. That's why there's always plenty of smoke there. But Fritz will never be able to hold it. We bite off one small piece, then we bite off another. If Fritz wants to stay there, we'll eat him up."

Slipping around the crest of the hill, we headed back toward headquarters. Acres and acres of rich wheatlands spread out before us, their stubble lying yellow and warmly tinted by the late afternoon sun. Out in the plain the weatherstained peasants' cabins squatted serenely. It did not seem possible that the German lines at their nearest point were only two miles away.

"See that?" queried Smirnov, waving his arm toward the

broad wheatlands and the patches of fir trees cropping up darkly against the horizon. "We'll never give that up — never!" Then he pointed down below us near the gully's edge where a score of women were steadily feeding sheaves of wheat into a threshing machine. "You see," said the huge Ukrainian. "They've completed the harvest. German shells couldn't stop them. Fritz shells these fields, but what good does it do him? Ho-ho-ho!"

Inside the whitewashed dugout, where the guns' rumble fell suddenly far away and receded to a dull mumble, we sat down to enjoy tea with Smirnov and several of his staff officers. We had sardines and, of course, vodka; and then something which seemed too good to be true — genuine American Spam. For fourteen months I had forgotten such a thing existed and it seemed strange somehow to rediscover Spam in a deep dugout on the Rzhev front, thanks to Lend-Lease. "That's some of your American sausage. It's good," laughed Smirnov. "But why don't you put skin around your sausage?" As we drank the toasts I noticed that these were keen fighting faces around me. These were men who gave you an immediate feeling of confidence. They were strong and they knew their jobs. They also knew how to make a stranger feel at home, and they hammered me with questions about America and England and the war on the other side of Europe. "Is it for the political reason that they don't start the second front?" asked a dark-haired young major. "Is it because we are Soviets? After all, isn't it more important that fascism should be crushed once and forever?" Then the lieutenant colonel was pounding the table with one massive fist. "If you don't start the second front pretty soon," he boomed, "we'll lick the Germans by ourselves."

I asked about the Nazis' fighting methods on this front and Smirnov replied: "Without tanks the German infantry is nothing. It's only with superior weapons that they fight well. Without tanks and planes Fritz doesn't like to fight at all. Bah! What a race of warriors! Man for man we outfight them every time. Look at Stalingrad. Even with great superiority in planes and tanks they still can't take it. And wait until winter."

"What about the winter?"

"This winter will be several times harder on the fascists than it will be on us. Our men are stronger, much stronger. They're used to terrific cold, and this winter we'll use every lesson we learned from last winter. We have huge numbers of veterans from last year. Take my battalion. My men are young, but they're all veterans. The Germans have had to send a tremendous lot of fresh troops into Russia. All their new divisions have had no experience with the Russian winter — and they're all scared to death of it."

"What are German ski troops like?" I asked.

Again Smirnov roared with laughter.

"I happen to be a skier myself. In fact, I won a ski championship in the Red Army. The Germans — " He laughed again loudly and then put it in one word: "Lousy."

"Tell him about your German general, colonel," urged the major with a twinkle in his eye.

"Oh, my prisoner?" Smirnov poured another vodka. Obviously he was having a wonderful time. "Well," he continued, "when things were a little too quiet last winter, they let me do some raiding back of Fritz's lines. This time I took fifty men with me and we went on skis. We raided Porchov Novgorod, about seventy miles behind the lines. It was midnight and terribly cold, so we caught Fritz with his nose inside his coat collar. Didn't even have to shoot at the sentries. A peasant woman told us a German general was living in the town hall. That was my borsch. All I wanted was a taste of that general." Smirnov pounded the table and his officers grinned. "The woman showed me the upstairs room where the German commander slept. So I posted my men, took off my skis, and climbed up the drain pipe. There was Fritz sleeping like a baby. He didn't have time to squeal more than twice, but he squealed like a pig. I hit him with the butt of my revolver and stuffed a pillowcase in his mouth. I tied his hands and feet and brought him down. A German general was too good a catch. We had to bring him back alive. So I slung him on my back and we got into the forest as fast as we could travel. What a load that pig of a Fritz was! Ho-ho-ho!"

"The trouble with these damned Germans is they eat too much," continued the lieutenant colonel. "Most of their *lebensraum* is in their stomachs. This General Hoffmann wasn't so tall, but he weighed nearly two hundred pounds."

"General Hoffmann? Was he any relation to the General von

Hoffmann who invented the plan for invading Russia?"

"He was a Lieutenant General von Hoffmann — I think a brother of the other von Hoffmann, or a cousin. Anyhow, I slung him on my back like a dead pig and we started back on our skis. I carried him the first three miles and then we passed him around every mile or two. With that general on our backs it was a long way. We had to untie him every few miles and pound him all over to keep him from freezing. When we finally delivered him at our headquarters he looked like he wished Hitler had never been born. Ho-ho-ho! We had plenty of fun on that trip, okay. . . . Yes, Fritz has had plenty of surprises in Russia. But wait until this winter. He's going to get lots more to surprise him. Fritz will get his bellyful of Russia, all right."

It was long after dark now and it would be mean driving across the prairie without headlights. Smirnov escorted us down across the gully and ordered one of his men to accompany us. He was booming *"horoshos"* all the way. When we said good-by he almost cracked my shoulder-blade. "We'll meet you Americans somewhere in Germany," rumbled the happy warrior from the Ukraine. "But you'd better start soon." As we ferreted our way across the wheat-fields, rockets and flares were shooting up all along the front. The outline of the front glowed at intervals for many miles to the south and southeast.

3

"Some of the fellows will want to murder me when they find out I've sneaked off to the front," I remarked to Ehrenburg.

"Oh no," said Ehrenburg with his sardonic smile. "I'm the one who'll be assassinated for this. Not by an agency correspondent, but by one of the special correspondents. They'll never believe the idea wasn't mine. What a way to die when your country is full of heroes!"

But we had great luck in leaving Moscow because a Red Army commissar needed to get back to the Rzhev front, and this commissar, who traveled with us, was Emma Wolf. She was a dark-eyed, black-haired little slip of a woman, not more than five feet two, and she couldn't have weighed much over one hundred pounds. She looked very slight but decidedly trim in her Russian military tunic and she wore her revolver as naturally as an

American frontiersman. She was a *polytruk,* but her rank was equivalent to that of captain. She had been the first woman to be assigned as a front-line commissar with the Red Army. She wore a Red Star medal and I learned she had been wounded in action. But in every sense Captain Emma was an unusual person. She was remarkable in her modesty, in the gaiety and wit which her own private sorrow had never dimmed for long, and for her quiet courage. In the first week of the war Captain Emma, her husband, and her son had all enlisted together. Her husband had been killed many months ago. Her sixteen-year-old boy served in the same Guards division with her. She did not look more than thirty, although she told me, laughing: "You'd better add ten years to that." Her hair had a short mannish cut because it had been shaved off recently when she caught typhus, but neither the haircut nor her uniform could suppress Emma's femininity any more than the horrors of battle had curbed her irrepressible spirit. Emma was also completely unique in my experience because she was the only person I have ever encountered who translated to me in three languages all at once — almost in one breath and all in the same paragraph. Captain Emma usually started in French or Spanish, then she would slip into the other Latin tongue when the going seemed easier; and then, when things began to get complicated, she would throw in a few twelve-syllabled jawbreakers in German. If I had spoken Italian she would have tossed that into her linguistic cocktail as well.

Captain Emma's husband had been an anti-Fascist Italian who joined the Garibaldi Battalion of the International Brigade, so she went with him to Spain. She escaped from Bilbao on a submarine and finally got to France on one of the last Loyalist planes. Fascism, first in Italy and then in Spain, had taught Emma how to hate. When she told me this I thought of something Ehrenburg had once written: "Without hatred war is something shameless. Only hatred as vehement as love justifies war." These were things which Emma did not talk about much, nor did she discuss her own war record except as I plied her with occasional questions during the days that we traveled and worked together. Ehrenburg had his own reporting to do, so it was Captain Emma who relayed questions and answers for me wherever we went.

"Yes, I was wounded — in the head here," she admitted when I made a direct query. "But I had killed twelve Germans before that happened. No, not with my revolver. That was during attacks, with my rifle or tommygun."

We had journeyed in an arc from General Zigin's army corps to that commanded by Lieutenant General Leliushenko on the southeastern side of Rzhev. A Red Army officer led the four of us — Ehrenburg, Captain Emma, Major Arapov, and me — through a trench into the side of a mound of earth, covered with young pines. He opened a door and said: "This is your house." It was a splendidly built and very clean three-room dugout, the same guest dugout in which Wendell Willkie had been quartered for a short time only a few weeks previously. There was a big stove in the dining-room and a Red Army girl even brought towels and placed them on the beds in the other rooms. In the midst of the badlands and shell-torn woods of this front sector this dugout really seemed almost as luxurious as a hotel. While lunching there one day — it was the day they served a few strips of raw bacon and it looked so wonderful that I ate one strip raw as it was — I managed to get Captain Emma to talk about her life as a front-line commissar.

"I'm rather small, it's true," Emma said. "But if a woman is going to be a commissar at the front that's really an advantage. Whenever I lead my soldiers in an attack you should see how gladly they follow. When a woman is advancing against the enemy, naturally the soldiers feel they must be braver than ever. I love to go with our men. They are wonderful in battle. . . . Sometimes my son goes into the attack beside me. Then you should see the soldiers when they see a mother and her son going forward together. Twice before my husband was killed the three of us went into battle side by side."

She paused suddenly and I realized then what lay beneath her façade of jests and laughter and her good comradeship. After a moment she resumed, her voice even once more.

"Bombs and gunfire really don't bother me. I almost always sleep well at the front too. It was only after my husband was killed that I couldn't sleep. For a whole month I could scarcely sleep at all. Then I realized finally that I must concentrate all my strength and all my thought on each day's battle. I must only live for winning the war. Because I still have Vladimir it is easier to do. He is a soldier, but he also writes articles and verse for the division's newspaper. Yes, it's fine to have my boy in the same unit with me. But sometimes it makes it harder, too. When I know he's in an attack — somewhere not far away — but I can't be with him. But I know I can't do my job right if I let myself keep thinking about him or wondering if he'll come back. Then it's really hard. . . . Do you know, it's not difficult to have no fear about yourself. But it's much different and much more difficult not to have fear for someone you love. One has to remember that any one life does not matter. Just as one must remember that the question in this war is not fascism or bolshevism. This war is only one thing — *fascism or humanity*."

Sitting across the table from me, Captain Emma was just a slender little woman who might have been sitting at home — except that she, Emma Wolf, could not possibly be sitting anywhere so long as this war is on. She did not dramatize herself, and she did not indulge in gestures or postures. She was at the front simply because she could not think of being anywhere else, and because she understood why she had to be here. If enough people had only understood why, I thought, then this war would never have happened.

Another day I asked Emma if she thought of anything she would like to say to American women, and her reply was characteristically simple: "I would like American women to know that we have fought very hard for sixteen months now, yet despite our great losses in dead and wounded and despite all the suffering which we must yet endure, Russian women have never lost their courage. Each Russian woman knows the meaning of the words of Dolores Ibarruri. You remember what Pasionaria said — 'It is better to die standing up than to live on your knees.' Well, we know what that means and what it costs." Captain Emma paused and then added slowly, almost reflectively: "All the sacrifices which our women make are made modestly — without big words."

I was reminded of the incredible labor I had seen Russian women doing everywhere; of the millions of Russian women who worked ten or twelve hours seven days a week in the factories; of the millions of women now harvesting the crops all over the Soviet Union; of the girl soldiers who policed the roads all the way from Moscow to Kalinin and on every highway; of the girls who manned more than half of Moscow's anti-aircraft batteries; of women railroad engineers and brakemen, women bringing the cargo boats up the Volga; of the Russian girls we had met everywhere along the front.

"They do this," Emma was saying, "out of a necessity of their hearts."

4

On the outside it seemed just another cabin in another Russian village squatting on the broad prairie some eight miles from the front lines. Inside the door, however, I found myself in a newspaper composing room — the only one I've ever known that actually went to war. Inevitably Russian women were part of this war job, too. Five young girls were busily setting type as Ehrenburg, Captain Emma, and I walked in. The top headlines and half of the front page were already lying in format on the table. Within a few hours the two-page tabloid, the *Son of the Fatherland,* would go to press. This was a typical front-zone newspaper, of which the Red Army has several scores, each published for separate divisions.

But the *Son of the Fatherland's* press room astonished me even more than its composing room. The editor, Regimental Commissar Mikhail Nosov, led me out through the barn which is always attached to Russian peasants' cabins. Before the war Nosov had been a journalist in Minsk. Parked against the rear of the barn we came upon a large truck, well camouflaged with tree branches. Editor Commissar Nosov opened the back of the van and remarked: "There's our press." The press was only three and a half feet square, but clean and shiny. It was bolted into the floor of the truck which also had built-in drawers for the type, a small electric motor, and a tiny stove in one corner. This was the Red Army's newspaper on wheels — and I had never heard of a newspaper on wheels before either.

"We can publish in the forest in a hole in the ground — well, we just travel with our division and publish wherever the front is," Nosov said with a smile.

Alexandra Stagkina, who had a pre-war experience of six years as a typographer, was in charge of the press. Her husband had joined the army on the first day of war. "I've had no news from him for more than a year," Alexandra said. "I think he is dead. If he is dead I think I should do the same as he did. If they will let me I want to take his place in the army."

Back in the cabin's composing room the five girl typesetters, all in uniform, worked with flying fingers. One, a pretty and slender blonde from Moscow, smiled at my question. "This life is more interesting because we change all the time," she answered. "Of course I don't mean I want the war to last forever. We've been on the southern front and many places along the central front. I can't remember how many headquarters we've had."

Editor Commissar Nosov pointed to a buxom brunette, really an Amazon, who was twenty-one and called Nastia. "That girl," he assured me, "can work eighteen hours a day without getting tired." Nastia had flashing dark eyes and wasn't averse to using them. "Tell her it's too bad I'm married," I said, and Nosov translated. The girls burst into peals of laughter. You could always count on the Russians for friendliness and a sense of humor. But, in truth, all of the young Red Army women that I saw in hundreds along the front looked as if they could work eighteen hours a day without any particular strain. Most of Russia's young womanhood, it seemed, were so husky and lusty as to give any medium-sized male a definite case of hesitation. You could understand how Russia had been ruled by three or four empresses in a single century, and why Russian women seemed to have been bossing their good-natured males ever since the days of Catherine the Great.

In a cabin next door Nosov had his editorial room, with a large map on the wall and one typewriter which had to be shared by several soldier reporters. One of these, Grigori Verhovsky, had been so badly wounded at the front that he had spent five months in the hospital. Major Arapov had told me that the *Red Star,* the army's daily paper, had had fourteen of its staff members killed in line of duty up to that time (October 1942). "Men don't like to talk about their own heroism," Verhovsky told me. "But they'll always tell what somebody else has done. When we find out about such cases, then we interview the men and we run photographs of those comrades who have been especially brave.

In that way their whole regiment or division knows immediately what they have done. That kind of recognition means a lot to the men — and it's one of the best ways to build their morale."

Verhovsky showed me copies of half a dozen different front-line publications for Red Army units around Rzhev. One of these, called *Forward against the Enemy,* had a special issue for the Red Army's September offensive against Rzhev. In its columns I noted these items: a list of officers and men who were newly decorated on this front; the sketch of a captain cited for valor; a photograph of a commander of a mine-throwing detachment, who had wiped out sixteen Germans while his men destroyed one hundred more; a cartoon and two poems contributed by soldiers; the announcement of a contest for the best words and music for a Red Army song; and a feature article stressing the importance of snipers. These Red Army divisional or regimental newspapers and news sheets were as personal as a small-town daily — but most intelligently "pointed" to instruct the troops, to boost their pride in their own unit as well as their patriotism, and to fan their hatred of the enemy. As I observed the scope of this army newspaper-on-wheels and the ability with which it was organized, I wondered what the British or American armies could show to compare with this. As far as I knew, we had the *Stars and Stripes,* but the Russian army's daily newspaper, *Red Star,* was admitted by foreign military attachés in Moscow to be in a class by itself — for technical articles by highly placed officers in all branches of the army, for its emphasis on instruction of soldiers, for its constant shaping of the soldiers' mental attitude toward the existing war situation, and for maintaining morale. I had never heard of any other army in the war which also published divisional papers *in the front zones;* nor of any other army with morale-building specialists so carefully trained and working so closely with their men as the Russians' commissars. Was it an accident that the Red Army was still undefeated and still stronghearted after fifteen months of unparalleled punishment and reverses? Everywhere I went along the Rzhev front I found incessant evidence of planning, of leadership, and especially of an extremely intelligent system which had been hitched to hard work. We Americans thought we knew about all there was to know of the psychology of advertising. But what about the psychology of fighting men? No, it was no good hiding behind a comforting patriotism. Every other armed force I had ever seen, including the first-class Wehrmacht of Germany, could learn a good deal from the Red Army.

"Have you been bombed very much?" I asked Nosov.

"We're always being bombed," laughed the editor commissar. "Look behind this cabin. Fritz dropped some eggs there yesterday. Once we were caught in a very big raid. I put all my staff in trenches we had prepared near by. The fascists dropped bombs all around us, but nobody was hurt. Once we were completely cut off by the Germans along with one of our divisions. We all dropped our newspaper work and used rifles instead. Oh yes. Of course the girls fought. We resisted for ten days and finally the division fought its way out. We saved everything. We didn't even lose a stick of type."

Before we left, Nosov insisted he must have our pictures for his next issue. This little isolated village, where German planes passed over many times a day and the guns rumbled most of the time, scarcely seemed a place in which to find a photographer. But the *Son of the Fatherland* had its own staff photographer. Everything in this army was organized. In more than a year of slashing advances the Nazis had even failed to disrupt the Red Army's front-zone newspaper-on-wheels. Mikhail Nosov summed up his unique publishing job in this manner: "The first task of our paper is to show the soldier how to fight better — how to fight with fewer losses and with higher morale. That's why we give so much instruction about sniping. We keep insisting that every soldier must be a sniper. We say: 'Every day every soldier must kill one fascist.' When soldiers read those things every day they remember them. And the soldiers know this is their newspaper because it goes with them wherever they fight."

5

From Lieutenant General Leliushenko's headquarters we swung south to reach another sector where a Guards division was biting closer to Rzhev. We traveled in style that day because Ehrenburg had so much prestige he even procured a jeep. That was really a tribute to Ehrenburg's status with the Red Army, for in nearly a week we saw less than twenty jeeps along this entire front — a revealing indication of how far Lend-Lease still had to go. Jeeps were the only vehicles in the world capable of going places over these almost impassable roads. They seemed to be made for battling the endless bogs and ditches of the vast Russian marshlands. A jeep could travel five or six times as fast as any other vehicle in these front sectors and get through, time and again, where nothing else could. When Ivan the Terrible saw one he growled enviously: "That machine goes everywhere." In a neat balance of enthusiasm and humor the Russians called the jeep "the goat." Transportation was one of their most formidable problems, and twenty or thirty thousand jeeps would have contributed greatly toward turning the tide against the German armies. Unfortunately, not more than a few hundred jeeps appeared to have reached Russia yet; so a jeep at any headquarters or on any front was a prized possession and in use virtually night and day.

Thanks to our Lend-Lease "goat," we made much better time, and after days of jolting, for once our spines were not subjected to a sharp tattoo from ruts and ridges. After a couple of hours the terrain changed completely. The badlands dropped behind and the road twisted through rolling country. Here many trucks growled steadily toward the front and occasionally big guns on caissons, around which the jeep slid easily. We rode on through several villages which could scarcely be recognized as such. Only the broken walls of one or two cabins remained above ground. Everything else had been leveled to the earth by shells and bombs, and in one such desolate spot, surrounded by debris, stood two slender, freshly painted red obelisks, each crowned with a star. They marked the graves of Russian officers who had fallen here recently. Beyond this ruined village the land extended in long graceful swells. It was rich wheatland, caught in the fighting zone and so unplanted, but it wore a warm sheen beneath the bright October sun. And now, quite suddenly, these slopes and crevices were filled with life. Every tight gully and side hill was populated with men of the Red Army.

Until a month ago this had been the front line, and the line was clearly traced in red-earth parapets which hugged the slopes and ran on and on, seemingly without end, across the countryside. The line of red clay cut along the middle of the slopes with a steady row of dark rectangles above it. The rectangles were the doorways of hundreds of dugouts which burrowed snugly into the hillsides, and their parapets made a kind of crude sidewalk which meandered and zigzagged across the landscape. Reserve regiments were now quartered in these dugouts, and in many places smoke curled from stovepipes which barely protruded from the grass. We stopped near a long gully which was crowded by cave-dwellers and their homes. Scores of soldiers were washing their clothes in the stream at the bottom of the gully; others were carrying wood or drinking water, and others were preparing meals at outdoor kitchens.

The Red Army men who crowded around us were deeply tanned, hard-muscled, and uniformly rugged. Most of them seemed under thirty; all were well clad and appeared well fed. A huge iron kettle over a near-by fire was filled with a cabbage and potato stew with hunks of meat mixed in it — a far better dish than most civilians in Moscow had seen for many months. *"Horosho!"* grinned a big Slav sergeant whose immediate anxiety was that we should remain for dinner.

As everywhere, the soldiers plied me with questions about America and the second front. While trying to answer them I was fascinated by the soldiers' faces. There was as wide a variety of racial features here as I had seen at the Supreme Soviet's meeting in the Kremlin, yet one quality seemed common to all — the quality of peasant strength and steadiness. A brown-eyed young corporal from the Kuban said he had been an automobile mechanic before the war. "We are fighting," he said, "and we know that you in America want to help us, but we don't know how or when." . . . How was Fritz getting along on this front? . . . "Fritz?" laughed the corporal. "He's learning about Russians — and pretty soon he'll learn a lot more." These soldiers were the sons of the simplest families in the Soviet Union, but their questions were invariably intelligent. I did not see any face that was moody or appeared tormented by doubts. They were very businesslike about their work and I noted a general respect for their officers. The more I saw of Red Army commanders and men, it seemed that this was a truly democratic army. Riding on and talking with Major Arapov, I got a better insight as to why this was so. Arapov told me he was born in a small village near Voronezh. His parents had been peasants. Therefore under the czars he could never have hoped to become more than a corporal or a sergeant in the Russian army. "I went to college and studied engineering," Arapov said. "Then I entered the Red Army artillery school to get my commission." In this army Arapov, the son of peasants, could become a major or a general. It was this equality of opportunity that was one of the main sources of strength in the Red Army quite as much as in the American Army. Despite their very rigid discipline you sensed this in the Russian soldiers.

By the time we reached the division's advanced headquarters there was a good deal of firing up ahead. German planes were also passing over quite often, but they were Messerschmitts and high up. Nazi bombers did not seem to be numerous in this sector, or they concentrated on troops in the forward trenches. Eventually we were led to a mass of wheat rubble and chaff on a gentle slope, underneath which the GHQ dugout was located. Ehrenburg had been telling me about the Georgian general who commanded here. After one very hot battle he had shouted: "Bury the dead. Send back the wounded — and the rest go forward!" When we met Major General Tshantshebadze he looked like that kind of war dog. He was built like a bull, he had the beak of an eagle and his large head was absolutely bald, as smooth as ivory. He escorted us down into a rough dugout which had a small alcove with a table in it. Four persons could just manage to crowd in on each side of it.

"The Germans have been trying to counter-attack here," the general said, "but we have them pinned to the ground. Yesterday and last night we flung them back and they paid plenty for it. The fascists always try to get an overwhelming strength in one narrow sector. When they can't get it they crawl into their holes again. Fritz never attacks here twice in the same place. As soon as he meets stiff resistance he tries somewhere else. The Germans are always trying to feel out a weak spot. Then when they can't find one, they wait for more reserves. Soldiers that must always fight with an advantage — bah! We shall show them. Even with a disadvantage our men can outfight them. Every week we are nearer to Rzhev. It is slow and hard, but we keep making progress. When the snow comes we'll see how much they can take.

"Yesterday the fascists sent in twenty tanks with their infantry," General Tshantshebadze added. "We threw them back. They don't like it, but they can't shake us off. Yes, they keep using their mortars, and that's the one thing the Germans know how to use. But they never can dodge our big guns. And when we use Katusha, or her big brother Androusha [another secret weapon], you should see them wilt."

The general rubbed his hands gleefully and poured out a second round of vodka. Then he plunged into the eternal questions about the second front, now and again grabbing my knee and half-crunching it to stress what he was saying. "I esteem the American people — please know that," he said. "You Americans have great technical ability and we've always admired you for it. But as the world's most advanced industrial nation what excuse can you make for not being ready to fight?" I explained how American senators and congressmen had voted against the fortifying of Wake and Guam, and how many of them had even voted against selective service long after the fall of France. "There is something in the structure of democracy which seems to make it impossible to prepare adequately for the disaster of war," I concluded. "But please believe me when I say that the great majority of Americans want to fight this war, and intend to fight this war. If I didn't know that I'd be ashamed to be an American."

General Tshantshebadze grabbed my shoulder in one huge paw and squeezed it hard. "I see you understand," he said, and filled up the vodka glasses again. We were soon eating another plenteous and splendidly cooked meal while the general punctuated stories of the front with great gusts of laughter and stinging slaps on my leg. "The other night I decorated twenty-five of my men. Guess what one of the soldiers said when I had pinned on his Red Star. He stood very straight and said: 'Our job is clear. We must kill the German soldiers. Because if we kill enough German soldiers, then Hitler will have to kill his generals.' Ha, ha, ha! That's one way to end the war fast, eh?" Then the general turned toward me impatiently and pounded my knee again. "Damn it, when are you Americans going to begin to fight?" he exclaimed. "Come on. Let's drink to your success when you do begin."

The general had a fine German military radio in his dugout, a trophy of the recent fighting, and he showed it to us with great pleasure. Ehrenburg went with him to give a pep talk to some of his men and the divisional commissar suggested that I get a little sleep. I had slept very little for seven nights, but I knew I was too keyed up for it now. I stretched out on the bench, however, and tried to rest. In the main dugout several soldiers were sitting. For more than an hour, until the general and Ehrenburg returned, they spoke only in whispers. It was a remarkably considerate thing to do. I lay thinking about the extraordinary consideration that Russian army men had shown for me everywhere we had been. One night Arapov, who sometimes seemed to have a surly disposition, had been supposed to share a bed with me. I awoke in the morning to find him sleeping on the floor because he knew I would get more rest alone. It seemed there were no limits to the Russians' interpretation of hospitality. Now these soldiers, conversing only in whispers, tried to assure me some badly needed repose. But the Germans spoiled their generous intentions by opening up some very heavy mortar fire. When we clambered up into the night the near horizon to the northwest was seared with lightning flashes and a single huge orange blotch glowed and hovered and danced over Rzhev.

I had already had more vodka than I like to drink, but the baldheaded eagle-beaked Georgian general treated vodka exactly like tea. I begged him to go light on the farewell round, but it took a great deal of firmness to make any impression on a man like General Tshantshebadze. Finally he poured two thirds of the contents of my glass into his own and declared with a roar of laughter: "All right. Since we Russians are doing most of the fighting, I'll drink most of the vodka. When you Americans are fighting as much as we are, we'll drink glass for glass." The Georgians are renowned for the sharpness of their wit. After an evening with this Georgian I understood better what a fencing match Winston Churchill must have had on his hands with Joseph Stalin.

Through the gun-lashed night we rode back to our luxurious

dugout at General Leliushenko's headquarters, where a wood fire was blazing cheerfully in the stove — a welcome sight after a biting cold ride — even at two in the morning. My Russian companions were now in a perfect mood for several glasses of tea and much conversation. This time I fell asleep in the same room without worrying whether they shouted or whispered.

In the morning I met a group of young Red Army commissars, the men whose chief preoccupation was to keep their soldiers' fighting spirit high. They were a very keen-faced group of officers and their questions were equally keen. "Our men are much disappointed about the second front," one captain said. "They say it will never come. It's very difficult for us to persuade them that the British and Americans are real allies and will fight in the west. I know the American people from your literature. I know the Americans are honest, energetic, and valiant, and also good businessmen. Americans do not merely talk — they act. But now they only talk. Why is that?" The commissars asked many questions about the international and political aspects of the war, and their questions were unfailingly sound. They asked about the quality of American arms and if the United States as yet had many troops in England. One major asked a question which, it seemed to me, revealed the Russians' practical and psychological approach to fighting a war.

"What does the American and British press do to implant hatred of the enemy?" he inquired.

"Not very much," I replied. This front-zone sector of the Russian front somehow didn't seem to be the place to admit that an enormous number of Americans had never considered whether hatred might not be an essential factor in the successful waging of war. Because their cities and homes had been destroyed before their eyes, because millions of their people had died, the Russians understood why hatred need not be something to be ashamed of and why it was a powerful weapon for both winning and shortening the war. These commissars were mostly between the ages of twenty-two and twenty-seven. They were intensely serious and they also bore the mark of unquestionable leadership.

"They are fine men and very intelligent," I remarked.

"And also courageous," said Captain Emma.

6

"At last we're going to my division," Captain Emma said jubilantly.

But to do so we had to ride across what had been a battlefield for many months and rely upon the unpredictable Ivan the Terrible and his equally terrible and unpredictable car. From the army corps' GHQ our trail first wound through a great wilderness of stumps. The stumps all stood about three feet high because the snow had been that deep when the Germans leveled this entire strip of woodland last winter. The so-called road finally turned westward into the chewed-up badlands and marshes. For miles there was nothing but jagged and ugly wasteland, most of it torn by shells and bombs. Countless trucks and tanks had gouged deep ruts and mudholes, so Ivan had a continuous struggle to keep from getting bogged down completely. We jolted over pine logs or inched along with the car's axle scraping ridges of caked clay, but we kept moving. Rzhev lay close on the horizon, ahead and slightly to the left.

The day was fine again and mortars and artillery were exceptionally active all along the front. Aside from their puffs of smoke the whole desolate prairie, spread flatly in the sunshine, seemed deserted. Emma said there had been many villages off to the right and several to the left. "Where there are a few trees, standing in groups, there used to be houses," she said. "Now there's nothing left but some of the trees." As we proceeded we passed the charred debris of peasants' cabins, often without so much as the foundation stones remaining in place. I could understand that, because old abandoned trenches twisted out on either side of the road and there were hundreds of horseshoe-shaped machine-gun nests built of clods of turf. Everywhere rusted barbed wire lay in great tangles, and sometimes a tilted blackened carcass of a tank or the burned-out wreckage of a German plane. The October sky was deceitfully serene. As we proceeded within four miles of the front a steady humming, like that of giant bumblebees, rose above the growl of our car. This time the planes were coming closer and coming from an enemy direction. Leaning out the rear of the car, I couldn't see a thing up above, but I could hear plenty. That reminded me that there were a good many trucks on this ditch-infested road. It would be just as well not to get stuck behind a long row of trucks—not with Nazi bombers about. But Captain Emma was chattering away as if going on a picnic.

Then a series of heavy crunches shattered the prairie off to the left and slightly south. Huge columns of black smoke spurted up into the sky, one after another. They looked much less than a mile away, and the bumblebees up above were roaring very loudly now and so was the Russian ack-ack. "The fascists are trying to hit one of our communication lines," Emma remarked calmly. Privately I thought it might be a good idea to get out and see if any bombers were directly overhead or coming our way; but Emma didn't seem at all concerned and now I was discovering she had told the plain truth about the advantage of women as front-line commissars. A man can hardly afford to get nervous when a hundred-pound woman alongside him apparently has no nerves at all. Ivan the Terrible had his Tatar features screwed up in one of his fiercest gorilla faces and was sending our car careening forward over ruts and ridges. He plunged it out into no-man's land and around half a dozen trucks which made a marvelous target for bombs. Ivan growled to himself and for once failed to get stuck in a quagmire at a critical moment. I breathed easier with the trucks behind us. But just as he hurdled the car over some pine logs and back on the road again, the earth shook under us once more. This time there were more than a dozen jarring crumps, to the right of us this time and considerably nearer.

"The Germans must be attacking on our front," said Captain Emma, otherwise not so much as lifting an eyebrow.

Both the artillery and machine-gun fire crackled sharply now and the smoke clusters above Rzhev, straight across the prairie, were becoming steadily heavier. In a short time, however, Ivan turned to the right into the soggy torn marshland. We passed another village that was now nothing but crumpled bricks and heaps of refuse lying between lonely shade trees and Ivan skirted innumerable bomb craters as he dodged soft spots in the marshes. Most agreeably, the bombing had turned to the south of us, for the badlands had become a problem commanding all of Ivan's powers of concentration. Then a Red Army lieutenant came galloping up and blazed a trail around the treacherous spots of the scarred and water-soaked battleground. Finally we stopped not far from a haphazard stand of very young pines. The headquarters of Emma's division was planted deep underneath these pines.

Captain Emma threw her arms around her colonel with a joyous cry. It was as if she had come home for Christmas and surprised the family. The colonel smiled broadly and everyone was talking at once. Her son? Oh, Vladimir was fine. I could catch that much, although all that was necessary was to see Emma's face. We pushed down a narrow corridor and into the dugout and I exclaimed at the lay-out and coziness of this underground house. "Yes, this was a German headquarters until two weeks ago," said Guards Colonel Shafranov. "We found everything upside down. A couple of fascist officers had even left their overcoats. They left in a terrible hurry. Yes, it's very comfortable here. It was kind of Fritz to build it for us." While Emma was demanding all the news about her regiment and her friends, I inspected the Germans' de luxe dugout. There was a large kitchen alcove alongside a huge stove built of clay and tiles with a big oven in the lower section. The great chimney of the stove served as one wall of the main living-room, off of which were two bedrooms. What surprised me most about the living-room was the fact that it had standard-sized windows with real panes of glass on two sides. They created the impression of being in an ordinary house after nightfall. Behind the windows I discovered there were ventilation shafts, running up to the surface, some twelve feet above. By opening the windows fresh air could be kept in circulation below. This main room served as the colonel's office, and a table beside one of the windows would seat eight persons comfortably. The bedrooms were each furnished with two iron bedsteads, a table, a chest of drawers, and shelves. German officers had lived in this dugout through the previous winter.

I had barely finished a quick look around when a boisterous human tornado blew in through the door and swept Emma almost off her feet. He was a round-cheeked, curly-haired man of about thirty, who wore a close-cropped blond mustache. Divisional Commissar Pavlov laughed with great gusto despite the fact that his voice sounded as if he had a chronic case of laryngitis. Guards Colonel Shafranov, who was forty, was as quiet-spoken as Pavlov was effervescent. The colonel was a broad-shouldered powerful man who made his words count. Captain Emma had told me that as commander and divisional commissar they made an exceptional team. Their division had been honored with the coveted "Guards" designation a few weeks earlier. In the Red Army a Guards unit receives a higher level of pay in all ranks, but the Guards medal which every member wears on the right side of his tunic represents unique prestige for a distinguished record in battle.

"In the last few days the Germans got reinforcements on this side of Rzhev," the colonel said. "This morning they opened up with an artillery barrage and then attacked with tanks. But we've beaten them off. Recently the enemy has been attacking four or five times a day. But since we smashed the fascists' 87th infantry division we control all of the northern bank of the Volga. They attack and bomb, but they can't do anything more about it."

"The Germans have been trying out some new bombing planes with music," croaked Pavlov. "They have sirens attached to the bombs and they make a terrible noise. They thought they'd scare our men. Those fascists are fools. They don't know the Russians."

Pavlov sounded like a bullfrog when he laughed, and he laughed as often as Smirnov, the artilleryman. His colonel had three decorations; Pavlov wore the Red Banner and two wound stripes. As we talked the windows rattled frequently from the barrages on the front, less than two miles away. Suddenly a great crescendo of explosives drowned our speech. It sounded like a huge bundle of hundred-foot firecrackers going off all at once — a whole series of tremendous booms which seemed to put the earth into a fit of convulsions.

"That's Katusha," said Colonel Shafranov with the shadow of a smile.

"That's what gives the Germans a bellyful," barked Pavlov. "But you should hear Androusha. Androusha breaks your ears."

I listened to the rapid concussions with heightened interest because Katusha was the secret weapon about which all Russians boasted gleefully, but about which correspondents had nothing more than a vague idea. It was generally believed that Katusha was some kind of multi-barreled mortar which fired shells that contained several smaller shells and plastered an area with successive explosions. In the hospitals soldiers had told me that Katusha killed everything within a wide radius of the place where her explosives landed. Now, as I heard Katusha for the first time, I realized that she sounded more terrific and destructive than anything I had heard on any war front. But now the Russians had Androusha, a bigger Katusha. Until I came to the Rzhev sectors I had never even heard mention of the super-Katusha. This was merely another reminder that the Red Army is full of surprises; that its weapons were much better than the outside world had realized. Dinner was just ready to be served when the colonel's telephone rang. "Our planes bombed the lower side of Rzhev a little while ago," he said. "There's a big fire there now. Would you like to see it?"

We went out through the long trench and up on top. Straight across the darkened prairie Rzhev was blazing. Flames and golden smoke swirled skyward in a tremendous billowing mass. The fires leapt so luridly it seemed the whole city must be ablaze and that Rzhev was very near. As we watched, the sharp, short bark of tommyguns and the staccato bite of machine guns reached our ears. The tempo of the day's battle was holding into the night. Returning to the dugout, the colonel explained that the Germans had launched two attacks during the afternoon while we were coming up from Leliushenko's headquarters and they had bombed heavily at the same time.

"You see this is the anniversary of the Germans' October offensive against Moscow," the colonel said. "The fascists always like to make a show on their anniversaries, but they'll get nothing out of this one."

I had learned by now that whenever Russian officers have guests they heap the table high and expect you to have an enormous capacity. There were a great many hungry people in the Soviet Union, but not among the fighting men and least of all near the front. We began with sardines which had been captured from the Germans, which of course justified a toast in vodka. After that we had meat with wonderful fried potatoes, and finally a separate course of Russian stuffed griddle cakes. The colonel told about the narrow toehold which his men had seized across the Volga more than a month ago and had held against terrific pounding ever since. The land lay in a hairpin curve of the Volga, a narrow strip not much over a mile wide. Because the Germans had bombed it so ruthlessly it had come to be known as Hell's Elbow. The Nazis had used artillery, tanks, and planes against it time and again. "Our men never gave up a yard of soil," the colonel said quietly. "Tomorrow you can talk with my lieutenant colonel, who has led the defense of Hell's Elbow. He will tell you just how it goes there."

We talked for several hours that night and I soon understood why Captain Emma swore by her commander. There was a measured strength and unmistakable sureness about Colonel Shafranov. Once he looked me straight in the eyes and declared: "Russia will be the last country in the world to capitulate. We shall fight to the last man." You could scarcely have found a more contrasting team than the colonel and his commissar. Where Shafranov was serious and reflective, Pavlov was jovial, dynamic, and bubbling with words; yet they seemed to work very closely together and the colonel appeared content to let the other run away with the conversation rather regularly.

"Here's something the German planes dropped today," Pavlov said. "They drop a new one on our front-line positions almost every day."

He handed me a propaganda leaflet printed in Russian. It contained a picture of Stalin standing beside a scowling-faced Churchill. Stalin was holding up a platter on which a dead Russian soldier was stretched out, his blood dripping over the edges. Stalin was saying: "My friend Churchill, for the sake of our friendship I've sacrificed millions of lives of Red Army men in the past year. How many more do you need?" On the back of the leaflet was a printed pass "valid until the end of the war for an unlimited number of privates, officers, and political workers of the Red Army." It stated that, according to Hitler's new order, those who surrendered voluntarily would be treated especially well and promised that the German command would not publish the names of any who surrendered.

"I can get you plenty more with the same theme," Pavlov

added. "The fascists have been dropping them for weeks now. But our men don't even read them. They tear them up or use them for toilet paper, unless I order them to save some for me."

At this time Rzhev was the only zone along Russia's 1,800-mile front where the Red Army was able to dictate the strategy and impose terms of battle upon the Germans. All around Rzhev the struggle was positional warfare, but the Russians were steadily attacking and blunting the edge of the Nazis' counter-attacks. As the colonel admitted, the entrenchments here were more like those in the first World War and so were the Red Army's tactics of gnashing and gnawing at the enemy's lines. The Germans had fortified Rzhev tremendously because it was their closest approach to Moscow. With the Russians fighting in part of the city, Rzhev was curiously like a Stalingrad in reverse. Here it was the Germans who were on the defensive, but the Russian divisions' task was slowed down greatly by the Nazis' superior strength in tanks and planes. Every tank and plane that could possibly be spared had to be used by the Red Army in defense of Stalingrad.

"Which is more important for you to have — superiority in tanks or in planes?" I asked Colonel Shafranov.

"Both is best," said the colonel. "But if you can't have both, then tanks are more important. Planes can kill many men, but they don't gain ground. To gain terrain you need tanks and infantry. The Germans have made as many as six hundred bomb flights over the narrow sector of Hell's Elbow in a single day, but even with that they couldn't recapture the ground. Aviation is powerful against industries, communications, and enemy morale. But it isn't of first importance in a war of positions. A good officer puts his men up close to the enemy's trenches, and then they can't bomb his troops without bombing their own. In my view, the tank is most vital for attack, but it needs air protection to be most effective."

Colonel Shafranov was a man who could make his point clear with very few words and sometimes with a twinkle in his eye. "I'm sorry I can't speak English," he said toward the evening's end. "When the second front opens we will all speak English. Now, you see, we have no practice."

I was quite certain that the colonel was giving me his own bed, but he wouldn't listen to my protests. "I'm commander here and I don't have to go without a bed," he insisted. Although the bombardment was still rumbling, I slept well, and upon rising I felt quite strong until Pavlov poured out a big glass of vodka as a prelude to breakfast. I think only the Russians or the Finns would quite be capable of drinking vodka before breakfast, but it seemed as though the stamina of American males was at stake; so I took the firewater in one gulp and got warmed up faster on a chilly morning than I ever had before in my life. The commander from Hell's Elbow, after a night of brisk engagement, arrived in time to eat with us. Lieutenant Colonel Polevoi had a face which was memorable for its chiseled quality and for its deep lines of fatigue. He was a Ukrainian in his late thirties, more slender than most Slavs, but he looked like a blade of Toledo steel whetted down to its keenest possible edge. His face was haggard and dead tired, but you could feel the man's willpower and self-control. He spoke without dramatics, as the best and bravest fighting men usually do.

"When we struck across the Volga our men had no cover whatever," Polevoi said. "There were only the German trenches and they faced the wrong way. We had to dig in as we fought, but we drove the fascists back until we held the whole elbow. Then the enemy poured shells and bombs on our troops day after day. But they can't blast us out. We are still holding and we will hold."

"But when you had more than six hundred bombers on you in one day, in that narrow terrain, how could you possibly hold?"

The lieutenant colonel's eyes lighted as Emma translated my question. Then his jaw snapped tight and he made a swift gesture with his right fist. "By moral force," he said in a sharp tense voice. Then he swung his closed fist down a second time and again his jaws snapped.

"By moral force," repeated Polevoi.

I thought suddenly of those American isolationists, including Charles Lindbergh, who were insisting during the spring of 1941 that Britain and the United States could never outbuild Germany's Luftwaffe. None of these people who had preached defeatism, I thought, had ever possessed eyes and cheeks and a chin like those of this Ukrainian officer. Those in every land who had spread the doctrine of appeasement and the glib thesis that "it's not our war and besides it's too late" had had many dangerous weapons in their arsenal — but they had never had the incomparable weapon of moral force. That was one great reason why, in the end, they had lost.

"We dug trenches and fortified our positions while we fought," Polevoi continued. "There is one spot where our most advanced positions are only seventeen yards from the enemy, and in another the fascists are less than fifty yards away. We stick close to Fritz. That's why he can't get rid of us. You must always press against your adversary. The closer you press, the less formidable he becomes."

In Colonel Shafranov's sector I talked with an anti-tank platoon commanded by a black-haired little Armenian lieutenant. At the time there were only thirteen men in the platoon, and among these thirteen soldiers were men who spoke six different languages, including Tatar, Ukrainian, Georgian, Uzbek, and Bashkir. This was typical of the mixture of races in the Red Army. The Soviets' emphasis on education had given all a common command of Russian and a common stake in the future of the Soviet Union. The anti-tank men were young and hardy and a number of them had been decorated or cited for bravery. Lieutenant Colonel Polevoi explained: "The Germans don't like to have to pay dearly for what they can't get. But when they go up against fellows like these, the Germans' tanks pay a real price. In our sector they've been showing very few tanks lately. Our men's resistance has never been broken down."

We had to keep a rendezvous with Ehrenburg back at General Leliushenko's headquarters that noon. I asked Colonel Shafranov if he thought it would be wise for me to describe the captured German dugout in which he lived, or could that by any chance increase the danger of his headquarters being bombed?

"They know where we are," laughed the colonel. "Describe what you like. Besides, we get bombed anyway."

Chapter XIV

PEOPLE NEAR THE FRONT

One cannot understand Russia with the head,
One cannot measure her with a yardstick.
Russia has her own conformation.
One can only believe in Russia.

Tutchev

What a little soldier! He looks like a boy — he is a boy!"

"Oh, that's Petya," said the regimental commissar. "Sure he's a soldier. He's been adopted by our regiment."

"Adopted?" I repeated.

"That's right," explained Captain Emma. "A good many war orphans have been adopted by Red Army units. Probably this boy is like the others. He has no home and no parents. They love being with the army, you know."

"I'd like to talk to him. How about getting him to ride back with us tomorrow?"

So here was Petya Kaputovsky, soldier of the Red Army, waiting for us as we prepared to leave the headquarters of Emma's division. He stood no more than four and a half feet high, but he looked very trim in his coffee-gray Red Army overcoat and he smiled shyly. Petya, it should be explained, is one of those musical Russian diminutives. It means Little Peter and you pronounce it "Peet-ya." Underneath his army cap with the red star on its front Petya's pink cheeks and soft mouth made him look incongruously boyish. He was only twelve, and twelve is very young to live the life of a soldier. He climbed into the back seat with Captain Emma and I sat beside Ivan the Terrible. Ivan had no paper for rolling cigarettes except a soiled back page from *Pravda* and what he produced, with the very ordinary Russian tobacco now available, was a monstrosity that looked like a slightly triangular cigar. Ivan usually started a minor conflagration when he lit his cigarette, which was more newspaper than tobacco. When Ivan had completed his ceremony we were off across the badlands and between numerous battles with mud and swampy ground I concentrated on Petya and his story. We had a truck to pull us out of bogs and through several brooks, so our navigation problems were simplified considerably.

What impressed me most about Petya from the start was the straight clear gaze of his handsome gray eyes and an almost childish gentleness in his voice. He had exceptionally regular features; in fact, he was one of the finest-looking boys I had seen in a very long time. His face was adolescent but clean-cut, the kind of face that would be better than a letter of recommendation anywhere in the world. Sitting beside him Captain Emma didn't seem much bigger than Petya. I noticed that he responded immediately to the warmth in her brown eyes and perhaps even more to her femininity. There had been no woman in Petya's life for a long time now. I let Emma do her own questioning most of the time, and her own interest guided her accurately. As she obtained another fragment of the boy's experiences, she translated carefully to me — sometimes prefaced by an exclamation of surprise — and I scribbled Petya's remarks verbatim in my notebook. The jounces and jolts made it difficult, but one who had been scratching notes in all sorts of positions for years could manage it. Sometimes our car was stuck in a mudhole and that made things easier. I watched Petya's face as he spoke and it registered as great honesty as a child's face will ever register. When we asked for more details about this or that, he never hesitated. I knew, as he proceeded, that I would willingly stake my life on the truth of what Petya was saying. One of my own boys, at his age, could not have spoken with more directness or with greater simplicity.

"I lived in a village near Kalinin," Petya said in his remarkably soft voice. "The Germans came in October. Right away they looked for all the Jews and all the relatives of partisans in our village. My father and many other men had gone into the forest to be guerrillas. The Germans came looking for people in every house. When they came to our house I hid under the steps and I took my brother Shura with me. Shura was nine years old. The fascists took my mother and my two younger brothers and my two sisters. They tied their hands with rope. Then they led them away and put them in the biggest house in our village. They put all the families of partisans and all the Jews they could find in the same house. We were terribly frightened, but we could see from underneath the front steps. When the Germans had filled the house with people they set it on fire — they burned it down."

Suddenly Petya's voice became dull and almost lifeless, but his eyes never faltered.

"How many people were in the big house?" I asked.

"There were very many — I think more than one hundred," Petya replied. "Many of the women and children were crying when they took them in. Then we heard them screaming and screaming when the fire began to blaze up high."

Petya stopped abruptly and looked away. His lips, which were very boyish lips, trembled for a moment. Emma looked at me, and what I saw in her eyes was something far more lasting and unstemmable than tears have ever been. What I saw was the personification of Ehrenburg's pronouncement that without hatred war is something shameless, that hatred too must be as strong as love is.

"Did you know any of the children whom the Germans burned to death in the big house?" This question I asked calculatedly, for I wanted to see if there would be the slightest hesitation or uncertainty on Petya's part. He answered without a second's pause.

"There was Kolia and Genia — they lived in our street. And Valodia. He was twelve, too, and we went to school together. There were others, but I don't remember their names. Then there were little children. Some of them couldn't walk and their mothers carried them when the fascist soldiers pushed them all into the big house. Then the Germans began setting fire to other houses. I knew they would burn our house too, and then we'd have to run out and be killed. It was getting dark and I told Shura we must crawl around behind the barn, and run terribly fast to the woods. So we crawled behind the barn and out into the field where the flames didn't throw much light yet. Then we ran as fast as we could. I was barefooted. But I didn't dare go into the house to get my shoes, so I ran barefooted. It was very cold. It was in October and in the woods the cold was very bad. But I knew that our partisans couldn't be far away and Father was with them. So Shura and I kept walking until we found the partisans. When we found them they told us that our father had been killed fighting the Germans.

"The partisans gave us something to eat and tied some rags around my feet," Petya went on; "but they were having big fights with the fascists, so we couldn't stay with them. A man went with us to find a Red Army unit. We had to go at night and we walked all that night because the Germans were always coming closer. Next day we found our Russian soldiers. Then they sent Shura away to be put in an orphanage. But I said: 'I don't want to go into any children's home. I'm big enough. I can fight. I want to fight in place of my father.' . . . I begged the commander very hard. I begged so much that at last he let me stay. But I was very sick for a long time. I couldn't sleep. I kept remembering my mother and brothers and sisters and the fire — the way they cried — "

Petya's small voice fell away into silence. I did not dare look closely at the face, which was mostly child yet partly young man. Captain Emma looked at me and I looked at her. We didn't say anything for a while and then Emma said: "Nerves." Providentially Ivan the Terrible maneuvered us into another bog and it was ten minutes before the car was crawling ahead again. Then Emma asked another question.

"After the commander said I could stay I was very happy," Petya told us with a sudden smile. In a twinkling his eyes became lustrous. "They gave me a uniform — a real Red Army uniform. And then the soldiers gave me shooting lessons. First they gave me lessons with a revolver, and later with an automatic — but I don't know the machine gun yet."

Petya's face clouded momentarily as he made that confession, but he added swiftly: "But I know the German automatic very well."

It was a relief somehow to hear Emma's laughter before she translated, and Petya smiled at me with the frank pleasure of a boy describing his first air rifle on a Christmas tree.

"At first I went on scouting trips with our soldiers in the forest," Petya said. "Then one day we had a fight and the Germans shot me. Not bad — just a little. Here in the knee. I was in the hospital, but when I came back the commissar wouldn't let me go on scouting trips any more. I cried and cried, but the commissar wouldn't let me go. I didn't like that commissar any more. They gave me new work as a messenger after that. But I liked the raids lots better. But now I like our division and regiment very much. It's a Guards division — and I like Commissar Pavlov very much." Petya's eyes were shining again.

"Don't you have plenty of bombs around here?" I asked, and Petya nodded his head vigorously.

"Yesterday and the day before we had lots of them. And one day I was riding on horseback, taking a message to another regiment, and the fascists sent over many mines. They were big ones and one exploded quite close — maybe a hundred yards away. I crouched down over my horse's neck and I made him gallop. We ran away from that spot very fast.

"Oh yes, I've got a horse," explained Petya, whose gray eyes were still dancing. "He's just three years old and small and brown. He's very good-looking and I call him Rocket. I learned to ride horseback with my regiment. First they used to send me with a motorcyclist to carry messages. But the roads got too bad for motorcycles, and then they gave me my own horse."

"When will you go to school again, Petya?"

"Oh, after the war I'll go to school. There's no time for lessons now. We have to fight."

"And what would you like to be when you finish school?"

Of course it was Captain Emma who relayed the question, and Petya looked at her uniform and at the commissar's red star on the sleeve of her overcoat.

"I want to be the same as you and Commissar Pavlov," he said. "Or perhaps an aviator. I don't know yet. If there isn't any war, then I'll be a peace aviator so I can make long voyages."

"Perhaps you'll fly to America some day, Petya."

"Yes, that would be fine. . . . Do American boys like airplanes too? Yes, I'd like to see America. Once I saw an air battle with two American planes against a Fockewolff and it came down burning and smoking. We all cheered and yelled for the American plane. I think American planes must be very good."

There was a brief silence and then Petya wanted to know what kind of money we have in America. I found a dollar bill in my pocket and asked him to keep it as a souvenir. When I pointed to George Washington's head I was surprised that the boy nodded quickly as if he recognized Washington without any help.

"If you don't lose the dollar, when you come to America you can buy a meal and ice cream and some candy with it," I said.

"Where is it you can buy ice cream and candy?" asked Petya with great swiftness. . . . Stupidly I had forgotten that he was a soldier in the army and he had probably not seen a single store of any kind since his village was burned one year ago.

Now we were on the main road, such as it was, and Petya was going to return to his regiment in the truck. I emptied the last tobacco out of its blue Edgeworth tin and Petya thought it had a wonderful odor. He sniffed it deeply and sniffed it again. So I handed him the tin, thinking it might please him as something different and from far away. Petya stuck his nose inside the tin to see if some of the smell was still there. Then he turned to Captain Emma, his face illumined with a rapturous smile and his gray eyes shining.

"I'm going to give it to the commissar," Petya said softly.

2

It was after midnight, our car had reverted to a cough and a wheeze, and the hill was very steep. Ivan the Terrible had become even more irascible and pigheaded than his ordinary normal. Evidently the Tatars are among the world's most stubborn and independent-minded people. Major Arapov, who could become exceedingly churlish and harsh-spoken on occasion, could do nothing whatever with Ivan. Arapov would shout orders at Ivan, and Ivan would knit his narrow brow tighter than ever, growl angrily to himself, and do precisely as he pleased. Since the Soviet Union had gone through its periods of purges, it was beyond me how Ivan the Terrible had escaped liquidation long ago. At this moment, in fact, I would have cheerfully participated in the liquidation of Ivan, and the major had become so furious he actually became speechless. At this delicate juncture Ivan produced his chef d'œuvre of the entire trip. He walked slowly around the car, exploring the terrain on every side, and then backed the car downhill into the very hole he had just walked around. I expected Arapov to knock Ivan twenty feet (if he could do it), but this was one occasion where a Red Army officer yielded to the unchangeable and irresistible. From that time on, everything was thoroughly Russian.

On top of the hill we found several log cabins and, by great luck, an army doctor from Novosibirsk. These peasant cabins were being used as a base hospital in the front zone and the medico brought us to his own humble headquarters. A tall blonde girl immediately set the samovar to purring. Somebody brought in a couple of stretchers for extra beds and we soon were devouring our bread, cheese, and caviar and chatting with the Red Army doctor. But the real Russian touch came when, in response to a word from our host, an officer walked in with an accordion. Here we were, at two o'clock in the morning and with the front only a few miles away, being treated to a serenade of typical Slavic songs; some gay and fiery, others sad and melancholy. In the dim light of the kerosene lamp we sipped tea and smoked and listened, and I noticed the lines of pronounced fatigue in the medico's face. As he spoke and moved he had the gentle manner of a man born to the medical profession. Now the Red Army lieutenant was playing that popular Russian song about "my beloved village, may you sleep peacefully." I had heard that song often in Moscow and should always remember it. There is in it the nostalgia and the yearning of the great Russian folksongs. The lieutenant sat on the edge of the cabin's only bedstead and the light flickered on his bronzed features as he played. We were all tired, and Dr. Lojken certainly most of all, but this somehow was better than sleep.

The lieutenant leaned closer over his accordion, and his fingers began to dance. A sprightly Siberian folk dance rippled out from under his precise swift fingers. On a mattress in the corner, just behind me, lay a pale-faced little girl. The music had awakened her, but apparently it had in no way surprised her. She smiled at us coyly as if to say: "What fun to have company and music in the middle of the night!" She had a bandage around her head and she looked as if she had not had enough to eat for a long time. When Captain Emma gave her a piece of chocolate from our supplies, she nibbled at it very slowly, obviously wanting to make it last as long as possible. Now and then she flashed her coquettish smile at us and then hid her face for a moment beneath her blanket. But she always popped her head out again in a few seconds.

Now, however, this Siberian folk dance was too much for her Slavic soul. The little girl suddenly jumped out of bed and skipped gracefully across the room, twirling lightly on her thin bare legs. Then, as precipitously and with a merry laugh, she ducked back under her coverlet once more. The accordionist played on — *Kalitchka* and *The Young Birch Tree* and *Kazbek* and *Proshtai* and others which I did not know. The guns boomed fitfully along the front. It was after three before we went to bed.

The combined oven and furnace of clay-built stoves in Russian peasant cabins is a huge affair about eight feet long and six feet high. The top of this oven in winter constitutes the choicest sleeping-place in the house because it is the warmest, and for that reason Grandma (Baboushka in Russian) usually sleeps there. This place of honor was rightfully allotted to Captain Emma, so she climbed up into Baboushka's cubbyhole on top of the oven. Soon in the darkness, from behind Emma's curtain, we heard a long deep sigh.

"Poor little Baboushka," exclaimed Ehrenburg ironically from his stretcher in the corner. We all laughed. It sounded very funny at the time, perhaps because Emma was so amazingly young in spirit and appearance and so utterly unlike a wizened old grandmother. After that we slept for nearly four hours, but in the morning Emma had become Baboushka for the remainder of our travels. Before leaving that day we visited Dr. Lojken's hospital wards in the adjoining cabins. The doctor was attached to a mine-thrower's battalion and the wounded here were all men from his own outfit. Most of them had been wounded in engagements of the past few days.

"Will you take Rzhev?" I asked a husky youth from Novosibirsk.

"Rzhev!" exclaimed Ivan Kondratyev. "We'll take back everything the fascists have. When winter comes the Germans will be in a nasty spot." Then Ivan laughed confidently: "Fritz will forget everything — even his wife."

3

Ivan the Terrible may not have been an ordinary Tatar. In fact, I don't believe he could be described as an ordinary anything. Nevertheless Ivan, who growled back at Red Army majors and apparently did pretty much as he damn pleased in a highly bureaucratic land, and war or no war — well, this Ivan, cantankerous and annoying and incurably individualistic, opened for me vast fields of conjecture about Tatars and the Tatar character. Maybe Ivan wasn't a typical Tatar at all. Maybe he was just a mistake. At any rate, with Ivan's recurrent moods and provocative orneriness, I began to think it's all very well, that saying about "scratch a Russian and you find a Tatar." But scratch a Tatar, and then what do you find? In one short week I had seen enough of Ivan the Terrible to have no desire personally to experiment by scratching a Tatar. No, thank you kindly. I'd leave that little scientific research job to some of Hitler's "master race." They could have it. And if they thought they'd get somewhere trying to boss around a country full of Ivans, well, they could have that too.

In all the time that he had nothing to do while we were at various headquarters for the past several days, Ivan, the super-Terrible, had thoughtfully neglected to patch up the faulty gasoline feed-line in our car. That's why we were back on a cough-wheeze-and-poof schedule before we even reached the main road to Staritsa and Kalinin. And that's how we dropped in so unexpectedly, about ten o'clock that night, upon Mama Ikaterina Roubtsova and her two daughters. It must have been written in the stars, because we had abandoned our original route only an hour earlier, and our car's motor coughed into supreme silence for the umpteenth time just in sight of a row of log cabins. At that moment I would never have guessed that Ivan had accidentally done us a favor. We were all tired, plenty tired, and this meant losing another day on the return trip to Moscow.

Major Arapov — who by some miracle had still not shot Ivan — went to the first cabin in sight and a few seconds later beckoned us to follow. A smiling young woman, blonde and self-possessed, stood at the door. Like most peasants' cabins this one had a single large room, plus a small alcove off to one side. and very little furniture in it. In the left corner, as we entered, stood a cheap iron-poster bed with a wrinkled-faced peasant woman of sixty or more curled up in it. Mama Roubtsova didn't get up. She just chirped cheerfully: "Come in. Come in." Two soldiers were also in the room and another plain-faced young woman wearing a gray sweater and a blue beret. She was Antonina, Mama Roubtsova's daughter, and the blonde woman, who was the more attractive of the two, was Galina, her daughter-in-law. Galina's home and all her possessions were in German-occupied Smolensk. We learned these things little by little as Antonina and Galina started heating the samovar for tea and collected all the chairs in the house — precisely three — so that Ehrenburg, Arapov, and I could sit down. Meanwhile Mama Roubtsova had rolled over on one side, brushed the sleep out of her small, knowing eyes, and cocked her head upon the pillow where she could observe and hear everything. She had unmistakable Slavic peasant features, a slightly turned-up nose, and, as we observed bit by bit, an extraordinary amount of vitality. Undoubtedly she had worked like an ox on the land all her life, but the land had broken neither her body nor her spirit.

Ehrenburg, who keeps pulling at a pipe as tirelessly as I do myself, had lighted his charred old brier. He sat hunched forward near the lamp, his mop of gray hair all awry, his thick eyebrows ruffled, and pulled slowly at his pipe beneath the sharp curve of his nose. Ehrenburg had a way of looking like the description which my friend Derso gives of himself — like an archbishop in the act of committing a heresy. As a writer for the Red Army's newspaper Ehrenburg really ranked with the Soviet soldiers as a Delphic oracle, or at least as a high priest of Russian resistance. Often he had something of a Delphic manner also; an imperturbable and philosophic bearing, spiced with realism and frequently with dashes of bitter irony. But with the plain Russian peasants I noticed he was always his kindlier self. He liked to talk with them and he knew how to make them talk.

"They didn't bomb today," said Mama Roubtsova from her corner bed. "Probably because it's Sunday."

She cackled gaily at the idea that Germans would think of sparing people on Sunday. The younger women were apologizing because they had nothing but tea to offer us. They had no bread in the house, but we had enough bread and cheese and still a little pressed caviar to share with them. Meanwhile Antonina was telling us about the Nazis when they took this village.

"The Germans came in October and stayed until December 31," Antonina said. "They took all the pigs, cows, and chickens and they searched every house and took everything they wanted. Look. You see, we have no furniture left. We managed to get this table after they had gone. Look in the cupboard. You see there are only a few plates left. Everything else they smashed or stole. They shot my father. They killed many people in this village and everywhere in this district."

Antonina told it without emotion, like an old story that's been told too many times before. But Galina was Ukrainian and she had the vivacity and intensity of that sun-filled land. "I came with those who came back in January," Galina interrupted passionately. "All the people in this village met us sobbing, with tears running down their faces. Most of them had had some member of their family killed by the Germans, and everything they owned destroyed or stolen. It was terrible. Mama and Antonina were here all the time." Ehrenburg, still hunched over and scarcely moving, without a trace of emotion save for a steady glint in his eyes, asked another question.

"One woman who lived just down the road became a partisan. The Germans killed her. Another young woman — Zoya was her named — a good friend of ours — was locked up by the fascists. I don't know what they did to her, but she committed suicide with a razor."

"How many civilians did the Germans kill in this neighborhood?" I asked.

"In this district they killed a hundred and twenty-eight people," Antonina said. "Eighteen of these were hanged — and most of those they killed were not guerrillas at all. They had done nothing. One man by the name of Tichkin they hanged six times. Each time they cut him down before he was dead. Then they hanged him again. There was one girl who was a partisan. She kept shouting: 'Long live Russia.' They cut off her tongue before they shot her."

"They cut off her tongue?" I repeated incredulously.

Ehrenburg reiterated my question and Antonina looked me straight in the eyes.

"They cut off her tongue and then they shot her," she said in the same level voice. "I knew the girl well."

"That's true," exclaimed Mama Roubtsova from her pillow. "We have friends who saw it happen. Almost always the Germans killed our people in front of everyone in the village. They liked to do it that way."

"The girl's name was Pania Zemiatova," Antonina continued. "She was twenty years old."

Once again, as with Petya, there was not the slightest hesitation about precise details. We had changed our route unexpectedly on account of bad roads. The car's feed-line had gone bad and finally broken down. We had stumbled accidentally into this cabin, and its occupants could not possibly have known we were coming; they did not even possess a telephone. What object could a simple peasant woman like Antonina have in lying to us? It was perfectly plain, as it had been plain when I talked with peasants in Lotoshino, Pogoreloye-Gorodichtshe, and other villages liberated from the Nazis, that these were terrible truths. I had seen peasants weep as they narrated what had happened in their villages. Nowhere in the world do peasants weep for nothing.

"At Lukovinikovo — that's the next village — the Germans accused a boy of stealing food," Antonina said. "The boy ran away. So they hanged his father instead and left his body hanging in front of his house for four days. In another village the fascists hanged a boy because he had a small knife in his pocket — and a man because they found a piece of wire in his coat pocket. The boy was only eight years old."

As the three women talked, first one and then another, we learned that Mama Roubtsova's son, Galina's husband, was missing and there had been no news from her son-in-law, Antonina's husband, for more than six months. "I don't think the others will ever come back," Galina said in a low voice. "We shall be three women living alone. . . . I had to leave my mother in Smolensk. Probably she is dead."

Galina was pouring the tea now and Antonina suddenly reappeared with a huge pitcher of milk. "Last spring we got another cow," she explained. I gazed at the milk as if my eyes were betraying me. It was wonderfully pure, rich milk — one of the great gifts of life that we Americans so wrongfully take for granted. I had learned better. In fifteen months I had tasted milk only twice. I drank one big glass greedily, and then I remembered the bottle of vodka I had been saving for some special occasion. Certainly this was the right moment. I fumbled around in my knapsack and held up the bottle of vodka — and you should have seen little old Mama Roubtsova leap out of her bed. She gave a joyful cry and hopped right out in her worn cotton nightgown, as spryly as a girl of twenty and with her gums bared in a broad smile. Antonina and Galina perked up immediately, too. I don't think I ever had so much pleasure at extracting a cork from a bottle. But I reaped an undeserved reward, for no one else had any interest in the milk after that and I must have drunk more than a quart. If it had been possible I'd gladly have paid ten dollars for that fresh cool milk. Galina brought the only glass which the Nazi soldiers had not broken, and the vodka was passed, round-robin fashion. No one had to be urged to take seconds. You never have to do that with Russians and vodka. Mama Roubtsova showed us photographs of her dead husband, her missing son, and her son-in-law, who might be missing. Then she handed us the picture of the young woman, Antonina's friend, who had killed herself with the razor. When Mama Roubtsova told what a strong-willed and fine person the young woman had been, her voice broke and tears came to her eyes.

"Now, Mama, don't cry," said blonde Galina sharply. "You must grit your teeth, Mama. We must kill Germans instead."

Galina began to talk animatedly about other things, yet everything in the end came back to their shattered lives. "Today we dug potatoes," she began spiritedly. "I never did it before. You see I was brought up in a city and my husband worked in the bank and we lived very well. We had everything you could want to eat. We often had caviar and sometimes ice cream. But now we women do all kinds of work. Russian women are strong, you know. If there were no men to fight, we would fight. In this village we take turns as guards against parachutists. If you had come here alone — " (turning to me with a merry laugh) "we'd have caught you, and very quickly." In a moment Galina's lively face had darkened.

"If the war hadn't come our lives would have been so gay," she said. "Now all our lives are ruined. They'll never be the same."

Then, with volcanic fierceness, she added: "We must destroy the Germans. Once and forever, we must destroy them."

I was thinking how pitifully little it means to read in a newspaper that 10,000,000 civilians have died in Russia, or that more than 5,000,000 soldiers have been killed and wounded. To know and understand tragedy one must live with tragedy. We may try — a very few of the many may try — yet no man really knows death, anguish, and impoverishment until these things come inside his own close circle; until they come to him. Ehrenburg sat hunched up near the table, brooding and silent and looking more than ever like a pipe-smoking cockatoo. There was still a little vodka and I passed the family glass around. Mama Roubtsova sat on the edge of the bed and the two younger women on the mattress on the floor, and when Galina began to sing the two soldiers came across the room and lounged near them. Galina had a clear soprano voice. She was a Ukrainian and it seems that almost all Ukrainians sing well.

"It is evening," sang Galina. "From the edge of the river Katusha goes to her home."

Then she sang other songs, and Antonina, the two soldiers, and Arapov joined in. There was one which had a perfect Slavic mixture of melancholy and passion. "I like that," Ehrenburg said. "The words don't make much sense. Maybe that's why I like it." Then, as they all sang its chorus together in fine strong voices, he told me the words.

It turns. It turns. The blue globe turns.
It turns. It turns and can't fall down.
Where is the street? Where is the house?
Where is the maiden whom I love?

Once again it was long after midnight. The others sang the songs of their big Russian land and Ehrenburg and I sat, puffing our pipes, listening and thinking. I was thinking of the heartbreak this drab cabin had seen, of the kindliness and generosity

I had found here, of the unfathomable strength and deep renewal of people who could still sing like this after so much sorrow.

It turns. It turns. The blue globe turns.
It turns. It turns and can't fall down.

People may fall down, but there are people who can never remain down. In Spain, in Finland, in Greece, in China, and now in Soviet Russia I had seen and known such people. Systems of government might be one thing or another. Governments might rely upon mass illiteracy, as Franco's regime in Spain does; or they might teach tens of millions to read, as the Soviet regime (along with some other extremely severe dictatorial measures) had done. The blue globe turns, and now it drips with red. Everywhere the people remain, and millions of them are down. Does it seem likely that they will remain down? "We shall be three women alone," Galina said. But now she sings and her blue eyes are shining. Nazism and its armies could destroy and has destroyed many things. This is a thing that Nazism can never destroy.

Mama Roubtsova pulled out another mattress from somewhere and was spreading it on the floor. She motioned me toward her bed. I should take her bed and she would sleep on the mattress, such as it was.

"I can't do it," I said to Ehrenburg. "Please give her my thanks. But I can't deprive a sixty-year-old woman of her bed."

"It's no use, Stowe," Ehrenburg said. "You've got to do it. No Russian can forgive you if you refuse his hospitality — and this is all the hospitality this woman has got."

Mama Roubtsova curled up with Antonina on the mattress beneath the window near my bed. Galina went to her tiny alcove room to sleep with her four-year-old boy, Yura. The others, Ehrenburg, Arapov, and the two soldiers somehow shared a mattress in the middle of the floor. And I, because I was a guest and an American, retired in shameful grandeur to Mama Roubtsova's bed. This was a Russian peasant's conception of hospitality. In a very few hours, it seemed, I had seen a very great deal of Russia and the Russian war. Perhaps that was why I did not sleep well.

In the morning, before seven, Antonina went off to the near-by collective farm to dig potatoes. A few minutes later Galina, neat and smiling, departed to do her turn in the army telegraph office not far away. Mama Roubtsova fried some splendid potatoes for us for breakfast. I still had a little chocolate I could give her, but that was all. Little Yura, blond like his mother and extraordinarily sturdy, was sitting in the front seat with Ivan the Terrible when we went out. I could see that he had an aching longing for a ride in an automobile, but he didn't whimper or fuss when Mama Roubtsova lifted him out. Yura stood on his strong brown legs. Already you could see in him a self-reliant and sturdy man. "Where is the house? Where is the maiden?" There would be a house and a maiden for Yura some day. Yura gazed at us without speaking, but without a hint of a tear. As we rode away he waved a solemn-eyed *dosvydanya*. That was my farewell to the Rzhev front.

Chapter XV

SELF-PORTRAITS BY GERMAN PRISONERS

There are to be no more private Germans. Each is to attain significance only by his service to the state. . . . Thus, to express it in more emphatic terms, there are to be no more mere human beings *in Germany, but only Germans.*

Friedrich Sieburg

In two different sectors of the Rzhev front I talked with newly captured German soldiers. Both Ehrenburg and I talked at great length with them because they represented the latest sampling of Nazi Germany's "master" warriors. Ehrenburg called them the autumn Fritzes. Early in June I had visited an old monastery, far from Moscow, where more than six hundred Nazi prisoners were held. I wondered whether these October Germans would be less arrogant, less sold on Hitler or perhaps occasionally possessed of some slight moral scruples.

I found that they were not.

These German soldiers were frankly worried about the second Russian winter and about the Wehrmacht's failure to take Stalingrad on schedule; but I couldn't find a single young German, during several hours of conversations, who betrayed the least concern over the barbarous crimes which Hitler and the willing German *Herrenvolk* had committed among and upon more than 160,000,000 enslaved European peoples. I was looking for some manifestation of a German conscience — some honesty of thought — some sense of shame — some revulsion against a system of wholesale savagery and licensed plunder.

At the beginning of the fourth year of Hitler's war this is what I found.

Lieutenant Horst Krausgrell was a Luftwaffe pilot, aged twenty-one, from Offenbach-am-Main. Since he was twelve years old the Nazis had had complete control of Krausgrell's schooling and thinking. It was quickly apparent that they had done a thorough job. Beneath his bandaged head the lieutenant's face was chiseled and his eyes were hard, without light or emotion. I sat directly across the table from him and questioned him in his own language, not worrying at all about my inevitable grammatical errors.

"Why did Germany invade Poland?" I asked.

"Poland was a friend of England," Lieutenant Krausgrell said.

"Why did Germany invade Norway?"

"To keep the English out."

"Why did you go into Holland?"

"That was the only way we could defeat France."

"But why did you bomb Belgrade and occupy Yugoslavia?"

The German aviator seemed at a loss for an answer and finally said: "I can't remember where Yugoslavia is." After his memory had been jogged on that, and he had had time to cast about for an explanation, he remarked: "We invaded Yugoslavia because there were British agents there."

"So you feel the presence of secret agents justifies an attack, without warning, upon any country?"

Krausgrell made no effort to reply.

"How do you justify the wholesale execution of Poles, Czechs, Norwegians — of civilians in every country occupied by German troops?"

"I never heard of civilians being executed by us," said the Nazi lieutenant, squirming a little. "But if they were, then it was because they were working against Germany."

"So if they were working to free their own country — that means working against Germany — they should be shot?"

Krausgrell hesitated. After all, he had no desire to be shot himself. "Well, if not shot — they should be imprisoned."

According to this German officer's testimony, both the Nazis and Germany had an absolutely clean record. They had never terrorized or murdered. They were only protecting Deutschland. "After we defeat Russia," he said, "we will knock out England. . . . I think we will stay in Europe." Why? No, not because the U. S. A. wouldn't make fine plunder; simply because "America is too far." This was the type of young Hun that Ehrenburg was ideally qualified to handle, and as he took over I simply wrote down the dialogue verbatim.

"I'm sure you have a nice house in Offenbach-am-Main," Ehrenburg began with the faintest trace of irony in his voice. "Your house would please me very much. I think I'll go and live in your house. Do you understand?"

"No," said Lieutenant Krausgrell; and for once I think he was speaking half the truth.

"What are you Germans doing in Russia?" Ehrenburg fairly hurled the words in the young Nazi's face, in the manner in which Germans are accustomed to have their superior officers talk to them. "You Germans have shouted for years about the terrible wrongs of Versailles. What are you doing now in Norway, in France, all over Europe? Do those houses belong to you? Is Russia your house or mine?"

"No. Russia is your house," admitted Lieutenant Krausgrell, suddenly jolted and uneasy.

"But you want to live in my house. Very well. Your house in Offenbach would suit me perfectly. I need more room. Do you understand?"

The German aviator did not attempt to answer, so Ehrenburg fairly spat another question into his face: "Do you think you are right to invade Russia?"

"I think it was necessary," said Hitler's finished product.

"Have you a head? Answer my question — Is it right?"

"But der Führer said — "

"To hell with your dirty Führer," blazed Ehrenburg. Then he switched his inquiries to discover what kind of education these candidate-conquerors of the "master race" had received. The only German writers Krausgrell could mention by name were Goethe, Schiller, and Lessing. "I also read *Freiheitskrieg,*" he said.

"This is *our* war for freedom," snapped back Ehrenburg.

"But Communism goes into all lands," persisted the young German.

"What land has Soviet Russia invaded?" demanded Ehrenburg.

"There were Communists in Germany," said Horst Krausgrell. "No, I never saw any Russians in Germany, but I read about it in Hitler's book."

"Did you ever read any books by Thomas Mann?"

"No. I don't know Thomas Mann."

"Who wrote *Die Lorelei*?"

"Heine."

"Heine?" asked Ehrenburg. "Heine was a German?"

"No. A Jew."

"What are the words to *Die Lorelei*?"

"I've heard it sung, but I can't remember the words."

"And you Germans, you sing a song which was written by a Jew?"

Lieutenant Krausgrell winced as if lashed across the face with a whip. This, obviously, was the worst insult that could be heaped on a German warrior. His face became crimson. Germany's invasion and occupation of a dozen countries could all be justified with a glib phrase. The reminder that a great German folksong had been written by a Jew was the only thing that could make him blush. Ehrenburg turned away in disgust and I reverted to the war situation.

"We thought we'd defeat Russia this year," the young Nazi admitted. "Now I think we'll do it next year. Then we'll defeat England. No, we can't smash them both in one year, but I think we'll win the war."

"Why?"

"Because we've had all the victories so far," answered Krausgrell revealingly. "Perhaps America will send one or two million men to England, but Germany can still hold the Atlantic coastline of Europe."

"But to smash Great Britain you'll have to invade England."

"No, we won't invade England. We will win with U-boats and airplanes."

Every argument that the German aviator made came straight out of Dr. Goebbels's propaganda basket, but at last he disclosed one chink in his armor of confidence.

"We have had very big losses in men," he confessed. "More than 500,000."

"Only half a million?" I countered.

"Our people are tired. They feel these losses."

"But only half a million dead? Why, that's cheap. Look at all the countries you've conquered. Look at all the *Lebensraum* you've got!"

"For the future Germany it may be cheap," said Lieutenant Krausgrell, "but for our generation our losses are very heavy. It's a big price to pay."

"But the Poles, Norwegians, French, Greeks, and all the others have lost many more men than Germany."

"Yes. There are several millions of dead on the other side," the young German answered, much as if he was talking about dead pigs. "And we have killed ten million Russians. But just the same, half a million dead is much for us."

"Why don't you count all those European people who have starved and all those who have been executed by the Nazis?"

Lieutenant Krausgrell, twenty-one years of age and a member of the generation that will be Germany for the next forty years, had this reply:

"But in those lands the Germans are *Herrenvolk*. If people in those countries persist in working against the Germans, what can they expect?"

2

Next came a German corporal, aged twenty-eight, from Schleswig-Holstein. The only thing remarkable about him was that he was a colossal liar. He had been stationed in France for five months; he had eaten very well, he admitted, but he swore that he had never tasted a morsel of French food. He had now been in Russia for ten months. "I have never eaten Russian pork or chickens," said the corporal. "They were forbidden to us. Russian cows were forbidden, too. We never touched any Russian bread."

"Why are all the people of Europe against Germany?" Ehrenburg asked.

"I don't know."

"Is Hitler right?"

"With the German people he is right."

"Do you believe what Hitler says?"

"Yes."

"So Germany had a right to make war because Hitler said so?"

"I don't know."

"Can Hitler lie?"

"I think not," said the German corporal.

"Was it right for you to come here?"

The corporal hesitated. Then, probably out of fear, he answered in a low voice: "No. We had no right to come here."

One of the most revolting specimens of Hitler's Greater Germany was Under-officer Joseph Winterhaller, who had studied theology and had planned to take the robes of the church. He came from Württemberg and was in his twenties. He was blond, round-headed, and plump-faced. Although he had specialized in theology, Winterhaller gave no indication of having raised any moral questions in his mind. When I pressed him about the right or wrong of the German unannounced attacks and terror bombings of cities like Warsaw, Rotterdam, and Belgrade he replied evasively: "I'm a little man. I can't judge." As for the Norwegians, he admitted it might be better if they were free.

"Doesn't Hitler say plainly in *Mein Kampf* that all non-Teutonic peoples are inferior? That the Germans must be the masters, the *Herrenvolk*?" I asked.

"I've never heard about *Herrenvolk,"* said Winterhaller.

"You live in Germany, where the newspapers and radio speak all the time about the Germans as *Herrenvolk,* yet you never heard that phrase?"

"No, I haven't heard it," lied the completely Nazified young German who had studied to be a priest.

"You must know about the scores of thousands of Europeans who have been executed by Germans all over Europe," I insisted.

"It's a misfortune for all Europe," said greasy Joseph Winterhaller.

"Who is guilty, then?"

"I can't say."

"Are the Russians guilty?"

"No."

"Are the Dutch?"

"No."

"Is Germany guilty?"

"Perhaps — but England is really responsible."

"What about the thousands of civilians shot in Poland, Czechoslovakia, and Yugoslavia? Is England responsible for that?"

"I never heard of civilians being shot in any of those countries," said Winterhaller.

I looked at him for a moment and said nothing. It seemed to me, that within a year from the war's end I would be hearing millions of Joseph Winterhallers bald-facedly denying there had ever been a Gestapo or concentration camps, that there had ever been any crime or any murderer except Hitler — whom, *natürlich,* no German had ever willingly listened to or heeded. Except for Hitler, more than eleven years of Europe's horror had been "enemy propaganda." I could hear Winterhaller expounding all this to some profits-hungry American who wanted to start an export business with Germany. I beckoned for someone to take him away.

Under-officer Kurt Decker, a Saxon from Reichenbach, was the only German prisoner I saw near Rzhev who answered questions honestly. He had originally been a socialist, opposed to Nazism, but like millions of other socialists he had fallen in line after Hitler triumphed. He had chestnut hair and blue eyes, and his cheeks were sunken. He had belonged to the recently routed 87th infantry division, which had entered Paris on June 14, and he had remained for many months in France. Since Decker was not at heart a Nazi and because he represented a great mass of Germans upon whom the outside world counted for an eventual uprising, he interested us particularly. Before the Nazis came to power, in 1932, he had been without a job and had gone to France and found work.

"The French gave you work when you had no work in Germany," Ehrenburg said. "So you thanked them by invading their country and eating their food."

"We had to go," replied Kurt Decker. "But I didn't have anything against the French."

"Were the French and their government peaceful?"

"Yes."

"And the German system means war — Hitler says so?"

"Yes. But what could we do against it?"

"Are you proud that your country does things like that?"

"But we must have work," said Decker — as if even he, a former socialist, must somehow justify the Nazis' war.

"For three years you Germans have done nothing but destroy all over Europe. What do you say about that?"

"I can't lie. It's not right. It won't come to a good end."

"Tell me what you yourself think of Germany's conduct."

"One comes seldom to think what it means," said the once liberal and democratic Kurt Decker. "In the army we can't talk about it. We can't say what we think."

"Do you claim that the Poles, the Czechs, the Norwegians, and all the other people of Europe are responsible for this killing and destruction? I ask a *moral* question."

"Morally we are responsible," Decker answered straightforwardly.

"Why do you only think that when you are a prisoner?"

"It's impossible to do anything against the Hitler regime. In Germany the party members live and everyone else vegetates."

"You don't fight against Hitler, but you come to Russia to fight *for* Hitler — and you admit that what he has done all over Europe is wrong."

"Without weapons the people can't fight against the Nazis," the former German socialist insisted. "At this time you can't do anything in Germany against Hitler."

"But you have weapons," snapped Ehrenburg. "You could do something if you were willing to die doing it. You kill others to make slaves out of nations. You will not die to make yourselves free."

Decker shook his head fatalistically. He had been born a sheep. He had eaten the green pastures which belonged to others so long as it was convenient to do so. He knew he was living on plunder and other peoples' corpses. Perhaps the idea was a little unpleasant to him. Still you must not ask him to lead a revolt or to die for a more honorable and decent Germany. The Nazis were devouring Europe and he, Kurt Decker, was a soldier. "One comes seldom to think what it means."

3

At the prison camp in June I had talked with scores of German prisoners and they, like these new prisoners near Rzhev, were mostly between the ages of nineteen and thirty. The Nazis had controlled everything they were taught, had heard and read since they were adolescent or very young men. Among all these young Germans I found only one who was outspokenly anti-

Nazi, and only one other who had a slight sense of moral aversion to the system and crimes of Hitlerism. It seemed most emphatically indicated that the great majority of Germans below the age of thirty had been hardened, perverted, and criminalized to a point where any spiritual change in them would be extraordinarily difficult, if not impossible. They had been deliberately trained *not* to think — and also *not* to feel. They had been schooled to stamp out the tiniest voice of conscience. All that mattered was what would make Germans rich and prosperous and powerful. They had accepted this as their only religion, and among the young Germans I could perceive scarcely a hope that they would ever truly renounce their amorality. This was the terrible and frightening thing about the younger Germans with whom I attempted to reason. They had no reason. Hitler had destroyed it years ago together with most, or all, of their humanitarian instincts. This is the generation of Germans which, short of some miracle, will confound and plague Europe and perhaps much of the world so long as it lives.

A great many of the German prisoners were fine-looking young men physically and many had faces which were handsome in a metallic way. They smiled easily and made every effort to be ingratiating — most of them anyway. Young German officers were particularly dashing, although they were the toughest and coldest men imaginable when you talked with them. But their outer appearance was all in their favor and I thought the average easy-going American would be very strongly inclined to overlook the record, to forget to probe for a sense of integrity or a sense of moral values, and just put them down as "nice young fellows." But when I got at their attitude, I found a great majority of these young Germans, regardless of their superficial attractiveness, were likable in the way that typical American gangsters are "nice young fellows." They were products of the Hitler *Jugend* and they were hard — even harder on the inside than on the outside.

A German lieutenant cockily told a British colleague that the Nazis would knock out Russia this year.

"Even if you did," said the English correspondent, "Britain and America are not going to make peace with Hitler."

"Oh yes, you will," scoffed the German. "Why not?"

Luftwaffe officers were the most unregenerate Nazis of all, and some of them were also the biggest liars. A twenty-six-year-old Berliner, Karl Bomfeld, admitted to me that he was a bomber pilot and had been in the Nazi air force since 1938. Then he proceeded to insist that he had never dropped a bomb — an astounding achievement after four years in Göring's bomber squadrons. Bomfeld even went so far as to claim he had been doing reconnaissance in a bombing plane. I think it is accurate to say that throughout 1942 the general attitude of Germans taken prisoner in Russia was that "anything goes," anything is right, so long as Germany wins the war. A few German prisoners, however, were turncoats and bootlickers. They were the first to climb aboard the band-wagon. They had climbed on Hitler's band-wagon because it offered them the most, and they would climb on anyone else's just as quickly. When they know they are defeated, of course millions of German sheep will do precisely that. But in either the hard-boiled Nazified young Germans or the bootlicker variety the absence of any ethical stamina was equally great and equally disheartening. These young Germans gave me the enduring impression that Adolf Hitler had destroyed infinitely more than other nations' industries, churches, and cities. *Hitler has destroyed the moral scruples of the greater part of an entire German generation.* Whether this generation can ever be redeemed I don't pretend to know. I only know that it will be a simply stupendous task, and I question seriously whether a minority of responsible and humanitarian Germans can hope to succeed in re-educating Germany's criminalized youth without a program of enlightened help from some international organization.

When we arrived at the big camp in the old Russian monastery, we walked right into an unusual meeting, which — more than a year later — has assumed a particular significance. In July 1943 there was considerable surprise in London and Washington when Moscow announced the formation of a National Committee for Free Germany among Germans inside the Soviet Union. Personally I was astonished that either the British or the American government should have been surprised. Stalin's speeches had drawn a very clear distinction between the Nazi regime and the German people. Inevitably that distinction implied Soviet Russia's willingness to co-operate with anti-Nazi Germans — and you cannot co-operate in a vacuum, nor can you undermine the Nazi hold upon Germany's people without a political approach. Marxists have always been realists. It sometimes seems that only the democracies are inclined to be ashamed of using their own best weapons. If we do not know how to present the great appeal and assets of democratic principles to Europe's enslaved masses, we can scarcely expect the Communists or monarchists or feudalists to refrain from sowing seed on newly plowed soil. Moreover, you win wars much more quickly if you know how to organize resistance and encourage revolt inside the enemy's camp. For these obvious reasons the establishment of a National Committee for Free Germany in Russia was a perfectly natural — and intelligent — development. It merely proved once more that the Soviet government had a plan and was on its toes. In the prison camp in June 1942 I saw some of the highly important spade work for the formation of this Free Germany committee.

Over the doorway a single English word was painted: "Club." I entered, climbed a staircase, and elbowed into a crowded hall. There were no chairs. The prisoners, in their soiled and shabby uniforms, sat on the floor, knelt, squatted cross-legged, or half-reclined resting on one arm. They were packed in tightly, several hundred of them, and others were standing against the walls. A voice was booming steadily in German as we edged inside. In a Russian prison camp the first speech we heard was in German and by a German! "What's going on?" I thought. "This is something special. . . ." It was.

These were typical strong young Germans, almost all of them under thirty, and as I found a place in a forward corner near the stage I noticed that most of their faces were lean and hard. These soldiers belonged to an artillery battalion of the Wehrmacht's 294th infantry division, or to the 62nd, 71st, and 113th divisions. They had been captured near Kharkov within the month. Two huge blue-lettered banners hung around the upper walls, likewise in German. I read: "German workers, defeat Hitler and his clique. . . . Free our *Heimatland* from Hitler's slavery." Both these slogans stressed Hitler — not the German people or even their army — as the enemy of freedom. The soldiers glanced at us with a cold curiosity and then turned an equally cold attention on the speaker. He was a German non-com and he shouted a lot, but for me there was no ring of conviction either in his voice or in what he was saying. His audience listened stolidly until he finished, and then only a few of them applauded. A second soldier spoke, again denouncing the Nazi system and again straining too much. His reception was as chill and spotty as the first speaker's had been. I felt instantly that both these men were band-wagon climbers, and the few soldiers who applauded very loudly had all the earmarks of stooges. Most of the flintlike or bored faces which I studied on all sides reflected a reaction similar to my own. So far this was a pretty poor show.

But all this changed very suddenly. A young corporal stepped forward on the platform at our end of the hall and began to speak. Within two minutes he had every German soldier in the place listening intently. Three fourths of the secret of real oratory is sincerity — and this man had it. He was saying things that he believed with every ounce in a finely built, broad-shouldered body. He had a well-shaped head, a high forehead and the carriage of a man. He was a corporal named — well, the name we were asked to use was Hans Mueller. Since he had a family in Germany that request was understandable. The man's moral courage alone merited much greater consideration than that. He was risking the scorn and epithets of all the comrades with whom he had served and fought. I learned later that Corporal "Hans Mueller," about thirty years of age, was a former housepainter and he came from Munich. He was a corporal and a housepainter — and what was he saying about another ex-corporal and housepainter?

"When our fathers went to war in 1914, they were told they'd be home for Christmas. They said it again in 1915, in 1916 — and then in 1917. Der Führer said this war would be won last year. But another Christmas came and again we were far from home. When Christmas comes this year it will be the same. Hitler has deceived us. He also promised he would put an end to unemployment. The way he did it was to bring us here."

Every soldier in the crowded hall was hanging on the corporal's words now. This German was not talking for small prison favors from the Russians. He was talking from his heart. Even I felt the power of his round and full German speech, rendered more effective still by his softer Bavarian accent. Corporal Hans Mueller pulled no punches. He struck straight out, and every now and then he struck home. I could see it in the swarm of faces before us.

"Two years ago, when the German Army was in Belgium, we thought we were on our way to England. But the German Army hasn't reached England yet. And now? No, England and America are not stupid. They know the vulnerable place. They know the weak spot, just as the Germans knew the weak spot when they attacked France through Holland, Belgium, and Luxembourg. And what will be the end of it? Always the best German blood is offered. For what? Is it necessary that German children should be put in uniform at ten years and then sent to war before they are twenty? Is that freedom? And what will be the end? Another Versailles — something worse than Versailles."

For the first time in nine long years these young Germans were hearing a fellow German say publicly what he thought. For the first time they watched a German soldier declare his convictions fearlessly and honestly. I assumed, of course, that Hans Mueller was a Communist. But whatever his political affiliations, he was a kind of German that his Nazified compatriots had long forgotten could exist. He was a German who actually defied their opprobrium or their hatred — who actually retained and practiced liberty of conscience and freedom of thought. And for the first time in many, many years I saw an audience of Germans who were being swayed — reluctantly and slowly, but swayed nevertheless — by speech which was based upon reason rather than pure emotion. For the first time I also saw German prisoners who were beginning to think. In spite of themselves many of these soldiers were beginning to think.

"They say our youth will be destroyed if the war ends," Corporal Mueller continued. "But that's not true. Our youth can yet be saved. In a free Germany it will be saved. The best sons of every nation are going to hell for one man — for Adolf Hitler and his gang. Destroy Hitler and the Nazi system, and we can be saved. We don't want weapons. We don't want tanks and guns. We want what every other people wants — freedom."

When this housepainter of another German generation sat down, a gray-haired professorial man took his place. He was Edwin Hoernle, a former Communist deputy in the German Reichstag. He declared that this war was "the same swindle" as the last war. He cited the newly signed treaty between Great Britain and Soviet Russia and warned that a second front was bound to come; that Germany could never fight successfully on two fronts. When he cited the millions of war profits being reaped by Krupp, I. G. Farben and other big German industries, the faces of his listeners became particularly thoughtful. "There are still many among you who don't understand, whose eyes are not yet opened," Hoernle said. "But you will live to know that I told you the solemn truth when I say Hitler and the Nazis can never win the war. They can do nothing but lead Germany and the German people into destruction. But you can help prevent this. You can work to establish a free Germany. You can save our people from the vengeance of the enslaved nations. You can lead the revolt which will destroy Nazism. This is the only way out."

4

Meetings similar to this were undoubtedly being held in every German prison camp in Russia. Thirteen months later at any rate, in July 1943, Moscow announced the formation of a National Committee for Free Germany. The committee's manifesto was signed by German writers, by fifteen German officers and soldiers, and by five former Communist deputies — among them the same Edwin Hoernle whose speech I remembered so well. Perhaps Corporal "Hans Mueller" was one of the German soldiers who emerged as a leader of the Free Germany movement. I should expect him to be. But was this development really at all surprising? I have learned that those who are surprised by the policies or actions of Soviet leaders usually have paid little attention to what Soviet leaders have said, or prefer not to believe them.

In his first national appeal after the German invasion, on July 3, 1941, Joseph Stalin said frankly: "Our war for the freedom of our country will merge with the struggle of the peoples of Europe and America for their independence and for democratic liberties." On November 6, 1941 Stalin publicly renounced imperialist ambitions. He said: "We have not and cannot have any such war aims as the seizure of foreign territories and the subjugation of foreign peoples. . . . We have not and cannot have any such war aims as that of imposing our will and our regime upon the Slavonic or other enslaved nations of Europe. . . . Our aim is to help these nations in the struggle of liberation they are waging against Hitler's tyranny, *and then to leave it to them quite freely to organize their life on their lands as they see fit. There must be no interference whatever in the internal affairs of other nations."*

One year later, in November 1942, Stalin came out flatly for the liberation of the enslaved nations "and restoration of their sovereign rights." Most significantly Stalin added: *"We have not the task to destroy Germany,* because it is impossible to destroy Germany just as it is impossible to destroy Russia. But to destroy the Hitlerian state — this is possible and must happen."

When the Free Germany Committee's manifesto appeared its main declarations were strikingly in harmony with the Soviet policy laid down by Stalin. "Germany must not die," said the manifesto. "If the German people continue . . . to allow themselves to be led to their doom . . . their guilt will increase. . . . If the German people, in good time . . . prove by deeds that they want to be a free people, and are determined to free Germany of Hitler, *they will then win the right to decide their fate themselves.* . . . The formation of a genuine German government is the most urgent task. . . . This government must establish firm order and represent Germany with dignity to the outside world. . . . This means . . . a strong democracy. . . . It means the restoration and extension of political rights and social gains; freedom of speech, press, assembly, conscience, and religious beliefs; freedom of economy, trade, and handicraft; guaranteed right to labor and lawfully to acquire property . . . confiscation of property of those responsible for the war."

Could the American and British governments have offered the German people a more democratic program as a reward for rising against the Nazi control? It is difficult to see how we could have done so. But Britain and America had still put forward no offer of hope for elemental justice for the German people. At the time that a free Germany program was presented by Germans inside the Soviet Union, the only Anglo-American program was wrapped up in AMG — Allied Military Government in Occupied Territories. The Soviets had been permitted to appropriate what should have been the chief thunder, and one of the principal weapons, of the democracies. The more suspicious of anti-Soviet elements among Anglo-Americans still might skeptically insist that "there must be a catch in it somewhere." But that, in the late summer of 1943, was pretty cold comfort for the utter lack of a British-American political plan for the submerged people of Europe. For those millions of Germans who were yearning for freedom Soviet Russia, through the Free German manifesto, underwrote a precise and broadly democratic program — while America and Britain still offered nothing, nothing but a detested and feared military occupation.

I concluded my dispatch about that significant meeting in the German prison camp with this paragraph: "Walking down the stairway and out into the rain-sodden prison courtyard, this brief drama reminded your correspondent that there are other Hans Muellers. In this war their work can be of great importance — *if* those who capture them, like the Soviets, are wise enough to give them their opportunity."

I don't suppose any officials in Washington read that paragraph or would have paid any attention to it if they had. In any event and in due course I learned how amazingly little thought was given to the necessity of propaganda work with Axis prisoners by American officialdom. At the end of April 1943 I received an urgent request to consult one of our American army officers about a "very important matter." The colonel, whom I saw in Washington, was serving in a vital section of the War Department. This is what he told me:

"On Saturday morning my commanding officer called me in and ordered me to draw up a complete program for our handling of war prisoners. He wanted it ready by Sunday night."

"You mean to say that we have no program whatever for sifting out pro-democratic prisoners from those who are hopelessly fascist?" I gasped, amazed.

"That's right," said the colonel.

This was only about three weeks before Bizerte and Tunis fell and the Allies bagged some 150,000 Italian and German prisoners. The United States had been at war nearly eighteen months, and the U. S. Army was just getting around to working out some kind of plan for handling prisoners. Nevertheless, we would be surprised — and many of us quite annoyed — that the Russians had had a plan and had it working even when they seemed to be losing the war.

The colonel wanted to know if I had any idea what the Russian plan for prisoners was and how it operated; did they sift out the promising from the incorrigibly Nazi prisoners, and so on and so forth? I could only tell him what I had already reported through the newspapers eleven months earlier, plus a few definite impressions. The colonel explained that America was bound by the Geneva convention for treatment of war prisoners (which the Soviet Union had not signed). The Geneva convention, he said, prohibited forcing prisoners to attend meetings of a political nature.

"But you don't have to force prisoners to attend such meetings," I exclaimed. "You can simply make meetings sufficiently attractive so the prisoners will be glad to come. You can show them Walt Disney propaganda films. You can encourage some of their own men to talk to them, as the Russians do. You can have prepared a whole list of democratic and anti-Nazi books printed in their own language."

"I know it," said the colonel sadly, "but we haven't done anything about it yet."

"My God!" I said impatiently. "Is this a war of ideas — or isn't it?"

I went away from that discussion wondering how any of us could pretend that the democracies really deserved to win the support of the peoples of Europe. *We have the most wonderful goods in the world — the goods of human freedom — but we have learned practically nothing about the art of selling these goods.* The Communists also have goods to sell. Their potential customers are legion — and they know how to sell, the believers in Communism. You also have to win a person's confidence before you make a sale. Americans are past masters at selling refrigerators or automobiles or any inanimate object. How much do we really know about selling the tremendous idea by which we enjoy the privilege of selling refrigerators? If Americans and

Englishmen are among the world's worst idea-salesmen in our present revolutionary epoch, can we blame the Soviets for that? . . . No, it seems we must abide by the letter of the Geneva convention for war prisoners. And who were the men who drew up that curious convention? They are the men who were completely incapable of defending democracy in Europe and the world. They are the men who handed their great chance to Mussolini, Hitler, and Hirohito on a platter. So now, in the midst of an unprecedented struggle for survival, according to the strange ethics of important bigwigs in Washington and London, we must honor even the most fatally strangling of provisions which were drafted by these blind and ostrich-like creatures who contributed fearfully toward bringing democracy to the brink of extinction. Sometimes I think that if democracy survives through our lifetimes, it can only be by the will of God or some higher providence — surely not because of the intelligence or courage of those whom our democracies have elevated to positions of power.

What kind of beginning did we make at handling German and Italian prisoners? I have a bit of first-hand testimony which, short of a miracle, has probably been duplicated in essence thousands of times. A war correspondent, who is an old friend of mine, returned home from North Africa on one of many ships crowded with prisoners. His ship brought German prisoners to vegetate (without being subjected to anything so subversive as democratic ideas, without doubt) in some camp in the middle of Texas. The prisoners were in charge of an American army major. One day a group of German officers went to the major in high dudgeon. They demanded that a German soldier should be shot instantly. This soldier, said the Nazi officers, had insulted them beyond expression — he had refused to stand up and salute when they passed where he was sitting. The American major was as upset as only a muddled son of democracy can be. He didn't want to shoot the soldier, but he disliked all this row by the high-handed and arrogant Nazi officers. So the major went and tried to talk the German soldier into being a good boy. That, apparently, was not a violation of the sacred Geneva convention. The American major wound up by disciplining the German soldier. The hapless German private was ordered to clean out and scrub the ship's toilets for the duration of the voyage, and the Nazi officers' honor was placated to that extent. At least it was a fit place in which to placate Nazi "honor."

When the American major had completed this masterpiece of statesmanship he said to one of the war correspondents: "That German soldier said to me: 'I'm a Social Democrat. Now I'm a prisoner and I won't obey Nazis any more.' Say, what's a Social Democrat anyhow?"

The American army officer, selected to handle our Axis prisoners, did not know that the Social Democratic Party is the socialist party. He didn't know that Social Democratic parties have existed all over Europe for years. He didn't know that the Social Democrats — who are as far from being Communists as the British Labor Party — fought to keep free and democratic government in Austria. He didn't know that some nine million Social Democrats resisted Hitler in Germany for years, and that German Social Democrats must be our first and most powerful allies inside Germany if ever we are to see a parliamentary and democratic government in Germany in this century. In short, the American major was a complete political illiterate. But nevertheless he was entrusted to handle German prisoners, and punished the very Germans who were brave enough and non-sheeplike enough to begin to show independence of their Nazi masters. How would a Russian prison overseer have treated this same Social Democratic soldier? He would have treated him intelligently, of course. He would have taken the soldier's part and marked him for future re-education. Any Soviet official would have made him an ally.

Does it seem likely that we Americans can win German prisoners, and through them the German people, to democracy when we place officers in charge of these prisoners who do not know the difference between a Social Democrat and a Wagnerian tenor?

It may be possible that enough of Germany's Nazified youth can still be redeemed to save Germany for democracy and, just possibly, to prevent Germany from going whole-hog into Communism. These things may yet be possible; but certainly they are not possible unless the Anglo-American lip-service champions of democracy have a plan — an intelligent and carefully conceived plan — and are bold enough to apply it. Hitler and Nazism have twisted and perverted the minds of millions of Germany's youth. We cannot alter such calloused, ill-informed, and amoral minds by goody-goody treatment. No one, in time within memory, has ever made a lasting impression on the Germans, either physically or mentally, without an intense and uncompromising hammering technique. If we give, or have already given, the German people to Communism, we shall have no one but ourselves to thank. The future belongs to men and nations with a plan.

When you think about it that seems reasonable enough.

Chapter XVI

THE EVOLUTION OF THE RED ARMY

Is it really true that the German-Fascist troops are invincible? Of course not. History shows there are no invincible armies and never have been.

Joseph Stalin on July 3, 1941

The German robbers want a war of extermination with the peoples of the USSR. Well, if the Germans want a war of extermination, they will get it.

Joseph Stalin on November 6, 1941

Our lives have not been lived in vain if we have brought up such stalwart sons, such valiant defenders of Moscow, Leningrad, Sevastopol, and Stalingrad whose courage is a source of admiration to the entire world. . . . There is such a thing as immortality, the immortality of peoples.

From a letter to Russian mothers written by the widow of Anton Marenko, Soviet author and teacher

Since I came home from Moscow, questions repeatedly asked me have been: How do you explain the discrepancy between the Red Army's poor showing in Finland and its extraordinary achievements against the German invasion? Did the Russians deliberately bungle the first stages of their Finnish campaign in order to fool Hitler?

The over-all answer lies, I think, in the fact that the Red Army has been in a process of steady and most intelligently directed evolution ever since December 1939.

Through prolonged reverses, losses, and adversity this evolution continued steadily until the Soviets' war machine became the most resilient of modern times — perhaps the greatest army of the twentieth century. The outside world does not sufficiently appreciate the extent to which the Soviet high command learned the lessons of experience in Finland. That undoubtedly saved the Red Army from possible paralysis or destruction in the first months of the Wehrmacht's onslaught.

I saw the first Russian prisoners which the Finns captured on the Karelian Isthmus and they were poorly clad and ill-equipped. Three weeks later I saw hundreds of frozen corpses of an utterly different, first-class Russian division at Tolvajaervi. From that time through the remainder of the Finnish war the caliber of Soviet troops maintained a high level while the use of Red artillery and air force became increasingly effective. In Finland the Russian forces started in low gear and with very spotty leadership. At that time Finnish officials privately assured me they believed the Soviets had expected the Helsinki government to capitulate to their demands without a fight; that Moscow had been misled by reports from its agents inside Finland. Later in the Soviet Union I saw indications that the Russians had counted on obtaining Finnish bases without war; then found themselves compelled to use force before they were completely prepared. That and the terrible winter of 1939–40, I believe, chiefly explain the early Red Army setbacks in Finland — plus, of course, the superb all-round caliber of the Finnish officers and soldiers.

In any case it is frankly admitted in Russia that a wholesale reorganization of the Red Army followed the Finnish campaign. This revision of formations, tactics, and command was carried out with great dispatch and energy. Actually Stalin and the high command had but fifteen months (from April 1940 to June 1941) to put these reforms ruthlessly into practice. Knowing perfectly well that Hitler would strike Russia the moment his hands were free in the west, the Kremlin's leaders enforced the utmost speed. Some qualified observers in Russia insist today that, in this sense, the Red Army's Finnish experience probably saved Leningrad and Moscow in the autumn of 1941.

Since the outbreak of the Finnish war until the present time the Red Army's evolution has been marked especially by farsighted planning; by an exceptional degree of administrative and technical flexibility; by consistent improvement in tactics and in weapons; and by a careful sifting of army corps and divisional commanders which has coincided with the building up of an impressive — perhaps a brilliant — general staff in which "young blood" is a predominant element. Of course their own qualities would have been seriously limited or vitiated if the Russian soldier had not meanwhile shown a superb fighting spirit and remarkable endurance. They would also have lost much of their practical significance if the Soviet government had not put into immediate effect a bold and vast scheme for transferring machinery and whole industries from such regions as the Ukraine and the Donets Basin — if it had not simultaneously pressed urgently the expansion of Russia's inner industrial fortress behind the Urals. Finally British and American war materials, even though slower in reaching determinant dimensions in totals actually delivered in the USSR than most Anglo-Americans appreciate, gave the Red Army's high command a positive assurance of steadily increasing armed strength beyond and above Russia's own indispensable growth in production. Although it has not been generally understood abroad, American Lend-Lease and British supplies (owing particularly to heavy shipping losses on the Arctic route to Murmansk and Archangel) had not yet become sufficiently great to be more than a minor factor in the Red Army's crucial defensive fighting along the Don, in the northern Caucasus, and at Stalingrad during the summer and early autumn of 1942. In particular the number of Anglo-American tanks and planes which reached their destination in time to be thrown into these critical battles, according to the best information available inside Russia, remained in the hundreds rather than the thousands until about the time that the Russians' bulldog grip on Stalingrad was demonstrated.

The first fifteen months of the Red Army's resistance — otherwise the astonishing defensive phase of the Russo-German war — thus represent an almost exclusively Soviet achievement. British aid and American Lend-Lease really began to play a role of great importance during the Russians' extraordinarily successful winter offensive of 1942–3, and increasingly so throughout the remainder of 1943. Only those Allied supply officers on the spot in the Soviet Union and members of the Russian General Staff itself are in a position to make authoritative statements fixing the extent of the military contribution of British-American supplies to the Red Army's recovery of the initiative. That, therefore, is another story which is not likely to be available in precise and documented proportions until the war is over. The transplanting of Soviet war industries and their remarkable expansion in central Siberia likewise is not a primary element in the Red Army's evolution, even though this unbroken and rising war production provided Soviet forces with the sinews which made possible first the preservation and then the development and perfecting of a great war-waging machine.

One comes back, then, to a mighty armed force which grew and tightened and strengthened under adversity. That was only possible through leadership, vision, and adaptability at the top. From personal observation I know that the Red Army proved it was not limited to the strategy and tactics which it employed in Finland. On the Karelian Isthmus the Russians relied upon massed artillery and steamroller concentrations of tanks and infantry to break the Mannerheim Line. In the long withdrawals from White Russia and across the Ukraine and the Don steppes Russian forces gradually perfected an elaborate method of defense in depth, and also anti-tank tactics as well as anti-tank weapons. Eventually, in the 1942–3 winter offensive and the 1943 summer campaign, the Red Army also demonstrated the conception, speed, and timing of first-class offensive ability.

Taken as a whole, these varied developments constitute a steady growth. I do not think it is an exaggeration to say that these achievements have been based in large measure upon high alertness and intelligence quite as much as unshakable moral fiber. Hitler inherited a powerful and technically expert military élite with traditions dating back to Frederick the Great. But the master strategists of the Wehrmacht were first checkmated and then confounded by virtually an upstart military machine which has since proved itself the equal or the superior of the great German Army in almost every category of armed conflict. This was not an accident, as we clearly see when we retrace the major steps of the Red Army's evolution in more detail.

2

One of the lessons learned in Finland had to do with the amount of authority that should be delegated to political commissars with the Red Army. Following the purges of 1936–7 the commissars had returned to the army with all the necessary powers to check on the loyalty of every officer. But in Finland they often showed themselves too zealous and too rigid in their control over strictly military decisions. I was later told that this had accounted for more than one Russian setback during the Finnish campaign. As a result steps were taken immediately afterward to curb undue interference of commissars in military matters.

It is significant that within one month after Hitler attacked the Soviet Union, on July 16, 1941, the Presidium Council issued a new decree specifying the precise functions of commissars in the Red Army. This decree did not refer to them as "political" but as war commissars. It was based upon Stalin's dictum: "If the commander is the head of the regiment, the regiment's commissar must be its father and soul." During and after Russia's civil war army commissars were primarily political. They were security officers who propagandized for the Communist ideology. Abroad there has been a tendency ever since to regard the commissars in this narrow light and hence to misunderstand and completely underestimate the vital importance of their work. In reality throughout the struggle against Germany the commissars have been a combination of army chaplain, educational director, propagandist, and efficiency expert. In the July 1941 decree the commissar's task of political and party work in military units was not even mentioned until its final and ninth article. Overwhelming emphasis was placed on his responsibility "for fulfillment of the fighting task." He is "the moral leader of his unit, the first defender of its material and spiritual interests"; he must "inspire the troops to fight," must popularize the best men and commanders and "carry on a merciless fight against cowards, panic-mongers, deserters. . . ." It was also his job to hear and remove just grievances of the troops. In a word the Red Army commissar's first task was the building of morale. It still is.

When I discussed the commissar's role with Brigadier General Philip Faymonville, chief the U. S. Army's supply mission in Moscow, I obtained the confirmation of the man who is one of the greatest foreign authorities on the Red Army. "The morale angle is the important one," General Faymonville said. "The whole Russian Army feels that wrongs won't go unrighted, that grievances will be heard, and that any serious delinquencies will be reported to the top. This has a most beneficial effect upon military commanders. The commander knows the morale of his men is high — and he also knows he's got to produce the goods himself. All question of sloppy performance of duty is banished. Another very important thing is this: the commissar system is one of selection, and a selective system is almost bound to bring the best men to the top. A commissar's life is no bed of roses. Commissars go into the attack with their outfits, and often lead them. When you have your best men in positions of great responsibility they're the ones who perform prodigies of valor. They win their men's confidence. Thousands of them have been killed, but other thousands of well-trained commissars have taken their places. The Russians also get something out of this system which we haven't got. It's a system which keeps officers, as well as men, on their toes. Our own inspector-general system does not go nearly so deep as the commissar system goes, nor does it operate so completely and swiftly."

Along the Rzhev front I talked with scores of commissars who ranged in rank from the equivalent of generals down to captains and lieutenants. They were impressively keen men and their quality as leaders was universally apparent. The war commissars shared the responsibility of command and military decision with Red Army officers of equal rank. This dual command, in fact, was what orthodox American and British officers usually criticized as confusing and impractical. Certainly it required a rare degree of teamwork between a divisional commander and a divisional commissar; yet in half a dozen Red Army headquarters where I remained overnight or conversed at length with both the military and commissar commanders, I observed a remarkable co-operation and comradeship. Cases of disagreement or incompatibility undoubtedly cropped up, but I never heard of instances of disagreement on a serious scale.

For the first sixteen months of the Russo-German war the Red Army operated with officers and commissars on the dual-command basis. Yet through all the withdrawals and reverses, culminating in the black summer of 1942, when the Nazis surged to the streets of Stalingrad and the foothills of the Caucasus, its fighting morale remained amazingly high. Allied military observers on the spot had to admit that the powerful leadership of the Russian commissars was a real and potent factor in this performance. In a prolonged defensive period on a scale and intensity unprecedented in all history, in a period of defensive anguish which tried men's souls to the extreme limits of spiritual endurance, the Red Army commissars may well have contributed the difference between collapse and continued resistance. Personally I question seriously whether the near-miracles of Leningrad, Sevastopol, and Stalingrad could have happened without the inspiration, example, and leadership of Russia's commissars.

Nevertheless the dual-command authority was finally removed in October 1942. Significantly, this was the moment when Marshal Stalin was preparing the first great Russian counter-offensive. Many Allied officers who had not been in Russia during the war leapt to the conclusion that the commissar system had failed and was being abolished. This seems to me a serious misjudgment. Doubtless the high command wished to give the military commanders in the field freedom of decision in a great and complicated offensive action directly ahead. By this time, too, Stalin had reorganized his General Staff and had evolved an imposing number of generals and colonels of established ability upon all of whom he could rely. The dual command was only one item among the varied and indispensable functions of the commissar. There was another factor which has been almost completely overlooked, I think, by Anglo-American critics of the commissar system. This was the fact that the Red Army, in sixteen months of incessant combat, had suffered heavy losses among its officers. In an army of over 300 divisions how could these officers be replaced? In its commissars the Red Army has something which exists in no other army in the world — a reserve officers' training institution which functions in the front lines and sectors, not in schools hundreds of miles removed from the actualities of combat. Under the dual-command system every commissar from the rank of lieutenant up to colonel and general had been going to school under shellfire. The commissars, especially those of higher rank, had participated in every strategic decision; had been in daily contact with commanders with twenty or more years of experience behind them; had seen which operations succeeded and which failed and why.

Thus the Red Army, thanks to the commissar system, possessed the finest battle-tried reserve of officer material of any army in the present war. Commissars of the rank of major and above whom I met were already excellent officers in every respect save that of specialized technical instruction; but they had some additional things which the average West Pointer would never acquire in the same measure. They knew all the intimate problems of their troops. They had an acutely developed political sense. They understood perfectly all the minute aspects of psychological leadership and the building of morale. Therefore the October decree provided that the most capable commissars should be withdrawn for courses of three or six months at officers' training schools. By the spring of 1943 the Red Army had thousands of former commissars back as well-trained military commanders, with technical knowledge added to their invaluable experience at the front. And these were men hand-picked long before for their exceptional capacities for leadership. Neither the German nor the other Allied armies could replace their officer casualties with new commanders of this caliber — if at all — in anything like such shortness of time. Meanwhile the remaining commissars, and other new ones, continued their invaluable work — still removing the soldiers' doubts and building their fighting spirit — with the one constructive difference of a single military commander in every unit. In short, the war commissar system had passed into what is likely to be its final stage of evolution in this war. Nevertheless its contribution to Russian resistance and ultimate victory remains almost immeasurable.

3

Following the reorganization of the Red Army after the Finnish war, and the revision of the commissar system in July 1941, Joseph Stalin found himself confronted with the need of making changes in his high command. During the Finnish campaign he had relied upon his old comrade of civil-war days, Marshal Klementy Voroshilov. The results had not been encouraging. In the first months of the Nazi invasion Marshal Semion Budenny, another of Stalin's close friends, had failed disastrously to hold up the German advance across the Ukraine, and Russia lost the vital coal and industrial sinews of the Donets Basin as a result. In late October 1941 both Voroshilov and Budenny were withdrawn to train new armies in the rear. This was the first step toward building the Red Army's present high command. Stalin must have found the decision difficult to make. But even in the case of old friends Stalin did not hesitate. That fact seems to testify to his peculiar value as a supreme commander.

From the time of the eclipse of Voroshilov and Budenny until the Russians launched their offensive on November 19, 1942 — that is, throughout the first seventeen months of the war — the commanders of the Red Army remained cloaked in an almost inexplicable anonymity. Except when lists of the recipients of high decorations were announced, the Soviet press rarely published the names of army corps commanders or other outstanding generals. Younger men, many of them surprisingly young, were becoming generals of various grades and were distinguishing themselves. But month after month they were denied the privilege of becoming popular heroes. Sometimes in Moscow we used to wonder why there were so few names on the Russian side of the war. Eventually we learned that the government's policy apparently barred publicity *until* Red Army commanders had completely proved themselves in battle and until victories on a great scale could be celebrated. In the long interim of silence the sifting out of colonels and generals and the advancement of the ablest continued unheralded to the Russian people or to foreign correspondents. In this way Stalin did something which neither the British nor the American democratic system seems to make it possible to do: he avoided the public ballyhooing of officers whose reputations did not yet rest soundly on combat performance. When at last the Russian people discovered marshals and generals like Vasilevsky, Voronov, Rokossovsky, Vatutin, and Golikov, these commanders were already turning the Nazi tide at Stalingrad and elsewhere.

The first evidence of important changes in the Soviet high command came in August 1942, when General Gregory K. Zhukov was appointed vice-commissar of national defense directly under Stalin. Until then this extremely important post had been held by Marshal Timoshenko, although Moscow newspapers carefully failed to mention that fact. Rostov had just fallen, suddenly and without the customary yard-by-yard Russian resistance, and Timoshenko commanded all the troops in that Lower

Don area. The censorship did not permit us to point out the fact that Zhukov had succeeded Timoshenko as Stalin's right-hand military man — and American editors forgot to inquire who had been Zhukov's predecessor. So American newspapers for the next five months continued to comment on Marshal Timoshenko's defense of Stalingrad unaware that the third old-time Red commander had been relegated to a comparatively unimportant zone because of the catastrophically swift German break-through at Rostov on July 25.

It was not until September 13, when the battle for Stalingrad was just beginning, that correspondents in Moscow got their first inkling of the dimensions of the collapse at Rostov, which (still unknown to us) precipitated the second and most drastic reorganization of the Red Army General Staff and field command. On that day *Krasnaya Zvezda,* the Red Army's official newspaper, declared revealingly: "We have everything to mince fascist forces at approaches to any town. All these possibilities were available during the defense of Novocherkassk and the German drive on Rostov. But they were not fully utilized. Some cowards and panic-mongers fled the field of battle and leaders lacked the decision to deal mercilessly with the cowards and faithless. Novocherkassk and Rostov, prepared for impregnable defense, were captured by the enemy." To the best of my knowledge, this is the only case in the Russian war to date where important towns were not defended with savage stubbornness — a remarkable record. In this case the commanders involved were held rigidly responsible. Timoshenko was probably saved from complete disgrace by Stalin's remembrance of the elderly Ukrainian warrior's past services.

But the disaster at Rostov revealed where fatal weakness still existed in the Red Army machine and paved the way for the great comeback from November to February 1943. The defense of Stalingrad was entrusted immediately to younger generals — men of strong physique and iron nerves and greater competence in modern warfare. Lieutenant General Vassily Chuikov, who commanded the Sixty-second Army inside Stalingrad itself, later gave Henry Shapiro of the United Press a vivid and most enlightening account of the fighting in the Volga city. Chuikov said that when he took command Stalingrad was already a flaming inferno. "Our units were tired," General Chuikov said. "There were many whining pessimists in the army. I threw these panicky people out of the army right away and set to work. I told our men we could not retreat beyond the Volga. . . . I believe that nowhere else in this war was there such bloody hand-to-hand combat. Nowhere else were bayonets and hand grenades used so widely as in Stalingrad. . . . Lieutenant General Rodimtzev's division was first to arrive there and received the fierce German blow. Rodimtzev told me: 'We will fight to the last man, but we shall not leave the city.' . . . Our soldiers had only one idea. Stalin had ordered us not to retreat."

At the time they commanded this battle, perhaps the decisive battle of the war, the names of Chuikov, Rodimtzev, and other generals with them were known only to a few thousands among Russia's scores of millions of civilians. But the crucial August reorganization of the Red Army command had been completed, quietly and most effectively. The Red Army's leadership was now being whipped into a remarkable team composed of military commanders of very exceptional merit; and the most striking feature of these men was their comparative youth. Very few of Russia's now famous marshals and generals are more than fifty; most of them are in their early or middle forties — yet most of them are fighting in their third or fourth war. In Greece I met colonels, and even lieutenant colonels, who were engaged in their fourth war and this was one of the secrets of the extraordinary achievements of the Greek Army. In Russia most of the army corps and divisional commanders whom I met also had the experience of several wars behind them. Leliushenko, on the Rzhev front, was a lieutenant general at the age of thirty-nine; Lieutenant General Rodimtzev, one of the heroes of Stalingrad, was only thirty-six. Colonel General Andrei Yeremenko, who commanded the southern pincers which recaptured Kotelnikovo and liberated Rostov, at fifty was one of the oldest army group commanders on the entire Don front. Lieutenant General Rodion Malinowski, who served with Yeremenko, was but forty-four. Such ages had become the norm in the upper hierarchy of the Red Army. But this combination of commanders who linked broad experience to extreme physical fitness and endurance now gave the Red Army a super-powerhouse of energy and skill at the top.

At last when the Red Army smashed the German and satellite armies back across the Donets and virtually to the points where they had started in June 1942 (the Russians' winter offensive from November 1942 to February 1943), the veil was lifted and the dominant personalities of the new Russian high command became known to the world. Stalin meanwhile — but only in the hour of victory — had emerged as a marshal, a title which his leadership had unquestionably won, especially since much of the grand strategy of Stalingrad seems clearly to have been his. Zhukov had also become a marshal. Vasilevsky, promoted a marshal in February, was Chief of Staff. These three planned the great counter-offensive. Marshal Alexander Novikov, chief of the Red air force, also had won his final elevation in the Stalingrad operations. Now, like Napoleon, Stalin distributed the greatest laurels after they had been won on the field of battle. Marshal Nikolai Voronov rose rapidly as the others had done. As chief of artillery, what Stalin calls "the god of war," Voronov's contribution to the destruction of the Germans' Sixth Army at Stalingrad was very great. There remains a long and growing list of generals, like Rokossovsky, Vatutin, Tulenev, Sokolovsky, Golikov, Konev, and Tolbuhkin. These are the commanders who proved in the winter of 1943, and will continue to prove until the German armies are smashed into capitulation, the wisdom and effectiveness of Stalin's reorganization of the Red Army's high command. It is doubtful if many further substantial changes in Russia's high command will occur through the duration of hostilities. The men were there — and they have been found. Youth was no obstacle to their swift elevation. They were chosen on merit and promoted on the basis of performance.

The significance of the victory at Stalingrad and the successful winter offensive can scarcely be exaggerated. The Red Army had already demonstrated its ability at defense in depth. Now it revealed its mastery of great encircling movements and annihilation tactics — and this against the previously most powerful mechanized army of this century. Nothing that Hitler's Wehrmacht had achieved in two summer campaigns in Russia surpassed the paralyzing speed, sureness, and timing of the Red Army's winter blows. Max Werner, author of *Attack Can Win in '43,* spoke authoritatively when he wrote that the German monopoly on encirclement had been broken, that the Wehrmacht's speed had nowhere equaled the Russians' speed of advance in early February, and that "some day the Red Army will resume its offensive, and then the Wehrmacht will have nothing to fall back on in Russia but its military strength."

The Russians' 1942–3 winter offensive showed clearly that the Red Army, under the battering blows of vicissitude, had evolved into a very great modern army. It had the capacity for vast and over-all strategic planning, it had the brains (the marshals and generals and co-ordinated General Staff). It also had boldness, nerves of iron, an astonishing endurance, and superb fighting morale. All that it needed beyond these qualities was something like equality in tanks and airplanes; and this equality was bound to come. In fact, it had been achieved in sufficient measure to stop dead the Germans' Kursk salient offensive effort within a few days in July 1943 and then strike back in the Russians' mighty summer offensive, which rolled up the great victories at Orel, Belgorod, Kharkov, Stalino, Bryansk, and beyond. To one who had seen the Red Army in its darkest days, during October 1942, its following winter offensive meant that Hitler's offensive strength in Russia would never be the same again and must inevitably be very sharply limited thereafter. But the Red Army's 1943 summer offensive meant only one thing: that the Nazis' Wehrmacht was finished in Russia. The Red Army had evolved, so far as this war is concerned, into an unbeatable machine. (This at last became plain, even to the most stubborn anti-Soviet skeptics abroad, when the Russians broke the Dnieper line in October and then captured Kiev and surged on to ward Rumania and Poland.)

4

Coincidentally with its strictly military evolution the Red Army has also undergone other changes of considerable psychological and political importance. Today much less than formerly does it have the conformation and appearance of a "workers' and peasants' army." In a series of decrees Marshal Stalin rewarded his victorious officers and soldiers during the winter of 1943 with embellishments which make the Red Army more of an élite within the Soviet state than any Soviet body has ever been in the past. Russian officers now wear huge shoulder epaulets adorned with gold stripes or ornate gold braid. Those above the rank of colonel also have bright red stripes on the sides of their trousers. Dress uniforms have become much more elaborate and there is something almost Napoleonic in the prestige which the Red Army officers, and in lesser degree the soldiers, now enjoy.

Russian soldiers still address their commanders as "Comrade Colonel" or "Comrade General"; but officers' clubs, as C. L. Sulzberger has pointed out in the *New York Times,* have now been established for the first time in the history of the Soviet Union. At the Rzhev front I saw Russian women in uniforms (the WAC's of the Red Army) performing most of the duties of orderlies at various headquarters. A few months later, despite the war's strain on Russia's manpower, it was decided that Red Army officers should have male orderlies to serve their meals, polish their boots, and perform similar routine services. A few years ago the suggestion that there should be male orderlies in the proletarian Red Army would have been denounced by most Communist leaders as something approximating betrayal of the Revolution.

The Soviet plan for postwar reconstruction, announced in outline form in Moscow on August 22, 1943, contains provision for nine military schools to train boys between eight and seventeen years of age to become officers in the Red Army. Named in honor of Alexander Suvorov, one of Russia's first and greatest military commanders, these schools recall in some respects the cadet boarding schools of pre-Revolutionary days.

All this indicates the new tone in the Red Army today. It is the tone of an élite military organization which places increasing stress on nationalism and less — considerably less — emphasis on revolutionary doctrines. The Red Army man has become the first citizen of the USSR, and new regulations require a correspondingly rigid attention to dress and conduct, particularly by officers. Throughout the first eighteen months of the war officers on leave in Moscow did not have to concern themselves about personal appearance beyond a reasonable degree of neatness. Often they wore their front-line uniforms and their clumsy-looking but warm felt boots and carried as many bundles as were necessary at the moment. These things are now strictly forbidden. A Russian officer must wear his best uniform in the cities; he must be a reminder to the general public that this army represents something special — that it has class *and* position. The Soviet people must be given reason to be proud of their army in every respect. The day has now passed when Muscovites look at the handsome uniforms of British or American officers with secret envy. Indeed, the Red Army officers have come to rate probably more privileges and public distinction than most representatives of the Communist Party.

Both physically and psychologically this is a new Red Army. It is adorned with the prestige of great achievements and the assurance of a lifetime of unprecedented power, based upon a record of unparalleled victories. But it has grown into this position through a coincident crescendo of nationalistic faith. It is no accident that the Kremlin, from the beginning, publicized this great conflict as "*the* patriotic war." That was the only way that the Soviet Army and the Russian people could be spurred to the supremest efforts. Nor was it by chance that the newest decorations initiated by the Soviet government were orders named after the great military heroes of Russia's past: the order of Alexander Suvarov, who won fame as conqueror of the Turks and the Poles from 1787 to 1795; the order of Mikhail Kutuzov, that stubborn old Slav who confounded Napoleon; the order of Alexander Nevsky, who repulsed the Teutonic Knights in the Battle of Chudskoye Lake some seven hundred years ago. Among the various Revolutionary decorations, including those of the Red Banner and the Red Star, only those of Hero of the Soviet Union and the Order of Lenin rival or surpass the distinction of these new nationalistic orders. In every respect, then, the new Red Army possesses an éclat which was unknown before the Russo-German conflict, and with the subordination of commissars to the military command its officers have emerged independent and trusted, members of a superior organism. The Red Army is more of a professional army, and more powerful and more honored, than at any time during the first twenty-five years of the Soviet Union's existence. These are understandable rewards for its record of steadfastness, ability, and great heroism as well as for its huge sacrifices. Does this new authority indicate a more influential role for the Red Army inside the Soviet federation in the next generation? This may depend in the end on whether it has served chiefly for the protection and security of the Soviet state or whether it becomes eventually an instrument for another imperialism. So far one can say truly that its chief motivating force has been Russian nationalism and Russia's security.

By now it is clear that the Soviet Union will emerge from this war with the greatest and most efficiently organized army in either Europe or Asia. The Red Army will be enormously powerful and its new military aristocracy will wear an aura of well-earned glory. But it will be standing guard over a country of which vast areas have been ravaged, whose 160,000,000 surviving civilian inhabitants (more or less) are destitute, and whose economy is gravely dislocated. Above everything else Soviet Russia will need a long period of peace for rebuilding and rehabilitation. The Red Army will be able to assure it.

Soviet Russia's present allies may easily become obsessed by fear of the Red military colossus, even though — in the absence of any reliable system of general international security — its size cannot really be considered out of proportion to the one sixth of the earth's surface which it is designed to protect. It may be easy to forget this fact. It will be more difficult for many of us to keep in mind the enormous price which the Russian people have paid for their national existence, and the very great saving in British and American lives which their heroism effected. Only in this way will the Western nations be able to overcome their fear, to strive to dissipate those suspicions and prejudices which are as common to Soviet leaders as to ourselves, and so to lay the new foundations for co-operation with Soviet Russia.

A nation which has sacrificed the lives of from fifteen to twenty million of its soldiers and civilians — perhaps more — and has emerged triumphant from the holocaust can scarcely fail to be conscious of its stature. Such a nation commands respect and deserves an exceptional effort at understanding. Admittedly understanding between the Soviet Union, Great Britain, and the United States will be difficult to attain for all parties concerned. Yet the obstacles to co-operation with Russia can scarcely be as great as our mutual and imperative need for a prolonged era of peace once the Axis coalition has been completely destroyed.

Part V—All of Us

Chapter XVII

CAN WE LIVE WITH SOVIET RUSSIA?

> *Communism, for all the claims of some of its propagandists, is a national and not an international product. It is brought about by internal conditions. If you fear it, you should so set your house in order that your social and political conditions will silence any demand for its introduction.*
>
> Sir Samuel Hoare

In the postwar era which looms ahead the world's most powerful nations — in respect to their combined military equipment, natural resources, and industrial capacity — will be the United States of America, the Soviet Union, and the British Commonwealth. When peace comes they will rank first, second, and third in this order and it seems highly probable that they will remain in these relative positions for at least several decades. What is new about this, and of enormous historical importance, is the fact that Soviet Russia has replaced Germany as the greatest power on the continent of Europe. But simultaneously the USSR, this young stripling of twenty-six years, has emerged as tomorrow's strongest military and industrial force in Asia. Within fifty years' time, or before this century ends, it is conceivable that the Soviet Union may equal or surpass the United States in combined *assets* and physical development. Even though America's standard of living were still considerably superior, that may be purely a secondary matter in so far as power and influence in international affairs is concerned; all the more so since the Soviet Union's population is virtually certain to more than double that of the U. S. A. during the next half-century.

This means that both the American people and the peoples of the British Commonwealth must accustom themselves swiftly to thinking of the Soviet Russian peoples as their equals on the plane of world power and world leadership. The Chinese, too, are struggling upward toward this commanding plane and one day they will arrive. But what we are seeing demonstrated day after day is the new and tremendous fact that the Russians and their federated Asiatic peoples have already arrived. What they do, as what we Americans and the British do, will hereafter have its repercussions around the world. The Soviet Union has grown up with even more startling rapidity than the United States grew up during the war of 1914–18. When America came of age near the close of the last war, no people on earth were so surprised or ill-prepared as the American people themselves. In regard to Soviet Russia today there is one very great difference. Six months in wartime Russia taught me very plainly that the Soviet Russian people *know* they have grown up. Throughout the 1920's and 1930's many in Britain's ruling class made the error of failing to recognize the changed status of the United States, and that failure has often served to embitter needlessly — and frequently at great cost — the relationships between us. Today, unless we are extremely careful, we Americans may make the same costly error in regard to the newly grown-up Russians.

If it is at all possible, we need urgently to look at the Soviet Union with fresh eyes; and the less emotion we indulge in, the more clearly we may hope to see.

The area of the continental United States is 3,022,387 square miles. The present area of the Union of Soviet Socialist Republics (including the Baltic States, occupied Poland, Bucovina, and Bessarabia, most of which will certainly remain incorporated in the Soviet Union after the war ends) totals 8,819,791 square miles. Thus continental Soviet Russia is almost *three times as large as the United States* — and, from its European borders to its Kamchatka Pacific outposts, the Soviet Union is considerably *more than 6,000 miles wide*. In a literal sense, then, Soviet Russia constitutes the largest single physically united political and economic entity in the world's history. In addition Russia will emerge from this war with the largest and most powerful army in Europe and Asia. Industrially she will only be outranked by America and Great Britain. In undeveloped raw materials she will lead the world's nations, surpassing even China and Brazil. In short, Soviet Russia is the new colossus of the twentieth century. The prosperity and peaceful existence of Americans and Britishers throughout the next fifty years will be determined in very large measure, perhaps overwhelmingly, by whether we can live on terms of decent friendship and reciprocity with this new Russian colossus.

Russia has suffered such deep injuries from the war that it will probably require twenty or thirty years before she can begin to expand to a point commensurate with her vast potentialities. Several five-year plans will be necessary for Russia's industrial recovery; and when that much has been achieved and exceeded, she will still have to supply an *internal* market for approximately 220,000,000 people, if not more. One sixth of the earth's surface and some 220,000,000 people form quite a gigantic market of themselves. If Americans are as technically talented and as organizationally efficient as we like to think we are, there would seem little excuse for us to fear the eventual large increase in Russia's industrial production. The truth of the matter is, of course, that we do not fear the Soviet Union physically because we have never had the slightest reason to fear an attack from Russia. What a great many of us have found reason to fear about the Soviet Union has been its political-economic system, the Marxist experiment — or the world revolution. That is what has prompted so many British-American citizens to ask: Can we live with the Soviet Union?

The truly extraordinary fight which Soviet Russia's government and people have put up against Hitler's war machine has now served to narrow this question very considerably — and also very pertinently. It is no longer so much a question whether we *can* live with Soviet Russia as it is a dead certainty that *we've got to try*. Between the peoples of the long-established democratic nations and Russia an ideological gap remains, although that gap has narrowed perceptibly in the course of this war. On both sides are prejudices and distrusts of long duration. Shall we be capable gradually of reducing or removing these prejudices, distrusts, and fears? Or shall we — British-Americans on one side and Russians on the other — exacerbate them by further blindness and increased blunders in international policies?

In this sense trying to live with Soviet Russia has already become perhaps our paramount problem as a nation and a great world power. If we cannot live with Russia, there can be no "world council" or world federation or any effective apparatus for international co-operation after the war. If we cannot live with Russia, there can be no peace for Britain or America; only another armed truce of crushing cost in taxation and in social disintegration at home. If we do not find the means of living equably with the Soviet Union, then we shall be led inescapably to contest her influence in both Europe and Asia — and in each realm we, either with Britain or without, will have the grave disadvantage of operating from the outer rim. Strategically, whether in a political or military sense, the Soviet Union occupies the "heartland" — the huge core of the globe's greatest land mass. Shall we solve this problem by aping Hitler and declaring that Communism and everything communistic must be destroyed? Would we, in truth, have any better prospects of success than Hitler had? Or shall we have far greater hopes of a peaceful future if we do our utmost to achieve an understanding and a policy of "live and let live" with the Soviet Union, and so facilitate an evolution toward moderation which may become a natural phenomenon in a nation and a revolution that have now come of age? These, at any rate, are questions which Americans and Englishmen can no longer dodge.

2

The Soviet Union has existed twenty-six years in exceptional isolation from the rest of the world's nations, chiefly because the leading Allies took up arms against the Russian Revolution after the last war, and because our governments for years refused to recognize, diplomatically and officially, an established fact. And because we thus encouraged the Soviets to build a Chinese Wall around themselves more than twenty years ago, we are handicapped today, since the Soviet Union is largely a land of mystery to us and because we know so little of the Russian people. Somehow we must get to know them if we are to live with them on a friendly basis.

What are the Russians like?

After a mere six months in wartime Russia I do not assume that I can give a completely accurate or completely balanced answer. On the other hand the chief task of a foreign correspondent, his first and fundamental job, is to study and try to understand people in foreign lands. I have worked at this job since 1926 — and I might add it is one of the most engrossing and intellectually stimulating occupations a man can have. One of the things that it cannot fail to do is to develop strongly a feeling for people as national entities and an awareness of racial characteristics and differentiations.

In the course of my stay in the Soviet Union what impressed me repeatedly and with great force was how remarkably much in common Americans and Russians have. In the course of seventeen years of work and travels on four continents I have never met another foreign people with whom Americans feel so easily and so much at home as with the Russians. It's true that the Russians also have certain marked differences in temperament and character. They have their Slavic soul and their Slavic melancholy and such Oriental qualities as a deep fatalism. Yet to a surprising degree Americans and Russians can be said to be brothers under the skin. An average American can be baffled completely by his first acquaintance with Englishmen or Frenchmen, yet feel almost immediately at home in his first contacts with Russians. I had found this to be true with White Russians whom I knew in Paris. It was equally true of Red Russians in Moscow or elsewhere. As I remained in Russia I tried to sort out the component parts of this Russian-American common denominator.

At the outset it must be stated that Russians almost invariably like Americans. They like Americans because we rarely stand on our dignity; because we have energy and get things done; because we are modern and have technical ability. They like our frankness and our sense of humor. The chief thing they are skeptical about in Americans, I think, is the soundness of our political judgment — but they have no doubt about the average American's heart being in the right place.

Interestingly enough, almost all Americans who have lived any time in Russia — no matter how anti-Communist they may be — develop a genuine affection for the Russian people. While I was in Finland I acquired a profound admiration and lasting friendship for the Finns; and when I praise certain Russian qualities I am not detracting in the slightest from my equally great respect for the Finnish people. But the Finns are more difficult for Americans or any foreigners to get close to, because they are essentially a lonely and somewhat distrustful people and every Finn seems to have his own tight little inner fortress. I think he would like to invite you inside, but he can rarely manage to do so. Americans are not used to that deep reserve (which the Englishman understands so well because he has so much of it himself), nor are the Russians used to it.

Ivan Ivanovich has the same feeling for bigness and at-homeness with what is big as the average American. The entire Bolshevik Revolution has been a national defiance of "it can't be done, it's never been done before." Until very recent times, at any rate, Americans have always responded zestfully to the challenge of what hasn't been done — and I think the enormous and amazing expansion of our wartime plants and production indicates clearly that Americans still possess a strong trail-blazing instinct. The people of Soviet Russia are also pioneers. Probably they are the greatest pioneers of this century, and their pioneering spirit is akin to an American pioneering spirit which we now give vent to in the world of machines and scientific exploration. Russians and Americans also have the same attitude toward machinery. I have seen their artillery, tank, and anti-tank crews and their pilots and their factory workers. It is astonishing to think that Russian peasants, sons and daughters of generations of illiteracy, have reached such a high degree of skill in twenty-five years. Captain Eddie Rickenbacker confessed: "I'd put Russian fighting pilots up against ours any time — which was a surprise to me." One cannot accuse Captain Rickenbacker of being a pro-Communist or a Leftist. Yet the whole tone of his press interview upon returning from the Soviet Union was that of an American who had discovered Russia and the Russian people. Rickenbacker, a firm champion of capitalism and free enterprise, apparently did not see much in Soviet Russia to give him nightmares. But he did find much to admire and he obviously felt very strongly the common — and, unfortunately, as yet unexploited — bond between our two peoples. I can understand Rickenbacker's reactions because they were my own. And when he says: "Let us keep an open mind," he is voicing words of great common sense.

I have mentioned the mutual Russian-American feeling for what is big. Both of our peoples are born in big lands, are used to great amounts of elbow-room and vast horizons. Both of our peoples have grown up keenly aware of national greatness and an expanding future. Hence both of our peoples like big ideas and like to do things on a big scale. It required real boldness for the Russians to embark upon such huge hydroelectric and steel projects as Dnieprostroy and Magnitogorsk. But the very unprecedented magnitude of these projects was what appealed most to Russian workmen. In Moscow I often walked past the skeleton of the great Palace of the Soviets, whose construction was interrupted by the war. I used to think: "Some day that's going to be the tallest building in the world, taller than the Empire State Building." What other people on earth ever even thought of constructing a building taller than American buildings?

Ivan Ivanovich is essentially democratic in the American manner. He has the same aversion to class distinctions. Even in a system which originally renounced the profit motive and has reduced free enterprise to an extreme minimum, the new Russian generation has grown up with the feeling that a man's progress depends primarily upon his intelligence, ability, and willingness to work. You might not expect this to be true in a Soviet society, but I am convinced it is true to a surprising degree. This is because the Soviet Union has opened the doors of education and technical training to all with ambition and ability in the younger generation. For the first time in Russia's history any peasant's son can aspire to a profession or a position of executive authority. In this sense, although political democracy is still far removed, there is an unprecedented democratic opportunity for scores of millions of young Russians. So Ivan Ivanovich understands and shares the American's pride in making a place for himself regardless of his humble beginnings. Like ourselves the Russians are a boisterous, somewhat crude people. Like us they have a tendency to grumble a great deal, but, as with us, much of that is pure habit or vocal exercise. Essentially they are a friendly and warmhearted people whose faults are obvious but whose strength and vigor are exceptional. And in the realm of hospitality the Russians have a naturalness, sincerity, and overflowing generosity which reminded me again and again of the extraordinary hospitality of the American people.

The sum total of these Russian characteristics and qualities — and even of some of their shortcomings — actually reveals a remarkably broad common denominator between the Russian and American people. With such a natural basis for understanding it seems a great pity that we still know each other so slightly and that an ideological gap threatens to keep us apart. For the United States of America and the Soviet Union are the two largest and most powerful geographical-political entities in the entire world. We are so great and so powerful that a firm Russo-American friendship, dedicated to peace and international co-operation and working closely with the British Commonwealth, could scarcely fail to assure peace throughout most of the world for the remainder of this century. Can such a friendship be achieved between America and the Soviet Union? I must confess that today it seems doubtful. But it is by no means impossible.

3

If we are to live with Soviet Russia — successfully, I mean — we must begin by recognizing that the Soviet experiment has come of age and also that it is in the process of a steady evolution. Especially, I think, we must determine to let bygones be bygones. Including our own American Revolution, there never has been an immaculate revolution; and those which will shortly occur in many European countries will be equally far from immaculate — rightly so because the tumors of inestimable crimes and injustices cannot possibly be removed without a surgeon's knife and coincident loss of blood. By our own serious delinquencies we have contributed to the acuteness of Europe's disease. We cannot hope, nor have we any ethical right, to deny to Europeans the only surgical operation by which they can hope to live again. We can only hope to diminish the pain and duration of Europe's hospitalization, and to give Europeans the inspiration of a democratic goal when they are able to walk again.

I am not a Communist, nor have I ever had the remotest idea of becoming one. Despite all the abuse and scorn (some of it justified) that has been heaped upon the species, I remain a liberal democrat — with a small "d" and without any party affiliations. Consequently I am not one to go into raptures over every aspect of the Soviet regime. I do not like its one-party system, even though that may have been the only means by which Russia could throw off the shackles of medieval feudalism. I do not condone the lack of freedom of speech and freedom of the press in the Soviet Union. I think the NKVD (formerly the Ogpu) is as repressive and often as brutally severe as any rigid nationally organized secret police system. Soviet Russia is certainly no nearer giving real liberty to its average citizen than is China. Restrictions and shortcomings such as these still exist under the Soviets and are very far from what I, as an American and a democrat, can subscribe to or should care to tolerate in my own daily life. Therefore I have no inclination to paint the Soviet Union as all white, and just as great a disinclination to paint it all black.

On the credit side any objective observer must as frankly confess that Soviet Russia has made astonishing progress in many fields. Since the Bolshevist Revolution illiteracy in Russia has been reduced enormously — from something like 80 or 85 per cent in czarist days to approximately 20 per cent or less. Russians with high-school or university educations are many times more numerous than ever before in the country's history. So are hospitals and clinics. Socialized medicine has been a tremendous boon to public health. The work of the Soviet Academy of Science and its talented members unquestionably exceeds anything that Russia has ever known. Russian workers have many benefits, in housing, in municipal or state care for the children of mothers who work, in recreation facilities, and so on, which mark very great advances over the past. It is difficult for an American to conceive the vast wheat-fields of Kansas, Nebraska, and the Dakotas split up into tiny strips of earth, each fenced off by hedges of piled turf so that the use of tractors and combines is impossible. Riding out toward the Rzhev front one day, Maurice Hindus, who is one of the great living authorities on the Russian land and the Russian people, pointed to the magnificent rolling wheat-fields and told me how he had never seen such a sight in Russia as a boy. You do not need more than this one vivid contrast to understand what great progress the collective farms represent. Industrialization under the Soviets has also been one of the outstanding national achievements of this century. Without this industrialization, whose cost in blood and sacrifice of the smallest creature comforts of Russian civilians over twenty long years can scarcely be conceived by us — without the great steel and tractor and tank and airplane plants, the Red Army could never have resisted and finally defeated Germany's invading legions. Without that industrialization, in fact, several millions of British and American soldiers would have had to die or suffer grievous wounds before Nazism could have been destroyed.

There are, then, very great accomplishments in Soviet Russia and these achievements cannot be brushed aside by the bitterest critic of Communism. In whatever name they have been done they still represent astonishing forward strides and long-term gains for Russia's huge population. In his books Maurice Hindus has made both the progress and its excruciating cost superbly clear for all who wish to know. He has not gilded over the liquidation of the kulaks, the transfers of population, the period of anti-religious campaigns, the purges, or other aspects of the darker side. It is by this hard and bitter road that Russia has groped and plunged her way forward into the twentieth century.

In the course of this mighty transition the Soviet Union has undergone numerous changes, and these have been greatly accentuated by the war. Unless we, in Britain and America, appreciate the nature and scope of these changes we shall be endeavoring to deal with a Soviet Russia of our memories or preconceptions instead of the Soviet Union which now exists. Russian nationalism — not international Marxism — has been the dominant force with which the Russian people have made their tremendous fight against Germany. In Soviet Russia the rallying slogan has been "the patriotic war," and that is precisely what it is. Great Russian warriors of the past, like Kutuzov, Suvorov, and Alexander Nevsky, have become the inspiration of the Red Army. The Soviets' wartime films are devoted to historical themes, such as one of the most recent based on the life of Ivan the Terrible; and their primary aim is obviously to arouse a great national consciousness. Even the Red Army officers' new and gilded epaulets are in the Russian tradition. Moscow newspapers, including the Communist Party's official organ, *Pravda,* have devoted such full attention to beating the drums of a proud nationalism that they rarely mention the class struggle or proletarian problems. This does not mean that the Soviet government has renounced state ownership of industries and natural resources inside Russia; but it does mean that the Soviet experiment has gone nationalistic, has turned inward, to a pronounced degree.

Much interest was excited in England and the U. S. A. when a Soviet news agency reported that the chairman of the Karl Marx collective farm in Kazakhstan, with other members of his immediate family, had bought war bonds to the value of more than 1,000,000 rubles and paid for them in cash. Other collective-farm managers had invested such amounts as 50,000 or 100,000 rubles in war bonds. These incidents prompted the *New York Times* to remark: "Many observers have claimed that communism was dead, but few can have suspected it was that dead. . . . Once again a utopian and doctrinaire system has been forced to bow to human nature. What emerges is a new 'capitalism,' the further development of which will be interesting to watch." Actually, the Soviet system has evolved to a point where a collective-farm family can become a "collective millionaire," but this is merely part of the personal-incentive methods — highly uncommunistic — which have been steadily growing since Lenin first put forward the New Economic Policy in 1921. In Russia's war factories the Stakhanovite system, which gives additional pay and bonuses to those who turn out the highest quotas of work, applies everywhere. Consequently, the least productive Russian workers may earn no more than 400 rubles a month while the best workmen in the same plant earn 800 rubles per month or even more. I met young Russian engineers whose monthly incomes were 2,500 or 2,800 rubles — perhaps as great a comparative advantage for a college graduate and specialist as usually exists in the United States. There are Soviet technical experts, as well as Soviet ballerinas, who earn 6,000 rubles a month; and that is nearly twenty times the wages of some workers. It is perfectly evident, then, that such Communism as has survived in Russia has been watered down very radically. It now applies chiefly to government ownership and operation of large enterprises. But inside these enterprises there are great variations in income and very definite incentives for personal initiative.

A similar change has occurred in regard to the state's attitude toward religion in Soviet Russia. The crusading atheistic societies of another decade have been abolished. Churches have been greatly reduced in number, but they are open — as I observed in Russia — and I never heard of any instances of persecution or governmental interference. It would be my guess that a considerable majority of the younger Russians accept Lenin's pronouncement that "religion is the opium of the people." That phrase is still engraved on one of the walls at the entrance to Red Square. Nevertheless you get the impression that the younger Russians are irreligious rather than anti-religious. As one of them said to me: "We think everyone should be free to go to church or not to go to church — and no one should try to compel anyone to do one or the other." Personally I think it very doubtful that religion will again become a predominant influence on Russian life in this century; but it seems quite possible that the Russian Orthodox faith may continue a slow growth without any serious governmental interference or may even win a certain amount of official encouragement with the passing of time. With religion as with socialistic practices, the trend in Russia is definitely toward moderation. The pendulum has swung very noticeably away from the radically Left extreme and back toward the center. That is another important evidence of Soviet Russia's coming of age.

Thus, I do not think it any accident that the Kremlin dissolved the Communist Party's international organization, the Comintern, in the late spring of 1943. As Anne O'Hare McCormick very justly said, this move showed that Stalin "is ready, obviously, to exchange the role of world revolutionary for that of world power." In the Soviet Union nationalism now predominates and it has superseded international revolution. The Red Army's emergence as a new aristocracy inside the state emphasizes this turn to nationalism. Even the establishment by the Soviets of a permanent-career diplomatic service stems from this same fundamental change. It would be foolish, I think, to assume for a moment that the highly indoctrinated Russian people will lose all interest in the progress of workers, labor unions, and the proletarian peoples in other lands. They will always watch the struggles of the most exploited and impoverished classes, whether in China, India, or South America, with sympathy and probably with the conviction that some degree of socialism offers their only final hope of betterment. But Soviet Russia's foremost preoccupation must be with her own internal problems for a long time to come, and the Soviets' leaders are keenly awake to their new obligations as helmsmen of a great world power. Even if this should prove to be an attitude of temporary duration, for a matter of ten or twenty years, it would still offer a unique and unparalleled opportunity for British-American statesmanship. So long as this new situation exists — and it must exist for a very considerable period — we in America and Britain have an unequaled opportunity to demonstrate that we want to live with Russia. And while the Soviet Union enjoys a new power and new immunity from foreign aggression, her leaders have an equivalent opportunity to show that Russia wants to live with the British-American nations.

4

We shall have a much greater chance of living successfully with the Soviet Union if we get it clear in our minds what circumstances govern her policies today and will inevitably govern them for many years to come. I believe three factors dominate and will continue to dominate the policies of Soviet Russia: (1) her need for security and a long peace; (2) her urgent need for rehabilitation of her people, her ravaged cities, and her industry; (3) her need for outside assistance and foreign trade with which to speed up this rehabilitation. Those in America or other countries who fear that the Red Army may be used as an aggressive or imperialist force after the war completely ignore the depth and crippling scope of Russia's war wounds. They also overlook two facts, one historical and the other geographical. In the course of centuries Goths and Romans, Frenchmen, Turks, and Teutons have made conquering sweeps over most or all of Europe — but Russian armies have never once attempted to conquer Europe. Why not? Primarily, I suspect, because the Russians have always had more living-space than they knew what to do with. No czar could ever incite the Russians with demands for more *Lebensraum*. And that brings us to the geographical fact — *space,* immense quantities of space. The Russians need very little, if anything, beyond their historical frontiers, which approximate quite closely their frontiers of 1940. On the contrary their greatest necessity is to restore and develop what they already have. The Soviet Union now has the opportunity to play the role of a foremost world power, but she can only maintain this new position of international leadership and authority if her wounds are swiftly healed.

Soviet Russia must preoccupy herself chiefly with peace, security, and rehabilitation because her war losses and sacrifices have been so staggeringly enormous. It seems almost impossible for Americans, in our remote security, to comprehend what these losses are. But we cannot measure Russia accurately, we cannot deal with her intelligently, and we cannot treat her fairly unless we make an effort to comprehend them.

A territory almost as large and as industrially important as a strip of the U. S. A. from Maine to South Carolina and as far west as Tennessee and Indiana has been occupied and fought over in Russia by more than 200 Nazi-Axis divisions for considerably more than two years. If we could transpose these long months of savage warfare into the above-mentioned section of the United States and substitute Buffalo, Pittsburgh, Cleveland, and Detroit for Dnieprostroy, Kharkov, Leningrad, and Stalingrad, with these great American industrial centers lying in ruins, we should still scarcely have begun to appreciate what war has done to Russia. We should still have to picture thousands of towns and small villages laid waste in New England, New York, Pennsylvania, West Virginia, Ohio, and several other states. We should have to imagine that approximately one third of the population of the United States (equivalent to some 60,000,000 people in Russia) had been swallowed up by the Nazi invaders, that millions had been sent to Germany in slavery, and that the fate of some 25,000,000 Americans was still unknown. We should have to imagine another 15,000,000 American civilians, with nothing left of their possessions save a few bundles and the clothes on their backs, swept from the Eastern states by the tide of war and pushed back across the Middle West and across the Mississippi — a helpless horde of refugees, existing under any kind of roof for more than two years. The equal of all this, and more, has happened in Russia since June 1941.

By the autumn of 1943 it seemed certain that the total of killed, wounded, and missing in Russia's armed forces must surpass 7,000,000 men — or approximately seven tenths of all the men who wear the uniforms of the U. S. Army and Navy. It is difficult for us to conceive of 7,000,000 Americans killed, wounded, or missing — still more difficult to conceive what gaps that would mean throughout our society. But there can be no doubt that another 8,000,000 Russian civilians — perhaps much more than 10,000,000 — have also perished from hunger or exposure or by Nazi executions. A total of 15,000,000 war dead in the Soviet Union means that Russia has lost nearly one out of every twelve persons in her population. Supposing that America, in less than three years of war, should lose one out of every twelve persons in our population of 130,000,000 people. If all these tragedies and disasters had been suffered by us, can you imagine with what stupendous relief we should greet the end of the war? Can you conceive what would be our consuming desires and necessities? They could not fail to be anything else but — peace, security, and rehabilitation.

The Red Army's soldiers have been warmly clothed and well shod only because more than 140,000,000 Russian civilians have been unable to buy new shoes, suits, or overcoats since the war began. A few million fighting men have been well fed because a great many millions of Russia's office workers, old people, and dependents have had barely enough to eat to keep them alive, while a great many of the old and the weak have died of malnutrition. Thus the Soviet Union's supreme postwar task is many times greater and more urgent than anything the United States has ever known. Its plight is on a much larger scale yet similar to that of the Southern states after our Civil War. But in Russia the destruction and dislocation is greater than anything known in modern times, except possibly in China. This is why the Soviet Union's need for many years of peace is cruelly imperative. No government, of whatever ideology, could ignore its obligations to a huge population emaciated and weakened to such a degree. The Soviet regime won the confidence of Soviet Russia's masses by its leadership in the war. It can only retain their confidence by an equally energetic leadership in the nation's reconstruction. But only a long-term and heroic program can ever rebuild Russia's ravaged cities and towns or reclothe and revitalize her scores of millions of civilians.

What must be done? Leningrad, once a city of 3,000,000 people, must be rebuilt. Rostov, Kharkov, Orel, Smolensk, Sevastopol, Odessa, Kiev, and Stalingrad all have been at least two-thirds destroyed. These nine cities are as important to Russia as our nine largest cities east of the Mississippi. There are also thousands of miles of railroads and tens of thousands of miles of highways, thousands of bridges, to be rebuilt. It will take several years for the Soviet Union to produce enough tractors, combines, and similar farm equipment to reach again her 1940 level. But thousands of factories must also be reconstructed and part of Russia's great central Siberian arsenal must be shifted to peace purposes, all at great cost and with expenditure of time.

Shortly after I came home I was in an elevator in Chicago and, standing directly behind the girl operator, I suddenly noticed she was losing a hairpin. Instinctively I reached out to catch it, thinking: "If she loses that, she can't get another." Please don't get me wrong about hairpins, but that was my Russian training. If it had been a shirt button, or a piece of thread, it would have been the same thing. If a man had been dropping some matches I should have reacted the same way. For ten years before the war the Soviet Union strictly limited production of consumers' goods in order to arm the Red Army for defense against Germany. But even so, when I visited Moscow in 1940, the big Mostorg department store and many other shops were crowded with what, for Russians, was an abundance of things. Almost all these things have been eaten up by the war and are irreplaceable until long after peace comes. For the average Russian civilian today there are no such things as toothpaste, toothbrushes, soap, cigarettes, buttons, pins, jack-knives, ordinary medicaments like aspirin, or hundreds of other articles which we in America (despite increasing shortages) still take for granted as simple necessities. For more than two years tens of millions of people have been unable to buy new clothes of any kind, except perhaps for one or two articles. Russian civilians today need many millions of pairs of shoes. All of this means that the Soviet Union will urgently require gigantic quantities of consumers' goods after the war ends, and it cannot begin to produce all of these items itself. In addition Russia must procure very large amounts of machine tools, machinery for coal mines, oilfields, hydroelectric projects, and numerous other developments. In the first postwar years a tremendous quantity of these materials, from foods to consumers' goods and machinery, will have to be imported.

Can we do business with Soviet Russia?

The answer is that we did a huge business with her in the 1920's — and we were paid for all of it. I touched upon America's coming trade opportunity with Russia during a talk in Worcester, Massachusetts. Among the old friends I saw there afterward was Herbert Stanton, vice-president of the Norton Company, which is one of the world's largest manufacturers of ball bearings and grinding wheels. Mr. Stanton said to me: "While you were talking, Lee, I looked around the room. I counted at least twenty men representing as many plants in Worcester. Do you know that all those plants, during the great postwar slump in 1921–2, were doing a rushing business — and most of it was going to Russia?" I told that story in Cincinnati and businessmen in that remarkably governed city added their testimony. Cincinnati, they said, had never known the postwar depression simply because of the millions of dollars' worth of orders its factories had from Russia. It's true that the Soviet Union now has a great industry untouched behind the Urals and can produce its own machine tools to a considerable extent. But it cannot begin to produce all that Russia will urgently need in the first postwar years somewhere ahead; and Russians have great confidence in the quality of American goods as well as in the ability of our engineers and technical specialists. Russia also possesses vast amounts of things, like asbestos, manganese, and platinum, of which America has a serious shortage, as the war has shown. Russia has other things, such as furs, timber, and caviar, which also provide the basis for reciprocal trade. Is it at all likely that we can find either as rich or as reliable a customer anywhere else in Europe or Asia? Perhaps if we do business with Russia as well as live with Russia, several millions of Americans will be assured of employment throughout the first postwar years. In more than one way friendly relations with the Soviet Union would be a mutually profitable enterprise. But that will necessitate a clear-headed attitude on the part of the American people quite as much as in Washington — and in the Kremlin.

5

The obstacles to Soviet-American or to Soviet-British co-operation are very real, the more so because most of them are psychological. On both sides the faults and errors of the past twenty-six years do not redound to our credit and even as allies these first three world powers have progressed very slowly in the direction of understanding. Many of us think the Soviet leaders have been holding back on us, and many of them think we have held back on them in regard to launching a second front, and fear we may take an anti-Soviet position during peace negotiations. The harvest of long years of distrust is mutual and unfortunately mutually costly.

In the course of more than three months of lectures across the United States one fact struck me most forcibly — namely, how very few Americans ever seem to have asked themselves a first and most essential question: "How would *you* feel, how would *you* react, and what would *you* do if you were a Soviet Russian citizen?" Quite frankly I met all too few Soviet officials in Russia who appeared to have asked the same question about us; but at least they did have the exonerating circumstance that their country was fighting on its own soil for its very existence and their millions of men were doing most of the bleeding and dying in this war. Nevertheless Americans, Britishers, and Russians alike cannot hope to find any durable solution *unless* we all make a new — one might say, an almost completely untried — effort to understand the other's point of view. And even if Soviet leaders should fail to do this, history will not absolve us — nor will international developments fail to punish us in future years — if we fail to go fully half-way to see and understand why Soviet Russia makes certain demands and puts forward certain claims. If we have the slightest hope for a tolerable world, we must be capable of this degree of toleration toward our Russian allies.

Many questions which I was asked on the lecture platform were revealing about American mental attitudes toward Russia. A few of them, I think, should be mentioned here. One question was this: "Is it true that the American identifications are removed from all military equipment so that the Russian soldiers and people are not aware of the aid we are giving?" If I had heard that as a statement from Dr. Goebbels I should not have been surprised at all, since this is obvious Axis propaganda playing upon anti-Communist sentiments in the U. S. A. I was glad to be able to answer this question precisely on the basis of personal observation. I had seen American tanks, airplanes, jeeps, and field telephones — to mention a few most important of our Lend-Lease materials — and of course every one bore all of the American marks of identification and every Russian knew where these materials came from. I might add that the Russians invariably showed both their enthusiasm and appreciation — but if they thought a weapon, like our first inadequate M-3 tank, could be improved they frankly explained how and why. Which is good sense when you're the fellow who is doing the fighting with that weapon.

A much more widespread American attitude is summed up in this question: "Remembering that by the German-Russian treaty Russia bought time at the expense of Polish, French, English, and Dutch or Norwegian lives, is she justified morally in her supercilious attitude toward our own lack of a second front?" This question merely shows how little we ourselves remember our own sins of commission and omission. A great many of us are still burned up about that "Nazi-Soviet deal" in 1939. But why was that treaty signed? What made it inevitable? It's true that the Russians bought time. But they only bought time nearly one year after the most tragic and flagrant piece of time-buying in our generation. At Munich Great Britain and France — who had barred Soviet Russia from her rightful place at that conference — "bought time" in a disastrously big way at the expense of scores of thousands of Czechoslovakian lives. Most of Czechoslovakia was much nearer to Soviet frontiers than to England, and it was also a Slavic country. Yet Britain and France refused to admit that Russia had any business to help defend Czechoslovakia's independence, and by selling the Czechs into slavery they gave the Soviet Union no other choice than to buy time from Germany. It is strange, and also dangerous, that millions of Americans still refuse to recognize so simple a fact as this.

We Americans also have an annoying habit of putting international problems on high moral ground while conveniently forgetting to remember our own moral delinquencies. For more than three years, while China was bleeding, we did something worse than buying time. We sold many millions of tons of scrap iron to the Japanese, from which they made planes and guns with which to kill, subjugate, and starve millions of Chinese. We also sold the Japs vast quantities of oil and gasoline. We were perfectly content to pocket the profits. Who, then, are we to talk about doing things at the expense of other peoples' lives? While the Spanish republican government — a freely elected democratic government — was battling against fearful odds for almost three years, we Americans refused to send weapons to Republican Spain. We, along with the French and the British, sold Spain's democracy down the river. We were not at all concerned with the *moral* right of the Spanish people to have the kind of government that a large majority of them had voted for and established. Where, then, can any of us in America presume to find a moral justification for condemning Soviet Russia's 1939 treaty with Germany? It is always easy to see the mote in your brother's eye. Nevertheless the record of all the Western democracies since 1918 is not such that any of us can afford to indulge in moral preachments. We may not remember these things, but we may be sure that the peoples of Europe and Asia will not forget them for many years to come.

Again and again Americans have asked me: "Why don't the Russians give us bases from which to bomb Japan?" At a time when American and British armies had not yet engaged even *ten* German divisions in any one place and the Russians were still fighting some *two hundred* German divisions, it seems incomprehensible that any of us should expect the Soviet Union to invite immediate hostilities with another *forty* Japanese divisions in Manchuria. If we were in the same situation, with the same ravaged cities and the same tremendous losses that the Russians have suffered, would we be likely to take such a step? But a very great many of us are fantastically incapable of putting ourselves in the Russians' place, or in the place of the British or Chinese — in anybody's place except our own still very comfortable seat in the transatlantic bleachers.

For an educated people, many of us do not seem to think very clearly, but we do become concerned about Soviet Russia's role in settling the peace. "Will Russia insist on dictating the peace? What voice will the Russians want in it?" To such questions as these the answer should be fairly obvious. Russia will undoubtedly want a voice in the peace commensurate with the international prestige and power which she has won at an extremely dear price on the battlefield. Russia will undoubtedly insist upon determining pretty largely just where her frontiers in eastern Europe will lie. "But will Russia co-operate with the United Nations in a peace settlement?" I fully expect Soviet Russia will co-operate so long as the United Nations do not ask her to sacrifice her own security in the west; so long as we recognize that the Baltic States, which were improvised as separate national states for the *first* time after the last war, have been an integral part of Russia for more than seven hundred years; so long as we recognize that large areas in eastern prewar Poland were populated overwhelmingly by White Russians and Ukrainians and belong inside Russia's historical frontiers. The Russians are absolutely convinced of their historical right to such territories as these, and who is going to be in a position to make them renounce these claims? If we are at all realistic, and if we have any proper appreciation of our need of Russia's goodwill, we shall not stir up acrimony and dissension by entering into any such futile debate. As a matter of cold fact, and whether we like it or not, Estonia, Latvia, and Lithuania are already federated republics of the Soviet Union and they are certain to remain so. If we were to insist that they be restored to a status which before 1918 they had never had for hundreds of years, the Russians might as logically reply: "First we suggest that you Americans return Texas and parts of Oklahoma and New Mexico to Mexico." To the Russians that would make quite as much sense.

One other question bothers a great many Americans: "Will Russia make a separate peace with Germany after she has driven the Axis armies off of Russian soil?" I am convinced this will not happen — unless the British and American armies fail to fight with reasonably large forces on the European continent. The only thing, it seems to me, that could persuade Soviet Russia to negotiate a separate peace with Germany would be a sharp feeling among Russians that we had deliberately let them down on a real second front. Such a shortsighted failure would probably be more costly to us than to the Russians, for we should thereby have sacrificed any strong voice in Europe's peace and opened the door to permanent misunderstandings with the Soviet Union.

Another angle of Russo-German relations cannot be ignored. These two prolific peoples are neighbors who have always alternated between periods of conflict and interludes of courtship. After taking a terrific beating from the Russians in this war it would be extremely German for the Germans to throw themselves into the arms of the Soviet Union within a decade. Economically the two countries are also largely complementary. Therefore — always providing that Moscow at last felt confident of being able to maintain the whip hand over a postwar Germany — the Kremlin may find it prudent or profitable to co-operate closely with the government of a conquered and weakened Reich. This could happen in one of two ways: either within the framework of an international system of security, or as a Soviet move away from or against the Anglo-American powers. It would seem fairly safe to assume that the latter development is unlikely to occur unless Stalin and his associates become convinced that friendly co-operation with Britain and the U. S. A. is hopeless of attainment.

If you or I were in Stalin's place we should probably prefer to steer a middle course if possible. As Russians we would prefer to avoid all danger of a race of armaments and ultimate rupture with Britain and the United States; but we should also be anxious to have the Germans in a position and in a mood where they would not be tempted again to wage war against the Soviet Union. If we had to choose between one risk or the other I imagine we would make sure of dissipating the nearest risk — the German risk. For this reason Russian policy is bound to strive to establish a basis of living with postwar Germany, just as British policy must seek a similar basis for living with postwar France. In these circumstances British and American statesmanship — if it is statesmanship — can only hope to win Russia's support and co-operation in the broader field of global security, by recognizing the Soviets' status as a first-ranking world power and providing definite assurance that our leading capitalist nations recognize fully such Russian interests as are legitimate in either Europe or Asia. To do less than this would be for Washington and London to precipitate an outright and formidable German-Soviet alliance which, in the long run, could scarcely fail to open the door to another and more gigantic competition for world domination.

We could commit no more costly error than to make intimate postwar partners of Germany and the Soviet Union. Nevertheless that very alliance, fed by obvious springs of self-interest for a prostrate Germany, can only be prevented by American and British policies dedicated to world security (necessitating another League of Nations or world council) and by American and British governments which are willing to go more than half way to win Russia to a common basis of co-operation. *In the cold logic of things it seems indisputable that the surest way to weld the military, industrial, and material resources of Russia and Germany into a single solid phalanx would be for Americans once more to adopt isolationism.* The same tragic result would likewise be assured if Britain and the United States, abandoning democratic practices and progressive ideas, attempted to impose ultra-conservative and reactionary settlements upon the smaller European nations and upon the peoples of the Far East. It does not seem reasonable that Russia would risk outright marriage or cohabitation with the Germans unless she felt that no other alternative remained. It is the business of Anglo-American statesmanship to show that other alternatives exist for Soviet Russia and that these alternatives are grounded in a common world citizenship and world leadership, shared with ourselves.

6

One of the things which most seriously threaten future Russian-American co-operation is a widespread American misconception of the nature and by-products of a war waged with allies. This misconception is rooted in another most prevalent and false American idea — that you can win friendship or love with material things alone. Too many of us today assume that our Lend-Lease aid to Russia in itself should warrant an undying gratitude among the Russians, whether or not we contribute our full and proportionate share to fighting Nazi armies on Europe's continent. Most of us do not like to admit the plain fact that Lend-Lease is simply America's way of "buying time." Since we did not have an army of any size, or a real air force or a two-ocean navy, we did the only thing we could do. We poured billions into Lend-Lease to subsidize the British, the Russians, and the Chinese to hold the breach until our own armies, planes, and battleships could take the field. Lend-Lease is just as great a piece of time-buying as the Russo-German treaty of 1939 ever was. And again like that treaty, Lend-Lease merely made it possible for us to get into a position to defend our own liberties while several millions of others fought and died.

My observations lead me to say that the Russians genuinely appreciate Lend-Lease, but they are quite as acutely aware of its highly practical and purely selfish motivation. We happened to be able to afford to buy time with billions of dollars. But neither the British nor the Chinese nor the Russians are so simple as to believe that we sent them these billions in Lend-Lease materials just because we loved them so much.

The only way that the American people can gain the complete respect of our allies, and also of the enslaved peoples of Europe and Asia, is on the field of battle. Our fighting forces have made an excellent beginning in the Solomons, in North Africa and Italy, on the sea and in the air over Europe, Burma, and China. But now that we are fully armed, these smaller-scale combats fall into their true perspective as opening engagements and not more than that. This fact explains a good deal about the Russian attitude toward an Allied front in western Europe.

In August 1943 the Red Army's daily newspaper, *Red Star*, stated significantly: "The Allied command carried out a well-prepared landing operation in Sicily. The struggle for Sicily, however, failed to divert a single German division from the Soviet-German front. . . . All of the German General Staff's attention is concentrated on operations against the Red Army, which now is bearing on its shoulders, *as for two years*, the main burden of the struggle against the forces of Germany. . . . By a second front we understand an operation by our Allies in the west which would draw from fifty to sixty divisions from the Soviet-German front."

By asking for an operation which would withdraw at least fifty divisions from the Russian front the Soviet leaders were certainly asking for a great deal; probably too much. Nor did they evaluate sufficiently the crippling effects of the great British-American bombing war against Germany's industrial centers and our blockade at sea. But let's try to keep in mind Soviet Russia's losses and try to understand the Russian point of view. What would a Russian have said to you or me in August? Something like this: "Your Anglo-American promise of a second front in Europe is now more than one year old and we are still waiting for your troops to land on the European continent. You have done well in Tunisia and Sicily, but you have also played it very safe. How can you justify playing it safe any longer? It is now more than three years since France fell. Britain has more than 3,000,000 men under arms. Is it unreasonable for us Russians to ask that the British, after over three years, should put at least 1,000,000 men on the continent of Europe? You Americans also have your war in the Pacific. But now you have been at war for almost two years. Can you honestly claim that the United States cannot now put 500,000 men into a European invasion? The Allies also have some 300,000 French forces under arms and part of them must be equipped by this time. We Russians couldn't wait until we had absolutely perfect conditions for fighting. We get the impression that the British and Americans are more interested in winning the war cheaply than in winning it quickly. But if you wait any longer, while you possess the armies and the equipment, you are again buying time with Russian corpses — and in Europe almost all the time for more than two years has been bought with Russian corpses. If you insist on our paying some 85 or 90 per cent in dead and wounded for the defeat of Hitlerism, how do you expect the Russian people and our government to feel? Under such circumstances do you expect us to go out of our way to please you when peace comes? We have lost millions of our best men. If Britain and the United States are truly great powers, let them prove it by their boldness and their willingness to sacrifice."

For us in America what does this boil down to? It crystallizes into the hard fact that, in a world war, the United States can win either the respect or gratitude of the world's nations only *through performance on the battlefield.* It means that we cannot have a great influence or any real voice in Europe's peace unless we win it by force of arms. Neither Lend-Lease nor fine phrases about the Four Freedoms will win us any moral authority in the postwar world. A determinant voice in any peace has never been won except by the sacrificial blood of the fallen and the boldness and courage of those who survived. Both for Britain and for America this is perhaps the biggest thing at stake in the final battle for Europe. Most of us may not acknowledge it or recognize it, but the Soviet Russians see it very clearly, and their future policies toward the United States and Great Britain will be determined by the amount of moral prestige that our armies win on European soil. Everything that has preceded has merely led up to this final and supreme test of our own title to rank as primary world powers.

As I write, it is too early to declare confidently that we shall meet this test, although it should be done and I have the belief that it must be done. For if the intervention of our Allied armies in Europe is on such a scale that it contributes greatly to the overthrow of Nazism and the liberation of the European peoples, we shall have achieved much more than the freeing of Hitler's slaves. We, British and Americans, will have won the right to the confidence and co-operation of Soviet Russia, and a respectable and honorable basis on which to begin to live with the Russians. With this as the culminating part of our European war record we shall be in a position to ask certain concessions from the Soviet Union which otherwise we should be in no position to ask. Unless we go all-out to finish off Nazi Germany, for instance, how can we expect Russia to feel obligated to join us in our war against Japan? The Russians would be able to reply: "You saved the bulk of your armies while we were taking enormous losses against the Germans. Our people are tired of war. Now it is our turn to economize in men." That could happen — but I don't believe it will happen *if* Britain and America have put between 500,000 and 1,000,000 men on European soil before the spring of 1944. If we wait until the spring of 1944, predictions are impossible. We must remember, however, that our own share in the closing phase of Germany's defeat cannot fail to establish the ratio of our future prestige and influence in Moscow. There are no short-cuts or by-passes to either diplomatic or moral authority, least of all in a gigantic global conflict. The Russians will search our actions — and for one thing in particular: do we mean democracy? Or do we really mean anti-Sovietism, anti-liberalism, or even anti-progressive democracy?

On the other hand it is equally true that up to mid-autumn of 1943 Soviet leaders had failed notably to make plain what their intentions and desires were for postwar Europe. The overtures of Churchill and Roosevelt for a meeting with Stalin had been neglected in Moscow much longer than seems justifiable. Russia's attitude toward her allies had been lamentably lacking in frankness, just as Washington's refusal to recognize Russian claims for her historical European frontiers had been seriously lacking in realism. The voice of the Soviet's officially inspired press was often carping and sometimes ill-mannered, although this may have been provoked on many occasions by disputable ideas nursed inside our own State Department. At any rate, Moscow's tendency to belittle the Anglo-American invasion of Italy and to insist that nothing less than a frontal assault upon western Europe would constitute a real second front merely served to rebuff those in London and Washington who labored most sincerely for improved relations with the Soviet Union. It appeared that the Kremlin had deliberately chosen to wait until its armies were victoriously driving the Germans well behind the Dnieper and until Russia's diplomatic bargaining position would be extremely strong. If we could scarcely blame Soviet leaders for their pragmatism and self-interest, the American and British people nevertheless had a right to feel that the time had now come for a powerful Russia to make a gesture of friendship in their direction. In other words, the responsibility either for increased co-operation or for gradual alienation between the Western democracies and Soviet Russia cannot fall entirely on one side. To avoid a race of armaments and eventual war between the Anglo-American powers and Russia concessions must be shared — in Moscow as well as in London and Washington. Because all parties have so much to lose through disagreement, and although periods of strain and uncertainty are inevitable, it would appear that compromises and at least a minimum of common ground must be found.

For most of us who live so far away from Europe's long-submerged nations a word of caution is needed. Many Americans are going to be rudely surprised if tomorrow Rumania, Bulgaria, or Poland — or possibly even Germany — should go Communist. Some of us would leap at such a development with the angry declaration that it was all the Soviet government's fault. Except for the Axis countries, I have traveled and worked in almost every European country since the war began; and in most of them I worked during a good many years before the war. I believe one thing about Europe is as inevitable as tomorrow's dawn. At the end of this war most of Europe's nations are going to the Left. The only question is how far they will go. They're going to the Left primarily for a simple reason which cannot be accredited to Soviet connivings or to the Comintern or an international Red plot. The majority of European countries are going to be more socialistic, more radical, and more Left-wing after the war *because Hitler has left them no alternative.* The Nazis have plundered and liquidated the middle classes all over Europe. Hitler, as some of us insisted years ago, has done far more for the progress of Marxism — and possibly for Communism — in Europe than all the socialists and all the Comintern agents that Europe has known in two decades. It is Hitlerism, not any revolutionary Left-wing movement, that has wiped out the middle ground of European society.

Therefore Europe's postwar nations, in a definite majority, will be much more socialistic than they ever were before 1939, and they will probably be governed by Left-wing coalitions of communists, socialists, and progressive democrats or republicans. No amount of hair-pulling or heeby-jeebies on the part of conservative American citizens will have the slightest effect upon this inevitable and rapidly approaching development. The social basis of most European nations is going to be changed; their political instruments (as newly evolved) will precipitate this change — and no AMG or other instrument of Allied occupation can possibly delay this for any length of time. We Americans, of whatever political preference, must face this fact and resign ourselves to the certainty that we are going to have to live with it. Nor can we afford to forget that these new European governments, built by liberated peoples who have a strong realization of how greatly Russian resistance has contributed to their freedom, will undoubtedly be inspired by a natural friendship or sympathy for Soviet Russia.

But the coming emergence of a Europe faced Left merely underscores very heavily our inescapable necessity of learning how to live with the Soviet Union. To live with this Russia we have got to use brain-power quite as much as machine-power. We have got to possess and know how to use moral assets as well as physical assets. We have got to have a definite long-term policy toward the Soviet Union — one that is based upon the realities of Russia as a new world power, not upon anti-Communist bugaboos or hysteria. It has been truly said that the great danger for Europe and ourselves after the war is not Russian influence, but Russian isolation. If we, the American people, are realists, we shall see clearly that the U. S. A. and the USSR do not have any clashing territorial needs or aspirations, and that we do not have any essentially conflicting interests. In the years of postwar reconstruction Soviet Russia will need us. If there is to be any hope of peace, we need Russia just as urgently.

Postscript. This chapter and the remainder of this book were written more than a month before the tripartite conference of British, American, and Soviet foreign ministers convened in Moscow in October 1943. The Moscow conference was a heartening and historic success in that it constituted the first great diplomatic collaboration between these three Allied governments since the war began. This progress was achieved chiefly, I believe, because Soviet leaders recognized that Russia needs us and because British and American leaders realized quite as keenly that their countries need the support of Soviet Russia through the final phase of the war and through the postwar period of readjustment. In this sense the Moscow agreements registered an unexpectedly constructive, a promising and hopeful first step toward a sane solution of Europe's postwar problems.

But the attainment of a goal at the far end of a long, rough, and hazardous road cannot be assumed or taken for granted simply because a group of pedestrians have taken an initial turning which is at once correct and the obvious turning to make. The Moscow conference, after all, must prudently be regarded as *only a first step* in the right direction and nothing more than that. We have not yet found an enduring answer to the question: "Can we live with the Soviet Union?" We have merely made an important and encouraging beginning. To complete successfully the trying task of Anglo-American-Soviet co-operation through the coming decisive months and years will require far more comprehension, tolerance, and statesmanship in London, Washington, and Moscow — and on the part of our three peoples — than any of us have yet demonstrated.

For this reason I have not felt justified in changing any of the context of this chapter and have also refrained from making any alterations in the two concluding chapters which follow. As a result of the Moscow conference we are entitled to harbor a much greater degree of sober hope than previously. But the early establishment of "a general international organization based on the principle of the sovereign equality of all peace-loving States" will require a consistently sober understanding — on the part of all of us — of the very great handicaps and hazards which still lie ahead. It will also require much more than a single encouraging and statesmanlike vote by the Senate of the United States. To live with Soviet Russia, and so to win the peace, will necessitate the greatest intelligence, foresight, and moral courage of which we may be capable for several years to come.

Chapter XVIII

SHALL WE WIN THE WAR, BUT LOSE THE PEACE?

We must face the fact that for nearly fifty years the nation has not had a settled and generally accepted foreign policy. . . . An agreement has eventually to be reached when men admit that they must pay for what they want and that they must want only what they are willing to pay for.

Walter Lippmann in *U. S. Foreign Policy*

It is only if we comprehend the revolutionary nature of the European struggle and the alignment of social forces in it that we can grasp the real issue between General Giraud and General de Gaulle. . . . That issue will be at stake not only in France but in every European country, occupied or Axis. . . . The question at stake is with what social forces in Europe, with what trends we intend to collaborate.

Dorothy Thompson

For more than twenty months, from Pearl Harbor to the conference at Quebec and afterward, the United States government made an amazing but frightening record. It waged war against the Axis oppressors and against the Axis ideologies without producing a precise political chart by which to guide and give purpose to our military blows. America and Great Britain alike continued to rely upon a vague set of "common principles" which were laid down in the Atlantic Charter before our own belligerency, 'way back in August 1941. The core of this declaration went no further than to state that the Anglo-American governments "respect the right of all peoples to choose the form of government under which they will live; and they wish to see sovereign rights and self-government restored to those who have been forcibly deprived of them." After America was in the war President Roosevelt also declared we were fighting for "freedom of speech, freedom of religion, freedom from want and freedom from fear." Together these two declarations amounted to an announcement that the great liner, S. S. *Democracy,* intended to cross the ocean. They did not explain how we intended to get impoverished and helpless prospective passengers aboard the liner. They did not indicate by what route S. S. *Democracy* would sail. They did not touch upon the practical problem of how we proposed to pick up passengers at more than thirty different ports of call. So S. S. *Democracy* has been under way ever since 1941 without a definite chart that either the navigators (generals and admirals) or the crew (soldiers, sailors, aviators, and civilians) could hope to understand clearly. Evidently it was deemed sufficient that we should all know that the co-captains expected to cross the ocean and get the liner to its various ports of call somehow.

For more than twenty months, while Americans were fighting the war, Washington revealed only a single clear and unmistakable policy in international politics aside from these distressingly broad generalities. This one precise policy was not a program for restoring democratic government to the enslaved peoples of Europe. It was not a program for encouraging revolts and revolution against the Nazi slave-drivers. It was not a program to win the Italian and German peoples to our own democratic principles. During more than twenty months of belligerency the one precise policy followed by the Roosevelt administration and our State Department — that is, the one policy as yet having a direct and immediate bearing upon our relationships with postwar Europe — was an increasingly sharp and stubborn policy directed against General Charles de Gaulle and the Fighting French movement. In other words, the only place where the Roosevelt-Hull administration committed itself with definite clarity was in opposing the only Frenchmen who refused to capitulate to Hitler and the Nazis in June 1940. The Anglo-American governments demonstrated a pronounced tenderness for Frenchmen who were Nazi-appeasers and collaborationists while rebuffing or conniving against those Frenchmen who were fighting on our side all along and who were pledged to a restoration of democracy in France.

Thus to a most tragic and dangerous degree a policy, which

all admit has originated chiefly in Washington, has alienated the most constructive and patriotic elements in the French nation; has aroused a deep skepticism of our democratic sincerity among scores of millions of enslaved Europeans; has encouraged the yes-men of Vichy and the band-wagon climbers who have been serving Hitler and Mussolini; and has kindled understandable suspicions and resentments in Moscow. The only known and precise wartime foreign policy of the United States remained an essentially antidemocratic policy which still threatens to cost us the confidence and support of France in the postwar settlement and for long afterward. If Washington had been working to persuade the people of France to go to the extreme Left and throw themselves without reservations into the arms of Soviet Russia, it could scarcely have improved upon its wounding and provocative actions over a period of more than nine months since the Allied landing in North Africa.

The ineptitude and blindness of the French policy of the President and the State Department were wellnigh equaled during the Allied invasion of Sicily in July 1943. Our troops had been in Sicily but two weeks when Mussolini was overthrown with dramatic suddenness. But the Anglo-American governments, whose chief aim was the elimination of Mussolini and Fascism, were caught flat-footed. Hundreds of thousands of Italian workers swept through the streets of Milan, Turin, and Genoa eager for revolt and awaiting a lead and a program from their liberators. But Washington and London had no plan for the collapse of Fascism, and they had no political program — no machinery to encourage democracy among the Italians. All that the announced champions of democracy had ready was AMG, a device for strictly military occupation. Under AMG we expected the Italian people, after being throttled by a hated dictatorship for twenty years, to remain docilely in a vacuum until such time as we might take them gently by the hand and lead them to the polls. Apparently American and British leaders had assumed that Fascism and Nazism could be smashed without precipitating revolutions — quite as if history did not show that no entrenched tyranny can be replaced without revolution. Mr. Churchill himself expressed the fear that Italy might be reduced to "chaos and anarchy." So the Anglo-American governments carefully made no appeal and no liaison with our natural allies inside Italy, the great mass of anti-Fascist Italian workers and peasants; and within six weeks, when Badoglio finally accepted unconditional surrender, we had achieved precisely both chaos and anarchy throughout Italy. But now the vacuum was on the Allied side. Those large numbers of Italian soldiers and civilians who in central and northern Italy bravely resisted German domination, fought without the encouragement of any democratic pledges from us. The American and British governments still offered no concrete reasons for either their sacrifices or their support.

Thus it is impossible to escape the conclusion that the English-speaking allies have committed serious errors in their initial dealings with both the French and the Italians. Military expediency, justifiable as it frequently may be, had been used much too extravagantly as a substitute for political ideas and democratic realities. The Anglo-American armies won North Africa and were now invading Europe itself without their governments having provided them with a political chart—without a synchronized propaganda weapon designed to arouse the hopes and enlist the wholehearted aid of Europe's enslaved scores of millions. Presumably we were to occupy and liberate Europe without a political thought in our heads and then, with a dazzling sweep of the hand, produce a new European order like a rabbit out of a hat. Approximately 300,000,000 Europeans, including the Germans, are in the market for a different kind of life. But as late as October 1943 neither the American nor the British government had addressed itself convincingly to these waiting millions or had revealed itself equipped to win the European peoples as permanent postwar friends and allies.

Why are we suddenly deeply concerned that the peace may be bungled and all the greatest gains that we are fighting for frittered away? Obviously we are concerned because our governments have been afraid or incapable of waging political warfare; because, thus far, we have not known how to arm our own people and the peoples of other nations with democratic ideas. We are concerned because our governments have been floundering along without a fixed political program and, too often it has appeared, without fixed political principles. Those who are afraid of the wrath and the uprising of the people, of masses of humanity who are potential friends, betray a lack of faith in the solidity of their own political systems or an uneasy conscience about what they possess. It does not seem that the government of the United States should lack such faith today or be beset by such fears.

At last there is a ferment in America, prompted by a gradually widening realization that the peace may be lost once more. We are coming slowly to see that the United States needs peacetime allies as well as wartime allies; and that it needs particularly a world policy. *But unless America's world policy is sternly democratic in its purposes — and in its functioning — we shall eventually find ourselves isolated and comparatively weak beside a new Europe and a new Asia, and the fighting of this war will prove to have been little less than a farce and a gross betrayal*. We have pledged ourselves, as Woodrow Wilson once pledged us, to the right of self-determination of peoples. In America we came to exercise self-determination through revolution. Would it be logical or consistent for us to demand that self-government for Czechs, Frenchmen, Bulgarians, Greeks, or Germans should only be achieved through immaculate conception? Such things simply do not happen in any betrayed and ravaged war-torn society. One may hope and strive to save Europeans from unnecessary excesses, at least in so far as possible. One cannot hope to deprive Europeans of the self-expression and self-cleansing which is rightfully theirs. With their own blood, their own skeletons, and their own anguish Europe's peoples have earned the right to revolt — and to decide what kind of government they will have, however radical or socialistic it may prove to be. If we in America and Britain do not mean to assure them this right, then we have lied to mankind when we lauded "self-determination"; we have destroyed our own moral position, and have been actuated all along by nothing more humanitarian than the desire for our national preservation.

Democracy means the opportunity for government through elected representatives of the majority in the name of all. If such an opportunity is to be given the European peoples, then it is the business of the Anglo-American coalition to address itself to the Italian people much more than to a Badoglio; to the Rumanians rather than to an Antonescu; to the Greeks rather than to an exiled King George; to the Germans rather than to Göring or a Wehrmacht general; to the Spaniards rather than to Franco and his antidemocratic clique. We have already drifted a dangerous way toward losing the peace because Washington and London ignored for much too long the desires and the popular will of the European peoples. Throughout 1941, 1942, and most of 1943 the Anglo-American governments jeopardized the chances of an enduring peace by avoiding the political problems, or by partially concealing them from their electorates, or by repudiating democratic principles in a considerable portion of their war-waging decisions and methods. If we examine British-American policies toward the French and the Italians since Allied occupation of North Africa, it becomes clear that this statement is not exaggerated.

2

Of necessity American intervention in North Africa and the accompanying "deal" with Admiral Darlan in November 1942 were governed by military expediency. A month later General Catroux, one of the most loyal and moderate French commanders, declared: "There must be an end to that expediency. It is most important to revise the agreement between General Eisenhower and Darlan. I have absolutely no trust in Darlan, whom I know very well." Nevertheless Americans remained faithful to the turncoat pro-Nazi Darlan long after the fate of the French fleet had been settled — until, in fact, an assassin's bullet had removed him from the scene.

From that time on, American leaders in Algiers, operating under orders from Washington, favored notably or worked closest with a long list of Frenchmen who had been notorious Nazi "collaborationists" or Vichyites while maintaining a strong opposition to General de Gaulle and adherents of the Fighting French. General Noguès, whose resistance at Casablanca had cost several thousand American dead and wounded, was obligingly left in power in Morocco by his conquerors. Both American and British pressure was exerted, quite inexplicably, to keep Pierre Boisson — a pro-Axis servant of Vichy — in administrative control of the vital West African port of Dakar. Peyrouton, a Nazi appeaser who founded the most inhuman concentration camps in France, actually received Washington's backing and became Governor-General of Algeria until the stench of his own presence forced Peyrouton to resign. By January, Geoffrey Parsons, Jr., reported from London to the *New York Herald Tribune:* "The shocking thing is that American officials who have been very closely connected with the political arrangements in North Africa express astonishment that America's allies should have strong feeling about people who have collaborated with Adolf Hitler. . . . The State Department has been almost psychopathic in its de Gaullist phobia. It would not even let Mrs. Roosevelt meet Mme. de Gaulle when she was here."

For many weeks General Giraud left Vichy's anti-republican and anti-Semitic decrees in force in North Africa and carefully avoided committing himself to restoration of a genuine French republic. This defiance of the fundamental principles for which we were supposedly fighting did not seem to disturb either Washington or London. Anglo-American representatives consistently opposed the Fighting French and Frenchmen with clean records, but forgave turncoats and welcomed Pétainists and appeasers. Apparently these were the instructions which Robert Murphy, Eisenhower's chief political adviser, had received. Mr. Murphy himself had defended the Munich deal to Edgar Ansel Mowrer and had revealed himself as a "passionate advocate" of Marshal Pétain to Walter Lippmann. Was Pétain helping the Allies defeat the Axis? If not, could an American admirer of Pétain be expected to rally the support of sincere pro-Allied and democratic Frenchmen in Africa? With such glaring contradictions in British-American conduct of French policy it was not surprising that one correspondent asked: "Can a blackmailing collaborationist always count on getting a better break from the American government than an honest fighter *against* the Axis?" In a few months the American government's handling of French issues had gone far beyond the justifiable limits of "military expediency" and had become, in fact, a repudiation of our professed democratic principles. Democratic Frenchmen were the last Frenchmen Washington seemed willing to trust.

In June fourteen of the United Nations recognized the French Committee in Algiers, but President Roosevelt told a press conference that legally "there is no France now." The President did not explain how there could still be a Czechoslovakia, a Poland,

and a Norway, but no France. In any case Washington and London withheld recognition of the French Committee — to what conceivable good? — for nearly three months and blocked Soviet Russia's recognition simultaneously. This move unquestionably aroused serious distrust of America's and Britain's professed democratic motives in Moscow. When recognition came at last from the Big Three, Russia's was unqualified — a frank and friendly gesture to French leaders and the French people. America's notification was grudgingly phrased and totally lacking in graciousness. It was true that Anglo-American officers had complained that General de Gaulle was annoyingly stubborn and temperamental. In Washington one or more somebodies had proved to be quite as stubborn as any Frenchman ever born — but at an excessively high cost in French goodwill.

How did this tragedy of errors begin?

The astonishing and unpardonable thing about it is that most Americans still do not know. Even the elemental facts in the November 1942 Franco-American agreements were not revealed until the following July — a full eight months after the events. Were the details of our negotiations with Darlan and Giraud made public in an official White Paper in Washington? No. Were they issued to the press in a prepared statement by the White House or by Secretary of State Hull? No. Were these vital historical facts handed to American correspondents in Africa or to American news agencies for publication in all American newspapers? No.

Something quite different happened. In the late spring Demaree Bess of the *Saturday Evening Post* went to Algiers. There General Eisenhower obligingly opened up to Mr. Bess his personal files — files which had not been available to any of scores of American war correspondents covering the entire North African campaign. Without direct authority from Washington General Eisenhower would not have made this great exception. Thus, as Walter Lippmann so justly pointed out, knowledge of the secret agreement between Robert Murphy and General Giraud became available for the first time through a "hand-picked" journalist. "The net result of the whole procedure," Mr. Lippmann wrote, "is the manipulation of public opinion by preventing an independent examination of the facts." This maneuver was as naked in its intentions as Gypsy Rose Lee. It was but one more step in an officially inspired propaganda campaign to support Washington's dubious and devious French policy.

In a series of three articles Mr. Bess revealed that "our agreement specified that we would obtain General Giraud's consent before admitting any 'outside elements' to our African expeditionary force, an obvious reference to the British and to followers of General de Gaulle." Mr. Murphy, incidentally, made this promise just one week before our troops landed and at a time when he knew that British forces were about to embark for North Africa. But apparently Washington felt we must have some French general other than de Gaulle, so the game was to get Giraud from France to North Africa. According to the Bess report, "the Murphy-Giraud accord stipulated that any expedition to French territory would be an essentially American expedition . . . with no participation of any outside elements, French or otherwise. . . . In making this agreement Murphy, of course, acted on orders from Washington."

So just one week after the American government had made this pledge to General Giraud it was broken. And then our representatives found themselves with Admiral Darlan on their hands and made another "arrangement" whereby Giraud had to accept playing second fiddle to Darlan. When you know even this much of the Murphy-Giraud agreement it seems pretty plain why Washington backed Giraud to the limit, once Darlan had disappeared. Our government had started the venture in French North Africa with pledges which it did not want publicly known. In regard to this "most unappetizing mess" Mr. Lippmann emphasizes the fact that "this profoundly embarrassing disclosure has been made not by the critics of administration policy but by its own chosen and specially privileged newspaper correspondent." The Demaree Bess revelations inevitably aroused a still more sharp criticism of the French policy of Roosevelt and the State Department, whose bias against de Gaulle had now become abundantly plain. American authorities on European affairs emerged in virtually complete agreement that Washington's policy was maladroit, that its dangers for future peace could not be ignored, and that immediate recognition of the French National Committee by our government was a first essential to get

Franco-American relations back on solid ground again. But week after week passed with this recognition still being withheld. "We have waited three years for the voice of France to rise again," remarked Samuel Grafton. "Now that it is heard we are childishly startled to find that it speaks French, and not English."

When General de Gaulle first reached Algiers, at the end of May, he spoke with a French voice. "The central power should be able to direct, materially and morally, the effort of France in the war," he said. "I say *morally* because it is most important that the men wielding power should be men able to give moral direction and worthy of the trust to be placed in them. You all know what I mean."

So here was a French leader who did not mumble dry and hollow phrases like tired-looking General Giraud. Here was a Frenchman who spoke like a leader, who stressed moral values and rekindled the pride and confidence of his compatriots. Here was a French chief at last with the spirit of Clemenceau and Poincaré — a man who refused to compromise where principles were involved and who spoke in terms of restoring the good name of France. That was why de Gaulle had become a symbol to millions of Frenchmen — because he was the one man who personified the honor and integrity of the France that refused to die and would rise again tomorrow. But some persons in Washington and London had taken a strong dislike to de Gaulle. By attempting to put him on a shelf they had merely made him stronger than ever with the French people and probably assured him of a dominating role in shaping the new France. Our "expediencies" had proved a boomerang. At the peace conference America and Britain could count upon paying the expense for this contradictory and bungling policy.*

Unfortunately Anglo-American intervention in Italy did not begin any more auspiciously in the political realm than it had

* The complete hollowness of Washington's efforts to prop up General Giraud and to suppress General de Gaulle was demonstrated on November 9, 1943, with unanswerable finality. Backed strongly by underground leaders, the French Committee of National Liberation ousted General Giraud from his role as co-president. Four other pro-Giraud members were also removed, including General Georges, who was reputedly appointed to the Committee upon the insistence of the Churchill government.

with the French almost a year before. However confusing the events surrounding Mussolini's fall and the acceptance of unconditional surrender by Marshal Badoglio later on may have been, one undeniable fact emerged: the democratic Allies failed completely to encourage, precipitate, and engineer an anti-Fascist (and therefore pro-Ally) uprising in Italy. At the moment the Badoglio government's surrender was announced, America and Britain had no contacts and no machinery available through which the mass of the Italian people could be brought into the fight on our side. If the Nazis had been invading Italy in our stead, would they have moved without their political and propaganda weapons fully prepared in advance? We already have the answer to this in Norway, Holland, Belgium, France, and elsewhere. It remained for the champions of democracy to fight with only one arm in Italy.

Why did we cripple ourselves in this fashion at the start? Once again, because we refused to use the waiting potential allies of our fighting armies; because some of our governmental policy-makers were afraid of the power of the people — and afraid of utilizing revolution and revolutionary methods to shorten the war and enhance the chances of parliamentary states in Europe. Ultra-conservatism inside the American State Department had a good deal to do with this shortsighted neglect. Professors Gaetano Salvemini and George La Piana, both Italian by birth and both prominent members of the Harvard University faculty, had followed Washington's official attitude very closely. In September, when Anglo-American lack of a political program left the Italian people helplessly adrift without directives or hope, Salvemini and La Piana wrote: "Our diplomats long cherished the hope that a coalition of ex-Fascist chiefs, clericals, monarchists and industrial and agricultural lords would one day unseat Mussolini and hand us Italy without fighting. . . . Our diplomats did not want a revolution. Our policy toward Italy before the Sicilian invasion raised doubts whether the ideas prevailing in Washington are compatible with our solemn avowals that we seek freedom and democracy for all in this war. Our State Department defeated the attempt to organize in this country an anti-Fascist legion open to Italian anti-Fascist volunteers from the concentration camps of India, Africa, England and America and under the direction of American officers. Such a legion, making possible the dropping of thousands of men from the air over Rome, Turin, Milan, and Genoa at the moment of Mussolini's demise, would have rendered the Italian revolution successful. But our diplomats prefer to conquer Italy inch by inch rather than allow democratic anti-Fascist forces to play any part in Italy's deliverance."

So we did not have — even when Badoglio surrendered — an Italian anti-Fascist legion to land by parachute all up and down the Italian peninsula and spread revolt and confusion behind the German lines. We had no inspired anti-Fascist soldiers to cut the Nazis' supply lines while the critical battle at Salerno hung in the balance, or to speed the entrance of Allied troops into Naples. It would be interesting to know how many tens of thousands of American and British soldiers have died or will die in Italy because of this colossal shortsightedness. Polish troops will march into Poland with the Red Army, and Czechoslovakian volunteers will enter Czechoslovakia with the Russians. Is it the desire of a few puny-minded men in Washington and London to leave no place for Europe's anti-Fascist masses to fight, except in the ranks of the Red Army? If the State Department prevented the establishment of an anti-Fascist legion to fight with our armies in Italy, that was little more than an important contribution toward the spreading of Communism in Europe; but it has also cost many American and British lives.

From the opening of the Sicilian campaign on July 10 until the battle for Naples was being fought at the end of September — and long afterward — the leaders of Britain and the United States made no direct appeal to the Italian people to fight for a free government. As once the Allied governments had been excessively considerate about the sensibilities of Darlan, Boisson, Peyrouton, and other Vichy-Pétain Frenchmen, so now they were equally tender toward King Victor Emmanuel, Badoglio and the elements which they represented. There was no open bid, in all this time, to all kinds and parties of Italians who opposed Fascism, regardless of whether they were Left-wing, Right-wing or moderates. In all these weeks Anglo-American leadership made no appeal to all anti-Fascist Italians and especially to all Italians who might prefer democracy. Until Badoglio had delivered the Italian fleet, that might have been a debatable step. But once Badoglio was where he had to remain on our side, it was high time for the democracies to thump their drums for democracy in a liberated Italy. As was the case in North Africa, the last thing the Anglo-American democracies were prepared to sell or to fortify was — democracy.

3

Why do the increasingly victorious United Nations face a definite danger of losing the peace?

In large measure this seems to me to have come about because both the British and American governments have been neither so realistic nor so idealistic (otherwise, genuinely democratic) as circumstances — and political strategy — have long dictated. It had been evident all along that no durable peace could be shaped without a comprehensive agreement between the Anglo-American allies and Soviet Russia. That Moscow was standoffish was equally apparent. But there was little or no effort to inform the American and British publics either as to the urgency of an agreement with the Soviet Union or as to the precise nature of the problems to be solved. The strength of Russia's case for recovery of the Baltic States of Estonia, Latvia, and Lithuania, for instance, had never been officially explained in Washington (or in London, I believe) previous to the three-powered conversations in Moscow in October. Realism and statesmanship would have required an intelligent preparation of Anglo-American opinion for at least some of the concessions which our governments would have to make to Russia. But the Anglo-American leaders had failed just as notably as they failed in the Declaration of Quebec to provide an international political program and to put democratic aspirations into concrete terms. This extended neglect by Prime Minister Churchill and President Roosevelt to fill in the broader outlines of a possible postwar settlement inevitably served to increase criticisms and doubts. Yet the public opinions of our two countries must finally accept or reject any settlement which may be reached; and among many people, throughout the past year, the feeling grew that they had been kept in the dark too long, and possibly about too many things.

I believe these are some of the reasons whereby we risk losing the peace: Because of the Anglo-American governments' delay in formulating a definite and comprehensive program for the nations of Europe and Asia. Because Washington's French policy, certain of its pro-Franco actions, and its previous dabbling with reactionary European elements has made future American collaboration both with Soviet Russia and with liberated European nations much more difficult. Because there has been too much that smacked of unregenerate imperialism in some of the Churchill government's policies and too much that was essentially antidemocratic in Washington's actions or omissions. Finally, we in the United States risk losing the peace because we have tolerated too long an antiquated and often reactionary State Department, whose leadership again and again has shown itself governed by a mentality much closer to 1914 than to 1944 and 1945.

I am convinced that a definitely democratic program is essential to winning the peace because the liberated peoples of all Europe will never accept a settlement which is largely imposed on them from above, while the peoples of China, India, and the rest of the Orient will never forgive a peace which smacks of Anglo-American imperialism. Nothing less than British-American liberalism in international affairs will build a solid foundation for peace because the world's peoples are much more wide awake, more demanding, and more powerful than they were in 1919. We are also compelled to be realistic about Soviet Russia's position and claims because neither Britain nor the United States is in a position to deny the foremost of Moscow's claims, and because there can be no real peace without co-operation with Russia. But for the American people the condition of our State Department should perhaps arouse the deepest anxiety of all.

In the September issue of *Fortune* Joseph M. Jones, for the previous six critical years an officer in the State Department, gave an authoritative picture of conditions inside the ugly old structure on Pennsylvania Avenue. He described the State Department as "one of the most inefficient organizations in the world" and he cited chapter and verse to illustrate this charge. "So great is the premium on caution and avoidance of error," Mr. Jones wrote, "that virtual unanimity among the higher officers is required. If officers do not agree they simply must talk until they do agree, until someone gives in and is willing to initial the action paper in dispute." As I read on I was reminded strikingly of the hopeless red tape and "play-it-safe" paralysis of Britain's Indian Civil Service which contributed so potently to the Allies' loss of Malaya and Burma.

Mr. Jones had the support of the best-informed Washington observers when he stated that the State Department's chaos "is magnified by the deep personal animosities, professional jealousies and ideological differences prevailing among the high officers." Nor could the dismissal of Under Secretary Sumner Welles alter the record of such men as Assistant Secretaries Breckinridge Long and Adolf Berle. Mr. Jones wrote as tactfully as possible of Secretary of State Cordell Hull, but there was still much food for serious thought in what he said. "The Secretary himself sets the pace and the tone, but these being at the speed and pitch of the reciprocal trade agreements program, the Department finds itself without leadership when confronted with the requirements of major diplomacy. It is widely observed that the Department's actions suffer from a two-year time lag. The Secretary, flanked by yes men of equal conservatism and caution, finds himself continuously pushed by a few more vigorous subordinates who are conscious of the requirements of the times."

These are things which I sincerely wish I did not feel compelled to discuss. I first became acquainted with Secretary of State Hull at the world economic conference in London in 1933, and at the Pan-American conferences (at Buenos Aires in 1936 and at Lima in 1938) I saw the great services which both Mr. Hull and Sumner Welles rendered to inter-American solidarity. Accordingly I have the highest regard for Cordell Hull's integrity and idealism, his sincerity and good intentions. I wish with all my heart that I could say that I believed Mr. Hull capable of leading and directing American negotiations for a world peace. But in all honesty — and despite my warm admiration for him in many ways — I must confess I feel certain that Mr. Hull is not equipped, either by vision, experience, or temperament, to fulfill successfully such a formidable task as lies somewhere directly ahead of us. Washington's wise men have insisted for some time now that there will be no change in the Secretaryship of State because President Roosevelt needs Mr. Hull's influence with Southern politicians for a fourth-term nomination. I hope these extremely realistic political observers may be wrong, for there are other places — such as the Supreme Court bench — where Cordell Hull's abilities and devotion to public service could be turned to much more effective use than in the State Department. It can be said without disrespect that we cannot hope to build a new world order except with men who combine the dynamism and boldness of middle age with a broad and intimate knowledge of European and Asiatic affairs. America does not lack men with these peculiarly difficult qualifications — but if we do not draft their services in high places now, in the midst of this supreme international test, it will be certainly not much more than an accident if we do not lose the peace.

(At this point a parenthetical remark seems necessary in regard to the Moscow conference which has been held since these lines were written. It is impossible for me — and for a good many other experienced observers with whom I have talked — to credit the promising agreements reached at Moscow so much to American diplomacy's good management as to force of circumstances and the willingness of Soviet leaders, or their anxiety, to go a long way to meet Anglo-American representatives. If one analyzes the composition of British, American, and Soviet delegations at the Moscow conference it is evident that the United States delegates were possessed of much less personal experience with Europe and with a much less impressive diplomatic background than the representatives of either Great Britain or Russia. The American delegation at Moscow could not be described objectively as a strong delegation. The four principal American delegates cannot be compared for background and astuteness with Foreign Secretary Anthony Eden; the British Ambassador to the Soviet Union, Sir Archibald Clark Kerr; Mr. William Strang, Permanent Under-Secretary of the British Foreign Office; and Lieutenant-General Sir Hastings Ismay. The Soviet's diplomatic representation was quite as impressive as the British.

Consequently, it would appear most debatable to hail the Moscow conference's success as primarily a triumph of American diplomacy. America's representation at Moscow was certainly far from being the most skilled and best-qualified diplomatic team that the United States could have sent to negotiations of such enormous importance. We are faced with other conferences of equal significance for America, for humanity and world peace. They will require men of the greatest experience, the best brains, and the deepest understanding that the United States government can assemble for international negotiations of exceptional delicacy. To this observer it seems imperative that every American should ask himself whether there are nearly enough men of such caliber in our State Department. From the viewpoint of America's future role in a world settlement we should also ask ourselves whether the Moscow agreements can be found, upon analysis, to have been the result of American good management — or merely of an American good fortune which is not likely to happen two or three times in succession.)

"Conservatism and caution," especially if they predominate over everything else as they have done for years in our State Department, are in no sense qualities by which to hew out new and workable solutions in a revolution-swept world. All along the line we must negotiate with Soviet Russia and with liberal or Leftist coalition governments throughout most of Europe; and their spokesmen will be neither conservative nor cautious, nor will there be any "two-year time lag" in what they decide to do. Nor will the representatives of the new China be lacking in a positive program and the necessary unity with which to defend it. If the State Department is merely overhauled superficially and in such a way as to eliminate the realism of men like Sumner Welles, we may expect our government to go to the most important peace conference since the Congress of Vienna with advisers who speak largely the language of 1910. In short, it seems lamentably but undeniably true to this observer that the United States cannot hope to play its justified part in winning the peace — that indeed we will run great risks of losing the peace — unless there is a radical and thorough change in personnel and methods in the State Department long before such a conference is convened. If the Republican Party has the intelligence to present this issue properly, it can scarcely fail to have a powerful weapon in the 1944 presidential campaign. But in order to serve the nation on this issue the Republican leaders will have to be frankly liberal and progressive where the New Deal's State Department has been retrograde and reactionary, or do-nothing conservative, on many vital international policies for the past several years.

4

Can we hope to win the peace while shutting our eyes to the prevailing and predominant trends among all European peoples and among nearly 800,000,000 Asiatics in China and India?

Can we win the peace by insisting upon treating the predominantly democratic French Committee of Liberation on a plane inferior to that enjoyed by the exiled governments of Holland, Norway, Poland, and Czechoslovakia?

Can we win the peace by treating General Franco's anti-democratic and pro-Nazi Spanish government with kid gloves, and by leaving Falangism enthroned in Madrid to poison our relations with all the Latin-American countries after the war?

Can we win the peace by lip-service to democratic ideals and institutions while covertly trying to sit on the lid of popular revolutions in France, Germany, Bulgaria, and a dozen other European countries?

If I have learned anything in reporting this conflict since September 1939, and around the world, I have learned that the only answer to such questions is an emphatic negative. No, we cannot. This is the road toward losing the peace irreparably — and this is the road which we have been traveling far too long in our international policies and in much of our diplomacy.

This fact has not become plain to the majority of the American people for one reason — and that a very disturbing reason. Our government and the State Department have kept some of the most revealing aspects of its French policy and various other policies cloaked in secrecy. The American people have not been given the facts upon which to base their judgment. It is tragic, and an inexplicable fault in our governmental structure, that the American Secretary of State or one of his chief assistants does not have to appear in Congress regularly and publicly answer questions about the administration's foreign policies. In Great Britain both the Prime Minister and the Foreign Secretary are compelled to place themselves at the disposition of the House of Commons — and must therefore keep British public opinion constantly informed on decisions having to do with foreign affairs. But an American Secretary of State, like all our Cabinet members, enjoys a most dangerous immunity from the direct probings and criticisms of the people's elected representatives. It is an anachronistic system and fundamentally undemocratic. In the coming peace negotiations we are bound to pay a considerable price for this archaic luxury — but probably we shall do nothing about reform on such a grave discrepancy as this for another fifty or one hundred years. American Cabinet members have always been peculiarly immune from defending their policies and actions directly before Congress. So in our great United States we often have Cabinet members who cannot even get on their feet and deliver a good speech about their own jobs.

It is not surprising, then, that Joseph M. Jones should report that State Department officers "are among the most insulated of all government personnel from the influence of American life and thinking." Career diplomats, however intelligent, are further handicapped by the fact that they are rarely of grass-roots origin; for most of them must have an independent fortune or income in order to fulfill their social duties as ministers or ambassadors, and they spend their lives completely out of touch with the common people in the countries where they serve. It was not an accident that I found in Madrid, only six weeks before the republican revolution of 1931, almost complete unanimity among our American Embassy staff that the Spanish republican movement was so weak it could never overthrow King Alfonso. Our diplomats, naturally, were not in touch with the opponents of the monarchy and its dictatorship. The only trouble was that they were proved to have been completely out of touch with — Spain! As Europe is liberated, will our representatives be just as out of touch with the revolutionary masses of Europe? If so, the people of Europe will inevitably go their own way without us.

Mr. Jones's six years inside the State Department convinced him that its officers "move in a sophisticated society, usually conservative politically and well-heeled economically, so their thoughts are seldom disturbed by the urgings of most of the people of this country." Beyond that, "they have no faith in the people; they refuse to inform them or appeal to them. They give the wordiest of lip-service to democracy and proceed to deny it in their day-to-day actions."

Virtually every qualified newspaper correspondent in Washington knows that this is a simple statement of fact. But with men of these habits, with men who have no faith in the people forming policies which determine our relations with the rest of the world, how can we expect the United States to play a statesmanlike role in the peace?

Inside the State Department men like Assistant Secretary Breckinridge Long and James C. Dunn are not distinguished for having exercised a progressive or predominantly democratic influence. As American Ambassador in Rome Mr. Long, according to correspondents who knew him at that time, never betrayed any real aversion to Mussolini or Fascism. More recently Long sponsored severe measures to exclude refugees from French soil from asylum in America. He was strongly isolationist. James C. Dunn, an intimate adviser of Secretary Hull, had an excellent reputation as a chief of protocol — the man who always knows the correct procedure for official functions, such as who should sit next to whom — until he branched out into political fields. Dunn has been a champion of General Franco, an apologist for fascist Spain, an anti-de Gaullist; and he is described in Washington as emphatically anti-Russian. Key men in the State Department of this general type, usually well protected from publicity, are credited with having toyed behind the scenes with the idea of restoring a feudal and reactionary Poland; and also of restoring Otto of Habsburg in Hungary or Austria — supposedly as buffers to Soviet Russia, although this would be the one way to invite Moscow to intervene strongly in central and eastern Europe. Nor have such State Department officers paused to consider the fact that most Hungarians and Austrians probably have no desire for Otto's return. Meanwhile, however, they succeeded in creating pronounced Russian suspicions of Washington's motives in seeming ready to align itself alongside feudalists, reactionaries, and political clericals in countries like Poland and Hungary (or possibly Italy). It seems certain, in any event, that Moscow made it bluntly clear to the American and British governments that she would not tolerate any eastern European federation or cordon sanitaire designed to maintain a group of hostile governments close to her borders. Such clumsy efforts at "fixing up" central and eastern Europe, without regard for the populations of these countries or the future expression of their desires, unfortunately remained largely cloaked from the American public at the time. But they go far to explain the aloofness to which Soviet Russia resorted for so many months. It is not possible to preach self-determination and the Atlantic Charter publicly, and flirt with or indulge in power-politics maneuvers secretly, without damaging seriously America's possibilities of understanding with the European peoples and with Russia.

The way to lose the peace is through betrayal of our own democratic principles, and the coincident betrayal of the democratic, liberal, and progressive aspirations of Europe's 260,000,000 enslaved people. Since Pearl Harbor the American government's actions have proceeded perilously far along the road toward these twin betrayals. Not because the American people have wanted it, and certainly not because President Roosevelt has intended it this way; simply because, on the political side of the war, our government's actions all too often have been sharply contradictory to our professed beliefs and alleged purposes. Again and again the State Department or the government has shown "no faith in the people." But it is the people who will underwrite or repudiate the peace — in Europe quite as much as in the United States.

The American people have a right to know precisely what decisions the President and the State Department are making in regard to the nations of Europe and Asia and relative to a postwar settlement. For unless the American people are taken into the government's confidence on these most vital matters — and taken into confidence well ahead of events — they may be expected once more to turn violently isolationist and to repudiate the peace. And if the United States returns to 1920, it will just as surely return to December 7, 1941, within another generation.

We risk losing the peace not only because of the contradictions in Washington and in the State Department, great and serious as these have been; but also because most of us in America, conservative and antisocialistic in our outlook, do not take into consideration with anything like sufficient seriousness and understanding the temper of Europe's and Asia's hundreds of millions of people. On these two continents more than two thirds of all humanity — or nearly four fifths of humanity if we include the Soviet Union — are possessed today by a totally unprecedented political awareness and a proportionate hunger for freedom and improved standards of living. After the last war Europe's people were by no means supine or spineless, nor were they lacking in revolutionary spirit. But over the past five years scores of millions of Europeans have known greater hunger and impoverishment, deeper humiliation and despair, and greater suffering and brutality than their countries experienced from 1914 to 1918. The difference in intensity in all these respects is very great indeed, and the difference in the psychological and spiritual consequences is correspondingly great.

This is why the popular revolutions by which the new Europe will be shaped cannot possibly be restrained in a rigidly ultra-conservative groove, and perhaps but rarely within a middle-of-the-road groove. This, too, is why Great Britain and the United States can maintain a moderating and effective influence in the new Europe — and also in the new world — only through policies and leadership which are unchallengeably democratic and consistently liberal and progressive in outlook. The one way for Britain and America to lose the peace with certainty would be to attempt to confront the remainder of the United Nations and the world with a reactionary program. If the liberated peoples — and those in the East who struggle toward liberation — should find us thus far removed from the political-economic consciousness of the twentieth century, inevitably they would come to regard the Anglo-American governments or peoples as nothing less than a hostile barrier to humanity's progress. The peace, let us remember, may be made by a few men at the top. But it will either endure for some decades or be blown sky-high by the explosive force of the world's masses from underneath. In this century they will not again be sold down the river with impunity. And they will not remain satisfied for any length of time with merely a limited ration of self-government and democracy. What they want the peoples of the world pretty well know by now; and where democracy comes largely into their wants, it must be a better democracy and much more closely integrated to modern industrialized society.

5

Eventually something like eight million or nine million American voters will come home from the war. If they bring with them a clear understanding of what has happened to the world and where the world's peoples are marching, our returned service men and service women will possess such electoral power that they alone might turn the scales and win the peace for America. Unquestionably those who are now in our armed services will exercise an enormous and probably unprecedented political force in the United States for the next several decades. Can we expect them to wield this momentous power intelligently and constructively? Or will they wield it blindly and within the narrowest limits of self-interest?

In North Africa *Time* correspondent Jack Belden (whose book *Retreat with Stilwell* remains one of the finest that any American war correspondent has written) talked with a group of 130 Russians who had been interned there after the war in Spain. Belden asked these newly released Russians what they thought of the political situation in Algiers and one of them expressed surprise that he should ask such a question. When Jack asked him why, the Russian replied:

"Americans generally do not show any political interest at all. When we came here we met American soldiers and were astounded by their ignorance. We've been shut up from the outside world for four years. But we knew more of what is going on in Europe than they did. Even the poorest peasant knows more of what this war is about than the American soldiers we have met. The people in Europe seem to know what they are fighting for, and they are at least partially educated politically. The British soldiers we've met are not so far advanced in their thinking as the people on the Continent, but they have a much greater understanding of the issues at stake than your soldiers." The Russian shrugged and then added: "Perhaps it's because you have always been such a rich country."

It is my observation that foreigners could make the same remark with justice wherever they have contact with men of the American forces. Any number of our war correspondents have commented privately upon the extraordinary indifference which is displayed toward the war's political issues and aftermath by the overwhelming majority of American soldiers, sailors, and airmen — including the officers. Our men in uniform, even inside the United States, are astonishingly ill-informed about current events and major developments between the Allied governments. Most of them read little more than the headlines where war and international affairs are concerned. Although our army has inaugurated so-called "orientation" courses in many camps, inquiry among those on the inside reveals that the higher-ups among the defenders of democracy shy away from encouraging discussions that might be described as "too political." Many of the officers who give these courses also treat them as a bothersome addition to the much more important military routine, or are themselves lamentably unfit to interpret or excite interest in international politics and the whys and wherefors of the war.

Recently I met a friend who had just come from the Marine Corps officers' training school at Parris Island. What he had to say was unfortunately all too typical. "The fellows never talk about the problems of the war and the peace," Mike said. "In fact, we rarely know how the war is going — we never even knew when Sicily had fallen. You see, they don't allow any radios in camp. Of course, there's hardly any time — only enough so you can scratch off one or two letters before going to bed. But we chat at meals and sometimes between exercises, and I've never heard anyone discuss what we're fighting for or what kind of peace we ought to have. You never hear anything like that. Maybe it's different with the privates and enlisted men, but that's how it is with our fellows — and they're college graduates, all of them. The only thing they teach us is how to kill. That's all, and that's all you're supposed to think about."

Could this official barrier to war information and discussion of war-provoked international problems be peculiar to the Marine Corps? A friend showed me a letter from a young American stationed at a U. S. Army officers' training camp. It was a memorable letter, written as a factual report but in a mood of passionate protest and despair. The writer again reported an utter lack of preparation of future officers' minds for grappling with the issues of tomorrow's world. "I shudder to think what the attitude of these men may be when the war is over," he wrote.

"In time of peace they could not imagine war. In war they cannot imagine peace. . . ." There was much more, most of it underscoring how American democracy is seriously neglecting the imperative task of preparing its soldiers for peace. But if some ten million American service men are not given a clear conception of the possible or probable nature of America's postwar relations with Great Britain, with Soviet Russia, with Europe, and with the nations of the Far East, how can we expect them to vote intelligently or to exercise constructive civilian leadership when peace comes?

In contrast I am reminded of the political commissars I saw at work with the soldiers of the Red Army; of their political discussion and free questioning, as it is carried on in every Russian division and regiment; of the Russian army and divisional newspapers, which contain no comic strips or sports columns (such as occupy so much space in U. S. Army publications like the *Stars & Stripes* and *Yank*). I thought again of Mike's further remark about the officer candidates of the Marine Corps: "Most of them haven't any idea what we are fighting for." I had heard that same comment about our fighting men in various parts of the world many times — too many times. Has this dangerous neglect of political education and discussion in our armed services happened deliberately or simply through shortsightedness? As far as I have yet been able to discover, it seems to have occurred chiefly through a combination of excessive timidity and lack of imagination at the top in many of our service commands. It appears, for instance, that the U. S. Army has been so fearful of being accused of playing politics or encouraging pro-New Deal or anti-New Deal sentiments among its men that it has frequently adopted a super-negative policy. This policy amounts to a naïve assumption that "there are no politics connected with this war." But our armed services seem to have dodged completely the question: How can the anticipated gains of any war be achieved and consolidated except through political arrangements? . . . Is it either wise or justifiable to ask men who go forth to die to shut both their ears and their minds to those things which alone can make their sacrifices of value to their country and humankind?

Consider the testimony of those who have been close to American and British soldiers in the war zones. From Allied Headquarters in North Africa Helen Kirkpatrick of the *Chicago Daily News,* a correspondent of exceptional ability and experience, recently wrote as follows: "Thinking men talk in terms of influencing events by their vote. *But* there are many more thinking men in the Army than are given a chance to think constructively. Their leaders seem reluctant to stimulate the men's thoughts for fear of controversial issues and political repercussions. The British are way ahead of us here. Their soldiers' paper, *The Union Jack,* takes up controversial subjects. Yesterday, for instance, one article was entitled, 'Some of You Must Go into Parliament.' The British Army's educational authorities issue booklets on all subjects, however controversial, and regular discussions take place in the ranks.

"In contrast the *Stars & Stripes* not only does not touch on controversial subjects but does not provide anything other than the bare outlines of the news. It lays great emphasis on sports and has a column of town gossip. Special services seem to be poorly organized here with representatives who often do not fully understand their jobs. *Controversial subjects are definitely banned and speakers are urged to avoid anything remotely political.* The majority of the Army and Air Force units do not get speakers and no reading materials are provided. . . . But anyone who has ever spoken before American soldiers knows they will sit on the damp ground and on hard benches for several hours listening to a description of serious subjects such as the Italian political situation, French politics and general war surveys. Furthermore they will hang around asking questions and showing every inclination to discuss these problems for hours on end. A vote taken among two units — one the Air Force and the other ground troops — showed that the majority would prefer serious discussions to floor shows. Yet they are provided with floor shows of fifth-rate quality."

You are entitled to wonder how much more Miss Kirkpatrick might have said if she had not written knowing that her dispatch must pass the army censorship. As it stands, however, her report is a most serious indictment both in its facts and in its implications. It shows, beyond dispute, that the U. S. Army's policy (at least in some of our most important war theaters abroad) amounts to a conspiracy to keep our fighting soldiers from thinking and from being even partially informed about the problems which will determine the kind of peace they will be expected to accept and support. This is not the fault of our millions of men in the armed services. It lies much higher up. This dangerous neglect, it is true, might have been excused during the first months, when every energy had to be concentrated upon producing efficient soldiers, sailors, and airmen in the shortest possible time. Does it seem reasonable — or tolerable — that the same blind suppression of political discussion should predominate in most branches of our armed services *two years* after the United States entered the war? What kind of material are we shaping for the super American Legion of tomorrow? Does not the native intelligence of our fighting men command a much more enlightened and constructive treatment? In a very large measure these young men will come home as products of the machine that has swallowed them up — they will come home what the Army, Navy, and Air Force have made of them.

Is it surprising, then — given this intellectual neglect — that among Allied troops from the U. S. A. to China the average American combatant has often been referred to in disparaging tones as politically illiterate, uninformed, and little interested in the deeper stakes for which he fights? And does this verdict promise either social progress, intelligent citizenship, or even social peace for the United States when our boys come home?

A thoughtful American must ask himself whether we have not been, and still are not, sowing a whirlwind. For we in America have been the last to understand that *what you put in the minds and hearts of our soldiers is just as important as the weapons you place in their hands — and possibly much more so.* We have not only removed the cream of our physical manhood from civilian life for several years. Despite our good intentions our armed services, in most cases, have clamped a lid upon their thinking processes. We seem to have conspired most effectively to keep them uninformed or ill-informed about the very world-changing events in which they are directly involved. To a dangerous degree our fighting services have contrived to immunize their men as much as possible from knowledge and reflection. Are such policies designed to develop and preserve democracy? Or will they not, more logically, work toward its ultimate diminution or destruction? The U. S. Army may bar discussion of "controversial subjects" in North Africa and Italy or wherever our soldiers go. But the postwar civilian world, in which most of these same men must take their part, will be rife with political debate and controversial issues. For the most part it appears that they will return and take their share of influence in these debates and controversies sadly unprepared and ill-equipped.

Ten million ex-service men will constitute at least one fifth of the future voting strength of the United States. And in all probability these millions of American voters will be organized into a semi-political force much greater than the American Legion has ever been. They will be expected to vote intelligently, to elect capable representatives, and to support constructive policies in a seriously dislocated national and world society. But they will emerge from the groove of an extremely narrow existence which has been dedicated to killing, destruction, and the ruthless employment of brute force. Have we concerned ourselves sufficiently with seeing to it that they emerge from this one-track military groove with wider interests, with sounder judgments, equipped with the materials necessary to the resumption of mature roles in a democratic state? It would have been an act of providential prudence on our part, perhaps, if — at the outset — we had determined to build armed forces in which liberty of thought and breadth of view had been treated as equally important as the capacity to fight, to kill, and to win physical battles. For if the battles of tomorrow inside America are not battles of intellect and the spirit, they must eventually degenerate into physical combat of the kind of which Detroit has already given us a bloody and ignominious warning.

Shall we win the war, but lose the peace?

After taking full cognizance of past mistakes and present obstacles one can only recognize that time has now become fearfully short, and that the odds against us — a complacent and non-politically-minded people — are fearfully long. If we, at home and in our armed services, knew clearly what we are fighting for;

if we understood plainly that fascism is an anti-human beast which dwells within ourselves quite as much as within the consciousness and appetites of our enemies, there would be far greater hope of building what has to be built.

For without awareness and without vision your world and mine, in America as outside America, will be lost.

Chapter XIX

TOMORROW IS A DIFFERENT DAY

The United States is the only great power which has not generally recognized the world revolution's existence as an inescapable fact. The proportion of its people who still imagine that after the war they can go back to the old social and international system — with a few minor changes, no doubt, but essentially the same — is still a high majority. . . . The most important single thing for the Americans to do now is to recognize that they, like the rest of the world, are living in a revolution.

Julian Huxley

America stands today as a symbol of freedom. The loss of this symbol will mean the loss of hope for white and black alike. . . . For in spite of selfish interests a new world is a-coming with the sweep and fury of the Resurrection.

Roi Ottley in *New World A-Coming*

It is strange how frequently in history revolutions and disorders are promoted by people who believe themselves to be conservative.

Count Carlo Sforza

Yesterday is dead and today is dying as swiftly as those who fall upon the field of battle. But at few epochs in human history has such a new and strikingly different tomorrow been in the process of being born. Shall we in America comprehend the nature of this new world? Shall most of us even prove capable of tolerating it? Or shall we endeavor to live out of joint with the times, and hence recklessly at war with the undeniable evolution of the great majority of mankind?

As I moved from one country or war zone to another nothing impressed me more than the frightening contradiction inherent in America's position in the twentieth century's revolution. Hundreds of millions of the world's peoples look to the United

States as the symbol of freedom and their greatest hope. But the American people are tragically unprepared, both mentally and spiritually, for leadership in a new universe which we can neither prohibit nor escape. While we Americans sleep or doze or keep our heads plunged in the sands, great masses of humanity, already awakened, are on the march. Most of them have assumed that what they mean by freedom and democracy is what we mean. Most of them therefore have assumed that Americans naturally understand what they mean. Only a comparative few of these rising, stirring, struggling legions of men and women realize that a large proportion of Americans are not at all certain about our own definition of freedom or about what democracy really implies in an age of machines and mass production. It is not yet plain but it will soon become shockingly plain how wide and dangerous a gap separates a large number of Americans from the overwhelming majority of peoples in Europe, Asia, and Latin America. Physically the United States of America leads the world. Politically and socially — and in some senses perhaps morally — the world is in the process of passing us by. Unless we learn to think much more clearly and unless we learn to adjust ourselves with far less venom and much more grace — as Dorothy Thompson has expressed it, unless we improve our *social habits* — the most powerful groupments of the world's society will have passed us by before this century ends.

For the most striking fact about America today is that the United States has become the last great stronghold of conservatism; perhaps even of reaction. This is still true even though our nation has had a liberal government since 1933 and despite the humanitarian motives of Franklin D. Roosevelt. Regardless of our unparalleled sources of reliable information and our unequaled opportunities for education, Americans as a whole understand less about where the world is going than many a Welsh coal-miner, Serbian guerrilla, or Rumanian peasant or a surprising number of Hindus and Chinese. In America we think much more of holding what we have got than of perfecting the political-social mechanism which we have inherited. But the world's masses are thinking — and acting — quite differently. More than 360,000,000 European peoples and more than 900,000,000 Asiatics are compelled to think chiefly of what they do not have, of what they have never or rarely touched or tasted — and why. They cannot afford to tolerate the complacency of well-fed and well-intentioned Americans. They know that they want to have, and that they or their children must have, an utterly different world. In the making of this new world they will not be denied even though the effort should require several generations. They will make it with our guidance and help — or they will make it in spite of the resistance of the United States and its voters. Their leaders know that they, the world's masses, are infinitely stronger than we. And if we reject their efforts toward liberation and progress, if we turn a deaf ear, their leaders also know that the government and peoples of the Soviet Union will never commit the same fatal strategic error. If America turns her back upon the world's masses, with the instinct of self-preservation they will know where to go. With such an alliance they cannot fail to be victorious in the end.

These are simply the A B C's of the revolutionary epoch in which we all live, yet most of us in the United States do not wish to admit their existence. From our own revolutionary beginnings we have become the most conservative people on earth — much more so than the British people are today. It is by no means a bad thing to be a conservative, providing one works steadily at the job of trying to be intelligently conservative. *But a successful conservative must know what things can be retained and what things inevitably must be changed.* A great many heads were chopped off during the French Revolution, and most of those heads had never made that vital distinction — what can be saved, what must be changed? This happened, too, in Russia's Bolshevik Revolution, and it will be happening any day now over most of Europe. In much of our contemporary world the die-hard reactionaries are living only on borrowed time. The abuses by which they have prospered have become too obvious and the conscience of mankind has been too long flouted and ignored. You do not have to be a Communist or a radical to recognize these facts. A man like Wendell Willkie can see them just as clearly. The wise conservative is like an able general; he knows what lines he can hold and where and when he must retreat. But here in America most of us harbor the assumption that the lines of a laissez-faire prosperity, already lost and irretrievable on its old scale and basis, can be restored if only the "right" man is elected in 1944 or in 1948. We do not care to admit that the old physical frontiers have reached their limitation in the United States, that the easy slipshod pioneer expansion is over, and that we now must turn toward the only frontier which in modern times we have never remotely approached. That is the frontier of political and social awareness, of intelligent planning, and of controlled direction of the machine-dominated civilization which we have built.

We do not see that we who are out in front are precisely those who are most likely to be left behind. But that is because we do not choose to see what is happening beneath the surface of the world conflict; because we persist in refusing to understand that this, in reality, is a formidable and unprecedented revolution from which we Americans are no more immune than a Burmese villager has been from the automobile or the motion picture. Machines have made a crowded world much smaller, but they have also awakened startling ideas about man's right to a better life. Machines have added to the dignity of many men, but simultaneously they have challenged the dignity of all men. Above everything else they have challenged the feudal conception that the majority of mankind should expect to be and remain less than free. The world's masses know this challenge. But we in America, who have contributed so largely to the spread of revolution-inspiring and revolution-making machines, are the last to comprehend the intellectual, moral, and revolutionary character of what we have distributed and sown around the globe. The machine has created an idea — but the idea dismays us. We did not expect the illiterate and impoverished hundreds of millions to accept this idea literally. Nevertheless they have done so, and as a consequence this twentieth-century revolution rings the entire globe and will not be completed in our lifetime.

2

Hitler, Nazism, and the war have profoundly altered society in every European country in a revolutionary sense. Vera Micheles Dean expressed this succinctly when she said: "By looting the conquered countries for the benefit of the Nazi war machine *Hitler has proletarianized Europe* in a way which the Communists could not have dreamed to be possible in so short a time. Property as a source of power may have become extinct in the conquered countries. . . . The ravages of Nazi occupation threaten to wipe out the middle class, from top to bottom, as the French Revolution laid low the monarchy and aristocracy. Under these circumstances some form of collective economy, whatever may be its political label, appears far more likely in Europe after the war than the immediate restoration of private property — and may, in fact, offer the only alternative to sheer anarchy."

To the average conservative American, and certainly to all Americans who are bitterly anti-New Deal, this must come as horribly bad news — "Hitler has proletarianized Europe." Yet Mrs. Dean has simply made an objective statement of an extremely significant fact. The middle class, that sturdy anchor of capitalism and that usually reliable instrument for transition and gradual change, has been virtually destroyed from Norway to Bulgaria by Nazism. Hitler has even gone so far as to plunder a considerable part of the upper class as well. The shrieking fanatic who was going to annihilate Communism has created tens of thousands of potential — with emphasis on *potential* — Communists for each one that his henchmen have killed. With its extreme ruthlessness Nazism has merely been a gigantic scythe slashing European society down to a single common level. As a consequence there will be no way for Europe to survive and restore itself except through a greater degree of collective economy — more socialism — than it has known in the past. For most Americans the very word "collectivism" is anathema, and many of us have disliked even such moderate socialistic institutions as have long flourished in Sweden, Norway, and Finland. Italy, however, has already revealed what is likely to be a widespread tendency: the grouping of parties and popular movements in a Left-center or Left-wing coalition. Something like this is bound to develop in France, Belgium, and other countries. But the Left parties in France were already strong enough to elect a Popular Front government in 1936. After more than three years of German domination and after wholesale destruction of the French middle class, is it likely that the French can fail to be much more Leftist and collectivist once they are liberated? I know of no sober observer who does not regard this as inevitable. As for the German people, because of their defeat their ultimate reaction must be expected to be even more violent. In the minds of most European people they have been betrayed by corrupt old-style politicians, by industrialists, by military careerists, by conservative clerical parties, and by foes of organized labor. Tomorrow at the very least they will demand a more truly liberal democracy — or they will demand outright socialism in one degree or another.

It is difficult for Americans to understand how stubbornly feudalism has clung to its entrenchments in many parts of Europe, what feudalism is, and why it cannot endure there much longer. In Spain, Hungary, and Poland in particular, feudalism has fought off reforms with the help of the church; and in Italy too the church has lost a great deal of its hold upon the people because it has too often failed to be *for* the people. There is much in Europe's social structure, then, which is synthetic or that has long been anachronistic because it has so blindly obstructed progress and betterment for the common people. But the intelligence of ordinary little people is much greater than most white-collar folk are accustomed to think. *Those who have suffered most from exploitation invariably understand quite clearly who has been for them and who has been against them.* The revolution which is now rumbling more acutely in Europe than anywhere else in the world will do one thing with disconcerting and perhaps terrible suddenness. Temporarily, at least, it will liberate legions of the disinherited. Most of these newly released peoples will be determined never again to be enslaved if they can possibly help it. Enslaved by whom? By another Hitler? No, I suspect they will see farther, much farther, than that. They will be determined not to be enslaved by the system, whether the system is chiefly feudalism as in Spain and Hungary, or feudal-capitalism as in the Balkans, or simply a virtually uncontrolled capitalism as it previously existed in France and elsewhere.

Liberated Europeans will be as disinclined to trust the high priests of their prewar governments, prewar industry, and prewar landed gentry as Americans were disinclined to trust bankers in 1931–2. It will not be enough to say to them: "Democracy is the best way of life." Europe's disinherited and newly bankrupt will merely reply: "What kind of democracy do you mean? Do you mean industrial democracy, trade-union democracy, and agrarian democracy? Or do you only mean the right to go to the polls?" Europeans will say: "We want clothes and food, and better clothes and better food than we had before. When there were big profits for the few we didn't get enough clothes and food. Don't ask us to go back to the old system. It wasn't good enough. But we do want freedom. If you can tell us how to get more clothes and food and a better life *with* freedom — well, we'd like to hear about that." But the liberated peoples of Europe will be hungry and impatient. They will not be afraid of words — least of all afraid of words like "socialism" and "collectivism." It will be easy for them to become convinced that only in such a direction lies the hope of a better life for them.

We in America were born with a fatally blind belief in what Eugenia Thornton has called "the divine right of democracy." We have always had democracy, so we assume its clothes will always fit us no matter how fast we grow or what we do. Louis XIV was never more sure of the God-given right of kings and of his immunity from the rights of the people than Americans feel sure of the divine immortality of American democracy. This is a very agreeable shrine at which to worship every second or fifth Sunday. The government should serve us as much as possible (we mumble in our ritual), while we serve the government and state as little as possible. You don't receive in proportion to what you give (we mumble); you simply make certain that you get as much as possible.

Sometimes, of course, we complain that we do not get better men in our government, in our national agencies and bureaus. But for the most part we leave the administering of our democratic institutions to second- or third-raters, just as the British have done in India, Burma, and Malaya. So the divine democrats have drifted along in their diabolically antidemocratic ways for a generation or more. And now, suddenly, the millionaire-making era is petering out and hereafter will be sharply limited by the stupendous cost of the war and the heavy tax burdens which will remain for decades to come.

The one-way "gimme-gimme" game which Americans have played with their government and their democratic institutions won't produce anything like the same number of lollypops any longer. We have turned our own and our children's eyes away from sacrifices for a national ideal and for the nation's welfare — except when a war makes it compulsory to look briefly in that direction. As soon as Germany and the Japs are polished off, we look forward to resuming the worst, as well as the best, of our peacetime habits. We will still educate our children for lip-service to the flag and for personal material success. In a universe where democracy is creaking in an obviously undivine manner, in a world where democracy is in serious need of overhauling — even of emergency operations in order to save its life — we are ready to let somebody else do something about it. *Very few of us, I gather, are ready to face the fact that America can defeat fascism abroad in this war, but will still be in serious danger of having an anti-liberal, anti-Negro, anti-labor, and guilefully "American" brand of fascism established inside our country within ten or fifteen years after peace comes.* When the reaction comes in the United States it may well come with the brutality and force of a tornado. Would you expect people who have lost the habit of serving democracy to know how to defend it intelligently when the day of reckoning arrives? There will be such a day — and almost inevitably within our lifetime.

The American people are dangerously unprepared for tomorrows' world because we have long forgotten how to deal with political ideas. The American has formed the reckless habit of concentrating most of his energies upon producing, devising, and selling material things. We are quickly at ease with the most intricate dynamo, turbine, or airplane motor. But we are immediately perturbed by much simpler political philosophies or innovations. In the realm of manufacturing or building, Americans will try anything, no matter how new, unconventional, or revolutionary it may be — and usually we make a success of it. But where we are concerned with a doctrine like democracy or with processes of government interrelated to industry, most Americans instinctively protest: "But you mustn't tinker with that." I think an American will tinker with anything he can put his hands on. But how rarely can he be persuaded to tinker with an abstract idea.

Thus we are one of the world's most progressive peoples in

such matters as industrial production, medicine, science, and inventions. Yet in political philosophy and in the exploration of democratic refinements we are peculiarly static. It is a popular American notion that Washington, Jefferson, Hamilton, and the others, guided by a kind of divine wisdom (from which our divine democracy descended), conceived and created the ideal mechanism for self-government — and that this Model-T of the founding fathers ought to be let alone. In fact, we shouldn't even talk about it too much, and if we do, then preferably in a slightly awed voice. With our customary youthful naïveté we ignore the fact that a tremendous industrial revolution has taken place since 1776, so our political Model-T is seriously undersized in proportion to the gigantic machines and industries which it is supposed to keep humming with a reasonable degree of efficiency and harmony. The New Deal, intervening at a moment of national economic collapse, improvised a number of gadgets, and some of them — as was to be expected — worked badly or not at all. Some of these gadgets also raised cries of horror on the grounds that they were "socialistic." The Tennessee Valley Authority was one of these innovations which a great many citizens denounced as being un-American, an affront to free enterprise, and supposedly socialistic. Yet if the Roosevelt administration had not insisted upon completion of the TVA "gadget," American war production would have been reduced and delayed so greatly that the duration of this war would have been prolonged by very many months — and by an inestimable number of additional American dead. The New Deal, with its disputable reforms and its failures as well as its improvements, nevertheless demonstrated that our top-heavy capitalistic structure can only be fortified by a continued and more skillful experimentation and a more scientific effort to perfect gadgets of political-economic control. In the realm of machines when a gadget doesn't work we try a new one. In the field of democratic government when a gadget fails we denounce it loudly, and often we seem to try to keep from thinking as long as possible afterward. Quite frequently we succeed.

Always preferring to work with concrete materials and always impatient for quick results, the American people are hypnotized by a deep aversion to political changes or to experimental efforts to improve our processes of government. So we tolerate the anachronisms and the gaps in our governmental structure: the cumbersome or inefficient rules or traditions in the Senate and the House of Representatives; the isolated position of our Cabinet members which enables them to hide many of their shortcomings or their incapacities from Congress and the public. In a world of tremendous change we, for the most part, are standpattists. And in consequence we are spiritually at a loss in and antagonistic to the revolutionary epoch in which we find ourselves.

There are some among us, but a dishearteningly small minority, who are intelligent enough to see that the old happy-go-lucky and devil-take-the-hindmost kind of capitalism is doomed in the United States as in all other capitalistic countries. They have understood that just as political freedom requires a certain mass discipline from all citizens, so freedom of enterprise necessitates a new degree of discipline on the part of industrialists, management and labor alike. One of these forward-looking business leaders is Eric A. Johnston, president of the United States Chamber of Commerce, who, when he champions a new capitalism, says:

"Only the willfully blind can fail to see that the old-style capitalism of a primitive, free-shooting period is gone forever. The capitalism which thrived on low wages and maximum profits for minimum turnover, which rejected collective bargaining and fought against justified public regulation of the competitive system, is a thing of the past."

These are words of industrial statesmanship. But America needs several thousands of Eric Johnstons, and there is no indication as yet that we have anything like that number or are likely to develop them for a good many years. We live in a world moving toward more and more collectivism, and most of us hope and pray we will not finally be forced to adopt a socialistic economy. What we refuse to understand, however, is that a middle-ground solution in our times can only be achieved through a definite willingness to experiment, ability to compromise, and the willingness of industry and labor alike to accept certain sacrifices. But the way is hard. In the fields of government and political economy throughout the past fifty years we Americans have not distinguished ourselves for those qualities by which a middle way can be safely attained.

3

When in December 1942 I came home from Russia, Iran, and Libya the previous seventeen months of war reporting had taken me around the world. Compared with the men who fight, I had not been exposed to danger very often and I had not experienced a great amount of hardship. Twenty pounds underweight was scarcely worth counting. Even so, these seventeen months had been the most difficult I had ever known in my life. I could feel their cumulative load inside me and I knew their marks would never completely wear off. . . . The squalor and misery of hundreds of millions of human beings in Malaya, Thailand, Indo-China, China, Burma, India, Iraq, Iran, and Soviet Russia; the betrayals of China's national cause by many of her war-profiteering businessmen and some of her well-educated leaders; the racketeering of the Burma Road. The nightmare of British blunders, inefficiency, and lack of leadership in Burma; the failure of the Cripps mission and the British government's unpardonable tardiness in making an effort to give India genuine self-government; the poverty and helplessness of the peoples of Iran and the rest of the Near East; the cost in blood and in scores of millions of undernourished or half-starved bodies which alone had enabled the Russians to keep fighting; the long road which the Soviet peoples must still travel before they can hope to have real democracy and the elementary democratic liberties . . . all this and more had given me moments of blackness and despair and disillusionment. Sometimes the impulse had been very strong to yield to an utterly negative defeatism; to say that nothing could be done and that man would always be dominated by greed and blindness; that we live like animals and that we would never learn better.

But those were moments when the spirit was tired and the heart forgetful. For the time being I had lost the faces of those who died, and had forgotten the grandeur of humble people I had known in Spain and Norway, in Finland and Greece, in China and Burma, in Russia and out on the wastes of the Libyan desert. These faces and these lives and sacrifices are stronger than moods of disillusionment and desolation. They are built of positive things. There is in them the timelessness of the spirit. There remains in their very memory a voiceless and untouched nobility which somehow makes all mankind more tolerable and in its immeasurable dignity, from out the stillness, points the way toward which we must stumble onward.

We shall stumble blindly, I know. We shall waver and turn aside and fall and be lost — and then we shall come back again and for another little while we shall keep to the road. We shall refuse to listen and we shall refuse to see, and then the searing flames will leap upward — consuming and destroying, but revealing what should have been plain before — and for a little while we shall see once more. I do not know how many generations or centuries it will take, nor how high the corpses may yet lie piled, nor how white and silently condemning the bleached bones of those who fell will lie at last beneath tomorrow's noonday sun. Sometimes I have wanted to forget that these things are true, but in my heart I know that the road is there and that the road is wide enough for all humanity to travel on and that the road is the only road because it encircles the entire globe and makes all the world one.

But that is the long, long view, the thing which alone makes today tolerable and which some of us must live by and live for through today and tomorrow. We must hold to that, or the war is a mockery. We must fight for that, or there is no peace. Above all we must fight the little betrayals and shut our ears to the false voices, for it is the little betrayals which have strewn the world's battlefields with the bodies of our brothers, husbands, and sons. If the betrayals had all been as great as Munich, we should have become frightened years ago and then peace itself would not have been betrayed.

So, inevitably, what we do now will save or betray tomorrow's peace. And because I am a reporter and because the school of nations and of peoples has been a stern school, and usually a cruelly realistic school — because of these matters of experience I know that the odds are definitely against Americans winning the peace. As a people we are still not prepared to play a role of leadership in the world. We are not accustomed to see and reject the little betrayals of our government and our national representatives. We have had little contact with peoples across the oceans whose aspirations and blunderings, desires and blindnesses, are so much like our own. We are less used to hardship than they. We are not used to sacrifices for the nation's good. We are more interested in the price of corn or the level of the stock market, in time-and-one-half overtime or in a larger income, than we are interested in making certain that we do not have to fight another war in thirty years. It is our supremely human habit to honor our dead — but like the other peoples of the world, we do not know *how to listen to our dead.*

We want to be left alone, and so for those who insist we are strong enough to live alone it will not be difficult to catch our attention once more as they did in 1940 and 1941. There will still be senators like Messrs. Nye, Wheeler, and Bennett Clark. There will be "Red-haters" and labor-haters, Coughlinites and Christian Mobilizers and countless others insisting that a single section of American society is all at fault. There will be defeatists who were wrong last time and are as likely to be wrong again. There will be men of little faith. What was it that Charles Lindbergh declared in St. Louis as recently as May 4, 1941? ". . . The claim that the American and British production of aircraft will soon excel German production is not true. . . . The idea that England, with our assistance, can equal Germany's strength in the air by 1942 or 1943 is a complete fallacy. . . . Germany has a head start and from the standpoint of research and production alone it will require years to overtake her. No matter how many planes we build in America and send to England we cannot make the British Isles stronger than Germany in military aviation."

There will be Americans who, having been as utterly wrong as this in our recent past, nevertheless will presume to tell us once more what cannot be attained, what is beyond America's capacity, or that America's moral leadership is of slight consequence to us or to the world. And there will be a great many persons who will forget that these people, the defeatists and the disciples of let-the-world-go-hang, have already been demonstrated to be out of touch with the realities of our times and the necessities of our relations with our now near-neighbors. Our boys will return from far places. Most of them, perhaps, will be perplexed by the complexities of other nations' problems or fed up with the surface manifestations of deep social disorders which they have never studied or been taught that they should try to understand. Being Americans, they will be impatient with the rest of the world, but they will perhaps be equally critical of our own United States. And there will be voices, isolationist voices and pro-fascist voices and other shrill voices, insisting that the cure lies in turning our backs on the world, in a militant and high-handed imperialism, or in severe repressions at home. These are postwar developments which we cannot escape. They are inside ourselves and so they will eat at our vitals. We shall need to be very grown up to understand which voices are true and which are false.

For people are saying, and will say more emphatically tomorrow, that we do not need the British. And some other people will say, as some already are saying, that eventually we shall have to fight the Russians — or, in any case, that we can never cooperate with the Soviet Union. As the war nears its end it will be more and more difficult for us to conceive that America is not powerful enough to live alone. How shall we conjure up with sufficient clearness a picture of the catastrophe which awaits us all if we fail to form a house of international safety; if we fail to make an alliance, or at least a permanent arrangement of cooperation with the British, with the Chinese, and especially with Soviet Russia? We pride ourselves upon being a literate people. But probably much less than five per cent of our adult population — and probably less than two or three per cent of our ten million men under arms — will ever read the logical and indispensable program for a safe American future which is outlined so precisely and unanswerably by Walter Lippmann in his *U. S. Foreign Policy: Shield of the Republic:*

"We should be lacking in candor and realism if we did not face the fact that the crucial question of the epoch that we are now entering is the relationship between Russia and that Atlantic Community in which Britain and the United States are the leading military powers."

But we do lack candor and realism. We have inherited a neurasthenic aversion to alliances because George Washington once referred to some alliances as "entangling." A major portion of our population harbors a deep-rooted distrust or fear of Soviet Russia despite the fact that there is no place where the national interests of our two countries conflict. Thus a great many of us still cling to the fatal idea that America can somehow get along in tomorrow's world without the British or without the Russians — and preferably without both.

We have also become accustomed to leave America's foreign policy chiefly to the President and a few supposed experts in our State Department. We, the ordinary run-of-the-mill Americans, have not been greatly disturbed that these experts were a motley mixture of upper-class socialites, reactionaries, and dead wood, with only a few firmly democratic personalities struggling to keep principles intact and policies realistic. We have tolerated an antiquated State Department. We have watched Washington's disastrous French policy. We have come to take it for granted that the State Department should not report frankly to us on the nature and details of its policies. While our men fight and die we have done virtually nothing to assure a sweeping reform inside the State Department which might make it capable, with new men at the top, of shaping a peace which will not betray our dead. Of what good can it be to save our democracy on the battlefield if we entrust its future position in the world to men who have often demonstrated no clear understanding of what the world's antidemocratic forces are or of what the inevitable fruits of appeasement, collaboration, and the little betrayals must be? If we want peace rather than another armed truce, we must have diplomats and negotiators who are capable of defending democratic principles at any cost. If we want democracy, we must act democracy and live democracy.

The peoples of the world have had enough of glib phrases, and the American people have had more than their share. But the earth's peoples cannot eat the Atlantic Charter or phrases which are equally vague and platonic. They have paid a terrible price, but in so doing we may safely assume they have learned a few elemental truths. Most certainly the great majority of European peoples have learned that any democratic government which will tolerate a Franco-Falangist regime in Spain after this war or will endeavor to support feudalistic and reactionary governments anywhere in Europe must be regarded as their potential enemy. Therefore, we shall be measured in the new Europe by our actions alone. The liberated Europeans, grouped in popular-front governments for the most part, will not dismiss any antidemocratic foreign policies of ours as merely a slip on the part of someone in the White House or the State Department. Nor will they admit that the United States government, or its people, did not know what was being done.

If, then, our representatives try to build peace with rotten timbers — or if we entrust second-rate, undependable, antidemocratic men to do the job — the structure of such a peace can scarcely be counted upon to resist the first high wind. But we live in a time of very high winds, and the danger remains great that our government may attempt to build the peace with such men and of such materials. We cannot quarrel with President Roosevelt's sincerity, idealism, and lofty humanitarian aspirations. But it will require greater political courage than Mr. Roosevelt has yet shown, or has had any occasion to show, to transfer such aspirations into the framework of a durable, workable peace. It will require leadership *which leads,* to the ultimate of that meaning; leadership which does not wait for public opinion to catch up with it; leadership which refuses to worry where the votes are; and also leadership which dares to defy those highly vocal sections of American public opinion which are still blind to the broader security of a shrinking world. In 1944, whether the elected presidential candidate be Democratic or Republican, America will desperately need a leadership which is concerned solely with rising as completely as possible to a mighty and fateful historical challenge.

Unfortunately our leaders, like the rest of humankind, are fearfully like ourselves; and politics and petty ambitions among all of us go on while our dead are still unburied far away. Few of our senators, congressmen, and prospective convention delegates have been gifted with any more vision or have been any better prepared to live in the midst of a world revolution than the rest of us. We are Americans and so we dream of material progress and of the physical conquest of time and space — and frequently of the more prosperous life which we feel our great country, for some unexplained reason, owes us. We are distrustful of international politics and rather ill at ease with abstract ideas. But we are adept with machines and it seems that our race was peculiarly designed to excel in an age of aviation — if only this age were not also an era of unavoidable political-economic experimentation and of stupendous change.

But how can we lead the world in the air if we incline to lag behind an important part of the world in the realm of intellect? We do not lack productive genius. We simply have more of it than we know how to control and direct. We do lack in political comprehension and in interest in the trends of government. We lack, too often, a progressive and probing curiosity about the political-economic problems of our age. If our foreign policy has been fifty years behind the times, can we claim to have been much more alert in our democratic and social thinking? But the peace will be won or lost where we lost the last one — in our hang-over prejudices of another era, in our complacent assumption of an unchanged world — in reality, then, in our daily habits and our daily lives.

* * * * *

Yes, yesterday is dead.

But only the weak or the incurably greedy will weep for yesterday. Tomorrow is a different day. It will belong only to those who are as clear of mind as they are strong of heart.

Today is dying as swiftly as those who fall and those who have fallen upon the fields of battle. If tomorrow is not a better as well as a different day, we can be sure that they shall not sleep.

Listen carefully and you may hear a faint echo from the graves on Guadalcanal and Bataan, from Norway and Poland, from Czechoslovakia and Yugoslavia, from Spain and Greece, from Flanders and Russia, from China and Malaya and Burma, from Holland and the Indies, from Tunisia and Sicily and Italy, and from battlefields named and nameless.

"We shall not sleep," the echo says. *"But neither shall you, my friends. Neither shall you."*

Index

A NOTE ON THE TYPE USED IN THIS BOOK

The text of this book has been set on the Linotype in a type-face called "Baskerville." The face is a facsimile reproduction of types cast from molds made for John Baskerville (1706–1775) from his designs. The punches for the revived Linotype Baskerville were cut under the supervision of the English printer George W. Jones.

John Baskerville's original face was one of the forerunners of the type-style known as "modern face" to printers: a "mod-ern" of the period A.D. *1800.*

The book was composed, printed, and bound by The Plimp-ton Press, Norwood, Massachusetts.